C000179871

The Reformer

Vasily Maklakov in St. Petersburg. © *State Historical Museum, Moscow.*

The Reformer

How One Liberal Fought to Preempt the Russian Revolution

STEPHEN F. WILLIAMS

Encounter Books
New York • London

First American edition published in 2017 by Encounter Books, an activity of Encounter for Culture and Education, Inc., a nonprofit, tax-exempt corporation.
Encounter Books website address: www.encounterbooks.com

Manufactured in the United States and printed on acid-free paper. The paper used in this publication meets the minimum requirements of ANSI/NISO Z39.48–1992 (R 1997) (*Permanence of Paper*).

FIRST AMERICAN EDITION

LIBRARY OF CONGRESS CATALOGING-IN-PUBLICATION DATA

Names: Williams, Stephen F., author.
Title: The reformer : how one liberal fought to preempt the Russian Revolution / by Stephen F. Williams.
Other titles: How one liberal fought to preempt the Russian Revolution
Description: New York : Encounter Books, [2017] | Includes bibliographical references and index.
Identifiers: LCCN 2017006458 (print) | LCCN 2017035181 (ebook) | ISBN 9781594039546 (Ebook) | ISBN 9781594039539 (hardcover : alk. paper)
Subjects: LCSH: Maklakov, V. A. (Vasilii Alekseevich), 1870–1957. | Politicians—Russia—Biography. | Reformers—Russia—Biography. | Liberalism—Russia—History—20th century. | Russia—Politics and government—1894–1917.
Classification: LCC DK254.M23 (ebook) | LCC DK254.M23 W55 2017 (print) | DDC 947.08/3092 [B]—dc23
LC record available at https://lccn.loc.gov/2017006458

PRODUCED BY WILSTED & TAYLOR PUBLISHING SERVICES
Design and composition: Nancy Koerner

Page 479 is an extension of this copyright page.

Dick Williams
and
Jack Powelson

*Who kept asking useful questions**

* They also proposed quite a few answers

Contents

III. Reform in the Third and Fourth Dumas

IV. The Slide toward Revolution

V. Postlude

Acknowledgments

I want to thank some of the many people whose kindness, scholarly prowess, and general helpfulness made this book possible, recognizing that I'll likely forget to name some key contributors. First, I'm deeply indebted to Lars Lih, Daniel Orlovsky, and Melissa Stockdale, who provided in-depth criticism and suggestions in their peer reviews and who engaged with me long thereafter. Many other scholars of Russian history also extended a welcome to this visitor from the world of law, ready to answer questions, point me to resources, chat about related (or unrelated) issues of Russian history, and offer useful suggestions. Among the many providing expert help (including partial readings) were Abe Ascher, Ira Lindsay, Jonathan Daly, Robert Weinberg, Albina and the late Igor Birman, Alex Potapov, Ilya Beylin, and Olga Zverovich, and Peter Roudik and Ken Nyirady of the Library of Congress. I am in debt to Abe for far more than his reactions to particular segments—his astute observations, encouragement, friendship, and laughter date back to nearly twenty years ago, when I first thought of doing real work in Russian history.

I'm also indebted to Peter Reuter, Peter Szanton, and Matt

Christiansen for readings of the whole book, and Peter Conti-Brown and David Tatel for partial readings, all from the perspective of intelligent, well-informed citizens. David Dorsen, Mike O'Malley, Amanda Mecke, Max Singer, Emmanuel Villeroy, and Jonathan Zittrain have provided all kinds of clues and ideas, as well as valued hand-holding and consultation.

Many thanks to Zhanna Buzova for hours spent untying the linguistic knots in Maklakovian sentences that first eluded me. I am grateful to the good people at Wilsted and Taylor Publishing Services for close copy editing and massaging the book to readiness for publication, and to Katherine Wong at Encounter Books for attentive support over the past year. Finally, thanks to all members of my family, especially to my wife, Faith, for readings, comments, and a well-calibrated mix of nudges and cheerleading.

The Reformer

"The only way to avert a revolution is to make one."
ANTOINE PIERRE BERRYER

Introduction

Why Maklakov?

In October 1905 Tsar Nicholas II issued the October Manifesto, opening the door for the first time in Russia's history to real-world political advocacy—advocacy that could affect the election of legislators, who in turn could pass laws controlling government action. This book is an account of the efforts of Vasily Maklakov, a lawyer, legislator, and public intellectual who used this opportunity to advance the rule of law in Russia. Though his efforts were clearly not enough to prevent the Bolshevik Revolution in October 1917,* they illuminate the kind of challenge that reformers face today in authoritarian regimes around the globe.

In the October Manifesto the tsar promised to allow freedom of conscience, speech, and assembly and to establish an elected legislature. He also took a pledge to the rule of law. Under the manifesto, a law could take effect only with the consent of the legislature,

* By the Western, or Gregorian, calendar, the revolution took place on November 7, 1917, which by the Julian calendar (Old Style, or O.S.) was October 25; hence, the "October Revolution." I will use Old Style indications for events that occurred before January 1918, in part because many of them became known by their dates under the Julian calendar.

rather than merely by decree of the autocrat, as before. And compliance with law would be an essential condition for valid executive action. If fully implemented, the manifesto would have created a government of laws.

As a trial lawyer, Maklakov regularly observed the practical qualities and defects of the rule of law in early twentieth-century Russia. He was renowned for being able to sway juries and judges with calm conversational logic. As a legislator he used his analytic and forensic skills to press for reform of Russia and reduce the risk of revolution, advocating, for example, a practical integration of peasants into Russian society and an end to religious and ethnic discrimination. He wrote for newspapers and intellectual journals on vital issues of the day. He appeared to move with ease between technical legal issues and the more philosophical questions of how law might enable the creation of a free society. His arguments delineate a Russia that might have been—a Russia struggling with corners of backwardness, to be sure, but liberal, open, welcoming previously unheard voices, and developing institutions that could channel conflict into lawful paths.

As participant and observer, actor and critic, Maklakov is an inviting lens through which to view the last years of tsarism. Born in May 1869, he received a degree in history before getting one in law. He was on the political stage from shortly before the October Manifesto until the Bolsheviks took power in 1917. Named ambassador to France by the Russian Provisional Government, he set off for Paris on October 12, but was unable to present his credentials before the provisional government fell. Although active thereafter as the effective dean of the Russian émigré community in France, he was also able to write the story of the revolution and its background in several books of lucid and engaging prose. Like any historian-participant, he occasionally spun events to fit his views at the time of writing, but through his contemporaneous speeches and writings we can detect cases where he adjusted history—usually only slightly—to reflect a new outlook. And his charm and capacity for friendship with people radically different from himself—Leo Tolstoy and the maverick Social Democrat Alexandra Kollontai come quickly to mind—created a trail of relationships far beyond the ken of most lawyer-politicians, however distinguished.

In the Russia of 1905–17, Vasily Maklakov may have represented the very center of the political center. As Leon Trotsky wrote of him in 1913, he "rose above all parties."[1] Trotsky's words were, in fact, an ironic sneer at Maklakov, but regardless of the intended irony, the words capture a truth. The moderate opposition—those who were neither self-proclaimed revolutionaries nor fans of unlimited autocratic power—was divided into two main parties. On one side were the Constitutional Democrats, or Kadets (the informal name derived from KD, the initials of their name in Russian). On the more conservative side were the Octobrists, who took their name from the October Manifesto and sought to advance the political system that it sanctioned. One might call the Kadets the center left and the Octobrists the center right. Though a Kadet leader, Maklakov combined elements of both the Kadets and the Octobrists. His insistence of thinking issues through for himself led to criticism from more partisan contemporaries. Paul Miliukov, the leader of the Kadet party and often an adversary of Maklakov, criticized him after the Bolshevik revolution (when both were emigrants) for having believed unduly in compromise[2] and described him with some disdain as having a lawyer's professional habit of "seeing a share of truth on the opposite side, and a share of error on his own."[3]

Maklakov deviated from Kadet and Octobrist orthodoxy on several key issues. The Kadets were firmly committed to a drastic agrarian policy: the state should take the land of non-peasant landowners, giving some compensation but not market value, and should transfer it to the peasants. But the peasant recipients themselves would not get full title—only a temporary right to use the land, subject evidently to endless further bureaucratic redistribution (a point the Kadets soft-pedaled in their quest for peasant votes).[4] Someone who favored serious protection for private property, though recognizing limits on that protection, could not be fully at home among the Kadets. But the Octobrists generally opposed equal treatment for Jews, Poles, and Finns and staunchly resisted anything like autonomy for Poles and Finns. This isn't to say that the Kadets were utterly indifferent to property rights or that the Octobrists were anti-Semites and extreme nationalists to a man. But anyone who favored the rule of law and private property rights *and* an end to state discrimination against Jews and Russia's "national minorities" was bound to be a bit uncomfortable in either party. Maklakov cast his lot with the Kadets, but the relationship was always a somewhat awkward marriage of convenience.

Maklakov brought to that marriage above all his skills as a brilliant and persuasive advocate, referred to in virtually every appraisal of him by his contemporaries. He had mobilized these skills for the first time in a controversy at Moscow University. A student chorus and orchestra had traditionally given a concert for the benefit of impoverished fellow students, but the famine of 1891 led to a proposal that the concert proceeds should go instead to famine relief. The issue was to be decided at a public meeting of the students, and those planning to speak for or against the change lined up on opposite sides of the auditorium. After Maklakov spoke in favor of famine relief, the line on the opposing side melted away, and the issue was resolved by default to his position.[5]

Maklakov used his advocacy on behalf of the Kadet party, both on the stump and in Russia's parliament, the Duma. At least he did so for goals with which he was in genuine agreement, such as judicial independence, limits on government arbitrariness, dispensing with restrictions on Jews and religious minorities, and constitutional treatment of national minorities. On issues where he could not embrace Kadet views, such as their confiscatory solution to Russia's agrarian problems, he generally remained silent.

Maklakov, in turn, enjoyed a position of influence in the party, being a member of its central committee from its founding until long after 1917. And he had the satisfaction of playing a pivotal role in mobilizing support for the party's electoral and (occasional) legislative wins. Assuming that the Kadets comprised, from his perspective, the least bad of the parties in existence, they gave him a political home without his having to try his luck at founding a new party—a course he contemplated but rejected.

Maklakov liked to quote Antoine Pierre Berryer's remark, "The only way to avert a revolution is to make one." Probably most Russian liberals agreed with the general idea, with everyone understanding that the idea was to obviate a revolution by means of drastic reform. But what kind of reform? Maklakov gave no explicit answer. But his work as a member of the Second, Third, and Fourth Dumas (from 1907 to the February Revolution in 1917) provides one indirectly. He seems to have believed that Russia could curtail government arbitrariness and supplant it with something resembling a Western emphasis on the rule of law. This vision permeated his public activities and writings. Even when advocating reforms that could be advanced on many grounds, he always highlighted the rule-of-law benefits.

As the rule of law was Maklakov's foremost reform goal, his greatest concern in strategy echoed Miliukov's phrase "the need to see possible merits in opponents' views." Especially in his historical accounts, he time and again expressed the belief that Russia's tragedy lay in a kind of twin blindness—a failure on each side to welcome, to use, and to benefit from the moderates on the other side. The regime and the opposition were each internally divided. Despite its autocratic character, the regime contained liberal elements interested in reaching out to the liberal opposition; the opposition, despite containing a powerful, and in many instances ruthless, revolutionary movement, also contained moderates who favored a gradualist path toward constitutional monarchy or at least some variety of liberal democracy. But the regime was reluctant to extend a hand to the liberals (confusing them with the regime's true enemies, the revolutionaries), and the liberals typically failed to grasp the hand occasionally extended (confusing the regime with the far right and discounting the far left's threat to liberalism).[6]

Maklakov's relationship to his brother Nikolai, also deeply involved in pre-revolutionary Russian politics, adds a special piquancy to his story. Representing almost opposite poles in the political spectrum, the two weave in and out of each other's lives. A biographer sketching a person's ancestry, upbringing, and schooling tends to rely on at least an implicit suggestion that these may partly account for the shape of his career and character. This biography will be no exception. But as to any causal link, the suggestion is muted.

Maklakov's parents had seven children who survived infancy. At a relatively early stage Vasily appears to have been at odds with his younger brother Nikolai, to the point that in October 1895, when Vasily was only 26 years old and Nikolai only 24, Vasily expressed a wish that there be no further correspondence between them.[7] Later, Nikolai seems not to have been so hostile—in a conversation about Kadets with a government colleague in 1913, Nikolai said in passing that he had a brother who was a Kadet and "he has a lot of good qualities."[8] Whatever the exact cause of the rupture, politics seems likely to have played a role. While Vasily was inveighing against the lawlessness of the ministry of internal affairs, Nikolai was an integral part of that ministry—indeed, he was the minister for two and a half years, from December 1912 to June 1915.[9] While Vasily was defending Menahem Mendel Beilis against trumped-up charges of murdering a 13-year-old boy in order to extract blood for mysterious Jewish rituals, Nikolai was helping to concoct the charges and orchestrate the prosecution. Nicholas II, whom we don't think of as a punster, was sufficiently struck to make a pun out of the brothers' initials, NAM (Nikolai Alekseevich Maklakov) and VAM (Vasily Alekseevich Maklakov). These are Russian pronouns, and Nicholas would commonly say (in a liberal translation), "We have two Maklakovs, one NAM (ours), one VAM (theirs)."[10] Actually, if he'd listened to VAM, he might have spared himself and, far more important, Russia endless grief.

It is a troubling clue to early twentieth-century Russian politics that Lenin declared, in a passage quoted in the entry on Vasily Maklakov in the first edition of the *Great Soviet Encyclopedia*, "The difference between any Maklakov and the Octobrists is completely illusory."[11] Given the differences, Lenin's lumping the brothers together, and both of them with the Octobrists, seems a triumph of venom over reality.

The rule of law has many definitions—as many, it's been said, as there have been people writing about the subject, reflecting an inescapable amorphousness in the concept. But certainly for Maklakov, as probably for most advocates of the rule of law, the central feature was the subordination of the executive to law, sharply limiting its possible arbitrariness. These limits require, for openers, judicial independence, clear laws rather than ones whose vagueness invites arbitrary and biased application, and remedies that give relief to the victims of government arbitrariness and disincentives to officials tempted to embark on lawless behavior.

These limits on government all relate directly to formal rules and structure. But these alone cannot assure the rule of law. Parchment tenure provisions can buttress courts' independence but cannot, alone, enable them to constrain a willful executive. As Alexander Hamilton argued, courts have "no influence over either the sword or the purse,"[12] and in a state where the executive's power is little tempered by an independent legislature, free press, or civil society, courts are unlikely to pose a serious constraint on executive authority.[13] Although independent courts may be the instrument for protecting the rule of law, their effectiveness is quite dependent on the "correlation of forces," both material and intellectual. Unless key segments of society respect the concept of law, and the laws at least broadly reflect those segments' interests, rulings applying the law are unlikely to command adherence. Getting to such laws of course requires compromise.

Maklakov understood this dynamic. In advocating advances

in the rule of law, he regularly tried to build intellectual and social foundations for a law-based state. An example is his work shepherding a bill for equalization of peasant rights through the Duma in June 1916. An imperial decree issued in October 1906 had taken serious but incomplete steps toward such an equalization, and Maklakov's bill had limited functions—turning the 1906 decree into a regular law and expanding it at the margins. But a persistent undercurrent of all issues relating to peasants was their widespread demand for the land of non-peasant landowners. In an effort to make the landowners see the benefits of admitting peasants to others' ordinary civic rights, Maklakov argued that so long as peasants were not admitted to full legal rights, they were likely to persist in demanding others' land.[14]

Similarly, arguing for repeal of the Pale of Settlement that kept Jews almost entirely excluded from much of Russia, he noted that the government had put itself in a preposterous bind, using incoherent and exception-filled rules to balance the anti-Semitic purpose with some opportunity for the rest of the country to benefit from the Jewish community's skills. He argued that because no civilized state could enforce the rules as written, they were an open invitation to bribery and corruption.[15] Maklakov's struggles for legislation were always grounded in a sense of how laws might fit—and reflect and nurture—citizens' consciousness.

Though Maklakov was a vocal and persistent avatar of the rule of law, his record was not unblemished. At the invitation of Prince Felix Yusupov, he played a role in the December 1916 plot to assassinate the shadowy religious figure Grigorii Rasputin. Though Maklakov's role started with advising the conspirators against the project altogether and then against particularly risky approaches, he allowed himself to be sucked in to the point where, as he later acknowledged, he could have been found guilty as an accessory. Why would he do such a thing? Perhaps the sort of civic zeal that moved the most honorable of Caesar's assassins? Perhaps a love of adventure, a raffish streak? After discussion of the issue in chapter 16, the reader will be able to speculate with more nuance.

Maklakov's efforts failed. But the failure is hardly shocking in view of the obstacles facing the rule of law in early twentieth-century Russia. The Romanov dynasty had ruled autocratically since 1613. It had occasionally assembled a *zemski sobor*, a gathering of politically weighty citizens loosely comparable to the Estates-General of pre-revolutionary France. These gatherings normally rubber-stamped decisions already taken, but they occasionally expressed an independent viewpoint. The last summons of a zemski sobor had occurred in 1684, to ratify a treaty with Poland. So politically active figures in the Russia of 1905 had had little experience in the arts of compromise needed to carry out the October Manifesto's experiment in self-government.

Nicholas II himself was by personality and character unsuited to the task of presiding over a transition to the rule of law. Though delegating much responsibility to his ministers, he nonetheless took many key decisions himself. His loyalty to Russia and general decency are not—or should not—be in question. But what of his capacity? His tutor, Konstantin Pobedonostsev, wrote that Nicholas had a good brain and analytical skills, but that he "only grasps the significance of a fact in isolation without its relationship to other facts, events, currents and phenomena."[16] If that deficiency is consistent with a good brain and analytical skills, one shudders to contemplate a mediocre brain. In any event, Pobedonostsev's comment seems wholly consistent with Nicholas's almost complete incapacity to address institutional issues, his largely mistaken confidence in his personal relationship with the ordinary Russian, and his refusal to talk an issue through with advisers. To the end he remained blind to the necessities of prioritization, of using a bureaucracy to sift through issues, and of delegating real authority to a person capable—unlike himself—of wielding it systematically and coherently.[17]

Despite his issuing the October Manifesto, Nicholas generally resisted genuine reform. In January 1895, while the public still entertained an initial glow of hope for his new reign, some rather conservative landowners active in local self-government had, very deferentially, suggested that he create a formal means for the public to communicate its views to the government. He dismissed their views as "senseless dreams." He issued the October Manifesto ten years later not because he had recanted his senseless-dreams epithet, or because he believed that Russia and the monarchy would benefit from institutional reforms, but because he saw the manifesto as the only way to defeat the revolution then in progress. To be sure, the regime contained officials dedicated to reform—without them the October Manifesto could not have been issued at all. But the tsar himself and the conservative rural landowners who were his main base of support saw no affirmative good in the institutions launched by the manifesto.

In recognizing Maklakov's position at the center of the political center, we've already seen the wide divergence between Kadets and Octobrists. But the members of those parties were the relative moderates. On their left stood self-proclaimed revolutionaries who boycotted the first set of legislative elections, and some of whom favored or practiced terror. On the moderates' right were fans of absolute monarchy, overlapping heavily with ardent anti-Semites, ready and often able to launch pogroms. Both extremes were unlikely to help develop the rule of law.

Nor was the mindset of the population hospitable to rule of law values. The peasants, the vast majority of the population, held virtually no formal rights but were subject to an array of obligations, including a duty, like the old French corvée, to perform the scut work needed to provide local services, such as road maintenance. Instead of rights, they had a vaguely conceived expectation that the state would somehow provide enough land for them to scratch out a living. People with such an expectation could hardly look favorably on the legal property rights of "landowners"—those from whom additional land might be drawn. (Historians use the term *landowners* only for non-peasant landowners; though peasants held about three times as much land as did the "landowners,"[18] their rights in most of that were too squishy to be called property rights.) With peasants' rights so limited, it's natural that their maxims relating to the law were generally negative, as, for example, "If only all laws disappeared, then people would live justly."[19]

Indeed, property rights themselves enjoyed little respect. In the West property rights could be seen as a source of independence and thus of a capacity to resist overbearing monarchs and the state itself. In Russia, by contrast, they were associated with the claims and interests of landowners, who had for centuries been dependent on the monarch to keep their serfs under control. There, property rights had no such luster as in the West.[20]

But the peasants had no monopoly on hostility to others' rights. One of Maklakov's sparring partners in the Duma, an arch-reactionary whom we'll encounter quite often, Nikolai Evgenevich Markov (known as Markov II), told Maklakov that "the gentry were enthusiastic about the nationalization of factories while resisting compulsory alienation of lands for the peasants. The industrialists had no objection to taking the gentry's land, and the peasants of course wanted it." Markov went so far as to tell Maklakov in the spring of 1907 that he anticipated revolution with pleasure, because it, in his opinion, would destroy what was evil in Russia—the bourgeoisie and capital. Another conservative contemporary, General Alexander Kireev, regarded Russians as prone to lurching from one extreme to another. Only "culture," which he thought Russians lacked, "enabled people to see two sides of an issue and respect alternative points of view."[21]

These attitudes seem intertwined with the weakness of Russia's market economy. Markets rely on the rule of law: without some protection of contract and property rights from government and other possible predators, market relationships are riskier and more costly (and thus more rare). And markets nurture the rule of law: people operating in markets learn to compromise, to work out mutually beneficial transactions that recognize others' rights.

While not only industry but also markets had grown in Russia since the emancipation of the serfs in 1861, a good deal of this was hothouse development driven by government (most dramatically in the case of the railways). Russia seemed to want the brawn of Western development without accepting the brains—the West's institutional infrastructure and mindset.[22] Market-friendly behavior and attitudes seemed not to jibe with Russianness. Russia's corporate founders and managers consisted disproportionately of tiny minorities, such as Jews and Russians of German ancestry. Even business leaders who were ethnically Russian and relatively independent of government, such as the Moscow merchants, were surprisingly devoted to the autocracy. And while Great Britain, France, and the states making up the United States had by the middle of the nineteenth century allowed individuals to enter business via corporations simply through filing routine papers, no such option ever existed in imperial Russia. There, corporations could be formed only at the discretion of officials, a rich opportunity for cronyism and bribery and a source of delay and expense.[23]

Government censorship, though disorganized and often ineffective,[24] posed a threat. In Maklakov's opinion it drove many reformist thinkers to avoid wrestling with structure or policy in Russia and instead to pen rather abstract comments on political issues in Western Europe. Until the October Manifesto they had little to gain by sober consideration of practical constitutional variations in the Russian context, especially as there had been no legislative body to take action. Maklakov quoted Bismarck's remark that nothing corrupts a party so much as a long time out of power. Having little prospect of acquiring power, such a party is little inhibited from making extreme criticisms or frivolous promises. So, too, he argued, for Russian intellectuals.[25]

Even Russia's literary elite had little regard for the rule of law. The most obvious example is Leo Tolstoy, a friend of Maklakov since the latter's college days, who at least purported to condemn all state coercion equally and to regard qualitative distinctions between governments as pointless or even dangerous. To characterize one government as "better" than another would be to offer an implicit justification of the unjustifiable.[26] Other Russian writers and intellectuals joined Tolstoy in measuring courts, lawyers, and the law itself against their ideas of perfect morality and perfect truth, rather than seeing them as a set of human institutions with some prospect of making the human institution of which they were a part—the state—less dangerous to morality and truth and more helpful to human flourishing. Thus Alexander II's judicial reform of 1864, a radical step toward creation of an independent judiciary and private bar, earned him no credit among Russia's foremost literary figures. Their disdain for the reform may account for some of the inroads into judicial independence that occurred after 1864.[27]

The weakness of civil society had implications for an aspect of the rule of law distinct from constraints on the executive, an aspect that Maklakov consistently pressed—achievement of the "order" in ordered liberty. Protection from executive arbitrariness is of limited value if, where government is inactive or ineffective, people lack the skills to work out their conflicts peaceably, through private negotiation or local political institutions, and have no ingrained resistance to rule by violence. The market's embryonic character meant that capacity for private negotiation was underdeveloped; and the central government's limits on the representativeness and authority of local government bodies (notably, the *zemstvos*), and its discretionary interference with their decisions, stunted their capacity. The fall of the tsarist regime in February 1917 and its replacement by a relatively inexperienced provisional government of contested legitimacy left a gap—to be filled, in many cases, with polemics, violence, and the threat of violence.

That said, the early years of the twentieth century saw rapid change in both the economy and attitudes. Elements of civil society—voluntary associations of every kind; a harassed but largely independent press; independent businesses and unions; groups who, though in competition, were able to negotiate their differences so long as the state kept its hands off—were beginning to thrive.[28] Bit by bit Russians were acquiring the experience essential to liberal democracy.

In an environment so uninviting for the rule of law, the question is less why Maklakov failed to achieve his ultimate goals than how he was able to make any progress at all—and I'll show that he did. The question on which he focused, how a liberal democracy can grow out of an autocracy, and the related question of nurturing the wellsprings of a productive economy where producers are motivated to create goods or services for voluntary purchase have been the subject of many recent books, such as North, Wallis, and Weingast's *Violence and Social Orders*; Fukuyama's *The Origins of Political Order* and *Political Order and Political Decay*; Acemoğlu and Robinson's *Why Nations Fail*; Mokyr's *The Enlightened Economy*; and McCloskey's trilogy, *The Bourgeois Virtues*, *Bourgeois Dignity*, and *Bourgeois Equality*.[29] This book is informed by their insights, but follows Tip O'Neill's maxim that all politics is local. Russia before the revolution had much in common with all autocracies, but with a Russian flavor. My hope is that a look at one individual's efforts—themselves informed by ideas at least overlapping with many current notions of evolution toward liberal democracy—can enrich our understanding of such evolution.

Although I read Maklakov's story as shedding light on the process of reform toward the rule of law and constitutionalism more broadly, this book is not a handbook—it's not a how-to-do-it guide nor even a tidy list of steps not to take. My far more modest aim is to tell the story for its own sake and with a view to helping us understand what reformers around the world face today—living under regimes that deny their citizens basic liberties. In the past decade we have seen so-called color revolutions in the post-Soviet space and the Arab Spring stretching from Tunisia to the Middle East removing old authoritarians but failing to replace them with liberal democracy. While Maklakov's story may make much of that shortfall seem natural, it may also provide grounds for hope that comparable figures will arise and have greater luck finding allies and forcing authoritarian retreat.

I. Origins of a Public Figure

CHAPTER I

Scapegrace and Scholar

VASILY MAKLAKOV'S CHARACTER and thinking resist easy pigeonholing and perhaps stem from his family's social and intellectual diversity. His mother, born Elizaveta Cheredeeva, was from a fairly wealthy and aristocratic family and was devoutly religious. His father, Alexei Maklakov, a "self-made man"—in his memoirs Maklakov uses the English expression[1]—was a professor of ophthalmology at Moscow University and a doctor at the Moscow Eye Clinic (and for some purposes, at least, its de facto director).

The parents' ancestors and relatives combined distinction with a touch of eccentricity. Vasily's maternal great-grandfather, an official with the civilian rank equivalent to a general, had three daughters, one of them Vasily's grandmother. Vasily knew her far less well than her sisters, as she died relatively young. One of the sisters, Vasily's great-aunt Raisa, was married to a soldier, who in the era when Maklakov knew him was a retired colonel spending all his evenings playing cards at the English Club. They had eighteen children, half of them with one patronymic, half with another—a phenomenon that Maklakov found unintelligible at the time (and evidently still did in his 80s, when describing it in his memoirs).[2] The other great-aunt, Mariia, never married. She lived on land that would have been very valuable if she had not given part of it to a church and if a railroad track had not prevented her from getting from her house to the rest of the property except by a roundabout route. This was no problem for her, as she never left her house. She rose at five in the afternoon and mainly enjoyed the company of other old ladies who played cards and read religious books to her. Maklakov, as her godson, had to go there for supper weekly until her death.

Some historians have suggested that Maklakov's opinions were a product of his class origins; one, for example, says that he was one of a number of "great landowners" among the Kadets.[3] That was indeed the background of many Kadet leaders, but not of Maklakov. In his memoirs he took some pains to explain that on his mother's side (the one with money), the original wealth came from salaries. Though her forebears owned small estates in the vicinity of Moscow, that ownership entitled them to very little peasant labor in the days before the serfs' emancipation, so emancipation itself inflicted no loss on them. Although Maklakov was technically a landowner because of land in Zvenigorod that his father had acquired for weekend and summer relaxation, the land occasioned expense and of course pleasure—but no income.[4]

Of his father's ancestors, Maklakov knew only his grandfather, a man who pursued several careers fitfully—doctor, entrepreneur, playwright, and translator. The entrepreneurship seemed never to pan out. His development of a special breed of cocks for fighting went nowhere; so, too, did his efforts to design a perpetual motion machine. He unsuccessfully urged Maklakov's father to join him at Monte Carlo to exploit a surefire gambling scheme. His efforts at dairy farming were effective at least in luring Vasily's family out to visit the site, leaving Vasily with a memory of washing pigs, who squealed when they got soap in their eyes. In the end, the grandfather developed a passion for literature, writing a play that was produced at the Mali Theater in Moscow, and he learned English and translated Shakespeare. In his later years he lived permanently at the house of a hospitable neighbor, Count Olsufiev—presumably a sign of some charm on his part, unless the count was a complete pushover. He and his second wife lived apart, although they were not divorced; whenever he learned that she was at Vasily's family's house, he wouldn't enter it.[5]

Vasily's mother had been well educated and spoke three languages besides Russian; her bookshelves were full of classic works in Russian and foreign languages, which she often offered the children. The good education was coupled with a religiosity that seems extreme by modern standards. Maklakov believed it explained her indifference to the stirrings of reform in the 1860s. When her children wondered why they, though faithful, could not move mountains, she explained that it was because their faith was too weak. She managed, he thought, to live the maxim that one should hate the sin but love the sinner, never getting angry and always defending everyone.[6]

Given Alexei Maklakov's career in science, he was naturally more inclined to empiricism than his wife. But he was skeptical rather than anti-religious. Seeing crowds of people taking off their hats and crossing themselves on Red Square at Easter, he mused, "Whatever the smart alecs say, what does this feeling come from?" It was probably typical of him to address the matter as a question. On one occasion young Vasily reported a conversation with a schoolmate who had offered an explanation of the origins of the universe: it had started, he said, with the appearance of a red-hot sphere. Vasily had asked, "Where did the sphere come from?" His father took delight and obvious pride in the response.[7]

Alexei had wanted to be a surgeon, but a shooting injury to his hand scotched that and also forced him to give up the violin. He redirected his medical interests to ophthalmology and, as Vasily saw it, pursued it with the spirit of a natural scientist, always looking for underlying explanations. The son's perception seems confirmed by Alexei's publishing ophthalmology articles in scientific journals in France. Life replicated Alexei's scientific intellect rather directly in his son Alexei Alexeevich, another younger brother of Vasily, who became a professor of ophthalmology at Moscow University and director of the Moscow Eye Clinic.

As was evidently true for all who worked in the Moscow Eye Clinic, the family lived on-site. The clinic had been founded with private funds in 1826 and occupied a large building in central Moscow that not only survives to this day but is still an eye clinic. Vasily and several siblings remained there until their father's death in 1895, so it was home to Vasily for his first twenty-six years.

The clinic gave Vasily a glimpse at the relation between accomplishment and privilege in late nineteenth-century Russia. One G. V. Grudev was chairman of the council nominally guiding the clinic. At the outset, so far as Vasily knew, he declared himself to be 84 years old, but after some years at that age he started losing years and worked down to 70. A passionate gardener, he had much of the hospital grounds set aside for his personal garden. Though his role was "purely decorative," no one was troubled at his holding a nominally responsible position: "on the contrary, all would have found it quite improper to remove him." Occupying the top managerial position was one G. I. Kertselli, also superannuated, who spent most of his day reading the paper. Actually running the place was a steward, Aleksei Ilych Lebedev, so much in charge that when any problem arose, one heard the phrase, "We must ask Aleksei Ilych." Below him, managing the clinic's lower-level personnel, was the clinic's porter, who bossed them around as a noncommissioned officer bosses the troops.[8]

The clinic's head doctor, Professor Gustav Ivanov Braun, extended the pattern of disconnect between responsibility and title, limiting his actual work at the clinic to giving lectures. At least in some instances he turned responsibility over to Maklakov's father, but it appears that most issues were resolved by consensus—one largely driven by conservatism. Maklakov: "I recall that my father complained about the impossibility of ever making improvements; his colleagues always found a reason to keep the old ways."[9]

There may have been a gap between his parents in political

inclinations. Alexei met his future bride while visiting her house, first as a doctor and then as a friend. He was evidently slow to open up about his interest in Elizaveta, for when he first did so, her mother said, "Finally, sir, at last." Vasily knew of the story and wondered whether Alexei's slowness was due to shyness, to concern about marrying someone of wealth, or to concern about the possible gulf in political sympathies between the families. But as he seems not to have heard his mother express political views, it seems likely that her religious perspective rendered politics unimportant. Alexei's own views were clear: he enthusiastically supported the emancipation and the other Great Reforms of the 1860s—above all, local self-government in the countryside (the *zemstvo*) and judicial reform, of which the key was a start on judicial independence. And he regarded the Great Reforms as simply the beginning of a process that should go much further. In a general way, these were the views of Alexei's friends, many of whom were active in the city council (its duma) and often talked of municipal and rural self-government. Alexei himself served at times as a member of the Moscow City Duma and of the Moscow province zemstvo. They valued their own culture and education and believed the state should make these available to others (without making them yield their place). If Vasily had a fault to find in these views, it was that they failed to grasp the less patient mood prevailing among the unprivileged.[10]

In 1881 Elizaveta and the children visited Red Square on the Saturday before Palm Sunday, as they had usually done. The children had such a good time that they asked her if they could skip their music lessons. In words with a curiously religious tint, she answered, "Yes, fine, perhaps I'll forgive you." The next morning she didn't come down to breakfast. Doctors came and gave prescriptions, but she lost consciousness on Monday. That evening the children were taken to her to say good-bye. Maklakov and his oldest sister tried to use the ultimate resource—they went to pray at the miracle-working icon of the Savior in a church on Ostozhenka, to which their mother had often taken them. But when

The seven Maklakov children,
with the youngest girl, Mariia, at extreme left,
Vasily third from the right, and Nikolai fourth from the right.
© State Historical Museum, Moscow.

they came home, their mother was no better. A little later Alexei told the children that she had died. Having borne eight children, of whom seven survived, she was dead at 33. For a long time Maklakov reproached himself for the failure of his prayers and for the lack of faith that this failure must imply. He was just short of 12 years old.[11]

By the time of his mother's death Vasily was enrolled in the gymnasium. His parents had disagreed on whether he should be sent there—his mother favored tutors at home; his father preferred the gymnasium for the exposure to real life, including its "dark side." The school, in fact, gave Vasily an early hint of some of the stultifying, oppressive, pedantic, and humorless qualities he was to encounter at the university. The students themselves did not represent an abrupt switch for him: they seemed to have been drawn from a similar social niche, being generally the children of such people as doctors and professors. One classmate was the son of a cook. With the revelation of this background and a suggestion from on high (probably the school administration) that the son of a cook didn't belong, "he grew in our eyes like a rare bird."

Maklakov did very well academically, never getting less than a "five," the highest grade possible. He was especially good at foreign languages and studied Greek on his own, just out of curiosity. (But he acknowledges in his memoirs that at an audience with the pope in 1904, he was unable to converse in Latin.) Though admitting that there were some excellent teachers, he deplored the teaching methods generally. For ancient languages there was a great focus on grammar rules, at the expense of reading literature. When a teacher took up actual thoughts expressed in classical literature, it was "like contraband." History similarly seemed to consist of pumping the students full of isolated facts. It seemed to Vasily as if the object must have been to kill any interest in history or literature. Reflecting on it later, he thought that perhaps the state's true goal was to weaken freedom of thought and any concomitant ideas of opposing the regime.[12]

The students responded rather creatively. One, the son of a professor at an agricultural academy, taught others zoology and the basics of evolution, making the subject interesting enough for Maklakov to take it up on his own. Another was able to give instruction in chemistry. As to discipline, they reacted with a "we, they" attitude: they met the school authorities with their united strength, learning to defend their own, never betray their fellows, and never help "the enemy."

It was on the disciplinary front that the school nearly bested Maklakov. The atmosphere is suggested by his story of a martinet, who, finding a student missing a button on his uniform, told him: "Today you've lost a button; tomorrow you'll go about without trousers; and the next day you'll be rude to supervisors. . . . Regicide! To the stocks." Under such a regime, it's hardly surprising that Maklakov got into endless scrapes, which ultimately put his access to a university education at risk. His bounding down a staircase elicited a reprimand from the school's director. When he repeated (quite a few times, it appears) a sardonic reaction to Alexander III's April 29, 1881, assertion of his commitment to "unshakeable autocracy," his name was posted for the offense of "stupid talk." He once used a rucksack buckle to carve a criticism of the school onto a desk; he was disciplined not for the vandalism (which, depending on the carving and the prior condition of the desk, may have been minor) but for "raising the banner of rebellion." Maklakov's own account of his scrapes is doubtless incomplete. A schoolmate from the class above him wrote in his diary years later, when Maklakov was quite famous and the schoolmate (M. M. Bogoslovskii) was a professor, "This demagogue, standing behind a column, cried out 'Marseillaise, Marseillaise!' and then sat down so as to hide himself."[13] The hijinks led to various marks of disfavor, such as being deprived of the special seating and public listing that normally celebrated high academic achievement. They also made him locally famous. One teacher at the school exclaimed, "Who is this Maklakov?"

The discipline problems came to a head on the verge of transition to university. During a language exam, Maklakov checked with a neighboring student on the translation of a word. The director happened to be passing by, heard the exchange, and ordered Maklakov to gather his papers and leave the examination room. The apparent cheating doesn't reflect well on Maklakov, but it's hard to assess. The director, speaking of it later, mistakenly described Maklakov's behavior as *helping* the other student; the fact that the director got it exactly backwards, as well as Maklakov's general track record, suggest that whatever was going on in Maklakov's mind, this was not an attempt to get better marks than his competence and diligence deserved. Because entrance into the university required that a student receive "full credit" for behavior, the school was in a bit of a bind. Full credit might seem a stretch under the circumstances, but it also would be hard to block the progress of so talented a student. The outcome was a deal. He was given full credit, but denied an honor that naturally would have been his—a gold medal for outstanding scholarship and conduct.[14]

In 1885, during Vasily's last years at the gymnasium, his father remarried. Lydia Filippovna Koroleva was a literary figure in her own right, author of a story published in *Vestnik Evropy* (Herald of Europe) that had won great praise from Turgenev; more important in the Maklakov family, she had written a children's book that Vasily and his siblings knew and loved. Her first husband had killed himself shortly after their marriage, and she had been the common-law wife of Vasily Sleptsov, a journalist, social activist, promoter of feminism, and writer of short stories and a novella who died in 1878. A distinguished Russian author, visiting Lydia in 1930 in the old-age section of the Soviet House of Scholars to talk with her about Sleptsov (she was nearly 80 years old), spotted on her desk "*Faust* in German, Marcel Prévost's *Les Demi-Vierges* in French, and the 1861 edition of Nekrasov."[15] She thus brought into the family the atmosphere of intellectual, literary circles. Among her friends was the great Russian historian V. O. Kliuchevskii. On one occasion six members of the Maklakov family (Lydia, Alexei, and Vasily, plus two daughters and another son) wrote to him jointly, explaining that a desire to see him had sprung up among all six at the same time and extending "a collective request" that he pay them a visit.[16] Among the other distinguished friends that Lydia brought into their circle were the writer Maxim Gorky and the lawyer who became the speaker of the First Duma, Sergei Muromtsev. Another close friend, who had lived abroad since his participation in one of Garibaldi's campaigns, was the geographer Lev Ilych Mechnikov, brother of Ilya Ilych Mechnikov, the Nobel laureate in physiology and medicine, and of Ivan Ilych Mechnikov, the model for Tolstoy's story *The Death of Ivan Ilych.* Maklakov found himself captivated by one of Lev Mechnikov's articles laying out a grand theory of history. It claimed to show a natural law tending to steady human improvement as work became specialized and people, acting on their own initiative, found their niches and ways of productive cooperation.[17]

Despite the gain in intellectual breadth for the Maklakov children, the remarriage took its toll. Maklakov observed that it was naturally hard for his stepmother to reconcile her literary ambitions with taking charge of a household with seven children. "Both sides," he observed, "suffered from the unusual relationship, though both, for the sake of our father, tried to hide it; he, of course, understood and suffered more than anyone."[18]

Maklakov graduated from the gymnasium in 1887 and then

proceeded to Moscow University, where his career looks a little like that of a perpetual student. He studied in three different faculties—natural sciences, history, and then law, ultimately taking his law degree in 1896. The two transitions—from natural sciences to history and from history to law—are fairly easily explained. He had been rather purposeless in choosing natural sciences. In view of his success in ancient languages at school, they would have been a more plausible specialty, but he rejected them, he later explained, at least in part out of a foolish spite toward the gymnasium. To the extent that he had been drawn to natural sciences by the excitement of public polemics on Darwinism, he was disappointed; the lectures were highly technical, probing, for example, details about grubs. Partly in response to this, he started going to lectures elsewhere in the university, most notably those of Kliuchevskii, whose lectures were "an aesthetic delight. . . . He was an actor, not a lecturer." Further, because of his involvement in student disturbances (of which more later), Maklakov was rather pointedly told that the natural sciences faculty had the highest proportion of participants in disorders and that he would do well to move to history. Maklakov was surprised by this advice, which coincided with what he'd been told by Jacques Elisée Rekliu, an anarchist geographer whom he had met in Switzerland through his stepmother's connection with Lev Mechnikov, and with whom he had long walks and talks about history and the prospects of mankind.[19]

A distinct episode precipitated the second switch, from history to law. Maklakov had done well in history, and Professor Paul Vinogradov, his friend, mentor, and hero (for his courage in expressing viewpoints that could easily lead to a professor's dismissal),[20] proposed that he stay at the university to be groomed for a professorship. But when Vinogradov sought the agreement of the history faculty's "tutor," Nikolai Pavlovich Bogolepov, whose consent was essential, Bogolepov declared, apparently on the basis of the political unreliability shown by Maklakov's involvement in student disorders, "So long as I am tutor, Maklakov will never occupy a chair." Vinogradov urged Maklakov not to take it too seriously: "Bogolepov's a fool; he won't be tutor for long." In fact, Bogolepov rose in the educational establishment, becoming minister of education in 1898. Unfortunately for Bogolepov, his activity as minister drew the attention of a Socialist Revolutionary student who walked into his office in 1901 and fatally shot him. Maklakov could not know of that denouement in advance. Even if he had, not only could Bogolepov have dampened his career prospects for another six years, but Bogolepov clones in the education establishment might have been able to do so indefinitely. Moved by Bogolepov's edict and his own doubts about his suitability for a purely scholarly career ("I didn't have the spirit of a true scholar, that is, a searcher after truth for its own sake"), Maklakov turned to the law.[21]

Much of Maklakov's university education naturally took place outside of classes. Because brushes with authorities played such a key role in his academic transitions, it makes sense to start with them. The administration and police seemed to wobble between heavy-handedness, driven by near paranoia at the thought of independent, united student activity, on the one hand, and a relatively laissez-faire attitude on the other. In late November 1887, at a university orchestra concert, a student named Siniavskii slapped a high university official, A. A. Bryzgalov, in the face. The slap was not Siniavskii's spontaneous individual act of protest against Bryzgalov's perceived hostility to students; he had been chosen to strike the blow by the members of a kind of "primitive conspiracy." Siniavskii was arrested, and student buzz designated the next day at noon as the time for a protest meeting in a university courtyard. An angry crowd of students gathered and then began to move onto the streets of Moscow. After a while Maklakov and other students drifted back to the vicinity of the university. The police chief, N. I. Ogarev, who unlike Bryzgalov was popular in Moscow, sought to calm things down by telling the students in the most peaceable tone that everything was over for the day and that they should disperse. Maklakov, though he claimed in his memoirs not to have been really involved in the disturbance, happened to be close by. He rather loudly answered Ogarev, "We won't disperse till you clear out the police." Ogarev shouted to the police, "Grab him." All this was in the sight of the students and, according to Maklakov, created a mild sensation.[22]

Somehow Ogarev and Maklakov ended up outside the cordoned-off area. Maklakov asked to be allowed to go back to the university, but Ogarev told him not to hope for that—they would not let him return. He then asked Maklakov where he lived. Maklakov said it was at the corner of Tverkaia Street, and Ogarev said, "I'll let you off at the corner." At the corner Ogarev asked his name. When Maklakov gave it, Ogarev asked, "You're the son of Aleksei Nikolaevich?" "Yes." "Then go home and tell your father from me not to let you out of the house." In fact he tried to go back to the university, but, failing in that, went home. The upshot was that he gratuitously got the reputation of a troublemaker. Or perhaps not so gratuitously: after all, he had directly challenged Ogarev with belligerent words and for a couple of days afterward was in the thick of disturbances on Strastnoi Boulevard. Mounted police broke these up, and the episode led to nearly two months without classes at Moscow University and five other Russian universities.[23]

The reputation of being a troublemaker stuck. Speaking years later as a deputy in the Third Duma on the issue of government policy on disciplinary exclusions from the university, he said that the precedents for such exclusions "are well known to me, though no worse to me than to many others, as I was once excluded from the university." Right-wing deputy Markov II shouted from the floor, "You behaved badly."[24]

Siniavskii was sentenced to three years in a disciplinary battalion. Maklakov recalled later that this was the first time he had seen someone sacrifice his life for something. It brought to mind his mother's stories of saints who were tortured because they refused to deny their faith. After serving his three years, Siniavskii returned to Moscow. Maklakov: "I got to know him; historic heroes lose something with close acquaintance."[25]

A second episode occurred two years later, on the death of the writer Chernyshevskii, author of the famous revolutionary tract *What Is to Be Done?* According to Maklakov, the younger generation didn't actually read him, but they knew his name, mainly from a student drinking song that included the words "Let's drink to the one who wrote, 'What is to be done?,' to his heroes, to his ideals." (Would the students have found this ditty very stirring without a great deal of vodka?) Students managed to organize a memorial at a church, and though they were not allowed to place announcements in the newspapers, the call to attend the event, launched by a so-called fighting organization, spread widely. After the service, the crowd poured out into Tverskoi Boulevard and made its way to the university. The police didn't intervene, and after some struggle among the students over whether there should be speeches, the crowd dispersed.[26]

But the episode didn't pass without regime reaction. Acting for himself and other students, Maklakov had asked a professor to postpone a lecture scheduled for the day of the memorial service so that they could go to the service. The professor agreed. When he entered the room for his next lecture, he was accompanied by the deacon, and the deacon and the professor jointly told the students that the professor's accommodation was regarded as a conspiracy and was the subject of a reprimand. When the professor finished his lecture, the students applauded at length.[27]

The university tutor at the time, Count P. A. Kapnist, followed up on the episode. Happily, he was far more tolerant than his successor, Bogolepov, the official who was later to drive Maklakov out of a scholarly career in history. Having assembled a group of students, he asked them what works of Chernyshevskii they had read; the answer—none. Maklakov volunteered that the students honored him not as a student of natural sciences or as an economist: they knew him through the drinking song. Kapnist cut him off, saying: "You can't cancel lectures because of a song." He went on to say that he wasn't going to give them a punishment or reprimand, but that his ability to defend them against state authorities was limited. He had selected them because they would know the ones who started the Chernyshevskii gambit; they should pass on to them what he had said. He also had special reasons for assembling this group of students. He had chosen some because they were on a stipend that could be cut off, some because they were recidivists, and specifically Maklakov, to whom he turned and said, "You, I asked specially because of your temperament. You need to think first, and then act. Learn to rule yourself before you may have to rule others."

While the students' memories were fresh, they wrote down Kapnist's talk, underscoring what they saw as "funny" parts. At home, Maklakov read the account to professors who were guests of his father and was surprised that they didn't laugh at the humor. They understood that Kapnist's action reflected a humane approach to the students and one that disappeared with the appointment of Bogolepov. Recounting the episode in later life, Maklakov concluded that it showed how much he and his fellow students failed to understand.[28]

Maklakov's third and last major run-in with university authorities occurred in March 1890. Students had assembled in a university courtyard with a view to organizing some kind of protest in support of a student disorder at Petrovskii Academy. Maklakov saw this from where he was working in the chemistry lab, and, because he was then hoping to advance student enterprise and independence through more-or-less legal means, he tried to persuade them to do nothing that would set that goal back. His argument encountered resistance, but before the students agreed on a course, Cossacks entered the space and surrounded them, and a group of nearly 400 people was herded first to the Manezh (a vast building in central Moscow suitable for exhibitions) and then to the Butyrskaia Prison. At the Manezh a number of students expressed satisfaction at his joining them despite his having opposed the demonstration; they chalked it up to solidarity, though he was there only because he'd been swept up with the others.

Life at the Butyrskaia appears to have been quite different in 1890 from what later generations experienced under Stalin and his successors. The students started two in-prison newspapers: one liberal, with the slogan "Involuntary Leisure," the other conservative, edited by Maklakov, with the slogan "Render unto Caesar the Things That Are Caesar's—and Also unto Caesar the Things That Are God's." A satirical column spoke of how a wise government in its work on popular education had in just two days opened a new institution, "Butyrskaia Academy." Reality intruded on these intellectual hijinks when two new groups of students were brought in (first a batch of seventy-seven, and then one of sixty). The earlier arrivals asked eagerly how the event was perceived outside. The answer was that the whole episode was being completely ignored. The discovery totally chilled the students' discussions of what "demands" to make upon the government.

In the end, students were called into the office in groups and told their punishments: for one group, nothing; for another, a trifle. Maklakov fell into a third group, which was punished with suspension for the rest of the term, but with the right to return to the university. This had a short-run consequence—it prevented him from going as a student delegate to an international student conference in Montpelier.[29]

But the suspension wasn't the end of the story. While he was pondering his possible shift to history, a friend of his father, N. A. Zverev, then an assistant to the university rector, brought word that the university had received papers from the public education and internal affairs ministries saying that because of his political unreliability, Maklakov was to be excluded from the university without right of return, a classification called a "wolf's passport." The family speculated on the possible cause—suspicious books he had been reading? people he had met on a trip to Paris in 1889?

His father consulted Kapnist, who told him to go to the root of the problem—St. Petersburg—and gave him letters to I. D. Delianov, the minister of public education, and to Pyotr N. Durnovo, then director of the police department and formerly a colleague of Kapnist in the procurator's office. Right after his father left for St. Petersburg, Vasily was called to the police station and told that as a political unreliable he would henceforth be under police observation.

In St. Petersburg, Delianov asked Vasily's father what Maklakov's offense might have been. His father replied that he was hoping to get the answer from him. But Delianov also said that if Kapnist would accept responsibility for Vasily, there would be no problem with the ministry of education. The minister then urged him to see Durnovo. The latter took the same position as Delianov on the effect of getting the tutor to assume responsibility. Kapnist agreed to do so, though telling Vasily he mustn't join illegal organizations. Technically, this included organizations forbidden under generally unenforced rules, such as those barring the *zemliachestvos*, largely apolitical student associations that were built on the desire of homesick students to see others from their parts of the country.

Years later Count Sergei Witte (finance minister from 1892 to 1903, and till April 1906, prime minister, and the empire's most influential minister throughout the period)[30] introduced Durnovo to Maklakov while all three were vacationing in Vichy. By then Durnovo had served as minister of internal affairs. The conversation drifted to this episode, and Durnovo told him that such things were done for small faults, simply to show that the authorities were watching and not to fool around, and that the orders were often revoked. In short, a trivial matter could terrify a student, even if the orders were revoked, and blight the student's higher education and likely his career if they were not.[31] For Maklakov, the immediate cause of his escape from this fate was his father's excellent connections—a point later harped on by Professor Bogoslovskii, the one so upset by Maklakov's shouting "Marseillaise! Marseillaise!" from behind a pillar.[32]

These close calls with government arbitrariness, and his escape through the accident of paternal connections, must have added zest to Maklakov's lifetime of efforts to expose and thwart exactly that arbitrariness. He saw them as a good summing up of the old regime and an explanation of why it had so few defenders later.[33]

It would be nice to be able to say that when we end discussion of these episodes we put paid to Maklakov's difficulties with the authorities, but it would not be true. Spontaneous civic association is the bedrock of civil society, and on this issue Maklakov's mind and nature put him at odds with the regime. Maklakov not only admired Tocqueville, civic associations' greatest proponent (he later participated in a project for translating many of Tocqueville's works into Russian),[34] but he also seemed by disposition to have relished joining and creating and enlivening such associations. The regime, by contrast, was instinctively hostile to just about any independent association of citizens. Once two or more people were gathered together for any purpose, no matter how innocent superficially, their thoughts just might turn to politics. Maklakov's behavior left him, at best, in subdued conflict with existing authority.

In his first two university years, the years of rather fruitless study of natural sciences, he appears to have joined two of the existing zemliachestvos, one for the Nizhny Novgorod region and one for Siberia, and he later participated in the formation of one for Moscow. The 1884 rules governing universities specifically named zemliachestvos as among the organizations students were forbidden to join.[35] He also joined other students in taking an existing organizational model, an institute formed by students in the medical faculty, seeking to spread it among all faculties. He believed that such organizations, reaching beyond the purely social goals of the zemliachestvos, were likely to be more effective. Indeed, the organizing students felt themselves to be acting on the militant-sounding maxim "He who wields the stick is the corporal," and, partly as a joke, they called the center a "fighting organization." That this did not lead to disaster seems to have been the result of Bryzgalov's successors' pragmatic decision to lighten the yoke a bit.[36]

Maklakov also had a hand in turning the student orchestra and chorus, formerly governed by the university administration, into a self-governing student organization. He and others formed a kind of "Management Board," half of the members of which were from the orchestra and chorus and the other half nonmembers, using broad student involvement to help justify student control. They secured student approval of the change by asking that the annual meeting be held in an auditorium, which they then packed with supporters; the effect was evidently strong enough to abort any official effort at rejection. Maklakov was elected president of the first board. To keep the elective principle fresh, the initial board members didn't run for a second term.[37]

Maklakov's involvement in the orchestra and chorus—specifically in advocating dedication of concert proceeds to relief of the famine of 1891—launched his reputation as a speaker. In the end, the choice of famine relief came at no cost to indigent students. Enthusiasm for the project (partly cultivated by getting popular professors to talk it up) led to not only a more than usually lucrative concert but also a successful subscription that raised double the usual amount for needy students.[38]

But the actual provision of famine relief gave rise to a typical imperial Russian minidispute. University authorities wanted the money distributed through a specific official organization created for the famine. The student board saw this as an invasion of students' rights. But it worked out a compromise behind the scenes, with the university *publicly* asking only that the money be given through *some* official entity. The board agreed, taking the risk that the full student membership wouldn't approve the official organization ultimately proposed (which proved to be the one originally named). The student membership voted its agreement, thus nipping a potential crisis in the bud.[39]

Though most events in Maklakov's as yet brief life underscored the hyperactive character of the Russian state, his university years also provided him with a dramatic example of the state's potential benefits. His older sister had often spoken of Mikhail Alexandrovich Novoselov, one of her gymnasium instructors, as a wonderful teacher and person. Maklakov, attending a lecture in the natural sciences faculty, found himself chatting with his neighbor, who proved to be Novoselov and who expounded his rather Tolstoyan ideas—that the state's reliance on force made it in effect dishonorable and that revolutionaries were no better, as they just wanted to secure the power of the state for themselves. He also believed that if people saw how a community that was not founded on force worked, they would be drawn to it and would want to join, just as people who see someone actually cross a dangerous river are inspired to take the risk themselves. Novoselov proposed to found a colony based on this principle, and did so in Tver province.

Maklakov, along with some friends, went to share this experience and emerged with conflicting thoughts. He deeply admired the simplicity of the participants' way of life; he mentions that that was the summer he gave up smoking. But he was equally clear that this was not for him. On his return to Moscow, he wrote Novoselov an enthusiastic letter, saying how the people there had found their true path, and that this was written in their faces. He soon realized that he'd overstated his position; Novoselov responded in terms clearly expecting Maklakov to return and join the colony.

In any event, the colony soon came to a tragic end. Neighboring peasants, learning that the colony believed one should never return evil for evil, tested it by stealing a couple of horses for no other reason than that they felt the need of them. The colony contemplated enlisting the aid of the local authorities, but decided against it, presumably on Tolstoyan grounds. The next day the whole neighboring village came, and the colony welcomed them, thinking they were acting out of conscience. But the peasants came to haul off everything they could—and did so. After that, no one wanted to remain in the colony. Novoselov himself became a priest.[40]

In the summer of 1889, when Maklakov was 20 years old and the French Revolution was 100, his father went to Paris for the World's Fair and brought him along. "Bliss was it in that dawn to be alive, but to be young was very heaven!" Recounting the trip in his memoirs sixty-five years later, Maklakov didn't quote Wordsworth's revolution-inspired exclamation, but he conveyed some of the feeling. "Later, any time a group of friends discussed the happiest minute in their lives, I always answered that the minute was the month I spent then in Paris."[41] It was the start of his life-long love affair with France, which he often visited and to which he returned as ambassador-designate in 1917, remaining until his death in 1957.

The trip started, characteristically, with a falsehood. For an underage child to go abroad required a doctor's certificate of illness and an endorsement by provincial authorities. Those authorities gave the endorsement without reading the papers. Why should they take the trouble? The whole exercise was a charade.

Maklakov was no simplistic fan of the French Revolution, but he was dazzled by the freedom enjoyed by the French. Political hawkers would press flyers into his hands—the presidential campaign of General Boulanger was then under way—and Maklakov at first, out of Russian caution, was afraid to hold on to them. He was struck by the common ground shared by antagonistic political actors. He fondly recalled the scene after a group of Boulangists invaded an anti-Boulangist meeting, leading to a rather violent debate, with antagonistic mobs swirling out of the meeting hall and into the street. Suddenly the strains of the "Marseillaise" were heard from the hall, and minutes later the two chief adversaries were walking off arm in arm, enveloped in the music. "The whole crowd in the street suddenly followed them, caps flew into the air, all sang and applauded and embraced. The Marseillaise, the republic —for a minute reconciled everyone."

And the French voters impressed him. Pro-republic, they were discerning enough to reject not only outright foes of the republic but also demagogues who would compromise it (Boulanger, for example). Maklakov felt that France's freedom had taught him a lesson in a kind of conservatism—a popular readiness to preserve a relation to the historical past. Russia, he thought, had nurtured no such readiness.[42]

His French revolutionary hero was Mirabeau, whom he admired, he said, not for his genius, but for his commitment to Berryer's view that "the only way to avert a revolution is to make one." As the French Revolution's most eloquent proponent of averting revolution through reform, Mirabeau was obviously the perfect model for Maklakov. Later, in Russia, Maklakov was given an eight-volume work that included a biography of Mirabeau and excerpts from his speeches, many of which he memorized and retained for life. Ariadne Tyrkova-Williams—Maklakov's longtime friend and colleague in the Kadet party and the only woman member of its central committee—reported that Maklakov would recite long excerpts from Mirabeau's oratory. His memoirs enthusiastically quote Mirabeau's self-description as "a man who does not believe that wisdom lies in extremes or that the courage to destroy should never give way to the courage to create."[43]

The Paris trip implanted in Maklakov a belief in the affirmative value of a free state, one that recognized the independence of individuals and of society and protected them from lawlessness. He linked this to the experience of the Novoselov colony, which obviously needed government to defend its legal rights from the crowd. He even wrote to Novoselov—one hopes not gloatingly—to argue that the state was necessary for the success of undertakings such as the Tolstoyans'.[44]

Gregarious as ever, Maklakov naturally sought out French students and, after brief frustration because he mistakenly looked first in the cheapest cafés, found the Association générale des étudiants de Paris, whose students welcomed him enthusiastically. He declared this event the decisive moment of his trip abroad. His links gave him access to the nitty-gritty of political campaigns in which the students were active—so different from politics and student life in Russia. His father was scheduled to go home before the elections, but Maklakov persuaded him to let him stay on.

On his return the Russian state hit Maklakov with an immediate reminder of its character. He had brought along books and cartoons relating to French politics and the revolution; border guards confiscated the cartoons. Wanting to share part of his experience, he wrote an article recounting the lively, innocent, and unburdened activity of the Paris students' association. Submitting it to *Russkie Vedomosti* (Russian news), the first of many pieces he ultimately published there, he was pleased at its acceptance, but dismayed that the editor had shortened it in the published version. He went to see the editor, who assumed Maklakov was coming to thank him. At the end, the editor said, "This will be a lesson to me not to have anything to do with young people who know nothing." Maklakov replied, "And it will be a lesson for me not to have to do with old people who're afraid of everything." In retrospect, he saw that the shortening had done no harm, preserving the article's message about the benefit of allowing Russian student organizations to associate with international ones.[45]

The French students had told Maklakov of an international students' meeting in Montpelier and said that only Russia was sending no delegate; they urged him to come. As the time of the conference approached, Maklakov found himself barred by his involvement in the disorders that had led to his time in Butyrskaia. Somehow a substitute was found, one Dobronravov. He participated and as a result was also excluded from the university for political unreliability. To assist Dobronravov's struggle for rehabilitation, the Paris students' association mobilized the French ambassador in St. Petersburg to vouch for his irreproachable behavior. Strange to think that such heavy diplomatic artillery was needed to address the Russian state's paranoia! Besides this, what may have been the standard remedy was applied: vouching by Kapnist as tutor (resting, in part, on somewhat unreliable assurances from Maklakov). But by the time Dobronravov's exclusion was canceled, he had unfortunately died of a blood infection.[46]

Before leaving Maklakov's time in the natural sciences faculty, we should have a look at his initial acquaintance with Tolstoy. An indirect acquaintance began very early, as he had been given—and very much liked—a copy of Tolstoy's account of his childhood. Later, in the second grade at the gymnasium, Maklakov had been sent with his brothers, because of diphtheria in the family, to the house of a friend of his father, V. S. Perfilev, the prototype of Stiva Oblonsky (of *Anna Karenina*). A man came in wearing a blouse and high boots, and Maklakov discovered that it was Tolstoy. Having already read the account of Tolstoy's childhood, Maklakov had hoped he would show him a little attention, but he became much more interested in the dog that Tolstoy had brought with him. He remembered Tolstoy's broad thick beard, not yet gray, just as in the photographs. The wife of Maklakov's host explained that in his clothing Tolstoy was imitating the simple people, and that this was all right for a brilliant writer, but that children were not to copy him.[47]

Later, as a student, he had another sighting of Tolstoy, seeing him walking along Nikitskaia Street, looking exactly the way he looked in a photo at the beginning of a volume of collected works. Maklakov followed him, and even ran ahead so as to have a chance to meet him, deeply envying the person Tolstoy was talking with. But he didn't dare approach and was content to contemplate him from afar.

After he'd gotten to know Tolstoy, Maklakov had an experience showing him how the writer's mere presence inspired a similar awe in others. Maklakov and a fellow student named Singer were at the Tolstoys' on the evening before Singer's father, a professor of mathematics, was to deliver a lecture on Darwinism at the university. Singer told Tolstoy that his father would use the occasion to attack Darwinism, of which Tolstoy was no fan. Maklakov and his fellow student had the bright idea of taking Tolstoy to the talk, naively thinking that he could come without anyone's noticing. Tolstoy agreed to come. Singer and Maklakov awaited him at the entrance and spirited him up a special staircase. Only a handful of people accidently spotted him as he entered. He sat in the hall behind a column, where no one could see him, but somehow word of his presence spread through the hall. People asked where he was and wouldn't accept Singer's and Maklakov's assurances that he wasn't there. The crowd's whispering, and some members' departures, made it impossible for the lecturer to proceed. Representatives of the event's organizers persuaded Tolstoy to come up onto the platform, in the hopes that this would quiet people. But no: members of the audience jumped from their seats, waved handkerchiefs, applauded, and shouted. Professor Singer brought his lecture to a close, and Tolstoy disappeared. Maklakov caught up with him on the street; Tolstoy, "normally so delicate and disinclined to show dissatisfaction, said with irritation, 'It's you and Singer who arranged all this.' "[48]

The famine of 1891 appears to have occasioned Maklakov's first actual meeting with the great writer.[49] Even before that, the famine triggered a kind of anonymous encounter. At the end of the 1880s Tolstoy had published an article criticizing the custom of student carousing on Tatiana Day. On the eve of the day in 1891, *Russkie Vedomosti* published a letter, signed only "Student," saying that if in the past one might not have heeded Tolstoy on this, it was indecent to ignore his point now. Evidently, the restaurants were empty the night of Tatiana Day; the "Student" was Maklakov.[50]

After efforts to ban discussion of the famine, the government retreated and allowed the public freedom to help the hungry. Tolstoy normally scorned charitable activity by the rich, seeing it as a way for them to justify themselves: "If a rider sees that his horse is being tortured," he said, "he should not try to buoy it up but should just get off." Seeing the popularity of attempts to provide food, he prepared an article criticizing the efforts. But his friend I. I. Raevski invited him to see the peasants and the volunteers' special cafeterias. Tolstoy came for two days and ended up staying two years, working tirelessly and becoming head of the social aid scheme.

Many came to help, often losing their positions and health to do so. Of course, all the so-called Tolstoyans came. In one of his appeals, Tolstoy endorsed a proposal that landowners offer to take in peasants' horses to feed them through the winter. He especially liked this kind of help, as it would connect a peasant with a particular helper. Maklakov responded to the appeal, and through his acquaintances and luck he arranged more than 300 such adoptions. After Tolstoy returned to Moscow, the Tolstoyans came to report to him what they had done and brought Maklakov along. This was the first time Maklakov saw him close-up and talked with him.[51]

In the course of famine work, Tolstoy often told an Indian story that nicely reflected his self-effacement and sense of irony.

Some sort of rich person, wanting to serve God, found a poor, sick hungry person under a fence. Obedient to God, he brought the poor man to his home, washed him, fed him, was kind to him, and showed him respect, and then rejoiced that he was able to do God's will. After a few days, the poor man, feeling that all this had been done not for him but for the other's soul, told the rich man, "Let me go back under my fence; it'll be easier for me there."[52]

In a later chapter we'll return to Maklakov's relations with Tolstoy, his analysis of Tolstoy's thought and life, and the ways they may have influenced him. For now, we need see only a snippet of their relationship in Maklakov's student years. Maklakov observed that Tolstoy, who jokingly called him an "old young person," didn't try to reeducate him. At some point in Maklakov's Moscow university life, Tolstoy asked him to join him for a walk, and in time that turned into a habit. While they walked, Tolstoy asked him about student life. It was flattering to chat with him, though Maklakov never understood why his stories might interest the writer. Later a conversation with Tolstoy about bicycling offered him a possible answer. Maklakov knew that Tolstoy bicycled a good deal around his country estate, Yasnaya Polyana; he asked Tolstoy why he didn't make these tours on horseback. Tolstoy explained that he needed an occasional complete rest for his mind. If he walked or rode, it didn't prevent him from thinking, so his mind got no rest. If he went by bicycle, he needed to keep an eye on the road and watch for stones, ruts, and holes, and then he wouldn't think. "I understood why my stories were necessary for him during our walks. He could avoid listening, but they prevented him from thinking and gave his mind a rest."[53]

We have seen how Maklakov ultimately abandoned history for law, and a word is in order on his history studies. Vinogradov took him under his wing and, responding to a failed effort by Maklakov to develop a students' circle for digging more deeply into Vinogradov's work, started a special seminar. Maklakov's seminar paper was based on a recently found fragment of parchment by Aristotle and tried to explain when and why ancient Athenians chose leaders by lot. To this day the question excites scholarly debate, but how Maklakov's answer stacks up against current learning need not detain us. For our purposes, his answer is most interesting in prefiguring his later advocacy of reconciliation and a spirit of compromise between the Russian government and its adversaries, or, more broadly, among the social forces at war in early twentieth-century Russia. He advanced the theory that in an Athens in which four clans of about equal weight contended for power, the strategy of having government chosen by lot did not manifest any particular political theory but simply provided a way out of what might otherwise have been a hopeless logjam.[54]

Maklakov's 92-page essay was published in "Scholarly Notes of Moscow University," with a preface by Vinogradov. As Maklakov later observed, "Of course no one read the Scholarly Notes." But he acquired over 100 copies and, at Vinogradov's suggestion, sent them to professors and other scholars. This didn't pass unnoticed in the scholarly world—a Professor Buzeskul, of Kharbovskii University, cited it several times in his two-volume history of Greece.[55] In his memoirs, Maklakov goes on about this at some length and excuses it on the grounds that it is a pleasant memory of the good past. He closes the account by describing an exchange that occurred while he was a member of the Third Duma. One of his sisters met a professor who had written a favorable review of Maklakov's essay. Knowing she was the sister of the deputy Maklakov, the professor inquired if she happened to know what had happened to the young scholar of the same name who had published work on ancient Greece and then had disappeared over the scholarly horizon. Learning that the scholar and the deputy were one and the same, he appeared for a long time not to believe it and then said with a sigh, "But we expected so much of him."[56]

Maklakov's university years included a tragedy that haunted him the rest of his life. He had met one Nicholas Cherniaev through the Novoselov colony, where Cherniaev's sister had lived. For a long time Cherniaev was his closest friend, and they saw each other daily. Cherniaev had been drawn to Tolstoy by his understanding of Christ's teachings and could never reconcile those teachings with the world. To him, activities of the state and of revolutionaries seemed the denial of those teachings. He solved it by concentrating entirely on science. Maklakov thought that Cherniaev was stuck in a dilemma from which there was no exit, and they silently agreed not to talk of these matters.

When Maklakov was working at home on a paper, Cherniaev's younger brother, a medical student, came and asked him to come home with him. Cherniaev, he said, had been burning his papers, and the brother feared some misfortune. Maklakov's paper was due the next day, and he didn't go. In memoirs written in his mid-80s, he wrote that he could not forgive himself for that. The next morning the brother came to his apartment and told him that Cherniaev had killed himself in the park, leaving a letter saying only that he'd used potassium cyanide and that no one was to blame for his death.

He had written letters for various friends, including several for Maklakov. One said that Maklakov had great talent, but nothing else, and went on in that vein. "I don't believe in your heart, nor in your strength. You always exaggerate; you show more than you are." He ended the letter with these words, full of passion: "I thought despite all that you loved me, but I was mistaken; you haven't taken notice of my life, and you don't notice anyone's life, anyone's grief. You are no Christian, and without that there is little value in all your talents. Farewell." He added a postscript: "I wrote this a while ago, and now with a few hours left alive I have lost my pride and approach you asking for a favor: don't forsake my Lisa [his younger sister]. Visit her, if only occasionally, bring her a book, and help preserve God in her." Maklakov observes that she herself preserved God in herself and became a scientist, like her brother.[57]

At the end of Maklakov's time in the history faculty, he accepted the invitation of a relative—the brother-in-law of his stepmother, an artillery general—to do his military service in Rostov. The venture was preceded by yet another Maklakovian scrape, this time for acting as the party responsible for a student party that he didn't attend but that got out of hand. He was banned from Moscow for three years after his military service—a ban that was soon dissolved. The military service was of a special type reserved for educated persons and known by the extraordinary term *volnoopredeliaiushchiisia.* The service proved extremely easy, as his relative was the principal person in town, and he had loads of free time and could live in an apartment rather than in the barracks.[58]

But on May 4, 1895, his father died of endocarditis, a then incurable disease leading to inflammation of the brain and aphasia, at the young age of 57. Maklakov said it was the end of his "spoiled life." He had basically lived his whole life in a state apartment, and now he and the remaining members of his family had to clear out. His military unit was moved to Moscow, the ban on his living there was accordingly dissolved, and the military required no more of him. He resolved to do something with himself—to change his life and turn to the bar.[59]

He and a brother and sister took an apartment together, and he arranged to prepare for the law faculty exams in a year. Because of the coronation ceremonies for Nicholas II, the exam date was moved up to March 1896, and the year that he could normally have counted on shrank to nine months. Though helped by such law as he had learned in historical studies, he was still compressing into nine months what would normally have taken four years to complete. He spoke of it later as "the great sporting achievement of his life." Although he occasionally took time off for skating at Patriarch's Ponds, he put a sign over the door to his room—"Guests should please stay no longer than two minutes." He was greatly helped, he reported, by a professor who secured for him a copy of the lectures of another professor, V.M. Khvostov, who had explicitly refused to be of any help to him at all. In the end he added a second degree to his earlier degree in history, both "excellent."[60]

CHAPTER 2

Trial Lawyer

MAKLAKOV'S DECADE as a trial lawyer developed his analytical and rhetorical skills, exposed him to facets of Russian life rarely brought home to a Russian intellectual, and gave him the opportunity to hone his powers of persuasion on countless juries of ordinary Russians. The simplest way to describe this period and highlight the features of Maklakov's character that it reveals is through a series of vignettes and anecdotes. I postpone to later chapters discussion of his two most famous trials, which occurred after he had turned almost entirely to politics. One was the Vyborg Manifesto trial, where Kadet Duma members were charged with distribution of offensive material in a call for civil resistance to the tsar's proroguing of the First Duma in July 1906 (see chapter 6). The other was the defense of Menahem Beilis, whose prosecution arose entirely out of Beilis's being Jewish (see chapter 9).

In principle a Russian could become a full-fledged lawyer—could move from "assistant" to "sworn attorney" (from *pomoshchnik* to *prisiazhnyi poverennyi*)—only after serving a five-year apprenticeship. Happily the apprenticeship rules allowed an apprentice to engage in independent representation of a client without reaching the position of sworn attorney. For the many talented Jews hoping to become lawyers, the rules had a more serious impact, often preventing them from even securing status as an apprentice. If they overcame that hurdle, however, the barriers to their becoming sworn attorneys were of largely symbolic effect—the regime's way of expressing its attitude toward Jews.[1] Apart from these pointless obstructions, the apprentice rules did little to achieve their nominal training goals; in the words of one observer of patrons and their apprentices, "the first did not supervise, the second did not help."[2]

Maklakov's apprenticeship was especially odd. In one sense, he had two apprenticeships; in another sense, none. A friend of his father, the very distinguished lawyer Fyodor Plevako, asked him to apprentice with him and even seemed to assume he would do so. But Maklakov declined because he thought that Plevako, awash in clients, had accumulated so many assistants that they included quite a few of "deservedly questionable reputation." Consultation with his mentor L. V. Liubenkov, an elderly justice of the peace, confirmed his intuition and added an additional reason for avoidance. In choosing a patron, Liubenkov advised him, "Don't go with a famous one; there you won't learn anything. Don't go with an unknown; there you won't find enough work. Go with one who isn't famous, but soon will be." Liubenkov believed Alexander Robertovich Lednitskii met that standard, and Maklakov signed on with him. Events, in fact, made that apprenticeship a dead letter, but the two became good friends. When Maklakov set off from Russia for Paris in October 1917 to take up his post as ambassador, the Provisional Government's wartime security measures kept his travel information largely secret; among those in the know, only Lednitskii came to see him off at the Finland Station.[3]

Though Maklakov turned up at Lednitskii's at the appointed time to start his apprenticeship, he never worked with him. Because of a chance case-scheduling shift, Maklakov stepped into the shoes of Plevako at the last minute as counsel for one of the defendants in a major trial. The client was acquitted. As Maklakov later recounted, "The defense went so well that it made my name. I became an independent lawyer."[4]

The trial involved a set of rather sensational swindles at the Northern Insurance Company. The newly appointed procurator for Moscow, Alexander Makarov, later to be Russia's minister of internal affairs (indeed, the immediate predecessor of Maklakov's brother Nikolai), handled the case himself rather than assigning it to a deputy. Just before the trial Plevako was called to the Caucasus to fulfill a prior obligation in another case. Talking up Maklakov with what Maklakov calls "typical Plevako hyperbole," he urged his client to enlist Maklakov as his substitute. Because time was short, the client had little choice and acquiesced in the substitution.

In the ensuing high-profile trial, Maklakov's client, one Setkin, was only small-fry. He had used clients' funds to gamble on the stock exchange and had lost. Maklakov's strategy turned on an important idiosyncrasy of Russian law. It gave the jury the task of finding not only the elements of the crime, including "intent," but also whether the defendant deserved to be held criminally responsible on a moral basis. Perhaps the most famous application of the principle had been in the trial of Vera Zasulich, who had indisputably attempted to assassinate General F. F. Trepov, governor of St. Petersburg. The defense was that years of deprivation and political oppression had developed in her "an acutely sensitive nature"; this provided enough of an opening to allow the jurors to acquit.[5] Under Maklakov's guidance, Setkin openly confessed his guilt, but to explain it he testified that he'd been led down that path by the atmosphere of easy profit on the stock exchange. He also undertook to compensate the injured.

Although all the defendants were acquitted, Setkin's case was special because he had confessed his guilt. Maklakov's closing speech turned that seeming liability into a strength, arguing that in the circumstances a verdict of acquittal "would not whitewash Setkin's acts." A reporter covering the trial quoted that passage and wrote, "I congratulate the young advocate on his choice of words that were direct, truthful, honorable, and worthy of the highest justice." Favorable publicity of this sort solved the standard problem of a young lawyer—how to find clients—and at least in that sense mooted Maklakov's need to serve an apprenticeship.[6]

Though the Setkin defense may have made Maklakov's name, it was not his first case. That came to him through his friendship with Tolstoy and his family. Maklakov lived with his brother and sister in a small apartment on Zubovskii Boulevard, a few steps from where Tolstoy lived, on Khamovnicheskii Alley (since renamed Lev Tolstoy Street), and they were constantly over at the Tolstoys'. One day Tolstoy asked him if he would represent a member of a sect who had been found guilty of the crime of "inducement to schism" in the circuit court in Kaluga and had been immediately locked up.

According to the client, all that had happened was that he had passed by a factory as the workers were leaving, and they, knowing him, started to make fun of him. He had evidently overdone his response, but he firmly denied any intent to stir up a religious schism. By providing bail for the defendant, Maklakov made it possible to get an immediate appeal to a Moscow court rather than a delayed appeal in Kaluga. "Appeal" here meant an opportunity for retrial in a higher court.

The defendant had not testified at the trial, so the conviction was based simply on the evidence set out in the accusation. Maklakov was sure that if he testified the court would acquit him. But the defendant didn't appear for the retrial, so Maklakov could only argue that even if the defendant said the words charged by the prosecutor, they showed merely a squabble, not advocacy. The court split two-to-one against the defendant. Thus, as Maklakov later said, his "first pancake was lumpy," which quite irritated him. It turned out that the defendant had been in the courthouse all along but was too scared to enter the courtroom. Maklakov appealed yet another level up, on Plevako's urging that the Senate (actually a court, not a legislative body) was more liberal on religious matters than the lower court. Here there was no retrial, just a review of the existing record. Maklakov notes that Tolstoy wrote to a friend on the court, asking that the matter be given real attention; he doesn't say whether such a letter was proper under the prevailing standards.

At this stage the prosecutor conceded that there was no inducement to schism; rather he claimed that the defendant had blasphemed by labeling the church "vegetable keeper." But the defendant showed that some sort of Orthodox missal used that very phrase to describe the church. This brought smiles to the judges, and they acquitted.[7]

Maklakov took quite a number of other cases revolving around religious conflict and idiosyncrasy, some (perhaps all) sent to him by Tolstoy.[8] Maklakov's accounts paint a picture of Russian life far outside the high culture of his upbringing. One involved *beguny*, a subset of the Old Believers—Orthodox Christians who rejected Patriarch Nikon's reforms, of which the most controversial one involved the exact configuration of the fingers and thumb while making the sign of the cross. *Beguny* is derived from the Russian verb for "run" or "flight," and the name seems to have been attached to this group because their rules of noninvolvement with the state, or even money, made life in regular society impossible; they lived apart in the forests of the northern provinces. This separate life made it possible for people unknown to anyone to take refuge among them; ill-wishers claimed that they harbored buyers of stolen goods.

The beguny Maklakov represented were a couple accused of ritual murder, supposedly killing an old man by suffocating him with a red pillow. The "victim" had disappeared after "unknowns" had visited him, but his body was later found in the forest. The procurator argued that analysis of his corpse showed suffocation by a red pillow and offered "expert" opinions in support. On examination by Maklakov, one of the experts explained that the supposedly suffocating pillow must have been red because the sect itself called this sort of death *krasnaia smert*, literally "red death." Maklakov guessed that the phrase was probably a shortening of *prekrasnaia*, meaning "wonderful." It appeared that the community had a practice of removing from its midst people who seemed on the verge of death, which the procurator claimed was for the purpose of suffocating them. Maklakov got the help of experts in Moscow to confirm his view, and although the local court wouldn't allow him to call them, he used their information to frame arguments attacking the local "experts"—one of whom was a theologian who relied entirely on the other expert.

Luckily for Maklakov and the defendant, an ancient *begun* approached him at his inn the night before the trial's last day and told him that when death approached a member of the sect, the dying person was taken away from people and earthly activity so that he would die a "clean" death. But this potential witness was infuriated at the thought that Maklakov might ask him to say this in court. So Maklakov used the explanation in his summation, weaving rhetorical questions into discussion of the supposed experts' testimony ("Why could there not be another, much more simple explanation?").

The jury acquitted, and Maklakov talked with several of the jurors at the train station just before he left the town. They said they believed that the death was caused by suffocation but weren't convinced that "these people [the accused] did it."[9] The jurors seem to have done their job right, focusing on whether the accused actually committed the crime charged; only on a subsidiary issue did they go off the rails.

Two other "religious" cases deserve brief mention. The old man who had helpfully explained the "red death" to Maklakov was later arrested for refusal to give his name. The state required identification upon request as a protection against convicted criminals wandering about. The normal penalty was to send the refuser into exile. Maklakov tried to build a record that the defendant had a perfectly innocent reason for his refusal, and he hoped to persuade the Senate that applying the law to such a person would be invalid. The old man's explanation was that, since the reforms of Nikon, the church had taken the mark of the Antichrist, so he must not disclose his name. The logic of this is not at all clear, to be sure, but Maklakov hoped the reason might prove compelling if described by the defendant in a manner expressing full respect for the judges' good faith. The trial judges in fact found him guilty but ruled that because of his age he should merely be confined in a charitable institution. Maklakov hoped the Senate would reverse the conviction, but the defendant declined to appeal.[10]

Another case involved villagers who had torn down a church in a religious frenzy. Moses Teodosienko, a preacher from another sect, had turned up in town telling tales that he, like his namesake, was going to lead them out of heathen Egypt. Teodosienko left, and then Grigorii Pavlenko, one of the locals, convinced the villagers that he was about to ascend into heaven, and this was going to take place in the Orthodox Church. The villagers went to the church expecting a peaceful event—mothers brought their nursing babies. When they arrived, they found the gates locked, and a "voice from heaven" told Pavlenko that they should break the lock. They did so and entered. Pavlenko and two other people sat on the communion table, which broke apart. At the sight of this, the crowd went crazy, smashing everything of value.

The authorities initially responded to these bizarre events with great anxiety, talking of shunting the case to a military court (thus making a death penalty possible). In the end they settled for a closed trial in a civilian court, charging Moses, Pavlenko, and several other villagers. The defense, allowable under Russian law, was "delirium" or "frenzy," which seems an apt label. To pursue it would require a special inquiry, but the presiding judge cut that short. He asked Moses if he considered himself insane, and when Moses shook his head in the negative, the judge refused to order a mental examination. All defendants were convicted and sentenced to penal servitude.

At this point the case was saved, or at least ameliorated, by Ivan Shcheglovitov, who, as Maklakov says in his memoirs, "was not yet the Shcheglovitov he later became" (an arch-reactionary in his role as minister of justice). As part of his current post, either in the

Senate or the ministry of justice, he wrote a report highlighting the defects in the trial, and as a result the sentences were changed to "settlement with special medical observation."[11]

Quite apart from referrals by Tolstoy, Maklakov served as defense counsel in quite a number of high-profile political cases, or, as he said, cases that raised social issues but that the authorities preferred to regard as merely personal crimes. A collection of high-profile political trials in the period from 1901 through 1905 lists six with Maklakov as counsel, dealing with political demonstrations (Sormovo, May 1, 1902, and Novgorod, May 5, 1902), printing and distribution of May Day leaflets by members of the Socialist Revolutionary Party (Voronezh), a strike with the slogan "Destroy the autocracy" (Ekaterinoslav, August 7–11, 1903), an uprising on the battleship *Georgii Pobedonosets* (August 16–26, 1905), and armed resistance to arrest in a May Day demonstration (1905).[12]

A good example of Maklakov's approach is his defense of a group of peasants in the village of Dolbenkov, who had reacted to various injustices by going on a destructive rampage. They were indisputably guilty. Maklakov's summation was printed in full in *Russkie Vedomosti*, a leading liberal Moscow paper. It outlines the ways in which the peasants had been provoked by their employer's illegal behavior and the local authorities' indifference. He depicts the violence of the peasants' reaction as a function of the state's own brutality and arbitrariness.

> But if you start to blame them, representatives of state authorities, then I ask you: You want to condemn them, but what have you done to remedy their boorishness [*grubost*]? You have worked on many projects, you have tried to make them passive, subordinate to authority, peaceful before higher-ups. But have you, state authorities, worked to soften their morals, to instill a revulsion against boorishness? And how have you tried to achieve it? In the same way . . . you handled these events, by threatening them with birch rods, that they might all be thrashed. By having Cossack whips whistling down the streets, avoiding no

> one, sparing not even the children and priests. There are cruel morals among us, but from on high as well as from below. We reap from them the boorishness that we've sown. Punish them for having finally rebelled, for having lost patience, but know that once they lost patience, once order was violated, once the crowd broke up, it was inevitable that it would do all that in fact it did. Blame them for boorishness! A bitter joke for them. They are what you have made them, and you can as little reproach them for this boorishness as you can reproach for illiteracy those who have never been taught, or reproach infantrymen assigned as oarsmen for their inability to handle the seas.[13]

The trial ended in the acquittal of eighteen out of sixty-three accused. Perhaps more startling, the court itself sent a petition to higher authority asking that those condemned not be deprived of freedom or even subjected to police supervision; the petition was granted.[14]

Maklakov regarded the court's behavior as quite characteristic of the Russian courts before 1903. Defense counsel could argue for favorable interpretations of the statutes, and because "the judges were still judges, the defense counsel spoke a language that was understandable even by judges of an opposite political viewpoint. . . . This common language was founded on respect for the law and right, not on subordination to will, such as that of the monarchy, the majority, the 'prevailing party,' or 'revolutionary spirit.' "[15] But the courts became more politicized when a new criminal code reduced the ability of officials to penalize political offenders administratively, and the authorities thus relied more on the courts. The result was more abuse of the judicial process, which Maklakov experienced in his work.[16] Jonathan Daly confirms Maklakov's perceptions. Starting in 1905 the government made a special point of appointing to provincial courts of appeal senators "capable of exercising 'leadership' in them."[17] We may safely take "leadership" as a proxy for readiness to advance regime goals directly and by exercising pressure on other judges.

Before turning to Maklakov's role in the broader efforts of

lawyers, notice how, in all these cases, but especially in the Setkin and Dolbenkov cases, he tries to picture himself in the skin of the defendant. So it is not surprising that after his imprisonment by the Germans for several months during World War II, he expressed regret that he hadn't been in prison earlier: "If I'd known what solitary confinement was like, I would have framed my defense summations differently."[18]

The rising liberation movement naturally affected lawyers defending political cases. Some developed the practice—Maklakov dates it to a trial in 1903—of going to trial and then walking out in protest, either against a specific ruling or simply in outrage at the accusation itself. In the first use of the new tactic, some peasant defendants had been whipped by order of the provincial governor, and the court ruled that such an administrative measure was not "punishment." Apparently (Maklakov's account does not make it clear) the ruling thwarted some sort of double jeopardy defense. At this point defense counsel collectively walked out of the trial, leaving the defendants to their own devices. The ministry of internal affairs threatened at least one of the lawyers with administrative exile but didn't follow through.

Maklakov recalled going to Poltava with other lawyers, not to defend but to demonstratively refrain from offering a defense. In the railway car, N. P. Karabchevskii, a very distinguished lawyer whom Maklakov describes as a lawyer of the "old tradition," expressed his mystification at being summoned to a project where his talent would not be needed. The assembled lawyers met on the eve of the trial. Karabchevskii and another luminary of the old school, P. G. Mironov, spoke heatedly against the new tactic. They could not understand why the "sacred work of defense, their whole raison d'être," should be cast aside. But the innovators prevailed.

On many later occasions lawyers deployed the new approach. More administrative threats followed, and some action. A few lawyers were exiled to Archangelsk or Vologda, but this only made them heroes. Although Maklakov's account suggests he occasionally went along with the new tactic, he was plainly not an enthusiast; a fellow advocate characterizes him as a "bridge" between the old and new styles.[19]

Writing later as a historian, he deplores the tactic, arguing that it sharpened the warlike atmosphere between state and society and distorted the nature of a liberal profession.[20] He saw it as part of a fateful move by the liberation movement toward alliance with the revolutionaries, an "anti-state" movement—meaning a movement that saw no value in government institutions designed, however imperfectly, for the resolution and compromise of conflicting interests. He calls this anti-state element the "Acheron," invoking Juno's declaration in the *Aeneid*,

> *flectere si nequeo superos, Acheronta movebo*
>
> (If I cannot deflect the will of Heaven, I shall move Hell.)

While the defense lawyers' new tactic might isolate the autocracy, it would do so at a cost, creating a liberalism of a new type, one that "after victory could not manage the state."[21] By scorning state procedures for justly resolving cases, the lawyers were undermining the tools needed for a liberal state and denigrating the sort of self-discipline and realism needed to shift the Russian state from autocracy to constitutionalism.

For virtually all the clients discussed above, Maklakov plainly worked without compensation. To support his fairly comfortable lifestyle—hunting and fishing in Zvenigorod and vacations in France, for example—he clearly needed paying clients. He appears to have had them in abundance. He had a preference for criminal over civil cases because, he said, he didn't like to work through the sort of large organized apparatus needed for full-scale participation in civil litigation. Rather, he operated as a "strolling player." Thus he liked to participate in such cases only to address some basic issue of principle or to speak in court. His records show involvement in major libel cases involving newspapers and in a large group of high-stakes commercial cases involving major Russian enterprises.[22]

Maklakov found setting fees a troubling activity. It embarrassed him to recall from childhood how little his father—a distinguished doctor and professor—had been paid compared to what he earned as a young and inexperienced lawyer. In civil cases fees were set by law and custom, and they varied with the amount at stake. Not so for criminal cases, and there the comparison with his father made him propose rather low fees. This led to some curiosities. In one case at an early stage of his career, he suggested 500 rubles, which he thought was suitable; the potential client said he needed to think about it. Maklakov assumed the client thought it too high. Then he learned that the client had hired someone else for 5,000 rubles; he evidently took Maklakov's proposal as a signal that he was a lawyer of low quality. Occasionally fellow lawyers protested that he was undercutting them by applying what they saw as his unsuitable comparison with his father. He sometimes tried asking the client to name a fee, but this too presented problems. If it was too low, Maklakov would just decline, as he didn't like to bargain, but that would irritate the potential client.[23]

In one case—one that his memoirs don't mention—his fee elicited public criticism. In 1912 he defended one G. E. Tagiev, an entrepreneur in Baku involved in oil, textiles, and fish, who was accused of mistreating an employee. An article by Trotsky made a snide suggestion that the case showed that Maklakov's integrity was for sale, and the editors of Trotsky's collected works say that the fee took a toll on his reputation.[24] Perhaps not a heavy toll, as he was soon reelected to the Duma (the Fourth) with a still higher majority than in his election to the Third.[25]

Maklakov plainly earned a good living, as shown by his frequent vacations in France. But at least in some respects he exercised considerable thrift, perhaps recognizing that the excess of his earnings over those of his intelligent and hardworking father was partly due to pure luck. We learn that later, in Paris, he always rode the subway second class; he explained it to a friend as part of a desire to avoid arrangements in his private life that might foster "closed compartments and categories in society which would forever separate one man from another."[26]

As we saw, Maklakov's association with Plevako launched his career, and the two remained close, very often serving together as joint defense counsel. (In Russia, contrary to British practice, private lawyers did not serve as prosecutors, so there seems never to have been a case where Plevako and Maklakov opposed each other.[27]) While he had good reasons for not apprenticing with Plevako, he regarded him as "the first lawyer in Russia" and noted that his name had become in popular speech a generic word for a master of eloquence and law, as in, "Find another plevako."[28] As both were famous orators of the era, the St. Petersburg Society of Lovers of the Oratorical Arts naturally sought out Maklakov to speak at a gathering in honor of Plevako after his death in 1908.

Maklakov speaks with some awe of Plevako's "ability to fluently find the necessary words and form them into correct and flowing phrases." "He never had to search for words or think over phrases. The words in an obedient crowd poured into perfect sentences, perfectly expressed thoughts." In one case a prosecutor in summation made a stupid statement, and Plevako wrote on his scratch pad the single word "Fireworks." When Plevako reached the issue in his response, he addressed it with a true fireworks of thoughts and words, including "quotes from the Gospel, reliance on statutes, examples from the West, a summons to the memory of Alexander II."

Plevako prepared drafts ranging from a complete speech to notes of a few words, but wherever his preparation fell on that spectrum, his final words bore only a slight relation to what he had written. Often the whole structure of the speech changed. He might use a successful expression or a pointed phrase from the preparations, but those were the exceptions, which only underscored the general rule.

After a case on which they had cooperated, Plevako was preparing an appellate brief, and Maklakov asked him to send him drafts. He did so—a whole slew of drafts (five or six) successively typed out by Plevako on his Remington. All were without strike-overs or revisions, yet all were quite different and had plainly been started afresh. When Maklakov spoke to him about it, Plevako said it was always easier for him to start from the beginning. He acted with words, says Maklakov, "the way a rich man might casually throw money to the wind."

As Plevako had no need for advance preparation to find the necessary words, what purpose did his notes serve? Only, says Maklakov, to assure himself that he had an abundance of material. As a result, if a new topic struck him during a speech, he could leave his plan without fear or regret.

When Plevako lapsed from spontaneity his oratory paid a price. Maklakov cites his summation in M. A. Stakhovich's suit against Prince Meshcherskii, a high-profile, politically sensitive libel case on which the two cooperated. Evidently nervous about the political implications, Plevako hewed fairly closely to his text, and in Maklakov's view the speech suffered from length and ornateness, drawbacks in Plevako's writing. Though very good, it fell short of his usual work. In another situation, Plevako sent a reporter a segment of a speech that had been written (or at least polished) after the speech was delivered; Maklakov thought it "a cold-blooded creation of the office, which lay like a pale patch on the brilliant background of improvisation."[29]

Maklakov seems never to have described his own methods. Apart from his awe of Plevako's spontaneity, there are other clues to Maklakov's approach—a preference for knowing in advance fairly exactly what he would say. His friend and fellow Kadet deputy in the Duma, Mikhail Chelnokov, told a mutual friend that on the eve of his speeches Maklakov would often go to him and deliver the next day's speech with the same voice and urgency as he would later use from the Duma tribune.[30] This suggests preparation down to the finest detail. Georgii Adamovich, who was Maklakov's first Russian biographer and had known him and many of his contemporaries, reports that listeners were divided, some believing Maklakov memorized every word and every detail, such as pauses for thought, and others believing that he could deliver a lengthy speech with advance preparation of only its general content.[31] Whatever the method (likely a combination of the two), the effect was one of conversational spontaneity. Vaclav Lednitskii, son of the Lednitskii for whom Maklakov almost apprenticed, affirms that Maklakov could write and deliver a speech so that it sounded like the spoken, rather than the written, word.[32]

In his reminiscence, the younger Lednitskii shares with us an eccentric detail of Maklakov's life. Summer and winter, he reports, Maklakov used to wear a Russian cap, which, with his beard, gave him the appearance of a sixteenth- or seventeenth-century Russian—hardly the convention for an up-and-coming member of the bar in the twentieth century. When he came to Paris in 1917 as ambassador-designate of the Russian Provisional Government, he replaced the cap with a beret.[33]

Maklakov's memorial address on Plevako ranged far beyond his oratory. Painting a picture of a fellow lawyer, a deeply patriotic Russian, a public figure, and a friend, the talk also portrays the portraitist himself and his time. As a foil for describing Plevako, Maklakov uses *Vekhi* (Landmarks, or Signposts), a famous book published the same year as his address, which skewered (or sought to skewer) the Russian intelligentsia. Without endorsing the book's accuracy, Maklakov notes a number of attributes that it ascribed to the intelligentsia, most notably irreligion and lack of national feeling. He argues that Plevako lay at the antipodes from *Vekhi*'s characterizations. Plevako was, in fact, highly religious and dedicated to the Orthodox Church, giving it large sums of money. But at the same time he was an ardent defender of the Old Believers in the face of their persecution by the church and the regime, and was reverent toward Tolstoy's theological works. For him, defense of religious freedom did not grow out of indifference to religion. Maklakov suggests he had a loose affinity for Tolstoy's view of the state: "By instinct [Plevako] was an anarchist, though intellectually he understood the need for the state."[34]

Besides the implicit anarchism, Maklakov depicts Plevako's ability to form a bond with the sinner, who, in his profession, was often the defendant. "He could penetrate the interest, the grief, the suffering of whoever he was defending. . . . He immediately saw what was best in a person, what to others might be invisible." And more broadly, in terms echoing the "Grand Inquisitor" passage in Dostoevsky's *The Brothers Karamazov*, Maklakov writes, "There was nothing that could make him sacrifice a person: no belief in the saving character of any specific form of government, no devotion to doctrine, none of the intolerance arising out of such devotion." Adamovich remarked that in Maklakov's summation for Setkin, pleading that even a verdict of acquittal could not whitewash him, his spirit and tone were Plevako's.[35]

In addressing Plevako's sense of national feeling, Maklakov tells the story of a winter trip the two took to defend a case.

> The harness came undone. I was angry not only that we were going to be forced to freeze in the field, but because all this happened close to the station, where there had been time to check how well the horse was harnessed. Plevako began to comically describe how the muzhik [peasant] got up in the morning, saw that the harness was bad, but hoped to get to the station; but when he got to the station he noticed that it nearly held, and hoped that he could make it to the farrier, and so forth. He preferred Russian thoughtlessness to American enterprise or German precision.[36]

While Maklakov may have felt more irritation than Plevako at the peasant's haphazard ways, he clearly shared Plevako's affection for the Russian people and their way of life. This was part of what it meant, for both of them, to love Russia.

In Plevako's case, sympathy for casual peasant ways may have arisen partly from identification. "His vagueness was legendary." Once, having asked people to his home, he found it necessary to change the time and place and then arranged meetings with them for another time, but in three different places. "At the named hour he was at still a fourth place. This sort of thing made him enemies, and led to unflattering legends, but only among those who didn't understand him. Many could not, and paid for it [in loss of the rewards of his company]."[37]

Maklakov's talk conjures up a Plevako who, far more than a brilliant lawyer, was a great soul.

> You can teach yourself much—logic, and rhetoric and real eloquence. But it's impossible to teach yourself such an understanding of life, such an attitude to people. To be an orator such as Plevako was, you need to be a person such as he was—not by talent, not by a gift of words, all that is secondary, but in his spiritual cast of mind, love of man, inability to indulge righteous or even justifiable hatred, in the ability to look at things not through the eyes of this world, which made him so unlike others.[38]

As the relationship with Plevako suggests, Maklakov was by no means a solitary lawyer. He became deeply involved in lawyers' voluntary associations. During the reactionary reign of Alexander III, the government generally tried to limit the rights of lawyers' assistants, but there had been a revival of the bar in the second half of the 1890s, when Maklakov was starting his career. Young lawyers started "wandering clubs," so-called because their meetings migrated from one member's apartment to another's. They talked about mutual problems and current affairs, but they also arranged for free advice to workers and peasants. Maklakov saw the wandering clubs as "breathing life" into the bar, trying to turn it from a group simply enhancing the members' professional skills and prosperity to one that served society.[39]

Among their activities were confronting and overcoming technical legal restrictions on service in the provinces by lawyers from the capital cities who had not advanced from "assistant" to "sworn attorney." The young lawyers largely succeeded, aided by the cooperation of judges who responded conscientiously, even though the presence of better representation for defendants increased their work. These trials in the provinces (Maklakov uses the term *uezd*, or "district") were not only helpful for the accused but "the most outstanding school" for the young lawyers. Defense was not a matter of rhetorical razzle-dazzle but was aimed at ordinary jurors; the jurors created a businesslike mood that the lawyers had to echo. Later, on the stump in Duma elections, he was impressed by the voters' similar seriousness of purpose.[40]

Lawyers involved in defense of political cases formed an association, and Maklakov naturally played a leadership role. On November 20, 1904, the association called for a constitution for Russia, and, according to fellow lawyer Iosif Gessen, Maklakov was quite proud of the lawyers for doing so.[41] But the association took a new turn as a result of the tsar's decree of February 18, 1905, which invited Russians to express their concerns about the state and its direction. The Union of Liberation responded with efforts to encourage the creation of other "unions" revolving around particular professions or concerns: there were unions for "agronomists and statisticians," for "pharmaceutical assistants," for "equal rights for Jews," and so on. Galai lists fourteen such unions, to which others were added. The association of lawyers providing defense in political trials now embraced the spirit of the Liberation Movement.[42]

It isn't clear whether Maklakov was very active in the lawyers' association after it was enveloped by the Liberation Movement's unions. Certainly in retrospect, Maklakov criticized it as having only one activity—the adoption of political resolutions, specifically what he called the "cliché template." The cliché consisted of a call for a constitution drafted by a constituent assembly, in turn to be chosen by "four-tailed suffrage" ("four-tailed" was the liberals' phrase for a universal, direct, equal, and secret franchise). He argued that the resolutions didn't arise from any professional skill or expertise, but only from the fact of the intelligentsia's having settled on the package. The peasant's union[43] had joined the cliché template, though, as Maklakov joked, they really wanted the landowners' land and regarded calling for a constituent assembly with four-tailed suffrage as "a cheap price to pay for land." In later chapters I'll consider his affirmative objections to the cry for a constituent assembly and the liberals' favored franchise, but for now it's enough to say that Maklakov saw the outburst of these preprogrammed platforms from synthetic organizations as a natural result of the autocracy's having so long stifled genuine expression of opinion.

> People close to the process knew that they represented only themselves. But the ease with which the inexperienced and disturbed society submitted to the intelligentsia's propaganda, and accepted any position, justified this imposture. Where there is not a true representative system, it's easy not only to speak for others, but to be convinced that you're expressing public opinion. The authorities' long policy of preventing the organization of society yielded its fruit. Through the decree of February 18 [1905], they turned the intelligentsia leaders into spokesmen of the people's will.[44]

In May 1899 Maklakov played a role at the Moscow Juridical Society's celebration of the one hundredth anniversary of Alexander Pushkin's birth. Unlike many ceremonial occasions, this one became famous in its own right. Sergei Muromtsev, a very distinguished older lawyer, later to be chairman of the First Duma, gave the main speech and used it to celebrate Pushkin as a seeker of freedom and independence. "Together with the memory of the poet we celebrate the victory won by Russian individuality over routine life and government tutelage." This brought the wrath of God down on the society, or, more precisely, the wrath of Maklakov's old foe N. P. Bogolepov, then minister of education, who closed the society, which was institutionally part of Moscow University. Before Muromtsev's fateful speech, there had been a preliminary round of brief welcoming talks, including one by Maklakov. One of the preceding welcomers had argued that the society should not involve itself in politics. Maklakov used his time by responding to this, arguing that law always posed the question of its relationship to right. In recognizing that law doesn't necessarily correspond to right, members of the society would have to discuss political values.[45]

It would be convenient to argue that Maklakov's life as a practicing lawyer gave him a good understanding of the thinking of Russia's people and of their true needs. Indeed, I think that is so. But we must be cautious: many of the other liberals were lawyers by trade but nevertheless prone to a doctrinaire utopianism quite alien to Maklakov.

CHAPTER 3

Friends and Lovers

MAKLAKOV WAS GENERALLY gregarious—obvious exceptions being the forced march to his law degree and his fateful neglect of his friend Nicholas Cherniaev. His friends included some relatively well-known Russians, of whom Tolstoy is by all odds the best known; and the archives include records of his romantic interests, some of whom were prolific letter writers.

He knew Anton Chekhov, and although he saw him at least once at the Tolstoys', had known him before then. Among their bonds was the Zvenigorod area, where Maklakov owned hunting and fishing land and where Chekhov had lived as young man. Chekhov in fact looked for a country property near Maklakov's, but, as he reported to Maklakov, the place he visited proved overpriced.[1] When Chekhov came to meet Tolstoy at Yasnaya Polyana, the Tolstoys' country estate, Maklakov happened to be on hand. Chekhov arrived on a morning train, and Tolstoy, who usually wrote in the morning, excused himself and asked Maklakov to show Chekhov around. After the tour, the two writers began to chat. Chekhov gave Tolstoy an account of his trip to Sakhalin

Maklakov and Olga Knipper, Chekhov's wife. © State Historical Museum, Moscow.

to study the penal colony there. He had traveled through Siberia to reach Sakhalin, and Tolstoy somewhat oddly responded to Chekhov's Sakhalin account by rhapsodizing about the miraculous grandeur of Siberia's mountains, rivers, forests, and animals. Chekhov agreed, and then Tolstoy asked, with surprise and some reproach, "Then why didn't you show it?" After breakfast, Chekhov shook his head and said to Maklakov, "What a person!"[2]

Maklakov also knew Maxim Gorky, presumably through his (Maklakov's) stepmother; Maklakov was evidently a prototype for one Klim Samgin, the main figure in a four-volume Gorky novel that is now largely forgotten.[3] Maklakov was also a friend of the great opera singer Fyodor Chaliapin. The origins of their meeting are unknown, but it may have stemmed from Maklakov's defense of Nikolai and Savva Mamontov in a securities trial,[4] Savva being a wealthy backer of Chaliapin. When Chaliapin was dying in Paris in the 1930s, Maklakov was a frequent visitor, entertaining him with the latest political gossip.[5]

Chapters 1 and 2 mentioned Maklakov's first meeting and early contacts with Tolstoy. Their friendship, together with Maklakov's reading of his literary and philosophical works, provided the background for several lectures Maklakov gave after Tolstoy's death devoted to Tolstoy's thinking and life and their role in Russia and the world. All the lectures look at Tolstoy both from the outside, as any scholar of Tolstoy might, and from the inside, as Tolstoy's much younger and much less renowned friend. Maklakov never hides either his profound analytical disagreement with Tolstoy's views on political economy, or his reverence for Tolstoy as a man of conscience.

Postcard from Vasily Maklakov on vacation with friends in Vichy, France, to his sister Mariia. Vasily is on the extreme left; Fyodor Chaliapin, the opera star, is third from left. © State Historical Museum, Moscow.

The pivotal lecture is the one on Tolstoy's "Teaching and Life," delivered in 1928 at a celebration of the centenary of Tolstoy's birth.[6] It tackles the origins of the philosophic outlook that Tolstoy had embraced by the mid-1880s, expressed in *What I Believe* (published in 1884) and summarized in the idea that evil must never be resisted with force. Maklakov himself appears to have been an agnostic. Letters he wrote near the end of his life reveal that he was at one time a believer and found his belief comforting; at some point he lost that belief and recognized that only genuine belief could provide consolation.[7]

Maklakov starts with the obvious truth that Tolstoy enjoyed all the rewards that the world can offer—nature gave him bodily strength, health, strong passions, ardor for life, and extraordinary literary gifts. Fate brought him wealth and allowed him not to worry about what the next day would bring or to bother with anything not fitting his taste or spirit. It gave him exceptional ties to the world and rewarded him with glory not only in Russia but throughout the world. It gave him, "as a crown," exceptional family happiness. Yet, as Tolstoy made clear in his philosophical writings, the prospect of death led him to believe that life was meaningless, to the point of tempting him to suicide.[8]

After some false starts toward a solution, Tolstoy found one in the core message of the Sermon on the Mount—not to resist evil with force, but to turn the other cheek. For Tolstoy, this rule of nonresistance to evil was *not* part of a system involving life after death, and it was *not* a rule whose force depended on Christ's being God. Indeed, Tolstoy often said (here Maklakov is presumably giving an eyewitness account), "If I thought of Christ as God, and not human, Christ would lose all appeal for me." He read the gospels as *not* promising eternal life, as *not* contrasting a temporary individual life with an immortal individual life. Rather, the contrast he saw was between an individual life and a life lived entirely for others. When our personal life truly turns into a common life, he reasoned, the meaninglessness of life disappears, and a new meaning appears that no individual death can destroy.[9] In his memoirs

Maklakov tells a story reflecting the intensity of Tolstoy's belief. In a conversation about not resisting evil, the wife of Tolstoy's oldest son (Sergei) asked Tolstoy whether, if he saw some attempt to violate his wife before his very eyes, he wouldn't intervene to protect her and feel sorry for her. Tolstoy answered that he would feel even more sorry for the rapist. Everyone laughed, and Tolstoy was quite angry, as he had not intended it as a joke, but really meant that someone who acted that way must be doing so from a very deep unhappiness.[10]

Maklakov's speech, though mentioning a theological critique of Tolstoy by biblical scholars, presses a practical argument—that if neither individuals nor the state are to resist evil with force (where forceless resistance would fail), evil will triumph. He points out as an example the vandalization of a Tolstoyan settlement that he experienced during his university years.[11] He then turns around and defends Tolstoy's perspective. He asks rhetorically: If you think that property prevents us from turning individual life into a common life, and regard individual life as meaningless under conventional worldly conditions, then is there anything strange in nonresistance to evil, in "voluntarily giving away that odious private property to anyone who might want it?" Thus, Maklakov reasons, any refutation of Tolstoy must be directed not at his conclusions but at his original starting point. If you accept Tolstoy's premises, a renunciation of force seems to follow.[12]

As the lecture and Maklakov's memoirs underscore, Tolstoy's basic kindness and common sense seem to have prevented him from following his own views with any consistency. In his memoirs Maklakov recounts how, on his return from his first trip to England, he gave Tolstoy an enthusiastic account of English government. Tolstoy was dismissive, saying that in principle there was no difference between English government and Russian autocracy. The conversation occurred at a time when the Dukhobors in Russia, members of a religious sect that rejected military service (on rather Tolstoyan grounds), had been subjected to ruthless oppression, including dispersal from their villages and forced resettlement, with the predictable result of widespread deaths from starvation and exposure. Tolstoy had responded actively, moving heaven and earth to help them migrate to Canada, raising funds, trying to stir public opinion, and giving them the proceeds from his novel *Resurrection.* Maklakov posed the obvious question: how could Tolstoy reconcile his indifference to the advantages of British government over Russia's autocracy with his making all these efforts? Tolstoy said, "Ah, lawyer, you've caught me." But then he added that the difference between the two was like that between the guillotine and hanging. In fact, from his perspective the guillotine was worse, because its evil was better concealed.[13]

The inconsistencies go on and on. Tolstoy energetically promoted the "single tax" ideas of Henry George, pressing the case in a letter to Prime Minister Pyotr Stolypin and urging Maklakov to introduce George-type legislation in the Duma. Such legislation would tax away the entire value of unimproved real estate (and the value of improved real estate not directly attributable to improvements). The state would thus confiscate that value and wipe out the real estate market as a source of information about development prospects (through the signals given by market prices). The foe of all state power advocates a monumental exercise of state power![14]

But Maklakov stressed Tolstoy's efforts to improve the lives of ordinary Russians, however inconsistent some of the efforts might have been with his philosophy: writing Russia's first alphabet books; writing the first works for children that rose above dreary, implausible celebrations of contemporary Russian life (a leading "reader" was a book called "Milord," with about zero resonance for a peasant child); actually operating schools in the vicinity of Yasnaya Polyana and teaching in them; and, of course, relieving the 1891 famine and rescuing the Dukhobors. Maklakov observes, "His activity for his country was such that if ten people had done it, rather than Tolstoy, one could say of each that they had not lived on earth in vain."[15]

Beyond these direct practical benefits, Maklakov pointed to a subtler, perhaps more far-reaching one—the way Tolstoy's teachings reminded people of the independent force of good. If his readers were skeptical on practical grounds, if they "held back from following his conclusions, like the rich young man in the Gospels, all the same they started to look on the problems of life with different eyes."[16]

And by raising questions about the meaning of life, Maklakov argues, Tolstoy—though excommunicated and buried without a funeral service—did more for the revival of religious interest than anyone. The danger to religion, he suggests, is not from those who deny it or even those who persecute believers, nor from the slogan that it's an opiate, nor from the propaganda of the godless. Rather, the danger comes from indifference, from lack of interest in the questions with which religion deals. And Tolstoy couldn't live without answers to those questions.[17]

The intellectual divide between the two was most acute in their views of the law, discussed by Maklakov in a lecture on "Tolstoy and the Courts." After laying out Tolstoy's belief that the state's exercise of force was itself evil (regardless of the net effect on evil), Maklakov points to the radical character of Tolstoy's objections. Tolstoy did not especially condemn the courts' form, their incompleteness, the inadequacies of their procedures, the cruelty of punishments, or judicial mistakes; rather he condemned the very principle of their existence. He saw Christ's famous instruction "judge not, that ye be not judged" as forbidding the very institution.[18] That attitude toward law, and even the rule of law, was very much aligned with the views of Russia's literary elite discussed in the Introduction.

Tolstoy not only condemned the courts as organs of state violence but also saw them as worse than more generally suspect institutions. The evil perpetrated by an executioner is obvious. But everything conspires to mask the evil of the judge. The judge who condemns someone to death doesn't carry out the sentence; it is not he who deprives the person of life, but the law; if the law is bad and unjust, that is not his concern—or so Tolstoy assumed![19] Maklakov cites Tolstoy's story, "Let the fire burn—don't put it out," observing that he could confidently quote passages of it from memory "because it was under the scrutiny of the censor so many times." The cause of the censor's hostile gaze was the story's seeming exaltation of criminal acts: one character's unlawful concealment of another's crime is depicted as fulfilling God's law.[20]

In his literary treatment of the courts, Tolstoy sometimes spoke not as a prophet inveighing against any state application of force but as a political figure and revolutionary. In *Resurrection* the law serves only to advance the interests of the ruling elite. This of course is a much more worldly message; as Maklakov observes, he is "speaking our language, addressing our concerns."[21]

Lawyers fare even worse than courts under Tolstoy's gaze. As the judge is worse than the hangman, because he can hide his guilt behind his role, so the lawyer is even worse than the judge, because he can even more persuasively distance himself from the evils wrought by the courts and the state. In his memoirs Maklakov recounts three occasions on which Tolstoy received lawyers at Yasnaya Polyana. The three lawyers (Oscar Gruzenberg, N. P. Karabchevskii, and Fyodor Plevako) were all very distinguished and often active for the defense in political trials; at the Beilis trial they and Maklakov constituted the defense team (with the exception of Plevako, who had died by then). Yet, except for Maklakov's special friend Plevako, they irritated Tolstoy with their thinking process and attitudes.[22]

Maklakov, of course, had dedicated his life to law and politics, activities that he believed would advance the welfare of Russians. He exalted the courts as guardians of the law. He concludes with another mention of Tolstoy's many actual efforts at improving life in this world, calling the relation between his beliefs and his life "an inconsistency, a touching, miraculous inconsistency."[23]

Through his work on the 1891 famine, Maklakov met Tolstoy at his home in Moscow and talked with him for the first time.[24] Tolstoy read his guests an article, and "everything seemed so natural and simple that I had to force myself to understand my good fortune and grasp where I was sitting. His wife, Sofia Andreevna, . . . called us all to the dining table." After that he was often at the Tolstoys' home, until Tolstoy's death.[25] "It was great luck for me. The whole world knows Tolstoy's literary work. Some know his religious thinking, often only in part and not fully understanding it. To know the living Tolstoy, to experience his charm oneself, was given to very few."[26] Most of what follows as to Tolstoy's character is drawn from Maklakov's direct knowledge. Here is his overview:

> For those who knew Tolstoy, there was no personal pride; on the contrary, no one could miss his dissatisfaction with himself, eternal doubt in himself, his touching shyness, his reluctance to dazzle, even his inability to play a leading role. . . . In Tolstoy everything was ordinary and simple. He never imposed on others the innermost principles by which he lived, never made them the subject of general conversation. If someone not knowing who he was should by chance find himself in his presence, he would not guess who was before him; he could not believe that this simple and kind old man, listening with such interest to the general conversation, was the very Tolstoy whom the whole world knew.[27]

Despite Maklakov's own conviction that Tolstoy's self-effacement was genuine, he recognized that it might seem a contrivance. As he notes, it put Tchaikovsky off when he met Tolstoy—simply, argues Maklakov, because of the mismatch between the real Tolstoy and the grand image held by the world at large.[28]

Maklakov was present at Tolstoy's last departure from Moscow for Yasnaya Polyana, from which he then started on the journey that took him to his deathbed at the railway station in Astapovo. The newspapers had carried word of the departure, and the square in front of the railway station was packed. Everyone rushed toward the carriage that was bearing Tolstoy and his wife and daughters to the station, and the Tolstoys were able to make it inside only by

Countess Sofia Tolstoy, with a dedicatory inscription to Maklakov, July 2, 1896.

using a special entrance. The crowd rushed to the train, and the wave of people carried Maklakov to the railway car with Tolstoy. Through the open window, Maklakov saw Tolstoy thrust his head forward, and, mumbling with an old man's voice, with tears flowing down his pale cheeks, he thanked the people for their sympathy, which he said he "hadn't expected." He didn't know what more to say, and, noticing Maklakov, turned to him with relief; no longer able to comfortably appear before the public, he was content to see a familiar face.

Maklakov closes the 1928 "Teaching and Life" speech with these words:

> At Astapovo, a few months [after the departure from Moscow], he said to those nearest him, "You've come here for Lev alone, but in Russia there are millions." He could talk that way and think that way. And the world loved him all the more that he thought that way. The world appreciated that Tolstoy, having received all the blessings that the world can offer, was not tempted by them. The world could not but be touched that, with access to all that, Tolstoy preferred a life according to God. And it was all the more striking that Tolstoy came to the precepts of Christ not because he was ordered by God but because he found them a sensible basis for human life. . . . To not consider Christ God, to not believe in life after death, to not believe in requital, and all the same to preach those precepts, to consider that joy consists for a human in renunciation of individual happiness, in life for the good of others, meant to reveal a faith in good and the goodness of man that no one in the world had ever had.
>
> The world did not follow Tolstoy, and it was right. His teaching was not of this world. But listening to Tolstoy's message, the world opened in itself those good feelings which the trivia of life had long since drowned; the world itself became better than it ordinarily was. Tolstoy did not flatter it, but stirred its conscience and lifted it to his level. And while Tolstoy lived, the world saw in him a living bearer of faith in goodness and in man. Thus the life of Tolstoy was so dear to the world that on November 7, [1910], when Tolstoy died, the world was no

> longer what it had been. Something in it died forever. But Russia, in which Tolstoy lived, and which he would not have traded away for anything, Russia, which he loved most of all—Russia, humble, poor and backward, which did not know what misfortunes lay before it, did not foresee that it would soon come to know by its own experience the whole depth of human vileness and cold-blooded indifference, Russia instinctively felt that on the day of his death it lost its protector.[29]

Did Maklakov's association with Tolstoy affect his own behavior as a public figure? If you look for specific impacts, you will find few. One of Maklakov's favorite words is the untranslatable *gosudarstvennost,* which has some overtones of "rule of law" but tends perhaps even more to connote the simple value of having a working state, standing athwart chaos. He often observed that even a bad state was generally better than no state at all; Tolstoy, of course, engaged in no such pragmatic comparisons. While Maklakov obviously did not like war, he was no pacifist: he believed there were circumstances where the consequences of refusing to fight were worse than those of fighting. But Maklakov's reasoning was almost invariably pragmatic and consequentialist.

One issue escaped Maklakov's general rejection of Tolstoy's political positions—the death penalty. (Even here Maklakov's position is qualified by pragmatism—he regarded it as essential in wartime.) Perhaps his most famous speech was his attack on a system of virtual kangaroo courts created by the tsar and Stolypin in the summer of 1906. The aim of this system, the so-called field courts martial, was to stamp out an ongoing wave of assassinations. Maklakov's prime target was the procedures of the courts: their extreme speed, the absence of any right of appeal, and a virtual presumption of guilt once the defendant was charged. We'll come to the speech in the discussion of Maklakov's role in the Second Duma. For now, the interesting feature is that his argument against the death penalty takes a Tolstoyan form. Rather than marshaling policy arguments (the uncorrectability of errors, the questionable deterrent effects, the consequences for Russia's reputation in Europe, etc.), he tells a story: Characterizing the procedure as "a legal rite of death," he invites the listener to observe the scene when the death penalty is applied:

> They lead a person, captured, disarmed and tied up, and tell him that in a few hours he will be killed. They allow his relatives to bid farewell to him—near and dear to them, young and healthy—who by the will of other humans will die. They lead him to the scaffold, like cattle to the slaughter, tie him to the spot where the coffin is ready, and in the presence of the doctor, procurator and priest, who have been blasphemously called to watch the business, they quietly and solemnly kill him. The horror of this legal assassination exceeds all the excesses of revolutionary terror.[30]

Of course Maklakov might have come to such a viewpoint, and to such a rhetoric, on his own. But the reliance entirely on description and the complete avoidance of policy arguments and consequences, smacks of Tolstoy.

Yet Tolstoy's influence on Maklakov seems most powerful at a broader level—in Maklakov's capacity to see alternative viewpoints, his practice of fairly discussing contrary claims even while advocating whatever approach he had come to regard as best. Earlier we saw his recognition of the contradictions between Tolstoy's theories and his life. What could give a man more readiness to see the other side of an issue than to enjoy the friendship of a man whose life was a world of contradictions; to admire—indeed to worship and even love—a man whose mental processes and convictions were virtually the opposite of his own; and to recognize this man, whose political judgments must have seemed almost crazy, as a beacon for Russia and the world?

Of course the child who responded to his classmate's proposition about the origin of the universe by asking where the red-hot sphere had come from was not likely to buy simplistic positions, to disregard the vulnerabilities of any contention. But Maklakov's long relationship with Tolstoy seems likely to have fostered his sense of truth's complexity.

Maklakov's extensive memoirs never discuss his romantic life. The Moscow archives of his papers contain a record of his divorce from Evgenia Pavlovna Maklakova in 1899,[31] but so far as I can tell have nothing else about the marriage. The archives also contain a good deal of correspondence of an "intimate character,"[32] but I'll address just two relationships of special interest (overlapping in time): with Lucy Bresser (whose stage name was Vera Tchaikovsky), a voluminous correspondent,[33] and Alexandra Kollontai, a major political figure in her own right.[34] Despite the silence of his memoirs on the subject, Maklakov seems to have been not at all secretive about his loves. Rosa Vinaver, wife of his Kadet colleague Maxim Vinaver, tells of a train trip from St. Petersburg to Paris, during which she conversed with him all the way until they were approaching Berlin. Maklakov said, "Here I must get out. I'm about to meet a very interesting lady." On the platform appeared Kollontai, "as always graceful and elegant," says Vinaver.[35] Recall that Maklakov named a happy family life as "the crown" of Tolstoy's enjoyment of worldly blessings; yet we really have no clue why he didn't seriously seek out that blessing for himself.

The relationship with Lucy Bresser involved at least a momentary brush with marriage. It began with Maklakov's providing legal representation in some dispute in which Bresser seems to have been involved as a relative of a party. Her first (preserved) letter to him starts as follows:

> I am writing this not to the dear companion of a night's journey from St. Petersburg to Moscow but rather to the unknown lawyer who sat with me in the Buffet of the Palais de Justice—whom I had the honor & intense satisfaction of thanking—of thanking for his efforts & success by a kiss.[36]

The breathless style continues for about four hundred pages over nearly a decade, with punctuation rarely taking any form other than a dash. Lucy was married to a Cyril Bresser, so any marriage to Maklakov would have required a divorce. Evidently Cyril wasn't ready to agree to one, so "apparently we shall have to find someone to swear that we were together—the difficulty is to make Cyril sue me for divorce."[37] The social stigma involved is suggested by Lucy's mother's reaction: "My mother calls me a prostitute & that I ought to be shot—if only someone would do it."[38] Maklakov (as quoted back to him in her letters, our only source) responded rather captiously to the need to show guilt under English law: Lucy quotes his rhetorical question: "Qu'est ce qui empêche de devenir coupable?" and in English, "What's easier than to become guilty?"[39]

More troubling, Maklakov seems to have reversed his position on marriage over the brief interval between June 8 and June 14, 1910. Bresser lays it out: "[O]n the 8th of June you reply to my question of divorce 'Ai-je l'intention de t'épouser.' Ah, il ne m'est plus difficile de le dire. Je le désire, je le veux de tout mon âme." ["Do I intend to marry you. It's no longer difficult to say. I want to, I want to with all my soul."] Then "on the 14th your first letter of doubt arrived—what has happened between 8th & 14th?"[40] If Maklakov ever offered a real answer, her letters don't reflect it back. In a sense, the question is why he ever proclaimed his wish to marry her. He seems not to have been the marrying kind (or, more precisely, the remarrying kind), and her letters suggest a flightiness, even to the point of incoherence, that boded ill for the long term.

The relationship, though featuring many a rendezvous that filled Lucy with delight, was persistently troubled by her dependency. Her letters are filled with requests for money. He met many such requests, but not all—or not completely. We don't know the exact words Maklakov used to resist the claims, but she clearly read them as suggesting that she was a kept woman. She saw the financial aid differently: his desire to be able to be with her at times that fitted his schedule necessarily impeded her freedom to pursue her stage career. She regarded his financial help as no more than compensation for that impediment.

Alexandra Kollontai, a Menshevik who evolved into a Bolshevik, could hardly have been more different. Like Maklakov, she was an impressive orator, stirring audiences with revolutionary fervor. Like Maklakov, she was named to diplomatic posts (in Norway, Mexico, and Sweden), holding the rank of ambassador after 1943; she had the advantage over Maklakov in that, unlike the Provisional Government, the government that appointed her remained in office. She was an articulate advocate of "free love," or at least "comradely love," and she lived in accord with her precepts. Her novel, *Red Love*, is a lightly concealed tract in favor of free love (or perhaps more precisely, against any feelings of sexual jealousy) and against what she saw as the triumph in the early Soviet state of commercial and managerial greed over pure communist ideals. The heroine's husband is generally seen as modeled on the lover with whom she had the most intense and extended relationship, a worker named Pavel Dybenko; *Red Love*'s heroine is named Vasilisa—in homage to Vasily Maklakov?

The two seem to have gotten on very well politically. One letter reflects Kollontai's reading of a series of Maklakov's speeches in the Duma: "The first speech on the peasant question was very powerful, exact and successful. The later ones less satisfying."[41] Curiously, at the height of the Stalinist bloodletting in 1937, she wrote to a friend expressing a positively Maklakovian skepticism about Russia's readiness for popular rule: "Historically, Russia, with her numberless uncultured, undisciplined masses, is not mature enough for democracy."[42]

Like Maklakov, Kollontai wasn't fully at home in her political party, though perhaps she was more vocal in her dissent. After the October Revolution she helped found a "Workers' Opposition," aimed at fighting bureaucratic encroachment on worker control in industry. Her (and others') ardor in the project helped precipitate a Communist clampdown on intra-party expressions of disagreement: in 1921 the party adopted resolutions condemning the Workers' Opposition and claiming the right to expel members for "factionalism."[43] As was true of Maklakov, she had a deep skepticism about her party's leadership. In 1922 she told Ignazio Silone, an Italian Communist who later left the party, "If you should read in the papers that Lenin has had me arrested for stealing the Kremlin's silverware, it will mean simply that I have not been in full agreement with him on some problem of agricultural or industrial policy."[44] Despite all this, she was the rare Old Bolshevik to die of natural causes (so far as appears), a little shy of her 80th birthday and just a year before Stalin's death.

The two also shared a distaste for party partisanship—a distaste different from, but in keeping with their dislike of intra-party discipline. In 1914 a Bolshevik member of the Duma, Roman Malinovskii, was exposed as a double agent. The Bolsheviks were deeply embarrassed, and their Menshevik rivals piled on with criticism. Kollontai, then still a Menshevik, expressed her disgust to Maklakov. "The dirt we try to throw on Malinovskii above all makes us dirty."[45]

Consistently with her views on romance, she rather playfully teases Maklakov at his suggestion that she might be jealous. "Have you forgotten that that intolerable, though perhaps interesting feeling, has completely atrophied in me?" Then she teases him further about rumors of the "intimate side" of Maklakov, rumors that there was some pretty Jewish girl that he had had to marry.[46] The idea that someone moving in sophisticated Russian circles in the early twentieth century would "have" to marry someone seems a bit outlandish, but perhaps the rumor mills had generated such a story. Despite Kollontai's amusement at the thought of her possibly being jealous, she sounds a touch possessive. She is plainly eager to see Maklakov whenever their paths might potentially cross, giving details as to how to reach her, and is openly disappointed when he goes through Paris and fails to get in touch with her at a time when he knows she is there. She says she does not want to lose him, and that she has not lost faith in him.[47] The correspondence suggests there may be something simplistic in a purported total denial of jealousy: how is the line drawn between that and love's natural eagerness to be with the loved one (and presumably not in a mob scene)? This may be why *Red Love* reads more like a tract than a novel.

Kollontai's letters, especially one of them, devote a good deal of space to an analysis of their relationship. A letter sent in July 1914, on the eve of World War I, suggests she found in him an almost mesmerizing charm coupled with a frustrating remoteness:

> When we parted yesterday, . . . it was as if a melody had been interrupted, not allowed to play to the end. And today yesterday does not disappear, thoughts about proof-correcting [she was a busy writer as well as a revolutionary] flee to yesterday, look for something, there's not regret that the melody was interrupted, not sadness, there remains rather a smile, a small smile at us both. Isn't it funny that we're so similar? . . .
>
> Our interest in each other is surprisingly intellectual! It isn't boring—to the contrary! All the same—nothing in the heart trembles, is on fire. And it's funny that each of us pushes himself to move to feelings. Together—we're easy, not bored, but somehow relate as comrades. And we rebel against that. . . . You were far from any emotion, but when we went to the hotel you suddenly felt uneasiness; isn't that natural? . . . And we both tried to find the right mood. But the question remains a question. Are conditions responsible for the fact that this interest always remains intellectual? . . . all the same, I've a right to have a really good relationship with you. I give you what is due and I know your value. Today I even sketched your silhouette in my notebooks. But, you know, there is something unclear, not individual about you—your relationships with women. To characterize you—one needs to find other strings to [the structure of] your soul. You aren't one of those who would be characterized by your love life. And that's especially curious in you, in whose life so many kinds of women have always been intertwined. But do you really distinguish between them? . . .
>
> Do you ever hear the effect you have on a woman's soul?

> You simply have no ear for that. In this we are not alike. I, unfortunately, hear very well what develops in my partner's soul, and it horribly complicates relationships. But there is another mark that brings us together [she never seems to say what this is]; but you do not love that, her individuality, nor her love for you, but rather your own experience. You forget the name, face, the specialness of the woman, however fascinating she may have been, but you never forget if you yourself went through something sharp, special. You know this. But what must exasperate them, your future loved ones, is your absolute inability to reflect the image of the loved one. Especially for women who are not too gray, they much more than men love to have a mirror in the face of their partner, in which they can be loved. But you, among the very rarest varieties distinguish only "gender" and "species," like a naturalist. Those poor women! A question interests me: how is it then that you captivate them?[48]

Kollontai's questions, of course, remain unanswered, as do our own more prosaic or bourgeois questions about his failure to find—perhaps ever to seek—what he called the "crown" of worldly blessings, a happy family life.

II. A Radical Tide

CHAPTER 4

Into Politics—and Early Signs of Deviance from Party Dogma

An official investigation into the needs of agriculture elevated Maklakov from a distinguished young lawyer to something of a public figure. Russia's finance minister, Count Sergei Witte, in 1902 urged Tsar Nicholas II to order an inquiry into agrarian matters through a Special Conference, headed by Witte. The conference, in turn, created committees of inquiry at the province and district (*uezd*) levels of government. One such committee was organized for Zvenigorod, where Maklakov owned land for hunting and fishing.

Maklakov found the committee's discussion dispiriting. Count P. S. Sheremetyev, the chairman, quite rightly tried to give preference to peasant participants, but they tended to raise very narrow, specific complaints that could not readily be reframed as ideas for remedial legislation. Even when peasants got the idea that the committee was interested in identifying general problems, they gave up easily when they were told that the committee had no authority to adopt solutions—"There's nothing we can do." Maklakov did not think the peasant committee members were stupid; rather he thought that they lacked experience in the sort of reasoning required to analyze and address social and political problems. As to offerings from the intelligentsia, he found that, although they often spotted concrete questions and fundamental evils, they offered no solutions.[1]

Though by his account he had generally viewed agrarian problems with the "indifferent eyes of the city dweller," Maklakov believed that his rule-of-law ideals might well offer solutions. After seeking the blessing of a mentor, L. V. Liubenkov, he prepared a brief report, which he later disparaged as "rather elementary." But it drew from a basic premise that agriculture is a form of industry, so that its flourishing depended on social characteristics similar to those required for other industries, primarily freedom of initiative and security of rights. His eight-page memo not only offered a devastating critique of government policy in the countryside, at least as it worked in practice, but also developed the themes that preoccupied him in the Duma: the arbitrariness of government behavior; the absence of impartial, law-governed courts that might protect the peasants; and the solidarity with which officials backed up their subordinates' abuses. He pointed specifically to the "land captains," a special type of official created in 1889 that wielded both executive and judicial powers and whose arbitrary behavior even included interference in peasant efforts to vote in zemstvo elections. He deplored the government's failure to encourage (indeed, its active frustration of) private initiative and the prevailing "police point of view." All this, he thought, led not only to distrust of government but also to skepticism of the very idea of law. And he assailed the separation of peasants into a separate estate.[2]

The memo generated controversy. Many members of the local committee regarded it as not germane to the needs of agriculture. When Maklakov was addressing the issue of government responsibility for lawlessness, one of the land captains on the committee said, "Now seriously, V.A., what relation does this have to agriculture?" But then a peasant with a peasant coat (*armiak*) and a long beard, who had never taken part in the discussions, unexpectedly stood, turned to the chairman, and said, "Your honor, this [referring to Maklakov's depiction of pervasive government arbitrariness] is the most important thing."

Maklakov's theses passed the committee unanimously. Sheremetyev wanted to publish a book of the reports, but the provincial governor would allow it only if Maklakov's paper were excluded. Sheremetyev refused to submit unless Maklakov agreed to the omission. The matter was ultimately settled by publishing only Maklakov's "theses" (which he had articulated carefully as argument headings) and the comments of others, excluding Maklakov's development of his theses. V. M. Gessen, later a fellow Duma deputy, asked him for the report, and in a book on the work of the Special Conference he dedicated more attention to Maklakov's theses "than they deserved," as Maklakov wrote in his memoirs. But the report and the rather enigmatic comments on it stirred up the educated public's curiosity and attention.[3]

The paper's moderation—in contrast to the usually extreme expressions of members of the Liberation Movement—found support. In his memoirs Maklakov noted sardonically that "even" his brother Nikolai (then a tsarist official in Tambov) wrote to him expressing satisfaction with the memo. "In those days it didn't take much to become a hero of society."[4]

As a direct result, he was invited to join *Beseda* (meaning "Symposium"), a tiny "semi-conspiratorial" organization whose members were important players in the Liberation Movement and, later, in the nonrevolutionary political parties competing for power in the legislative elections made possible by the October Manifesto. Its membership was limited to people engaged in "practical work," meaning that they held elective office in Russia's embryonic system of local self-government—a duma in the city or a zemstvo in the countryside. The criterion was a natural one, as Beseda had been formed in response to a 1903 memorandum by Count Witte that had attacked the compatibility of zemstvo self-government with autocracy and, at least implicitly, indicated that, of the two, it was zemstvo self-government that ought to go. Beseda was created precisely to oppose that idea. Maklakov held no elective office, but Beseda made a special place for him as "secretary."[5]

Viewpoints in Beseda represented a broad range of reformist but nonrevolutionary opinion. Liberal constitutionalists favored a representative legislative body. The Slavophiles, who believed Russia could be better reformed by restoring healthy Russian practices than by adopting Western ones, split into at least two camps. Liberal Slavophiles favored reforms altering the structure of government but falling considerably short of an elected legislature; conservative ones favored policy reforms, but with no changes in the structure of the autocracy. Liberal Slavophilism was represented by Dmitri N. Shipov, whose vehement reaction to the Witte memorandum had been the spark for Beseda's founding. Though constitutionalists of a moderate or liberal flavor soon came to dominate Beseda numerically, they never sought to make it purely constitutionalist, if only because doing so would have cost the organization the liberal Slavophiles' potential influence over the government. Maklakov identified its unifying principle as a commitment to some degree of self-government, which was the essence of the zemstvo. At the time he joined, he was already a friend of a majority of the members.[6] Perhaps surprisingly for such an elite group, it seemed not to take itself too seriously. By tradition, Maklakov reports, the first day of its meetings was devoted to what was jokingly called "collection of gossip"—information not generally available about what was going on in the corridors of power.[7]

By the time of the October Manifesto, its members had dispersed politically, mainly to the Kadet and Octobrist parties, and Beseda ceased to meet. Maklakov later wrote a brief elegy.

> "Beseda" left me the best of memories. . . . To the end it personified the youth of Russian liberal society. It was pervaded by lively and powerful illusions about the healthy and peaceful renewal of Russia, illusions that later weakened. It had not yet

> lost faith in the authorities and was full of faith in Russian society. . . . The historical interest of *Beseda* lies in its representing one of the stages of development of Russian society, when it had not yet forgotten the traditions of the '60s [the Great Reforms], but recalled the cooperation of the authorities and society and prepared for more of just that cooperation.[8]

The Russian Revolution of 1905 began on Bloody Sunday, January 9, in the wake of Russia's disastrous performance in its war with Japan. Father Gapon, a charismatic activist priest, led a throng of workers toward the Winter Palace to deliver a petition to the tsar. Government troops opened fire on the marchers, killing 130 and seriously wounding 299, according to official figures.[9] One can hardly imagine behavior more sure to arouse nearly universal hostility toward the regime. It triggered strikes, violence, arson, and killing in the cities and countryside; it nearly precipitated the regime's collapse.

There is, oddly enough, a little-known counter-story to Bloody Sunday that tangentially involves Maklakov's friend Alexandra Kollontai. In 1961 a woman who said she had been a 19-year-old weaver in 1905 told one I. A. Isakov that she found herself in the first row of marchers, facing soldiers led by an energetic, trim, and well-dressed officer trying to prevent the crowd from continuing toward the Winter Palace. All was peaceful and quiet. Suddenly, a cleanly dressed person rushed out of the crowd up to the officer, who seemed to expect some sort of word or request from him. The man pulled out a revolver and shot the officer. The officer fell, and then the soldiers began to fire at the crowd. The weaver escaped. Later, in the 1930s, she told the story to Kollontai, with whom she was well acquainted. Kollontai cautioned, "Masha, don't tell anyone of this story. It could do you great harm."[10] Of course the story's value depends on the veracity of the weaver and Isakov, which can't be verified. But Kollontai clearly recognized the physical risk to anyone offering evidence impugning a key element of Russia's revolutionary iconography.

In any event, Russian society, including Maklakov and other Beseda members, responded to the accepted account with vehemence. The Assembly of the Moscow Nobility met just a few days after the shootings to discuss possible "addresses" to the tsar, ultimately endorsing the most conservative of the drafts, one presented by F. D. Samarin (formerly of Beseda), supporting the troops' action. Though not directly opposing reform, Samarin urged that it be postponed until war and internal rebellion passed (there had been little internal rebellion at that stage). Maklakov says that he "never took part in nobility meetings," explaining (perhaps in jest), "I would have had to obtain a uniform," but in nearly the same breath he reports that, at the request of Prince S. N. Trubetskoi (a professor of philosophy and liberal constitutionalist, also of Beseda), he did take the floor to contest Samarin. He argued that Samarin's view—first peace and quiet, then reform—was just what had gotten Russia into its current position. Without reform there would be no peace. Writing about the episode later, Maklakov said that after rereading Samarin's speech he didn't see it as quite the "unconditional reaction" he had seen originally.

Samarin's address prevailed, getting 219 votes, while a more reformist address received 147 votes. The moderates decided to issue a separate statement explaining their opposition to Samarin's position and tasked an all-Beseda committee of Trubetskoi, N. A. Khomiakov (a liberal Slavophile), and Maklakov to draft the statement. A line supplied by Trubetskoi attacking the bureaucracy and accusing it of both paralyzing Russian society and dividing it from the monarch drew great applause, even from the rightists. As a way forward, the minority statement called on the tsar to summon freely elected representatives, whose presence could reconcile the tsar and the people. By contrast, the action of the assembly's majority stood out against a background of overwhelming public sympathy for the victims and condemnation of the regime. In retrospect, Maklakov thought that, although the liberals didn't prevail, their efforts at least qualified the image of the Moscow nobility as supporters of aggressive reaction.[11]

The Beseda records (under Maklakov's custodianship as secretary) suggest that Maklakov's attitude at the time was more hostile to the monarchy than one might suppose from a study of his later writings. As a historian he pointed with horror to another politician's seeming indifference to the burning of manor houses.[12] Yet his January 1905 remarks at Beseda seemed to express a good deal of schadenfreude at the woes of the autocracy and gentry. He argued that the agrarian disorders "make autocracy a much more dangerous profession." Though seeing the disorders as possibly making ordinary people more reactionary, he had an answer. The task before Beseda, he said, was to convince the public that the disorders are "the consequence of government lawlessness" and thus turn them into "weighty evidence of the crisis of the regime."[13] At least at this stage—before the October Manifesto of that year and the Fundamental Laws of 1906—Maklakov's language, though aimed at nudging the regime to curb its arbitrariness, seems fairly indifferent to the risks of revolution.

Indeed, Maklakov had earlier been instrumental in promoting cooperation between Moscow adherents of the Union of Liberation (the center-left precursor of the Kadets) and local Social Democrats and Socialist Revolutionaries. The group failed to form any real bloc because of the Social Democrats' refusal to collaborate with "bourgeois elements," but the Moscow Socialist Revolutionaries and members of the Union of Liberation did cooperate for a while.[14] So at least before the October Manifesto, Maklakov saw benefits to acting in concert with the revolutionary left.

As part of the accelerating political action of late 1905, the Kadets held their founding congress at the Moscow home of Prince Paul Dolgorukov, between October 12 and 18. Maklakov spoke up twice. The first occasion was in response to a policeman who had entered uninvited. Nikolai Teslenko, who was presiding, tried to persuade the intruder to go. Maklakov asked for the floor and started to speak of the sanctions, including imprisonment, that a policeman risked by entering a house unlawfully. The policeman decided it was best to leave; Teslenko and Maklakov shared plaudits for this happy outcome. Maklakov credited his selection for the Kadets' central committee in part to this effective action and in part to agitation on his behalf by his colleague in political trials, N. K. Muravyov.[15] From then on he was continuously reelected to the committee until long after the Bolshevik revolution.

Maklakov's second intervention was substantive. In a discussion of the party's possible platform, he suggested that they bear in mind that one day the Kadets might become the government. An ideal polity, he thought, should obviously identify and protect its citizens' rights, but a polity whose government lacked the capacity to enforce the law could hardly do so—it could not provide the order of "ordered liberty." Thus Kadet ideals, he argued, called for the party to support allowing the government reasonable authority. This remark, he later reported, produced a storm of righteous indignation; one colleague told him that that the party must never think as the government, but always as a champion of the rights of man. The criticism was renewed years later, after most or all of the surviving participants had emigrated. It seemed to him that this position showed how ill-prepared the party was for the practical work of governing in a constitutional structure.[16]

Maklakov's two brief interventions capture his relation to the party. His legal and rhetorical skills made him useful, and his memoirs make clear that he found a deep satisfaction in political work on the party's behalf. At the same time, he seems never to have been really content with the party's overall direction. Paul Miliukov, in one of his works in exile, described Maklakov as always having been a Kadet "with special opinions," a judgment Maklakov reports without dissent.[17] Later, as a Kadet deputy in the Second, Third, and Fourth Dumas, Maklakov relished the independence that its Duma delegation gradually acquired vis-à-vis the party leaders; he seems never to have been content with the party's general drift. Maklakov's aversion to tight party allegiance seems to have been a bond with his friend Fyodor Plevako. The latter, elected to the Duma as an Octobrist, showed no devotion to (or really much interest in) the abstractions of the party program. At political meetings in the elections to the Third Duma, Plevako and Maklakov appeared as champions of their parties, but Plevako's "tolerance and respect for opposing views disarmed opponents and angered friends and associates."[18] So, too, as we'll see, for Maklakov.

On October 17, in the midst of the Kadets' congress and rising unrest, Nicholas II confronted a choice between repression and retreat. He chose the latter, issuing the October Manifesto.

> We impose upon the Government the obligation to carry out Our inflexible will:
>
> (1) To grant the population the unshakable foundations of civic freedom based on the principles of real personal inviolability, freedom of conscience, speech, assembly, and union.
>
> (2) Without halting the scheduled elections to the State Duma, to admit to participation in the Duma, as far as is possible in the short time remaining before its call, those classes of the population which at present are altogether deprived of the franchise, leaving the further development of the principle of universal suffrage to the new legislative order, and
>
> (3) To establish it as an unbreakable rule that no law can become effective without the approval of the State Duma and that the elected representatives of the people should be guaranteed an opportunity for actual participation in the supervision of the legality of the actions of authorities appointed by Us.[19]

From the perspective of what became standard Kadet doctrine, the manifesto had serious weaknesses. First, the tsar expressed his "will . . . [t]o grant" the civil liberties named, but that was not the same as granting them. Second, the principle of "universal suffrage" didn't live up to the egalitarian "four-tailed" suffrage (universal, direct, equal, and secret) that the Kadets demanded. (As the electoral law of December 11, 1905, would show, it was easy to combine nearly universal male suffrage [giving the vote to males over 24 years old, excepting students and military in active service] with a strong tilt toward the propertied classes. As a result of the mathematics of the indirect structure, in which curiae of landowners, peasants, town dwellers, and workers chose electors who then directly or indirectly chose Duma members, the vote of one landowner was worth the same as those of two town dwellers, of fifteen peasants, or of forty-five workers.)[20] Third, the manifesto obviously did not call for a constituent assembly and thus kept the tsar very much in the picture for the ultimate crafting of any possible constitution.

But the manifesto stated a commitment to core principles of the rule of law. In the hands of a reasonable and independent interpreter, paragraph 1 had the potential of developing into a full-fledged bill of rights. Paragraph 2 meant that even if the votes of many citizens might be diluted, all or nearly all men would participate in the governmental process, thereby acquiring a say in legislation and experience in thinking about government and politics. Most important, paragraph 3 barred the tsar from changing any law without the consent of the (as yet uncreated) Duma, a wholly independent institution, and promised the "people's representatives" a role in ensuring the legality of the laws' administration. The manifesto thus would bar the executive, the tsar, from acting on the basis of his will alone, either by ignoring the law or by changing it unilaterally. At least as a promise, then, it brought the government under the law—the most vital but the most elusive component of the rule of law.

The Kadets who had gathered at the founding congress generally recognized the manifesto's historic significance. As described by Alexander Kizevetter, a Kadet leader and historian, a man named Petrovskii rushed in from the editorial offices of *Russkie Vedomosti* (Russian news) and made his way to the podium. The presiding Kadet, Maxim Vinaver, interrupted the speaker and read out the manifesto. Writes Kizevetter, "The autocracy was over. Russia had become a constitutional monarchy. Citizen freedoms were proclaimed. Mitrofan Pavlovich Shchepkin, gray with age, trembling with emotion, said, 'Now at last we are free.'" Kizevetter reported in his memoirs that no one could stay at home, but instead poured into the streets of Moscow, congratulating each other as if it were Easter.[21]

Maklakov seems to have shared the general delight among liberals. Certainly in his speeches in the Duma over the years from 1907 to 1917, he invoked the manifesto constantly, not merely as a legal standard by which to measure the government's acts, but as an inspiration, as the founding of a new order, as a sacred text.

Miliukov, the party leader, shared none of this. He publicly responded, "Nothing has changed. The war continues."[22] When the Kadet party's founding congress ended the next day, the party issued a statement (*postanovlenie*) that conveyed the same spirit without using Miliukov's exact metaphor. Looking at the October Manifesto, the statement almost completely ignored the doughnut and focused relentlessly on the hole. Imagine if King John had preemptively issued rather than negotiated the Magna Carta, and the barons had responded by pointing out the gaps between it and a detailed constitution meeting all of their political dreams. The Kadet statement started by saying that the manifesto and Witte's accompanying report gave "far from full recognition" to the basic principles of political freedom and the equal and universal electoral rights demanded by the Liberation Movement. The October Manifesto, in fact, did recognize basic principles of political freedom, even if they were not exactly the ones demanded by the Liberation Movement, and even if full elaboration was left to the future (as under the American Bill of Rights). After making the important point that the manifesto didn't repeal the extraordinary security laws (which allowed officials of the ministry of internal affairs to exile people for up to five years without any recourse to judicial process), the statement went on to argue that for various reasons the Duma soon to be elected could not be recognized as a genuine popular representative assembly, so that (non sequitur alert!) the Kadet party's goal must remain as before—a constituent assembly elected on the basis of four-tailed suffrage.[23] In short, the statement reflected Miliukov's insistence that society and the authorities remained at war. In a zemstvo congress about a month later, Miliukov offered a resolution recognizing the October Manifesto as a "precious achievement" of the Russian people. But his zemstvo congress audience represented a far more moderate body than the Kadet party; Miliukov was sugar-coating his views to enlist its support for the Kadet program.[24]

Soon afterward, Witte launched a set of negotiations aimed at forming a cabinet relatively acceptable to the nation. First he asked Dmitri Shipov, the leader of liberal Slavism, to call on him, and asked him to join the cabinet as state controller. Shipov declined the job offer, but proffered some advice. As Witte had clearly invited Shipov in order to learn a zemstvo viewpoint, Shipov advised him to turn to the zemstvo leadership, in the form of the Bureau of Zemstvo Congresses, and ask it to send him a delegation. Shipov expected that at the Bureau's scheduled meeting on October 22 he would have a say in naming the delegates. But the process moved too swiftly. Witte sent the invitation to the Bureau by telegram, which (in Maklakov's words) "whipped up" the Bureau's self-confidence. Seeing the request as a sign of the government's weakness and a capitulation, the Bureau began to act with great self-confidence.[25]

Before Shipov could meet with the Bureau, it formed a small committee that included, either as a member or at least an attendee, someone who wasn't involved in zemstvo matters at all, Miliukov himself.[26] Miliukov managed to arrange the selection of F. F. Kokoshkin as leader of the delegation, a choice that Miliukov himself recognized as signaling to Witte that the zemstvo bureau was not ready to compromise.[27] The committee charged the delegation to tell Witte that the *only* solution to the present situation was to call a constituent assembly, to be chosen by a "four-tailed" franchise; and that a constitution "granted" by the tsar would be completely unsatisfactory. (This insistence on immediate democracy at the outset, including a democratic method of generating a constitution, seems based on Miliukov's belief that a developed and organized democratic society "can be created only by an active political life,"[28] that is, that the onset of democracy would itself be enough to generate the skills needed to make democracy functional, to enable it to survive amid countervailing forces such as reaction, populist demagoguery, and interest-group machinations.) Obviously Witte could not accept such terms.[29] Witte soon thereafter invited Miliukov himself in for consultation, and, curiously, Miliukov's direct advice to Witte was quite different from the standard Kadet notion that the *only* way forward was through a constituent assembly. Writing of it later, he explained that with Witte he conceived of himself as acting in a non-party capacity:

> I came [Miliukov reported] not as representative of anyone but in my capacity as a private person, whose advice was sought by the highest representative of the authorities of the moment, when it was being decided what direction Russian history should take. And on the question then put to me by Witte, what should be done, I decided to answer according to my conscience and personal conviction, not binding myself to the generally approved political formulae of my intellectual fellow travelers. I wanted to take the discussion down from academic heights to the sphere of real life.[30]

Miliukov's explanation of his answer does not really bridge the gap between his public position and his advice to Witte. If important decisions "for Russian history" were at stake (as they were), it would be startling to think that Witte would want anything other than Miliukov's *real* views, or that he would prefer notions from the "academic heights" rather than ones from the real world. It seems a sad commentary on the politics of the Kadet party that there was such a gulf between its leader's "conscience and personal conviction" and the "generally approved political formulae" that he and his "intellectual fellow travelers" had enthusiastically adopted.

The substance of Miliukov's advice was no less otherworldly. He told Witte that, although he still thought that a constituent assembly was the ideal way to get to a constitution, it was unsuitable in the circumstances and that the tsar should just grant one. Yes, he acknowledged, society would complain (in part because Miliukov himself had been constantly insisting that only a constituent assembly would do), but in the end it would work.

Specifically, he proposed that Witte arrange translation of either the Belgian or the Bulgarian constitution (presumably chosen as reasonably liberal written constitutions, and, in the Bulgarian case, one that had survived since 1879 in a country with scant liberal tradition), get the tsar to sign it the next day (whichever constitution it happened to be), and publish it the following day. Miliukov's constitutionalism seemed to be wrapped in a passion for labels, for form regardless of substance: when Witte refused to use the word "constitution" and explained that the tsar was against it, Miliukov, by his own account, broke off the discussion, telling Witte, "It is useless for us to continue our conversation."[31]

Maklakov says, with some justice, that Witte must have taken the constitutional proposals as a joke. At stake was a new order for a huge country of different ethnicities, different "estates" (a historical legacy that Maklakov was determined to eradicate),[32] and different levels of education. Its political relations were encrusted with complications that had accumulated over centuries. And Miliukov was saying that for this transition, it was enough to adopt the constitution of one of two very small countries, with apparent indifference as to which it should be.[33] All told, he took a "flick-a-switch" view of how to transition to liberal democracy.

Maklakov's critique of the Belgian/Bulgarian solution operates on two practical levels. The first is the matter of political power. The tsar had not been *defeated*. To be sure, his issuance of the October Manifesto had not delivered the hoped-for calm. Indeed, a major insurrection had arisen in Moscow right after its promulgation. But as suppression of the uprising in December was to show, the regime could protect itself. It was naïve and even arrogant to think that under those circumstances the tsar would accept the role of a figurehead in a purely parliamentary regime.

The other element of absurdity in the Belgian/Bulgarian option lay simply in the broader issues of social and political evolution. If a new regime in Russia was to live as a rule-of-law state, it could not instantly transform all the actors' accustomed roles by fiat. Change to an alternative system of arbitrary rule would be simple enough. But in Maklakov's view transformation to the rule of law was a different story: people's old practices, expectations, and habits of mind inevitably shape their behavior to some degree, and Russia's historic ones would not match the kind of full-blown democracy that Miliukov contemplated.

After the failure of negotiations between the Kadets and Witte, revolutionaries launched a general political strike in Moscow with the hope—which proved well-founded—that it would develop into an armed uprising.[34] (Some school students were accused of having started the uprising. Maklakov defended them, and a fellow lawyer and observer wrote later that "never did Maklakov's talent sparkle so brightly" as in the defense, laying bare the weak spots of the prosecution and leading to acquittal.[35]) In Maklakov's view, any constitutional regime would have felt obliged to suppress it. Witte's choices were whether to do so in alliance with liberal society or with the right. Even in an autocracy, a prime minister needs allies. Finding himself unequivocally rejected on the liberal side, Witte predictably turned to the right, unleashing Minister of the Interior Durnovo to repress the revolution.

Maklakov makes no bones about the savagery of this repression. He describes the use of artillery against neighborhoods, selective shootings of individuals on lists provided by the *Okhrana* (secret police), and the slaughter of students for no offense other than being a student at large on the streets of Moscow. He recounts one poignant case, in which a father kept his student son at home all day, but then ventured out into the streets with him at night, with the son wearing a coat that covered his student clothing. Police wrenched the son from the company of his father and hustled him off; the father saw him again only in a morgue.[36]

It is of course speculation that repression by a government at least loosely allied with the liberals would have been less savage. But Witte in his diary entries repeatedly laments his isolation at this period.[37] It seems plausible that, if he could have pointed to some liberal support, he might have adopted, or persuaded the tsar to adopt, less ruthless methods of repression.

Instead the Kadets stood aloof, if anything signaling sympathy with the revolutionaries by organizing medical aid, never uttering a public word of criticism of the revolutionaries, and never expressing any recognition that government—any government—has some duty to prevent popular violence. In the central committee of the Kadet party Maklakov and N. N. Lvov favored Kadet condemnation of the uprising but didn't prevail.[38]

The Kadet response to the October Manifesto and its aftermath was in Maklakov's view a failure on many fronts. The most immediate effect of their refusal to work with Witte was the de facto rightist control over suppression of the Moscow uprising. More broadly, it strengthened the right and undermined moderates in the bureaucracy. It also meant, in Maklakov's view, the abandonment of a key opportunity for the sort of activity required for constitutionalism. A leitmotiv of his writings is the idea that a workable rule-of-law state requires that citizens follow certain behavior patterns, developed and nurtured by experience. Foremost of these is the habit of compromise, of recognition of the rights and interests of others. He quotes Bismarck as saying that the essence of constitutionalism is compromise. Bismarck's view has been seconded by a quite different political figure, Bill Clinton: "If you read the Constitution, it ought to be subtitled: 'Let's make a deal.' "[39] Russian autocracy, of course, provided few chances for that experience—the zemstvo being the most notable exception. The October Manifesto offered such an opportunity, and, at least as a party, the Kadets turned their backs on it.

The next major step in the regime's halting embrace of constitutionalism was its April 23, 1906, repromulgation of Russia's Fundamental Laws, revised to reflect the commitments made in the October Manifesto. In the next chapter I'll tackle the question of whether those laws moved Russia seriously toward the ideal of the rule of law. Before that, we should consider Maklakov's involvement in an effort in Paris, just before the promulgation of the revised Fundamental Laws, to thwart the government's effort to float a massive loan (2.25 billion francs) with the aid of the French and, to a lesser extent, the British, governments. Apart from its intrinsic interest, the episode is probably the strongest ground for an argument that Maklakov was just Monday-morning quarterbacking in his later writings accusing the Kadet leadership of radicalism and folly in 1905–1907.

Indeed, at first blush, his behavior sounds rather extreme: working abroad to defeat a key foreign policy initiative of one's country. Perhaps, in fact, it *was* extreme. Under our Logan Act, adopted in 1799, it would be a crime for an American to carry on correspondence or conversations with a foreign government with the intent to "defeat measures of the United States."[40] Because Russia (so far as I know) had no equivalent of the Logan Act, the key issue was political and not legal: activities of this sort might tar the liberation movement as at least non-patriotic, perhaps worse. I will lay out the facts, primarily as presented by Maklakov himself in his 1936 memoir-history, *Vlast i obshchestvennost* (State and society). That account squares well with the published scholarly accounts; where they diverge substantively, the scholars offer no evidence supporting their contradiction of Maklakov.[41]

Maklakov had participated actively in the election for the First Duma, both campaigning for party candidates himself and, as head of the Kadet speakers' bureau, guiding others. By April 1906 he felt entitled to some time off and, following his long-established predilection for vacations in France, headed to Paris. On the train he had the company of Paul Dolgorukov, who went on directly to the Riviera from Warsaw (and who, as we'll see, turns up later in Paris and engages in anti-loan lobbying). One of the scholars of the subject speaks of Maklakov's having got "the idea to go to Paris and join the protest against the loan," but it seems safe to reject the insinuation that he went to Paris to participate in the protest, given the absence of any supporting evidence and Maklakov's longtime practice of taking French vacations.[42]

Once in Paris, Maklakov met one or more of the friends whom

he regularly saw there,[43] learned that his old friend S. E. Kalmanovich was in town, and was brought by friends to an event in honor of Kalmanovich's daughter's wedding. People at the party were somewhat astonished to learn that liberals in Russia had not fully shared the Paris emigrant community's concern that the imminent loan would strengthen the autocracy vis-à-vis the liberals. Maklakov's friends brought him to meet Pierre Quillard, a French poet, an ardent Dreyfusard, a champion of oppressed nationalities, and a leading member of the *Société des amis du peuple russe et des peuples annexés*. Frenchmen of a liberal or socialist bent, with the Société in the lead, had already conducted a vigorous—but quite unsuccessful—public campaign against the possible loan. Quillard proposed that Maklakov prepare a memorandum against the loan for submission to French government officials. Good connections between members of the French government and Société figures such as Quillard and Anatole France ensured delivery of such a memo.[44]

Maklakov agreed, and a copy of the resulting memo, evidently later obtained from French foreign office files, was published in 1961.[45] In a chapter of his 1936 memoirs-history, *State and Society*, addressing the loan, Maklakov acknowledges that he submitted such a memo but never quotes from it, presumably because he had neither a copy nor access to the foreign office files. His account of the memo is (naturally) shorter than the memo itself, but quite accurately reports its basic thesis, which was entirely political, not legal. It made no legal claim—such as the left had been circulating in France—that the loan would be unlawful without Duma approval. In *State and Society* he said that he then believed that until promulgation of the Fundamental Laws the tsar's powers continued;[46] the memo is in full accord. The memo argues instead that the loan would represent an intervention on the side of autocracy, relaxing its need to accommodate the burgeoning liberal democracy. Although one of the scholars writing about the anti-loan campaign says that "no reference to this memorandum has been found in Maklakov's major works," in fact *State and Society* refers to the memo and gives its gist.[47]

But in two respects Maklakov's account of the memo might be said to shade the truth. First, without actually saying so, the memo rather subtly gives the impression that Maklakov speaks for the Kadet party. In a few places he uses the first person plural (*nous* or *notre*), saying, for example, that he's going to discuss the reasons "why *our* party, in harmony with the great majority of the nation, consider the foreign loan proposed by our government as disastrous [*funeste*] for the interests of Russia and dangerous for those of France."[48] His later account doesn't acknowledge that he had seemed to act as a representative of the party.

Second, though Maklakov's memoirs-history made clear the basic claim that the loan would help the survival of an absolutist regime, it gave little clue of the memo's scathing portrait of the autocracy:

> The dilemma is clearly posed: the absolutist party must either yield to the national will, and abandon its dream of restoring autocracy, or it must immediately make a supreme effort to provoke a conflict and suppress the Duma. . . .
>
> If it is the former, the current practices of the government will continue, that is, the dilapidation of the Treasury, the weakening of industry and of commerce for want of the necessary liberties, the massacre of Jews and of ethnic minorities, of liberals and intellectuals, the destruction of what remains of the universities and schools, the suppression of the few liberties conceded to the press, the total ruin of agriculture, the final exhaustion of the country's last vibrant forces, the daily increasing disorganization of the army and the fleet, and finally permanent recourse to more and more onerous loans ending in the inevitable bankruptcy.[49]

Besides savaging the autocracy and drawing on French sympathies for representative government, liberty, and ethnic fairness, the memo targets concrete French interests: France's desire for military advantage; firming up its entente with Russia; and its hopes of ever being repaid.

The memo also claims that a decree had "annihilated" the authority of the Duma by creating a higher legislative body, the State Council, in which half the seats were to be held by appointees of the government,[50] and whose agreement would be necessary for most legislative action.

Although the memo might seem to track the most intransigent voices among the Kadets, it does acknowledge that the ministry *had* contained at least two liberals, M. M. Kutler and Vasily Timiriazev. But it nullifies whatever sympathy that might have won for the regime with the observation that they had been removed, which the memo ascribes to the influence of "a court camarilla" of grand dukes and others.[51]

The memo never had the slightest chance of affecting the loan. Although it was formally executed on April 22 (n.s.), the loan contract had been signed April 16,[52] and the memo bears a legend at the top saying that it had been conveyed to the French foreign ministry on April 18. When Maklakov and two other Russians (Kalmanovich and Count Anatolii Nesselrode) met with Georges Clemenceau (then minister of the interior, but soon to start his first period as prime minister, from late 1906 to mid-1909), the minister made clear that the loan had been a done deal for some time.

In *State and Society* Maklakov gives quite a full account of the interview with Clemenceau.[53] The meeting was rather secret, conducted in a little office apart from Clemenceau's main office, evidently because his holding the meeting poached on the territory of the minister of foreign affairs, Léon Bourgeois, behind whose back they were meeting. Clemenceau explained right off the bat that the loan had been agreed on, so there was really no occasion to discuss its merits.[54] The conversation instead turned to the Russian liberals' general strategy. Clemenceau was astonished at their quest for universal suffrage: "Didn't we understand," he asked Maklakov, "that any people needs a long time to be weaned away from their prejudices and crudeness, before they can be allowed to take charge?" As an example of such crudeness, he recalled how the

French, much more experienced in these matters than the Russians, had reacted like "lunatics" to a mere proposal to inventory the contents of churches (after the Separation of 1905). "You don't know what the strength of the authorities will be under an inexperienced population." Though Clemenceau was famous for saying that the Revolution must be accepted "en bloc," he was aware of its weaknesses and recommended caution and moderation: "Anything can happen except what you expect."

Maklakov raised the issue of resisting the oath to the autocracy, which was to be demanded of incoming deputies (and which his memorandum had complained about). Clemenceau "grabbed me by the arm: 'Don't do it. What does a vain word cost you? For the devil's sake, don't fight over a word. Leave them their words and titles, and take the substance yourself.'"

In a brief exchange on the loan itself, Maklakov explained how the loan would be a powerful weapon for the old regime in its struggle with the liberals. Clemenceau: "Ah, I understand you. You'd like to seize the government by the throat. You ought to have thought of it sooner."

Maklakov closed his account of the conversation by explaining why he had made it so complete: It was "so characteristic—in it spoke the real Clemenceau."

After the Clemenceau interview, word reached Maklakov that Raymond Poincaré, then finance minister, would like to meet the Russians.[55] Nesselrode refused to go, and Kalmanovich had left town. Maklakov met with others in a café, where their conversation was overheard by an official in the Russian embassy. (While Maklakov noticed this sign of Russian intelligence operations, doubtless there were many he didn't detect.) He was not eager to go, but Dolgorukov had arrived in Paris from the Riviera, and Maklakov proposed that they go together, which they did. Poincaré spoke of a condition that the French were proposing—that no money could be expended without consent of the Duma. Maklakov said it was completely useless, because a French condition could not amend the Russian constitution. (Presumably the French could not, after the execution of the loan, add a new, binding condition to the delivery of the loan's tranches.)

Just before Maklakov and Dolgorukov returned to Russia, the French foes of the loan asked them whether they would join a public campaign against it, and specifically whether they would do so as representatives of their party. This proposal obviously called for consultation with the party's central committee; in view of their imminent return they did so by telegram, which they sent "in clear." The central committee didn't answer, thus implicitly rejecting the idea. Maklakov chides himself for the carelessness and irresponsibility of sending an open telegram, thus giving "arms against ourselves." The self-reproof is surely right, though one wonders if the telegram added much to the secret police's dossier on the Kadets' activities in Paris.[56]

Concluding his account, Maklakov addresses an issue he had raised at the beginning—the principle that Russia should be united in relation to foreigners.[57] In justification of his conduct, he says that if he had acted in accordance with that principle, he would have brought on himself "the indignation of the whole of Russian society." Such an idea was no part of the liberation movement as it then existed. As an example of prevailing standards, he cites Miliukov's refusal, on the occasion of the parliamentary delegation's visit to London, to take part in a possible collective Russian response to an article, apparently attributed to Ramsay MacDonald, that ranted not only against the Russian government but against the tsar himself. Because of Miliukov's resistance to any rebuke by the delegation as a whole, the only Russian answer was from its chairman, Khomiakov. The refusal to defend the country, he says, wasn't personal to Miliukov. "In 1906 I sinned not individually, but from our general sin."

Even if we assume that the MacDonald episode was parallel, the exculpation seems dubious—at least by the standards that Maklakov developed later. First, his post-1917 account of Russian politics is replete with broad criticisms of "society" and its militancy; so how could the assumptions and predilections of society justify his conduct? Second, he could have just kept quiet in Paris, or at any rate not ventured beyond conversations with his Russian and French friends.

Though Maklakov's writings and Duma speeches are filled with criticism of the regime, none appears as vehement as that of the anti-loan memo. In *State and Society*, as we'll see, Maklakov gives a reasoned defense of the new Fundamental Laws—which had not been issued at the time of his memo. To be sure, I've found no Maklakov defense of the Fundamental Laws contemporaneous with their issuance. Despite that gap, it seems quite possible that the newly revised Fundamental Laws may have led him to appraise the regime more generously than he did at the time of his memo to the French and to believe that the powers granted the Duma gave it a decent chance at fulfilling the promise of the October Manifesto.

CHAPTER 5

A Constitution for Russia?

On April 23, 1906, shortly after the failure of Maklakov's efforts to defeat the French loan and four days before the opening of the First Duma, the regime issued a revised set of "Fundamental Laws." These were the product of a committee, chaired by the tsar, in which officials of varying predilections pressed their views on Nicholas.

Once the Fundamental Laws were issued, the tsar and his supporters, on the one hand, and the liberals, on the other, had motives to deny that the new laws and the October Manifesto amounted to a "constitution." The tsar resisted the thought that his commitments deserved that label (which would imply a real shift of authority), clinging to the notion that the autocracy had been a good thing for Russia and that he must pass it on to his son intact—or at least as intact as possible. Many of the liberals, who fervently sought a constitution, tended to deny that one had been granted; to acknowledge that this had happened would weaken their claim to more limitations on the tsar's power. They called it a "pseudo-constitution."

Clearly the Fundamental Laws fell short of the Kadet leadership's hopes. They did not sweep aside the property-weighted "curias" of the December 11, 1905, electoral law, which made citizens' votes indirect and unequal. They kept the State Council as a legislative body; because a bill could become law only with its consent as well as the Duma's, its authority qualified the Duma's, even though leaving the Duma a veto over new legislation. And the new laws did not make the government responsible to the Duma, that is, they did not require a cabinet resignation on the loss of a key vote, as under British practice. Thus the system they created was neither purely parliamentary nor politically egalitarian. But this outcome, and the disappointment of the Kadet leadership's hopes, is quite understandable in light of the tsar's apparent power to endure. Despite those drawbacks, the October Manifesto and Fundamental Laws imposed serious constraints on Russia's executive.

Writing about the Fundamental Laws after the revolution, Maklakov focuses on the degree of constraint on government: first, the extent to which the Fundamental Laws advanced Russia toward the rule of law or, more broadly, liberal democracy, and, second, their possible service as a platform for future liberalization, democratization, and reform. These criteria tend to converge; the difference is between their actual and potential results. By those criteria, he found the Fundamental Laws pretty good, and thus found the Kadets' intransigence in the First Duma—based on the gap between the Fundamental Laws and Kadet goals—self-defeating.

Maklakov's post-revolutionary assessment of the Fundamental Laws, stated most systematically in his 1936 history-memoir, *State and Society*,[1] gave them a high grade. (In chapter 7 we consider claims that the grade was inconsistent with his positions in 1906–7.) But his 1936 analysis omits their most glaring deficiency for purposes of the rule of law—their failure to cabin the lawlessness authorized by the extraordinary security laws. The executive authority, wielded largely by the ministry of internal affairs and its satraps (such as the provincial governors and the land captains), retained the authority to exile, imprison, and fine citizens without check or review by any independent institution. So long as the executive retained its powers under those preexisting provisions, the principle that it could (usually) act only in fulfillment of a duly enacted law was technically fulfilled—the extraordinary security laws *had been* duly enacted under the laws governing at the time of their enactment. But the Fundamental Laws *appeared* to allow the extraordinary security laws to continue in effect indefinitely.

In fact it isn't clear that continued enforcement of the extraordinary security laws was lawful under the October Manifesto and the Fundamental Laws. The security laws had been originally promulgated as "temporary," lasting only three years unless renewed (the three-year term was changed to one year in 1903). After the October Manifesto and the Fundamental Laws of April 23, 1906, the tsar annually purported to renew the laws himself, without a word of Duma approval. The provision for renewal might, on one plausible reading, be regarded as a lawful authorization to the executive to take future steps, as many laws do.[2] In the pre-Duma era, when the tsar was in substance both legislature and executive, the question had been rather metaphysical. On the sixth anniversary of the October Manifesto (October 17, 1911), a Kadet, Nikolai Teslenko, challenged the renewals of 1906 through 1910 as unlawful by asking the prime minister on the Duma floor what measures he was taking to bring action under the laws to a stop. The challenge passed handily (168–123), but had no legal effect. Arbitrary executive action under the laws continued unabated.[3] The episode exposed another gap in lawfulness under the new regime—the lack of any institution to resolve disputes between the government and the Duma on the meaning of the Fundamental Laws.

That said, we should be clear that the Fundamental Laws did create a real balance between the popular representative body and the tsar, barring the latter from acting without legislative authority and from generating *new* legislation without Duma consent. Two provisions addressed these limits, one explicitly, the other rhetorically. Both emerged from hard-fought battles in the special committee drafting the laws. The explicit provision was Article 11, which authorized the tsar to issue decrees, ukases, and so on, "in conformity to the laws."[4] If we put aside foreign affairs, some special provisions such as Article 87, and preexisting provisions such as the extraordinary security laws, those two simple prepositional phrases, if adhered to, would limit the tsar's executive powers to carrying out legislation enacted with the assent of the Duma. Article 11 was reinforced by Article 108, which allowed the Duma and State Council to question ministers (and heads of separate agencies) "in connection with apparently illegal actions committed on their part or on that of persons and institutions under their departmental authority,"[5] and thus to monitor the executive's compliance with the limits on its power. (Article 108 was the basis for Teslenko's challenge to the prime minister on the extraordinary security laws.) Oddly, Maklakov didn't mention an independent judiciary as another vehicle for making Article 11 effective. In any event, Article 11's restriction of tsarist decrees to rules "in conformity to the laws," and the provision for parliamentary power to interrogate the government on its possibly illegal acts, provided at least a scaffolding for the rule of law.

The atmospheric change took the form of deleting the word "unlimited" from Article 4's description of the tsar's power, so that it would now read "Supreme Autocratic Power" rather than, as it had since the promulgation of the original fundamental laws in 1833, "Supreme *Unlimited* Autocratic Power."[6] Maklakov lamented that in the special committee that resolved final disputes in the drafting of the Fundamental Laws, none of those favoring deletion of "unlimited" argued for it on the merits, as being beneficial for Russia and even for the tsar himself. Rather, they argued only that the October Manifesto in effect promised removal of the adjective (by requiring that enactment of law be contingent on Duma approval), so that to keep his promise the tsar must remove it. As a result, Maklakov argues, the tsar ever after regarded himself as having fallen into a trap on October 17, clearly an unhealthy attitude if he was to function as a constitutional monarch.[7] Certainly much of Nicholas II's later behavior shows that he never committed himself to the spirit of a limited monarchy.

If these were the key strengths of the Fundamental Laws, what were the vulnerabilities, the weaknesses that Maklakov's Kadet colleagues had denounced? The outstanding ones were first, Article 87's authorization of executive actions as temporary substitutes for true legislation, which required approval of the Duma, the State Council, and the tsar; second, the power of the State Council and the tsar to block legislation; and, third, special rules on the budget and the control of the military.

Article 87 certainly gave the executive the power to trump the legislative process *temporarily*. Its language framed many of the disputes that dominated politics from 1906 to 1917:

> [1] When the State Duma is in recess and extraordinary circumstances create the necessity of a measure requiring a legislative deliberation, the Council of Ministers submits it directly to the Emperor. [2] Such a measure, however, may not introduce changes in either the Fundamental State Laws or in the Organic Laws of the State Council or the State Duma or in the provisions on elections to the State Council or to the Duma. [3] The operation of this measure comes to an end if a bill corresponding to the adopted measure is not introduced by the qualified Minister or the Chief Administrator of a separate agency into the State Duma within the first two months after the resumption of the Duma's business, or if the State Duma or the State Council does not adopt the bill.[8]

The key sentence for most purposes is the third. It gave the government two options once it issued a decree under Article 87. First, it could introduce a bill in the Duma with the same provisions as the Article 87 decree; but in that case the law would die the minute that the Duma *or* the State Council voted it down. Under that condition, a simple majority of the Duma could easily kill an Article 87 decree it didn't like. Alternatively, the government could offer no such bill, in which case the decree would expire automatically two months after Duma sessions resumed.

Maklakov argued for Article 87 on the practical ground that in a country so huge it was essential to have some means for legislation to address urgent problems arising while the Duma was out of session.[9] He was quick to recognize that, as it proved, the government's applications of Article 87 went way beyond that. In fact, the government at least once exercised its power to recess the Duma solely to *create* the preconditions for exercising Article 87 (i.e., having the Duma out of session).[10] But Maklakov offered a qualified excuse for such excesses by pointing to the Duma's scant attention to legislation, its accumulation of unconsidered bills, and its obsession with trivial bills, known as "vermicelli."[11]

His more compelling defense of Article 87 was that a decree resting on the Article could not long endure in the face of Duma resistance. A simple vote of the Duma, without the agreement of the State Council or the tsar, would repeal an Article 87 decree (unless it simply died of its own weight through the government's failure to introduce a corresponding bill).

Of course the fear of being dissolved (and thus having to face new elections) might lead the Duma to refrain from voting down a bill supporting an Article 87 decree, and Maklakov acknowledges that that very fear explained the Second Duma's *not* voting down Stolypin's agrarian reform, which the Kadets vehemently opposed.[12] If fear of being dissolved drove the Duma's inaction, does such fear expose a major gap in the Duma's power (and thus in Maklakov's reasoning)? Superficially it might seem to, but Maklakov doesn't address the argument. He might have responded that dissolution was, for the government, a two-edged sword: it might lead to the election of an even more hostile Duma, as we'll see happened after the government dissolved the First Duma.

Maklakov also neglects the damage that a provision adopted under Article 87 could do between adoption and Duma reversal. The most obvious instance is the decree on field courts martial (discussed in chapter 7). It provided super-swift trials for people accused of revolutionary terror; the resulting hangings earned the epithet "Stolypin's neckties." Because the government never introduced a corresponding bill in the Second Duma, this decree expired after the first sixty days of that Duma; but its expiration obviously didn't resurrect the dead. Maklakov's omission is odd in view of his ardent attack on the field courts martial decree in the Second Duma. Nonetheless, the temporary character of decrees under Article 87 at least limited the government's use and abuse of them.

In another post-revolutionary book, Maklakov argued that where the Duma wanted to *improve* a decree in the process of converting it into a statute, it had an advantage: clearly the government favored the bill (it had introduced it), and the State Council (assuming it to be usually aligned with the government) would be reluctant to reject the amended law and thereby shoulder responsibility for destruction of the benefits provided by the Article 87 decree.[13] But as Maklakov's own experience in the Duma showed, the State Council could escape the bind by using a simple device: inaction—if it neither accepted nor rejected the amended bill, the decree would continue in effect without the Duma's changes. This is exactly what happened to one of Maklakov's most significant reform bills.[14]

What of the State Council? In his memo exhorting French officials not to loan money to Russia, Maklakov assailed the government's decree of February 20, 1906, which had established rules for the relationship of the Duma and State Council, making clear that legislation required the consent of both. This, he said, "annihilated the authority of the Duma."[15] Kadet rhetoric in 1906 was generally in tune with this view. The Fundamental Laws of April 23 retained the State Council's equal status with the Duma—the status that the February 20 decree had granted.

But in writing his history-memoir, Maklakov sees no such "annihilation." He argues that the State Council's blocking role was unlikely to prove powerful. Given its lesser political accountability, it was powerless, he says, without the support of the tsar, just as the Duma was powerless without the support of the country. In any serious conflict, public hostility to the State Council would ultimately fall on the tsar—at least it would do so as long as he retained the power to appoint half the council's membership. If he exercised his retained power to reduce the share of State Council members he could appoint,[16] he would, of course, cut into his public responsibility for the State Council's actions, but at the price of reducing his influence over its selection, and thus the likelihood of its blocking legislation at his behest. And Article 112 allowed the Duma, with the approval of the tsar, to resubmit a bill to the State Council even in the same session as its rejection (and to do so in later sessions without limit). Maklakov thus argued that the State Council was a shield the tsar could use "to deflect only a single arrow." He had made a similar argument in the Duma in 1911.[17]

Maklakov's argument as to the relative vulnerability of the State Council (and therefore of the tsar's possible use of it as a cat's-paw to prevent enactment of popular laws) proceeds in curious disregard of his own experience in the Duma. As we'll see, his advocacy in the Duma—above all the Third Duma (1907–12)—helped secure Duma approval for several reforms that either were then rejected by the State Council or never even came to a vote there. How then could he be so blasé about State Council, after its seeming frustration of his efforts? Perhaps his passage in *State and Society* assumes the possibility of Duma reforms riding on waves of popular enthusiasm more powerful than were actually enjoyed by the reforms passing the Third and Fourth Dumas.

Curiously, the Kadets seem not to have focused any attack on the *tsar's* power to defeat a provision by withholding approval. Perhaps they believed that victory on another pet issue—establishment of the principle that ministries must be responsible to the Duma—might well moot this power; the tsar as a practical matter would have difficulty acting except through the government. In any event, Maklakov argues that a tsar was unlikely to wield this veto. Whereas in a country with no representative body, or a silenced one, an autocrat or dictator could fairly easily resist the country's will, he could do so much less easily with a body like the

Duma on hand. Maklakov pointed to Article 112, which allowed the Duma to reconsider a bill rejected by the tsar so long as this didn't happen in the same session. This would enable the Duma to build a case for a vetoed bill. The resulting debates and their publication (protected by the free speech and publication provision of Article 79) would be dangerous for the tsar's prestige. Apart from a few matters adopted by the Duma and State Council on very thin majorities, Nicholas II's only exercise of this power was on a bill relating to the naval staff, in which the Duma doesn't seem to have been deeply invested.[18]

The Fundamental Laws had special rules relating to the budget and military affairs. Two key budget provisions are Articles 114 and 116. Article 114 precluded the legislative bodies from eliminating or reducing the amounts needed for the payment of state debts or other obligations. Maklakov defended that as suitable for a state with an underdeveloped sense of the rule of law;[19] the defense seems sound so long as the legislature could limit the power of the executive to incur obligations, which the Duma's general legislative competence would seem to include. Article 116 said that if a new budget should not be adopted by the beginning of a fiscal period, the prior year's budget would carry over. Maklakov offered two defenses. First, he pointed to the risk of demagoguery or "scatter-brained improvisation," illustrated by the Second Duma's near rejection of the budget, a rejection prevented only by the vote of Polish Circle deputies—because their party was primarily interested in advancing Polish interests, it acted as a kind of free agent on broader Russian issues. Second, he argued that, whereas for ordinary laws the status quo continues in the event of inaction, for the budget, inaction (in the absence of something like Article 116) would mean that "the life of the country freezes."[20] In the United States, where the government's spending is mainly authorized by continuing resolution, one can see his point.

As to the provisions making the tsar commander in chief and giving him broad authority over military matters (Articles 14, 96, and 97), Maklakov made a case that these powers were inherently suitable for a single figure. But he recognized that this would be less true if the government were "politically mature and the atmosphere normal." In any event, by leaving appropriations for the military in the Duma's hands, the Fundamental Laws gave it control over everything that needed money.[21] With an aggressive legislature, that seems likely to include virtually everything.

Maklakov seems never to have bothered with perhaps the most bizarre provisions of the February 20 decree, which purported to bar the Duma from having a committee work up a bill until the government had declined to do so itself.[22] Taken at face value, this would have delayed the Duma's work for little or no offsetting public advantage. In fact, the Duma seems to have paid these provisions no attention.[23]

Maklakov's defense of the Fundamental Laws as a step toward a rule-of-law regime, explained in *State and Society*, frames his attack on the Kadets' conduct in the First Duma.[24] Although he found their tone of unbridled hostility inapt and inept, his prime target was their insistence on giving priority to constitutional change at the expense of efforts to advance substantive legislation. Absolute priority for constitutional change would make sense if the October Manifesto and the Fundamental Laws left the Duma unable to mobilize public opinion for concrete reforms. But those documents gave the Duma ample means to stir up the public.

Although Maklakov's 1936 analysis varies in some ways from his positions in 1906, the key question is whether his ultimate assessment of the Fundamental Laws was sound. His belief that they provided basic language for the development of the rule of law and liberal democracy seems right to me. But parchment protections alone are weak. As Maklakov argued incessantly in the Duma, the October Manifesto could work *only* if the government and others acted with good faith—by which he appeared to mean respect for the law and willingness to seek compromise within the law. He constantly found that good faith missing on the government side. Looking at the history from the reformers' side, the real question is whether greater realism and moderation on that side might have coaxed the government toward good (or at least better) faith. Maklakov does not assert a firm answer to the question.

The tsar joined his promulgation of the Fundamental Laws with a critical personnel change. On October 19, 1905, right after issuing the October Manifesto, he had created a "council" of ministers that was to be substantially under the control of its chairman (only substantially because several ministers could still report directly to the tsar). He appointed as its first chairman Count Witte, who had advocated the creation of a council and chairmanship along these lines. The structural change and the appointment opened up a vista for the coherent formulation of policy. On April 22, 1906, just before issuing the Fundamental Laws, Nicholas relieved Witte of his post. He replaced him with Ivan Goremykin, an aging onetime minister of the interior hauled out of retirement. Goremykin seems to have been almost universally regarded as a cypher. On the eve of Goremykin's appointment Count Kokovtsov, whom Nicholas was about to name minister of finance, met with the tsar and observed that he feared that Goremykin's "personality, his great indifference toward everything, his utter inability to compromise, and his outspoken unwillingness to meet the new elements of our state life would not only fail to help us get acquainted with them but would serve to increase the opposition." The tsar acknowledged that Kokovtsov might be right, but said it could no longer be helped, as "he had offered Goremykin the office and could not withdraw his offer."[25]

The Kadets treated Witte's replacement as a cause for "elation."[26] They somehow imagined that his fall showed the Kadets' might and the regime's anxiety in the face of the liberal-radical opposition. In fact, although Witte's stands in the process of drafting the Fundamental Laws were sometimes conservative, sometimes liberal, and sometimes just confusing, his ultimate intervention may have been vital. After the drafting, the tsar held off signing for several days. Witte then made a pitch for going forward, and the tsar's decision followed almost immediately.[27] Maklakov may give Witte more credit than he deserves, but he seems right in his view that the choice was not between the Fundamental Laws as issued and some more liberal alternative, but between the Fundamental Laws as issued and retention of the old unlimited autocracy, in complete breach of the October Manifesto.[28]

But the foibles of Witte are not that important. The key is that the Fundamental Laws created a platform that reformers could use to advocate reforms in a national forum, to magnify their voices, and thus, at least occasionally, to win reforms.

CHAPTER 6

The First Duma

Take-Off and Crash Landing

IN ELECTIONS to the First Duma the Kadets captured a strong plurality—185 out of 478 seats. Three parties to the right won a total of 70 seats (the extreme right—zero). The remaining 223 seats went to leftists, many elected as "non-party," including a substantial group of peasants and intellectuals who later assumed the label Trudovik (from *trud*, for work). (The leftist victory would likely have been greater if the Social Democrats and the Socialist Revolutionaries had not boycotted the vote; of course they would have taken votes from "non-party" leftists.) The Kadets were exuberant, or, as Maklakov said later, borrowing a phrase of Stalin's, "dizzy with success." Said Alexander Kizevetter, who a year later would join Maklakov as a member of the Second Duma, "[If] the Duma is dissolved, that will be the government's last act, after which it will cease to exist."[1] This proved to be pure hubris.

On issues of substantive reform, there were major gaps between the Kadets and the regime. But the gaps did not add up to the sort of chasm that the brief story of the First Duma makes them appear. The regime—belatedly—announced policy goals of reforming peasant rights with a view to ending peasant isolation, equalizing their rights with those of other estates, and removing restrictions on their rights in the lands allotted to them in the emancipation.[2] (Thwarted in the First Duma, the government in fact adopted many of these reforms under Article 87 in the "inter-Duma" period between the First and Second Dumas.)

In the election campaign Maklakov had not been a candidate, but he had been in charge of a "school" for Kadet orators and had spent a lot of time out on the hustings. He read the voters as seeing in the Kadets an embodiment of Kizevetter's slogan "political freedom and social justice"—which Maklakov understood as an ability to improve life without revolution. He didn't see their support for the Kadets as based on love for, or even interest in, the structural changes championed by the Kadets: four-tailed suffrage (universal, direct, equal, and secret), deletion of the State Council's power to withhold consent from legislation, and Duma power to remove the cabinet. Paul Miliukov regularly called these issues the "three locks," which he saw as obstructions to a true constitutionalism. As for the general mood, Maklakov perceived the ordinary citizen as strongly disfavoring revolution, mainly because the citizen rightly sensed that he would be the victim of its violence.[3] This, of course, was the antithesis of the assumptions about popular feeling that seemed to underlie Kizevetter's idea that a Duma dissolution would trigger the regime's collapse.

What went wrong? Both sides plainly suffered from lack of experience: the government from never having had to deal with an elected legislative body, the Kadets from never having had to operate in a legislative body, much less to dominate one. Neither side had ever seen a *Russian* legislature at work. The educated on both sides were of course familiar with the French Revolution and the roles of the estates general and national assembly, but that vicarious experience didn't provide much of a model for revolutionary ferment with a happy ending.

Also important (again on both sides) was a "moralization gap," the ubiquitous human tendency to view the rights and wrongs of any clash in a way favorable to one's own side.[4] These two factors, inexperience and the moralization gap, surely helped generate, on each side, rhetorical sloppiness and a tendency to turn manageable disputes into hopeless gaps.

The first major misstep was the government's. At the outset, it appeared before the First Duma with trivial and absurd facsimiles of legislative projects, implying that it found the Duma itself a triviality. This failing was a side effect of the tsar's abrupt decisions to dismiss Witte on the eve of the First Duma and to have no holdovers in the new cabinet. Witte had in fact prepared a slew of proposals,[5] but Goremykin, the new prime minister, had so little sense of the moment that he failed either to seek them out, or to create substitutes, or to explain the deficiency. Witte had seen the prospect of reform work in the Duma as a sign of health. He had argued at the Council of Ministers' meeting of March 5 that "it is essential to immediately direct the activity of the State Duma to definite and broad but sober and businesslike work and thus make sure its work is productive."[6] And according to the memoirs of Count Kokovtsov, who had just concluded the successful negotiations for the French loan and had a long conversation with the tsar on the eve of becoming minister of finance, Nicholas II had obliquely echoed Witte's thought, saying (as paraphrased by Kokovtsov) that "the Duma, occupied with the responsibility of legislative work, might prove less revolutionary than I [Kokovtsov] feared," and that zemstvo circles "would not wish to take the lead in a new struggle between the government and the representatives of the people."[7]

Not to be outdone by the government's blunder, the Duma focused not on policy initiatives but on pursuit of constitutional change. The changes it proposed, stated in a formal address to the tsar, were not only improbable as a matter of politics (the bureaucracy had only barely extracted the tsar's consent to go as far as he did) but also were framed in terms that violated the Fundamental Laws' ban on Duma initiative for such changes (Article 107). The proposed changes were all the regular Kadet staples—extinction of the State Council's vote as a necessity for legislation, the four-tailed franchise, and ministerial responsibility to the Duma.[8]

The oddity is that the Kadets and their Trudovik allies passed up the opportunity to frame these changes in non-constitutional terms. The toughest needle to thread was the status of the State Council, which was fixed in the Fundamental Laws (see, e.g., Article 86, making the Council's approval necessary for the adoption of a new law). But, as the Kadets said in their address to the tsar, what concerned them about the Council was the way its members were chosen—half by the tsar, half by a franchise even narrower than that for the Duma. For changing both composition and franchise, the Fundamental Laws were no problem. Their only rule on those subjects was that the number of appointed members could not exceed the number of elected ones (Article 100). In other words, the Duma could change anything about the State Council's composition so long as it didn't *reduce* the relative weight of the *representative* interest, which of course was the last thing it wanted to do. As for suffrage, it was not defined in the Fundamental Laws but in the electoral laws of December 11, 1905; again Article 107 was no obstacle. Thus the Duma could readily vote for four-tailed suffrage and complete democratization of the State Council. Of course these changes, despite the legitimacy of Duma initiation, would have to secure approval of the State Council and tsar, clearly an impossibility. But a vote could have put the Duma on record, and perhaps over time developed support for its ideas, without an in-your-face defiance of the Fundamental Laws—defiance that came back to haunt the Duma (at least rhetorically) when the government invoked it to justify its decision to dissolve the Duma.

As for a requirement that the government be responsible to the Duma, nothing in the Fundamental Laws barred such a relationship. Maklakov argued that the practice would have been automatically "introduced to the degree that the Duma's prestige grew in the eyes of both the country and the tsar"; with a highly prestigious Duma in place, the tsar would find it politically impossible to appoint or retain a government that the Duma rejected.[9]

All told, despite Kadet laments that the Fundamental Laws' formal limit on the Duma's ability to initiate an amendment was an outrageous violation of the rights of the people,[10] it was in fact a minor barrier to their ideas for transforming the government's structure.

Besides their gratuitous attempted breach of the Fundamental Laws, the Kadets formulated at least some of their constitutional goals—notably elimination of the State Council as an obstacle to legislation—as *predicates* to "fruitful activity in the Duma."[11] It must have been obvious that, for the time being at least, the Fundamental Laws went as far as the tsar was willing to go. To tell him that complete transformation of what he had just wrought was a prerequisite to substantive action was to demand surrender—yet again—from a figure who clearly felt no need to surrender. And at least on Maklakov's reading, the Kadets' electoral victory reflected no great popular zest for the sort of constitutional issues that obsessed the Kadet leadership.

The Kadets matched their zeal on constitutionalism with a skewed vision of its content. They appeared to believe that the Duma, or at any rate its majority, represented "the people's will," with a corollary that its sole word was law, no matter what the costs in eliminating communication between government and Duma and in disregarding the constitutional provisions essential to the Duma's own existence. Thus when the War Minister, V. P. Pavlov, tried to voice the government's position on the death penalty, Kadets and other deputies hounded him out. One deputy, an "almost completely white old man [of the Kadet party] . . . banged his desk violently, jumped up, shook his fist and shouted: 'Get out, murderer, executioner, out.' "[12] When another deputy, Count P. A. Heiden, rose to insist on the value of some minimal decorum (suggesting that the scheme of government required "the deepest respect for the law and even for the person of one's foe"), a leading Kadet, Maxim Vinaver, rose to say, "All persons who openly defy the wishes expressed by the State Duma should not appear here on the instructions of ministers."[13]

The Kadets also insisted on identifying constitutionalism with purely parliamentary government. Thus V.D. Nabokov (a distinguished lawyer, son of a former minister of justice, and father of the famous Russian-American author), after encountering government resistance to Duma proposals, declared, "From the point of view of the principle of popular representation, we can say only one thing: 'the executive authority must submit to the legislative authority.'" While it's true that under a rule-of-law regime the executive can generally act only in accordance with legislatively approved law, the rule of law obviously does not require that the executive bend to legislative preferences that have not yet wended their way into law, as Nabokov assumed. Maklakov points out that Nabokov's statement pretended that the Duma was the sole legislative authority, while in fact, under the Fundamental Laws, the tsar (plus the State Council) shared that power,[14] as in many non-parliamentary constitutional regimes.

Even a very sophisticated lawyer such as Sergei Muromtsev could be blinded by a tendency to think of abstractions as categories whose *nature* compelled specific outcomes rather than merely as useful tools for organizing thought. On taking office as speaker of the Duma, he said: "Let our work proceed on the basis of the respect befitting a constitutional monarch [roar of applause] and complete realization of the rights of the State Duma flowing from the very nature of popular representation."[15] But the *nature* of popular representation does not in itself give any "rights" to a legislature. The rights flow from political settlements, forged in conflict between contending forces. Some such settlements may lay better claim than others to the label "popular representation," but it is the settlement that defines the legislature's rights, not the Platonic concept.

Whatever the Kadets' zeal for immediate constitutional reform, they could not in the end cleave to the notion that it must be a predicate to substantive legislation. In fact, the Duma did pass one piece of legislation—abolition of the death penalty. But here again rhetorical sloppiness sabotaged legislative accomplishment. The death penalty applied to civilians in Russia primarily because the extraordinary security laws (in the regions where they were in effect) gave provincial governors and the ministry of internal affairs authority to transfer cases to military tribunals, which, unlike civilian ones, had the power to impose capital punishment.[16] The Fundamental Laws were no obstacle to changes in this relationship: Article 15 said the tsar had authority to decree *where* the extraordinary security laws applied, but left authority to *amend* the extraordinary security laws themselves to the usual legislative processes. So the Duma could have attempted a neat surgical cut, excising the government's power to shift cases into the military courts. Instead it enacted language that seemed to ban the death penalty in all circumstances.[17] Of course the breadth of the Duma's bill ensured that it would not receive State Council endorsement. The State Council in fact referred the bill to a committee, which produced a bill that left intact the power of governors to transfer cases to the military courts. This denouement suggests that Maklakov was likely wrong to have suggested that the government would have agreed to a major cut in transfers from civil authorities to the military courts, although perhaps a more realistic bill from the Duma would have received more benign treatment from the government. In any event, his basic criticism stands: the Duma's bill—adopted unanimously and to loud applause—guaranteed continuation of what it sought to end.[18]

Even though they performed some substantive work, the Duma majority seemed little interested in such accomplishments. For example, in evaluating issues for possible legislative activity, some Kadets counted the prospect of government agreement and cooperation as a ground *not* to raise the issue. When a deputy suggested that the Duma's address in response to the tsar's include a proposal for expanded public education, a Kadet objected "that this subject would be accepted with delight by the government, which would add similar, politically inoffensive objectives for harmonious work with the popular representatives."[19]

Of course the Duma majority and the regime were hardly in agreement on policy issues such as the so-called agrarian question.

But true to form, apart from substantive disagreement, both sides framed their positions in a style that managed to be both inflammatory and muddled. Very broadly speaking, the Duma majority favored the redistribution of land (taking from the gentry, giving to the peasants), whereas the government favored enhancing peasant ownership, so that an enterprising peasant could forge ahead without the approval of the "society" or "commune" to which he belonged, and with entitlement to the full benefit of his enterprise. Within the left, the Kadet party favored redistribution with compensation, though it objected to compensation at market value and left utterly mysterious what principle *should* govern compensation. Yet in the address to the tsar, the Duma spoke of "obligatory confiscation of private lands," not mentioning compensation at all. It thus seemed to adopt the view held by parties to the Kadets' left.[20]

The government responded on May 13—the very speech in which it sketched out the reform program mentioned at the beginning of this chapter. But the government also overstated its position, saying that a solution to the agrarian question "on the basis of the Duma's proposals is absolutely inadmissible."[21] Nothing in the Fundamental Laws, however, seemed to bar the Duma's ideas, so it is hard to see just what made them "inadmissible." (If a court treated the October Manifesto as being of constitutional weight, it might have found its reference to "the unshakable foundations of civic freedom" to be a basis for invalidating uncompensated takings of land. But no one—least of all the government—was thinking of a court exercising that sort of freewheeling power.) The government could have contented itself with saying that it would oppose these ideas and, if they passed, with urging the State Council to reject them. Instead, it chose an inapt word that pointlessly infuriated the Duma members.

As the Duma's committee on agrarian matters hadn't reached agreement on any bill, and seemed not to be on the verge of any agreement, the Kadets had the idea of responding to the government's statement with an appeal to the people on the subject. But the absence of any Duma consensus meant that the appeal itself would lack any clear policy content. It stuck to vague phrases about compulsory confiscation and ended by saying that the Duma would not retreat from this position, "that any proposals not in agreement with it would be rejected." Again the language was pointlessly provocative. Many of the government's ideas were not mutually exclusive with the Duma's; if the Duma meant that only carbon copies of its ideas were acceptable (a quite plausible reading), then it was vetoing in advance any deal that would satisfy some of each side's priorities.[22]

Not to be outdone, the government gratuitously provoked the Duma with its reaction to a rightist campaign of telegrams to the tsar. The telegrams made a number of fantastic claims—for example, accusations that the Duma was plotting to seize the government and was working for dismemberment of the empire. Many attacked ethnic minorities, especially Jews, and some called for the Duma's abolition. Instead of either remaining silent or disassociating itself from the campaign, the government published the telegrams in the *Government Gazette* (*Pravitelstvennyi Vestnik*), thus seeming to express the tsar's solidarity with a party position—a solidarity plainly at odds with the position of a constitutional monarch. This led to a formal questioning of Goremykin by the Duma (an "interpellation") and a frosty but pointless exchange.[23]

One last substantive issue deserves mention: amnesty. The very first speech delivered in the Duma was a dramatic call for amnesty by a Kadet, I. I. Petrunkevich. The address to the tsar, while perhaps in form respecting the Fundamental Laws' allocation of the power of amnesty to the tsar (Article 23), nonetheless identified amnesty, for all crimes committed out of religious or political conviction, as a "demand of the popular conscience." The "demand," issued in a period when assassinations of government employees were averaging three hundred per month, and coupled with staunch Kadet refusal to condemn terror, seems highly provocative. A reader of a right-wing newspaper sent a letter to the editor that was nominally addressed to a Kadet Duma member, F. I. Rodichev: "Dear Mr. Rodichev, I am going to kill you for political reasons; please will you ask an amnesty for me in advance?" Maklakov in his history of the First Duma argued that an amnesty would make sense as a gesture of reconciliation celebrating the end of hostilities—a happy moment that plainly had not arrived. The Duma's position seemed to align it with the revolutionaries.[24]

On the night of July 8–9, 1906, little more than two months after it had assembled, the tsar dissolved the Duma under Article 105 of the Fundamental Laws. The tsar also issued a manifesto offering three reasons for the dissolution: (1) the Duma's supposed violation of Article 107, which denied it power to initiate changes in the Fundamental Laws; (2) the Duma's sending a mission to investigate the Bialystok pogrom, a pogrom the government had probably instigated and had undoubtedly failed to promptly quell; and (3) the Duma's appeal on agrarian policy. (The phrasing was somewhat more veiled, but these were clearly the sins the government had in mind.)[25] As legal matters, all three seem very weak. As we've seen, Article 107 didn't stand in the way of the *substance* of the structural changes that the Duma majority would have liked to make. While the Fundamental Laws didn't give the Duma the power to send investigative teams, neither did they withhold such a power. And the appeal on agrarian matters also violated no law.

What seems most surprising is that the government bothered with the explanatory manifesto at all. Article 105 didn't require an explanation, and the nature of the action suggests that the power was entirely discretionary. (Article 105 said the decree must provide for new elections and name the date when the next Duma would convene, but the inclusion of those details only supports the natural reading that the laws left the decision to dissolve entirely to the tsar, subject obviously to political constraints.)

The *actual* reasoning of the cabinet curiously did include the inquiry mission to Bialystok. But it also rested on the ultimate conclusion made by most of the ministers—and this seems to have been far more important—that the only alternative to dissolution was to name either a Kadet ministry or a government of public activists. "In either case, the result would be the same: the new government would be unable to stem the revolutionary tide."[26] These conclusions presumably came from the whole tenor of Kadet behavior in the Duma: failing to act as a serious negotiating partner for substantive reform, regarding emissaries of the government as ipso facto illegitimate and unworthy of being heard, treating the Fundamental Laws as illegitimate simply because they didn't establish a parliamentary regime, endorsing amnesty but refusing to condemn revolutionary terror, and doing little to staunch the flow of revolutionary rhetoric from Duma members on the Kadets' left.

Analyzing the matter in retrospect, Maklakov perceived himself and Miliukov as each seeing dichotomies—but fundamentally different ones. Miliukov tended to see Russia's great division as lying between autocracy and the constitution for which he longed, whereas Maklakov saw it as between the constitution, already achieved, and continuing revolution.[27] On the first premise, the Kadets must line up with the revolutionaries (or at least refrain from efforts to curb them); on the second, obviously not. Maklakov saw the first premise as a residue of the pre–October Manifesto alliance between the "liberation movement" and the revolutionaries, an alliance that made sense to Maklakov *only* until the October Manifesto and the revised Fundamental Laws opened the door to reform through peaceful political action.[28]

Maklakov argued that the Kadets' stance had two unfortunate consequences: first, a direct sharpening of the social and political divide; and second, the loss of a vital opportunity for political experience. He invokes Stolypin's observation, "In politics there is no revenge, but there are consequences."[29] As he viewed them, the obvious consequences were a shift to the right by the tsar and the forces around him, and by the Octobrist party, with a concomitant emboldening of the extreme right.[30] These consequences seem altogether natural. An insistence on the tsar's capitulation by a group that the regime had hoped were nonrevolutionary moderates plainly tended—from the tsar's point of view—to undermine the advantages of constitutionalism and cooperation. It strengthened a key argument of those who disliked constitutionalism and the rule of law, namely, that regime concessions along these lines would encourage revolution, not abate the risk.

The other general consequence was, in a sense, simply the converse of the first. Russia had no prior experience with the combination of the old regime and a popularly elected legislature. If that combination was to lead peacefully to a constitutional regime embodying the rule of law, it obviously required a degree of cooperation. Although I don't believe Maklakov ever quotes Aristotle, he clearly shared his view as to how humans acquire capacities for particular conduct: "Men acquire a particular quality by constantly acting a particular way . . . you become just by performing just actions, temperate by performing temperate actions, brave by performing brave actions." In their conduct in the First Duma, the Kadets, not for the first time nor for the last, passed up a chance to learn constitutional behavior.

In evaluating the Kadet and regime strategies, one is tempted to assign them ratings for their willingness to cooperate. Let us assume that the regime deserves to be rated lower than the Kadets. That lower rating doesn't mean that a different Kadet strategy might not have altered the outcome. If we hypothesize a replay of the game with a different Kadet approach, we can't casually assume that the government would not have altered its behavior.[31]

Though the dissolution violated no legal rule, it enraged the Kadets and their allies to the left. Members of those groups (most but not all of them Duma members) repaired to the town of Vyborg, which, because it was located in the Finnish part of the Russian empire, offered a legal regime more favorable to protest. There they adopted what became known as the Vyborg Manifesto. There were two competing drafts, a Trudovik version seeming to call for revolution by the army and navy, and a Kadet version calling for civil disobedience in the form of refusal to pay taxes or appear for compulsory military service. They chose the milder one; it could thus be said later that the Kadets had held their leftist friends back from repeating the error of the October-December uprising in 1905. The Manifesto brought forth virtually no response from the people summoned to resistance: Kizevetter later observed that critics called it a case of "shooting a blank."[32]

But the manifesto was not such a blank from the legal perspective. The signers were promptly charged with *distributing* offensive material, and thus were subject to a possible ban on seeking election to the Duma. A charge of merely *writing* the manifesto would have been far more accurate but would not have had this effect. When the case came to trial (only in December 1907, after the end of the Second Duma), the evidence linking the defendants to the distribution appears to have been too weak for a finding of guilt under Russian principles of aiding and abetting.[33]

In the central committee meeting just after the dismissal of the Duma, Maklakov had spoken very sharply against issuing the Vyborg proclamation. For that reason he didn't want to participate in the defense at the trial. But he did so, at the defendants' request; of the three defense lawyers, he gave his summation last. (Sixteen of the defendants also exercised their right to speak on their own behalf, emphasizing their political justifications.)

He reviewed the legal frailty of the prosecution's case, and the obvious reason why the government had chosen a crime for which the evidence was inadequate but the political consequences desirable (for the government). "Thus the criminal court becomes a weapon of political struggle, and its goal is to drive the opponents from the political arena." He then launched into a celebration of the rule of law, what he called his "confession of faith":

> I'm not speaking as a political comrade in arms of the accused . . . , nor as a lawyer who must painfully watch indifferently as the law is tortured before his eyes. I'm speaking as a person who has the weakness to think that the court is the highest organ of state power, as the law is the soul of the state system. A country suffers harm not so much from erroneous or imperfect laws, as

> from lawlessness going unpunished. However good the published laws may be, however good the legislative machinery, if there is no one to protect the laws, then no good will come of them for Russia. The preservation of the law from any violation, whether from above or below, is the task of the court. People may be dissatisfied with the courts, they may drag them into the struggle of political parties, they may threaten their tenure, but so long as the courts—independent even though much changed—stand guard over the law, so long will the state live.

Maklakov went on to express dismay at seeing the procurator (the Russian equivalent of a prosecutor, but also playing a role similar to an ombudsman's), "the guardian of the law," "publicly seek[ing] to violate it, [and] for the sake of political ends asking that a statute be applied that cannot be [properly] applied. . . ." Then he wound up:

> It is not of the fate of these people [the defendants], however close or dear they may be to me, that I'm thinking of now. For them your verdict cannot do a great deal [they had already been excluded from the Second Duma], but from it [the verdict] I await an answer to the tormenting question, with which many Russian people are watching this trial, "are defenders of our law to be found?"[34]

Another distinguished lawyer of the time wrote of the speech and Maklakov:

> Maklakov made a special impression with his speech. It was purely juridical, and in that lay the special quality of this orator of talent, who burned as no one else with passion for the law. Psychological experience, scenes of everyday life—all that touched Maklakov little, slid by his temperament, and in such matters he barely rose above the level of a good orator. But it took only some kind of violation of rights to strike his sensitive ears for Maklakov to be transformed. His speech then reached surging heights of power, he captivated and mastered his listeners.

> I've had to appear in defense with the best orators of Russia, but if I were asked what speech made the strongest impression on me, I would answer without hesitation: the speech of Maklakov in the Vyborg trial.
>
> When he finished speaking, the whole room was stockstill, then in a minute burst forth in thunderous applause.[35]

The court acquitted only two of the 169 defendants and sentenced the remainder to three months in prison and a ban on electoral candidacy. Russia's highest judicial body, the Criminal Cassation Department of the Senate, affirmed the conviction, over the dissent of three out of nineteen senators.[36]

Even before the trial, the existence of the charge itself had excluded most of the Kadet members of the Duma from eligibility for election. As Maklakov wrote later: "This affected my personal fate. When there were elections for the Second Duma, the majority of the well-known Kadets were ineligible, and in Moscow the party presented other candidates, of the second order, known to it from the electoral campaign for the First Duma. They were Kizevetter, Teslenko and I."[37]

CHAPTER 7

The Second Duma

Challenging Stolypin, Engaging Stolypin

Soon after the Second Duma met, on the very night before Stolypin was to address it for the first time as prime minister, the roof of the chamber collapsed. It was before dawn, so no one was hurt. The collapse itself was, of course, a bad omen, but some of the reactions were worse. Pavel Krushevan, the deputy from Kishinev and one of the so-called Black Hundreds (the label loosely applied to vitriolic reactionaries and anti-Semites), on seeing the devastated room reportedly said "Good," and "his face lit up with satisfaction."[1] On the left, a Kadet veteran of the First Duma insinuated deliberate government neglect, saying that inadequacies in the ceiling had been noticed in the First Duma and money appropriated for their correction.[2]

In the election campaign preceding the Duma's convocation, the government had harassed the opposition with a blend of repression and incompetence. At a campaign event where Maklakov spoke of what "we," the Kadet party, favored, a policeman interrupted to say that he mustn't do so, because the party was banned (as it technically was). Maklakov switched to "they," and that was apparently all right.[3] Another government tactic also depended on the party's unlawful status. Because of the indirect method of elections, voters chose only electors, who were typically people unknown or at least much less well known than the real candidates. Without lists linking them, voters were likely to get the electors' names wrong, so official lists were provided. But the government invented a new rule, which had not applied in elections to the First Duma, disallowing official lists for the illegal parties. The Kadets got around this with their own unofficial lists, which evidently functioned satisfactorily. These government shenanigans, plus cruder measures such as arresting and exiling candidates under the extraordinary security laws, largely backfired, producing sympathy for the candidates opposed by the government and bringing the Kadets closer to the hard left parties.[4]

As a candidate Maklakov sought allies to left and right. On two occasions he stressed the unity of the left (that is, the Kadets and those to the left of them). In one of these he invoked defeat of the Octobrists as a goal and argued that "in great struggles that define the path of history, only two armies fight." Despite this Manichean tone, in both instances his key pitch was that all on the left should get behind the Kadets, as the strongest party.[5] So he seems to have

Three Kadet leaders (left to right): Prince Paul Dolgorukov, Alexander Kizevetter, Vasily Maklakov, and N. V. Talenko. © State Historical Museum, Moscow.

been invoking leftist unity mainly as a device for promoting his own party—the least leftist of the leftists.

Maklakov made similar efforts to cultivate potential allies to his right. In the summer of 1906 he and some other Kadets met with representatives of the Octobrists, and an Octobrist splinter, the Party of Peaceful Renewal, to see if they could coordinate in the electoral campaign. The effort failed. Dmitri Shipov, one of the founders of the Octobrist party and then of its splinter, reacted to the government's field courts martial decree—of which more shortly—by saying that the Party of Peaceful Renewal could under no circumstances work with the Octobrists, who were acquiescing in or even supportive of the decree.[6] Maklakov's outreach activities seem to have been driven by one primary goal—enhancing the Kadet position wherever allies could be found.

The electoral results confounded the government's intentions in dismissing the First Duma. The most obvious effect was a hollowing out of the center. The Kadets and their adherents shrank from 185 to 99, or to about 19 percent of the membership. Slightly making up the loss to the middle was an increase for the Octobrists from 13 to 44. The Social Democrats, Socialist Revolutionaries, and Popular Socialists collectively rose from 17 to 118 (23 percent), while the Trudoviks edged up from 94 to 104 (20 percent). Those to the right of the Octobrists rose from zero in the First Duma to 64 in the Second (of whom only 10 seem to qualify as extreme rightist). Despite the shift to extremes, a centrist coalition on particular issues was conceivable. Excluding 2 percent classified as "extreme rightists," and running leftward so far as to encompass the Trudoviks, one could nonetheless imagine—perhaps with a good deal of optimism—a centrist majority of 58 percent of Duma members. If we add in 9 percent for the Polish Circle, who often showed a moderate bent,[7] this imagined coalition could prevail even in the face of losing most Trudoviks. Of course to assume that the Kadets themselves were centrist is, as we'll see, a stretch.

The new Duma represented not merely a shift to the left. J. W. Riddle, the U.S. ambassador, cabled to Washington: "The present

Duma has the reputation of being a less educated but more practical body than the one of last year. The leaders of the first Duma were doctrinaire professors of great learning and many theories, but with no experience of public administration or of business. In the present Duma this type is not at all prominent."[8] Maklakov agreed.

When Nicholas II dissolved the First Duma, he also appointed Stolypin, already minister of internal affairs, to be premier as well. As minister of internal affairs Stolypin had stood out in the Duma as articulate, self-confident, and relatively candid—going so far, for example, as to acknowledge the illegality of a police action, a concession that stunned the deputies by its novelty.[9] Stolypin used the time between the dissolution of the First Duma and the convening of the Second to issue a set of decrees under Article 87, implementing a mixed program of reform and repression. Two reforms stand out. First, a decree of October 5, 1906, eliminated many of the disabilities of peasants vis-à-vis the other estates. This was broadly welcome, and Maklakov was later, in the Fourth Duma, to take a lead role in trying to extend it. A second decree, issued November 9, 1906, adopted the government's preferred solution to Russia's agricultural woes: it enabled individual peasants to obtain rights in land that would be more like ordinary property than what they then held: they received the opportunity (either as individual families or as a village), to opt out of the process of endless redistribution aimed at matching landholding with family size. In large part because Stolypin presented it as a *substitute* for the left's solutions to Russia's agrarian problems (confiscation of gentry land, with some compensation, and redistribution to peasants), it was anathema to the left (including the Kadets); conflict between the competing visions for agriculture fueled political warfare throughout the Second Duma.

On the repression side of the ledger was the government's August 19, 1906, establishment of the field courts martial. The decree creating them came on the heels of an attempt to assassinate Stolypin at his residence on Aptekarskii Island, but the initiative and insistence on the decree came from the tsar, with Stolypin himself and Minister of Justice Shcheglovitov expressing skepticism.[10] The law enabled military officers with no legal training to act as prosecutor, judge, and jury, taking the accused from charge to execution in three days, with no possibility of appeal. As Maklakov pointed out, the law directed an official to send an accused to such a "court" when the crime was so obvious that there was no further need for investigation, terms that seemed to call for an automatic guilty verdict.

Just as the government manifested a real program in the run-up to the Duma opening, a stark contrast to the launch of the First Duma, so the mood on the left was more moderate. Miliukov himself sounded a less militant tone—"not assault, but an orderly siege."[11] The Kadet slogan was "Save the Duma," that is, avoid provocations of the sort that had precipitated dismissal of the First Duma. Maklakov endorsed this approach, arguing that at particular times it made sense to save the Duma, at others to strike the government with heavy blows.[12]

Another difference was a change in the Duma's rules, introduced by a committee under Maklakov's chairmanship. Maklakov and others believed that one reason for the futility of the First Duma was the waste of time in debate on bills that had not been through committee. To obtain the necessary clarity and specificity, Maklakov drafted, and the Duma in due course adopted, a *Nakaz* (rules or standing orders) that sharply limited debate over such inchoate measures.

The Second Duma's legislative life began with Stolypin's March 6 speech—the one that had been postponed because of the ceiling's collapse. The speech is remarkable for the scope and depth of reforms it proposed. As Stolypin's biographer Abraham Ascher writes, "If a liberal had delivered the . . . speech, a large number of deputies would have applauded most of it."[13] Of course Stolypin's agrarian reform proposal was offensive to the left, but that occupied little of the speech. Besides that, Stolypin proposed laws enshrining the civil liberties referred to in the October Manifesto; reform of local government on a plane of equal relations between all estates; reform of the local court system to bring the local courts under control of the rural electorate; a general policy of getting the government out of the way of labor-management relations; organization of medical aid for workers; religious toleration; subjection of officials to both criminal and civil liability for excesses; and, perhaps most startlingly, abolition of officials' power to impose administrative exile except in time of war or popular rebellion.[14] Imagine how Russia might have developed if the liberal Second Duma had put aside its conflict with Stolypin over agrarian policy and set out to enact such a program.

In fact, the Duma's leftist majority had resolved in advance to sit in stony silence regardless of what Stolypin might say. But one deputy, a Social Democrat, was bursting with such fervor that he assumed the tribune and delivered a scorching attack. The attack is familiar to history entirely because of Stolypin's response. His few words included these: "What the revolutionaries say boils down to two words directed to the authorities, 'Hands up!' And to these two words, the government with complete calm and confidence in its right can answer with two words, 'Not afraid' ['*ne zapugaete,*' literally, 'You don't scare us']."[15] In his history of the Second Duma, Maklakov wrote, "For many of us only party discipline prevented us from applauding. The impression on the country was tremendous. . . . March 6 was the apogee of Stolypin's popularity."[16] Maklakov went on to place the whole speech in context: "What was new and valuable was that he spoke as a true 'constitutional minister,' as the representative of a 'constitutional ideology,' understanding the rule of law and the need for an opposition to the authorities' policies."[17]

As we saw earlier, the government's efforts to quiet the revolution encompassed both reform and repression, the latter most clearly taking the form of the decree on field courts martial. The crude summary justice that the decree unleashed, almost invariably ending in a hanging, led to the epithet "Stolypin's neckties," a tag that ironically originated with a rather moderate Kadet, Fyodor Rodichev. That the government needed to take some action against terrorist violence seems clear: In the one-year period starting in October 1905 the killing and wounding of government officials ran at a rate of about 300 a month. Thereafter the rate slowed a bit, but when private individual victims are taken into account, the total over the years 1905 through 1907 reaches more than 9,000.[18] That, of course, is not enough to justify the lawlessness of the field courts martial.

When the Second Duma opened on February 20, 1907, the government knew that as a practical matter the measure could survive for two more months at the most. Recall that Article 87 gave the government only two options for a law enacted under that article. It could introduce a bill with the same provisions in the Duma; but in that case, the law would die whenever the Duma *or* the State Council voted it down; given the Second Duma's composition, it was sure to exercise this authority and kill the decree. Alternatively, the government could offer no such bill, in which case the decree would expire automatically two months after the Duma resumed its sessions. Knowing the decree's fate if it were introduced as a bill, the government offered none. The clock started running.

The Kadets nonetheless offered a bill affirmatively repealing the decree. The bill had no realistic prospect of having any effect, as that would require approval of the State Council and tsar, which, if possible at all, clearly would not occur until after the decree's legal expiration on April 20. But the Kadet deputies wanted to take action, and the field courts martial issue seemed the politically most promising area of activity. Maklakov joined the repeal effort enthusiastically, though he later regretted the strategy. In hindsight he believed that joining with the left in this way made the Kadets appear to be its allies in support of revolution.[19] Nonetheless, the repeal effort was the occasion of one of his most famous speeches in the Duma, and indeed the one of which he seems to have been most proud. We have already seen part of the speech in discussing his relationship with Tolstoy—Maklakov's assault on the death penalty.

His speech rested primarily on rule-of-law ideals. Stolypin

had argued that, in the interests of protecting the state from the revolution, it was sometimes necessary to sacrifice private interests. Maklakov turned this around, depicting the field courts martial as destructive not merely of private interests but also of the state itself. Anticipating the words later put into the mouth of Sir Thomas More by the playwright Robert Bolt in *A Man for All Seasons*, he said:

> Striking at the revolution, you have not struck private interests but have struck all that protects us, the courts and lawfulness. . . . If you defeat the revolution this way, you will at the same time defeat the state, and in the collapse of revolution you will not find a rule-of-law state but only solitary individuals, a chaos of state breakdown.[20]

He closed by saying that, if the government really meant to bolster the state system, as Stolypin had claimed, it should join those in the Duma attacking the field courts martial, and, not waiting for the decree to expire automatically, should itself declare that "the shame of killings by field courts martial in Russia will cease."[21]

In response, Stolypin acknowledged the legal merits of his Kadet critics' attacks, mentioning Maklakov by name, and going so far as to say that if he pursued that avenue he likely would not disagree with Maklakov.[22] But he offered the defense of necessity. He pointed to declarations by the revolutionary parties calling for uprisings, which of course were occurring, albeit in a scattered way. And, as we've seen, assassinations were running at a pace no government could tolerate. His speech ended by proposing some sort of accommodation with his critics:

> [T]he government has come to the conclusion that the country awaits from it not evidence of weakness but evidence of confidence. We want to believe that we will hear from you, gentlemen, a word of pacification, that you will cut short the bloody madness. We are confident that you will say those words that will have us all begin—not the destruction of the historic edifice of Russia—but its recreation, its restructuring, and its enhancement.

> In expectation of that word, the government will take measures to limit this severe law solely to the most extreme cases of the most audacious crimes, so that when the Duma directs Russia to peaceful work, this law will fall, simply by not being introduced for confirmation [under Article 87].[23]

The meaning of this offer may not have been altogether clear, but on its face it looked like a commitment to extinguish the activities of the field courts martial before their legally predetermined end (at least for all but extreme cases), in reliance on Stolypin's hope or expectation of some word from Duma members, at least from the Kadets, condemning revolutionary violence.

No such word came. Rather, the Kadet leadership treated this apparent olive branch as a stink bomb.[24] But Stolypin's meaning is to some degree independently verifiable by looking at the behavior of the field courts martial after March 13. The Social Democratic paper, *Tovarishch*, hardly an organ to downplay the state's bloodletting, collected the month-by-month figures.[25]

MONTH	DEATH PENALTIES
August (1906)	12
September	203
October	255
November	261
December	176
January (1907)	141
February	39
March	11
April	4
	Total 1,102

The downward trend is clear. It had been under way since November, but the decline steepened sharply in February, March, and April. Without day-by-day figures, and indications of the crimes for which the field courts martial were used after March 13, we can't precisely evaluate Stolypin's fulfillment of his apparent promise.[26] But despite those gaps and the preexisting decline, the record appears at least consistent with an effort to confine use of the field courts martial to the most egregious cases. Although the courts were sure to expire in any event (subject, of course, to the risk that the government might dissolve the Duma and radically limit the franchise, as it in fact did on June 3, 1907), this is a case where Maklakov's eloquence in the Duma may actually have saved lives from government arbitrariness.

In a letter to his friend Boris Bakhmetev, the Provisional Government's ambassador to the United States (unlike Maklakov, Bakhmetev at least arrived in time to take up the office), Maklakov said that the speech was the only one for which he received laurels in the press (an absurd exaggeration!), but that for him

> what made it important was not articles in the press . . . nor applause in the Duma; for me the important thing was the response of adversaries. I'll not forget how at the time of the speech I turned toward Stolypin, sitting on the ministerial bench, and saw his eyes, which he never took away from me. I continued to watch his eyes, and he didn't turn them from me till the very end; I was later told that he had talked about me afterwards. And the speech . . . was built on respect for authority, on the need to preserve it from what was dangerous for it, to save it from any mistakes that might compromise it. This was the idea that I pursued to the end, on account of which I often found myself divided from the Kadets.[27]

While the field courts martial decree itself was lawless, the authorities managed to make it more lawless by violating even the decree's own rules. In his speech assailing the decree, Maklakov exposed an especially flagrant example. Four people from the countryside surrounding Moscow met another outsider, who was a policeman. They asked him to join them, and all five spent several hours eating and drinking and in friendly conversation. After a while the policeman departed. The four then drank some more, and, perhaps drunk, wandered through the city and again met their friend. They asked him to rejoin them, but he refused, and they then began to fight with him, to drag him about by force. The policeman waved a revolver at the four. One of the four picked up a wooden snow shovel that was lying about and struck him on the head (as we'll see, the policeman died, but only *after* government injustice had run its course). All four were brought to a police station, sobered up, overslept, and, the next day, heard to their horror that they had been given over to a field court martial.

The members of the court expected something more like sedition and were amazed when they saw four bearded old people before them. They were horrified by the recognition that under Article 18 of the field courts martial decree there was only one punishment—the death penalty. They realized that death was impossible for such a fight. Although unable to state a legal justification for their verdict, they invoked the absence of aggravating circumstances, and sentenced the four to hard labor for an indefinite term, thinking it a punishment that no one could criticize as too soft.

They were wrong. Moscow's governor general, Sergei Konstantinovich Gershelman, overturned their decision. The verdict was put before him at ten in the morning, and at noon he cancelled it. In the evening he began another field court martial, condemned the four to death, and promptly had them hanged. Forget, for a minute, the savagery of Gershelman's decision: Article 5 of the field courts martial decree itself forbade any reversal of the court martial's judgment. But when an official found the rule inconvenient, he simply disregarded it.

As part of the October Manifesto's promise that Duma members would get "an opportunity for actual participation in the supervision of the legality of [officials'] actions," the Fundamental Laws entitled Duma members to question officials on the floor of the Duma. Maklakov thus pursued the attack on several occasions, asking for an explanation and responding to official efforts at justification. Among the official defenses was that the injuries inflicted on the policeman were more severe than Maklakov had originally reported—indeed, he had ultimately died of them. But the death occurred after the second trial, and thus in no way excused the government's lawlessness. Officials also cited legal exceptions, which Maklakov showed were inapplicable. The most extreme claims were those of Ivan Shcheglovitov, the minister of justice, and Alexander Makarov, then deputy minister of internal affairs, who would ultimately become the minister and Nikolai Maklakov's predecessor in that post. Shcheglovitov argued that there had been no unlawful reversal of a verdict; the first one had only been put aside without implementation! Makarov went further: Gershelman didn't reverse any verdict because the one he was accused of overturning did not, legally, even "exist."

Writing of the episode later, Maklakov drew the lesson that use of the Duma's interrogation weapon worked best when not entangled with a factual dispute, for which the Duma was ill-suited. (His account in the Duma had been inaccurate as to the scope of the policeman's wounds, but the error was irrelevant to the government's offense.) It was best, he thought, to focus on conduct that was unlawful even on the government's version of the facts. This particular exchange, he thought, brought an act of government illegality into the open under the scrutiny of the Duma. It made clear that the government could not defend itself with straight arguments, but rather was reduced to lies, sophistry, and demagogy—such as the theories vaporizing the first verdict. Stolypin's defense of state necessity was plainly unavailable.[28] Many of Maklakov's later Duma speeches pursued the same basic strategy.

Before turning to the Duma's demise and Maklakov's efforts to avert it, a word is in order about the Second Duma's treatment of two issues that had bedeviled the First: amnesty and terror. As to amnesty, the Kadets recognized that they had a jurisdictional problem: the Fundamental Laws (Article 23) assigned that power to the executive. But, wishing to press the issue, they placed it on the agenda but then proposed to send it to a committee to review the jurisdictional question. Maklakov spoke energetically for the referral to committee. He thought it clear that the tsar's power was exclusive as to the verdicts of ordinary courts, but very likely the reverse as to administrative decisions under the extraordinary security laws. He argued to the Duma that the committee could use the referral to develop a law eliminating altogether the system of administrative exiles and fines under the extraordinary security laws.[29]

As to terror, Maklakov seems not to have been very active. The Duma as a whole floundered. Its chairman, the Kadet Fyodor Golovin, succeeded for a long time in keeping it off the agenda, reflecting the Kadet concern that a resolution condemning terror would be seen as an implicit approval of the field courts martial and a betrayal of the left, while a negative vote would enable the government to paint them as sympathetic to terror. Maklakov worked to forge a compromise resolution acceptable to both the government and the Kadets, but the effort misfired.[30] There followed a swirl of draft resolutions, many aimed at trying to satisfy both sides by including a condemnation of the Black Hundreds' terrorist acts, which in at least some cases had been assisted by elements in the government. None passed. Looking at the issue in hindsight, Maklakov argued that, whereas the First Duma's failure to condemn terror had not been justifiable, the Second Duma's was. By that time, he thought, the government's own methods, including its use of *agents provocateurs*, were so offensive that any resolution should reach them as well. Of the rightists' arguments, he wrote, "They demanded condemnation of terror not in the name of the rule of law, but in support of the government."[31] Given that the authority for the field courts martial expired in April, that left-wing terror continued to predominate over right-wing or government-supported terror, and that the Kadets kept silent on left-wing terror even in their own newspapers (where they could have added balance in their own words),[32] the pass he gives the Kadets seems a stretch.

Although the divisions over amnesty and terror were severe and even raucous, the Duma-government split over agrarian policy was perhaps the key reason for the government's dismissal of the Duma and abrogation of the franchise. The government's solution to the problems of peasant agriculture was to establish, through its decree of November 9, 1906, a means by which peasants, acting either collectively as an entire village,[33] or individually against the will of the village, could convert communally owned property into individual "personal property," a status akin to conventional Western private property.[34] Fully converted land would be free from periodic redistributions to match up landholdings with family size and would be consolidated rather than scattered so that an individual peasant could cultivate it independently rather than only with the agreement of all the peasants in his commune. A peasant would no longer be, vis-à-vis the commune, in a phrase that Maklakov attributed to N. N. Lvov, "a rightless individual against a tyrannical crowd."[35] The Kadet proposals took exactly the opposite tack on private property: the first step was confiscation of gentry land at a value that was never specified but that was explicitly *not* fair market value. Their second step was to hold these lands as part of an ill-defined national land fund, to be allocated to peasants in some sort of equally ill-defined temporary tenancy, evidently subject thereafter to continuous bureaucratic reallocation.[36] Miliukov explicitly took the view that peasants simply wanted land and were not interested in the legal regime under which they held it.[37] The argument confirms Leonard Schapiro's comment that Miliukov's tragedy was "that he believed that he was a liberal, when he was in reality a radical."[38]

The government's concern was not that the Kadet program would become law. It could easily prevent that by having the State Council reject, or ignore, any Duma bill. The risk was that the Duma could destroy the government's program, dependent as it was on a decree under Article 87. For such a decree, all that was needed was for the Duma to vote it down.[39] With an anticipatory dismissal of the Duma therefore looming as a possibility, Maklakov was open to participating in a direct conversation with Stolypin. The background of the conversation, the conversation itself, and the reactions from left and right, tell us a good deal about the state of politics in 1907 Russia.

The first contact with Maklakov on the subject came through a Kadet member of the First Duma, S. A. Kotliarevskii, who had signed the Vyborg Manifesto out of party discipline although he thought it inexcusable. Because of the government's prosecution of the signers, he was therefore not in the Second Duma. He favored Kadet relations with cabinet members whose goodwill he trusted, such as Stolypin and Alexander Izvolskii (the foreign minister); he unexpectedly asked Maklakov if he'd be willing to meet with Stolypin. Maklakov saw nothing reprehensible in such a meeting and said he was willing. Kotliarevskii later called him to the phone; Stolypin was on the line, and they had a brief, rather guarded conversation. Maklakov surmised that Stolypin thought the phone was likely bugged. The next day Maklakov received a note of invitation, and met Stolypin that evening at the Winter Palace.[40] Maklakov discussed the meeting only with the Kadets ideologically closest to him—Mikhail Chelnokov, Pyotr Struve, and Sergei Bulgakov. In classifying them, it's useful to recall that Maklakov and the other three were among the eight Kadets who had attacked the field courts martial decree, something that only one Octobrist had done (Mikhail Kapustin); so the four were by no means reactionaries. (Struve and Bulgakov were later among the contributors to *Vekhi*, the collection of essays that assailed the Russian intelligentsia's rigidity, utopianism, and absorption in vague abstract principles.) The four nonetheless jokingly called themselves (and were called) the Black Hundreds, or the Black Hundred Kadets.[41]

Each of the four had occasional meetings with Stolypin after Kotliarevskii raised the issue, though only Chelnokov saw him at all regularly—in his capacity as Duma secretary.[42] At one such meeting, Stolypin made clear his anxiety about secret meetings of a Duma committee on agrarian matters, which he feared were building up to a rejection of the November 9, 1906, decree; Stolypin indicated that if rejection loomed, the government would dismiss the Duma preemptively rather than waiting for such a rejection.[43] The four moderates evidently caucused. Struve understood from a meeting with Stolypin that the latter would accept a good deal of amendment of the decree as a way of avoiding dismissal of the Duma, but not its transformation into a program of massive compulsory alienation—just the sort of measure that Kadet party rhetoric, and its agrarian appeal in the First Duma, had appeared to endorse.

The four met and agreed that the best strategy would be to ensure that any bill would receive a clause-by-clause reading: immersion in detail might lead to moderation. Chelnokov saw Stolypin and returned quite relaxed, conveying the impression that such a process was acceptable to Stolypin.[44] The premise appears to have been that Duma adoption of a *radically amended* version of the November 9, 1906, decree would constitute a rejection within the meaning of Article 87—and that seems a reasonable interpretation of the article. Thus amendments would meet Stolypin's demands only if they were moderate enough to allow him to get the amended version approved by the State Council and tsar.

Soon afterward, on May 10, 1907, Stolypin gave an extensive speech in the Duma on agrarian policy. Among other things, it discussed his agreement to compulsory alienation to help peasants use their land: to create wells and cattle pathways to pasture, to make roads, and finally to cure the scattering of plots. If the suitable Duma committee asked government representatives to attend, they could offer more details.[45] Maklakov himself thought that one might reasonably add instances of land that a peasant rented or that wasn't in use.[46] Given landowners' widespread practice of renting out land, it seems naïve for Maklakov to have thought that this would not be a deal-breaker.

In *Rech,* the newspaper edited by Miliukov and generally seen as the voice of the Kadet party, Miliukov responded to the Stolypin speech in his customary vein, saying that the proposal didn't deserve the name of compulsory alienation (curious that that should have transmogrified itself into an end rather than a means!) and was just a lie. The only object was to raise the price at which landowners could sell their land.[47]

Maklakov and his confederates now believed that the key was to ensure that the Duma as a whole didn't issue directions to the agrarian affairs committee that would be seen by Stolypin as likely to completely frustrate his goals. On May 26 this was achieved: the Duma voted 239 to 191 for a referral to committee without instructions (that is, without any specific mandate that the government might have read as foreshadowing rejection of its agrarian reform decree). Whether the Kadets and their allies to the left could have restrained themselves enough not to kill Stolypin's agrarian program under Article 87 seems at best questionable; even Maklakov's moderate Kadet ally Ariadne Tyrkova-Williams thought that in envisaging possible compromise he preferred "the wish to the reality." But as the four saw it, the only drawback was that the debate had included reminders of prior votes for compulsory alienation.[48] Overall, they saw the Duma's debate and action as meeting Stolypin's concerns well enough to save the Duma from dismissal.

Then on June 1 Stolypin asked for a closed session of the Duma and used the occasion to assert a claim that some Social Democratic deputies had been involved in terrorist activities. He asked the Duma to agree to the arrest of those involved and the removal of all the other Social Democrats from the Duma. The Duma set up an investigative committee that included Maklakov. Although the committee asked for more time to examine the allegations, it essentially found the government's claim baseless.[49] Meanwhile, back-channel contacts led to a meeting of the four moderates with Stolypin at 11:30 on the night of June 2. Stolypin met them immediately on their arrival, even though he was in the middle of a Council of Ministers meeting. After some general discussion of whether the Duma was working responsibly, Stolypin said there was one issue on which agreement was impossible—the agrarian one. The four were shocked; they thought they had worked out a possible path to agreement. As recounted by Maklakov, it appeared that Stolypin either mistakenly believed that the committee had adopted a resolution favoring mass compulsory alienation, or misunderstood the consequences of what had occurred, and thus was unaware that a procedure had been adopted that the moderates believed could yield an acceptable outcome. But Stolypin asked many questions, appeared to respond favorably to the answers, and gave the impression that their arguments had now removed this ground for dismissing the Duma—the main one, as it had appeared.[50]

Stolypin then turned the conversation in a wholly new direction, asking the four Kadets why they couldn't agree to remove the Social Democrats. "Free the Duma from them, and you will see how well we'll get along." Maklakov replied for the group, saying that Stolypin's demand was so extreme that "it would be shameful for us to look at each other if we accepted it." Stolypin asked, "So the Duma will refuse us?" Maklakov answered, "Probably. I am the most right-wing Kadet and I will vote against you." Stolypin: "Then there is nothing to be done. Only remember what I say—you have just dismissed the Duma."[51]

What can one make of this? Maklakov appears convinced of the sincerity of Stolypin's hopes for a compromise on the agrarian question, but we know with reasonable confidence that the tsar was by then emphatically eager to get rid of the Duma. A high government functionary, Pyotr Shvanebakh, reports being present with Stolypin late in the night of June 2 and hearing of a call from the four Kadets that they were interested in meeting him. All present "urged Stolypin not to lose time with the Kadet emissaries," but he rejected their advice and talked with the Kadets, by Shvanebakh's account, till 2:00 in the morning. After they departed, the group continued to wait. Soon a messenger from the tsar's Peterhof residence arrived, delivering documents signed by the tsar to change the electoral law, accompanied by a letter saying that he had waited all day for news of the dismissal of the "accursed Duma." He had sensed that something had gone wrong, and declared: "This is impermissible. The Duma must be dismissed tomorrow, Sunday morning. Decisiveness and firmness."[52] According to the American ambassador, the tsar had two weeks earlier told Sir Donald Mackenzie Wallace (a British observer who had been at times a journalist, at times a government official) that he intended to dissolve the Duma.[53]

Thinking their visit was not an official party act, the four Kadets had not told their colleagues about it. But S.D. Abelevich, a journalist for the left-wing daily *Rus*, had evidently been tipped off by the minister of trade and ran a story accurately reporting the Kadets' explanation of why they couldn't agree to hand over their Social Democratic colleagues. But Abelevich embroidered a bit, claiming that the visit somehow portended "some new combination the details of which are not known as yet."[54]

Just as Stolypin's colleagues had urged him not to bother with the four, their fellow Kadets—armed with the Abelevich article—at best scoffed at the failed mission, at worst regarded it as treacherous. Iosif Gessen, for example, writing years after the event, focused on the supposed terrorism of the accused Social Democratic deputies, and thought it absurd to hope that Stolypin would drop his demand to arrest them.[55] The furor in the party was such that Maklakov went to Miliukov and offered to resign; Miliukov, to his credit, refused and in fact calmed the others.[56] But Struve took the party outrage hard. It "struck him as symptomatic of an utterly self-destructive mentality," and drove him largely out of active party politics.[57]

It seems clear that well before the meeting the tsar had decided not only to dismiss the Duma but also to execute a coup d'état, unilaterally changing the electoral law (he did, on June 3, 1907). Stolypin and the tsar, however, were not identical, and it's entirely possible that Stolypin remained open to some saving change of events. But we have to consider his state of mind in the run-up to June 2. He could easily have been convinced, by earlier Kadet rhetoric and votes, and by behavior such as Miliukov's denunciation of his May 10 speech, that the Kadets (and obviously the revolutionary deputies to their left) would not compromise on agrarian reform. On that premise he agreed to implement the tsar's wish to dismiss the Duma (and to transform future Dumas by a unilateral change in the electoral system), proceeding by means of the bogus attack on the Social Democrats. By June 2 his apparent price—Duma acceptance of the removal of the Social Democrats and of the mythical plot—was obviously too high for Kadets with honor and commitment to the Duma as the pillar of a constitutional regime. But that hardly shows that he was acting in bad faith when he parlayed with them. Yet, even if the four moderates had convinced him on the night of June 2 that an acceptable solution on agrarian reform was possible, there was probably no arrangement that would have enabled Stolypin to withstand the tsar's commitment to radical, lawless action.

The Act of June 3 changing the electoral law was indeed lawless. The tsar purported to adopt it under Article 87, but that article expressly excluded its use for any change in the election laws for the State Council or the Duma. And the change was drastic, ensuring a strong majority of what the regime viewed as "trustworthy" representatives. Large geographic swaths of the country, such as Turkestan, lost representation entirely; the representation of the 11 million Poles fell from 46 deputies to 14; in the fifty-one provinces of European Russia, landowners would get almost 50 percent of the "electors"—the persons who in the layered system would actually cast the votes for deputies—against 26.2 percent for the urban population and 21.7 percent for peasants. In the countryside the tiered system assured that peasants reaching the status of elector would vote under the watchful eyes of landowners.[58] Of course this system produced, as intended, Dumas inclined to reach agreement with the government (at least relative to the First and Second Dumas). But the skewed franchise, and that franchise's unlawful origins, exacted a price in government legitimacy right through to 1917, when they impaired the Fourth Duma's ability to take over from the faltering Nicholas II.

An unbridgeable gulf between two of a country's institutions—as manifested in the June 3 coup—is hardly either novel in politics, or necessarily fatal to either institution. What was most ominous for Russia is surely that the dominant opinion on both sides regarded even *talking* with their political opponents as a worthless activity, or worse.

How did Maklakov view the coup? He is quite explicit in his memoirs that, despite his vigorous criticism of the Second Duma, he believed that in it the left had tempered the bellicose tactics of the First Duma, and that responsibility for the failure to fulfill the chance of implanting a constitutional monarchy fell squarely on the regime.[59] I've encountered nothing by him that might seem to excuse the government. Yet Soviet historians, ever reluctant to impute true constitutionalism to a "bourgeois" public figure, have latched onto observations by Maklakov on the floor of the Duma citing the 1762 coup removing Peter III and bringing Catherine to the throne, and the 1801 coup removing Paul and elevating Alexander I, as evidence of a belief that coups *can* lead to good. True enough. But his whole point in these passages was to *distinguish* those illegalities from a recent Duma act, which he regarded as not only unconstitutional (for infringing on Finland's constitutional liberties) but also likely to bear corrupt fruit.[60]

Maklakov had developed the same theme in an earlier article on the rule of law in Russia, noting instances when a legally invalid act is politically accepted, receives recognition, and becomes the law. He cited not only Catherine II's seizure of power but also the overthrow of Louis XVI in 1792 and of Napoleon III in 1870. (Americans might amplify the record by pointing to their own constitutional convention: given only a mandate to propose amendments for the Articles of Confederation, it drafted an entirely new constitution.) He specifically considered the June 3, 1907, coup, focusing on its juridical defects: although Stolypin explicitly defended the act as a coup, the government pretended, by cloaking it in Senate approval, to rest on a supposed continuation of the Senate's role of verifying legislation for failure to comply with the Fundamental Laws.[61] In his Duma speech and in the article Maklakov recognized the possibility that a coup d'état can "work," but he never suggested that the June 3 decree represented such a coup.

In assessing Maklakov's take on the core period of the Revolution of 1905, from Bloody Sunday in January 1905 to the June 3, 1907, coup, we have to distinguish between his acts *during* that period and his later analysis. While the validity of his analysis doesn't depend directly on when he reached it, contemporaneous parallel assertions would surely buttress it—the reverse for contemporaneous contradictions.

On some issues there were clear changes. His spring 1906 memo to French officials savaged the State Council's legislative role, which in *State and Society* he found quite harmless. And in articles published in *Russkie vedomosti* shortly before and during the First Duma itself, and in speeches pursuing election to the Second Duma, he seemed to endorse parliamentary supremacy almost as insistently as his more extreme Kadet peers. He scoffed at moderates who "don't recognize ministerial responsibility [to the Duma], who disown parliamentarianism." He even gave favorable mention to Nabokov's "pithy" summary of the parliamentary principle, which he later anathematized.[62] His early comments show no sign of the point he made later—that as the Duma manifested responsibility and usefulness, government responsibility to it would follow in the course of nature, as it had in Britain.[63] Giving a campaign boost to such a change, of course, is hardly the same as making it a precondition to substantive legislative work—the Kadets' strategy in the First Duma.

Indeed, his good friend and fellow moderate Kadet Ariadne Tyrkova-Williams noted in her diary on first reading *State and Society*: "Even Maklakov himself, as I recall, in the Duma and the Central Committee of the Kadet party, didn't speak against its [the party's] policies, and only after the events did these criticisms with which his memoirs are full come to mind."[64]

Her diary (plus the published records of the Kadet party) seem enough to convict Maklakov at least of failing to press his case in the party. So we have no way to be sure of his contemporaneous thoughts. But there are clues that they didn't change all that much, especially after the promulgation of the Fundamental Laws. His attack on the field courts martial decree in the Second Duma rested on its threat to the rule of law in Russia, and even his early response to the violence after Bloody Sunday proposed pitching any Beseda reaction as an attack on the regime's own lawlessness. And his meeting with Stolypin to save the Second Duma shows a readiness—at some risk to his position within the party—to seek common ground with opponents in the regime. His public posture was generally consistent with his later analysis.

We can learn something from a public debate between Miliukov and Maklakov that they conducted as émigrés in Paris, in a newspaper edited by Miliukov and a "thick" journal—the sort of intellectually (and physically) weighty periodical that dated from tsarist times. Maklakov had published the essence of *State and Society* in such a journal, and Miliukov replied both there and in an émigré daily that he edited. Throughout, Miliukov reproached him for the unrealism of his arguments (as he saw the matter), *not* for flipping his position.[65] Moreover, in his insistence on the inadequacy of the October Manifesto and the Fundamental Laws, Miliukov never attempted a comprehensive assessment of either document in constitutional terms. He thought it enough to say that they left in place the three "locks" (the State Council, the absence of four-tailed suffrage, and the absence of ministerial responsibility to the legislature), locks which he said "blocked the lawful path to construction of a normal constitutional regime."[66] But this critique is simply a restatement of the Kadets' constitutional *goal*, and an assertion (doubtless true) that the Fundamental Laws fell short of that benchmark. It tells us little about the scale of the change wrought by the two documents (on paper, to be sure) or about their capacity to generate improvement. This is odd, since only deficiencies along these lines could justify his response that "nothing has changed" and thus the Kadets' behavior in the First Duma. We are left to guess his argument as to why the two, evaluated as constitutional documents, did not represent not only a tectonic shift in tsarist policy but also a promising platform for the development of liberal democracy.

Beyond the supposed deficiencies in the documents, Miliukov's argument rested largely on the lack of any sincere commitment to constitutionalism on the part of the tsar and his ministers. He often mentioned Nicholas II's resistance to the *word* "constitution," as reported to Miliukov by Witte.[67] And he pointed to another clue to Nicholas's attitude—his well-known belief, based in part on a rather wishful assumption of unity between tsar and people, that it was his duty, in the interests of the people, to pass the autocracy on to his son more or less unimpaired.[68]

Of course the dispute between the tsar and society was over more than the word "constitution." The tsar's distaste for the word reflected his loathing for the thing itself. But while it is undoubtedly a plus when the author of a state document is sincerely committed to its undertakings, sincerity is hardly a sine qua non of effectiveness. After all, the October Manifesto was effective in producing *action* on the tsar's part—promulgation of the Fundamental Laws themselves. And when Englishmen and their successors over the centuries asserted rights in the name of Magna Carta, no one asked whether King John was "sincere" at Runnymede, or whether later kings "sincerely" accepted his commitments (which were thereafter embodied in English statutes). It seems improbable that such verbal commitments can ever do more than nudge the balance toward compliant behavior. As Learned Hand once said,

> I often wonder whether we do not rest our hopes too much upon constitutions, upon law and upon courts. These are false hopes, believe me, these are false hopes. Liberty lies in the hearts of men and women; when it dies there, no constitution, no law, no court can save it; no constitution, no law, no court can even do much to help it. While it lies there it needs no constitution, no law, no courts to save it.

Though Hand surely exaggerates, the basic idea is correct. Unless society has internalized the norm and is willing and able to exert pressure, holders of power will get away with violations. But a document can help on both counts—internalizing the norm and energizing society. The signer's state of mind is hardly a be-all-and-end-all.

In the end, what was the essence of the political difference between Maklakov and Miliukov? There was, surely, a difference in their weighting of the "liberalism" and the "democracy" in liberal democracy. Maklakov's great goal was control of government arbitrariness, Miliukov's the establishment of majoritarian democracy. This surely accounts for some of the higher value that Maklakov placed on the October Manifesto and the Fundamental Laws. But the far greater gap seems to me to lie in their ideas of the path toward liberal democracy from the centuries of Russian autocracy. Maklakov saw it as a long, hard slog, a gradual overcoming of the autocracy's near millennium-long deformation of Russian ways of thought. Miliukov saw it as something that a wise tsar could have accomplished in a minute, either by summoning a constituent assembly elected by four-tailed suffrage or by directly proclaiming a copy of the Belgian or Bulgarian constitution. The two men seem to be latter-day personifications of Edmund Burke's gradual reformism and Thomas Paine's revolutionary commitment to "reason" and its teachings.[69]

III. Reform in the Third and Fourth Dumas

CHAPTER 8

The Third and Fourth Dumas and Maklakov's Fight against Government Arbitrariness

THE DEMISE of the field courts martial ended one especially repellent form of government arbitrariness; others continued to flourish. They were prime targets of Maklakov's Duma oratory. In chapters 9 through 13 we consider many of his speeches linked to specific legislative proposals. But here we address a sampling of his attacks on the government's seemingly random acts of violence and injustice that were not pegged to any specific legislative reform, specifically its use of the criminal laws to affect the composition of the Duma; abuses of the extraordinary security laws; abuses by agents provocateurs; and the use of Article 87.

As Maklakov once said in the Duma, Russia was ruled the way an invader might rule a conquered country; he hoped the authority of conquerors could be replaced by authority "that has trusted a country, that does not exclude but nourishes, that does not destroy but creates, that does not mock but serves."[1] Russia's problem, he often said, was not so much the quality of its laws, as that the government paid so little attention to them. On the reform issues addressed in this section, Maklakov and his fellow Kadets generally battled together, arm-in-arm.

But first, to see the fetters constraining Maklakov at this stage, we should look at the composition of the Third Duma, elected under the truncated franchise prescribed by the June 3, 1907 coup. The Octobrists emerged from the elections not only in the center of the Third Duma but also as the largest party, with 154 deputies, more than a third of the 441 total. (The Octobrist numbers fluctuated over the Duma's five-year lifespan, with a general downward slope. Because of the party's openness, it was unclear what those numbers meant; the party leader, Alexander Guchkov, said at one point that there were no more than 100 to 110 "true" Octobrists.) The remainder of the members, working loosely from right to left, were: Rightists, 51; Moderate rightists, 96; Progressives, 28; Kadets, 54 (about half their number in the Second Duma and little more than 10 percent of the new Duma); Trudoviks, 14; Social Democrats, 18; plus three groups identified with nationalities and not readily classifiable on any ideological spectrum: Polish Kolo, 11; Polish-Lithuanian-Belorussian Group, 7; and Muslim Group, 8. As a social class, landowners were dominant, representing about 40 percent of the membership. A student of the Third Duma's social composition found it to contain a "surprisingly large representation" of the *narod* ("the people"), and the Octobrists, though center right, had the most diverse social representation, with one-fifth of the Duma's worker deputies and the same share of its peasants.[2]

Maklakov figured in the new Duma's initial self-organization. There was a move to make him deputy speaker, but just as the leftist majority in the First and Second Dumas had resolutely excluded everyone to its right from leadership positions, the Octobrist plurality of the Third Duma "repaid them in their own coin," as Maklakov later put it, and voted his candidacy down. Some members of the new Duma majority also wanted to throw out the internal rules drafted by Maklakov as relics of the old leftist Duma, but enough members—led by the new speaker, Nikolai Khomiakov—recognized that the rules had been aimed at fairness and efficiency, and so retained them; Maklakov was elected reporter and de facto chair of the committee on rules.[3]

Let us look first at Maklakov's arguments against the government's use of the criminal laws to eject members from the Duma. Recognizing that the rule of law depended on the "correlation of forces," on political realities that back up courts' ability to enforce constitutional rules,[4] Maklakov naturally fought to preserve the legislature's independence. Above all, he mounted a critique of the government's interpretation of statutes under which legislators who had run afoul of a broad range of criminal statutes were automatically excluded from the Duma—interpretations that helped the government use its prosecutorial powers to affect the Duma's composition.

In 1907 two members of the Third Duma, A. M. Koliubakin (a Kadet) and V. E. Kosorotov (a Social Democrat), were charged with crimes arising out of their political activities. Koliubakin had given speeches tracking the ideas of the Vyborg Manifesto, that is, calling for civil disobedience to protest the tsar's dismissal of the First Duma.[5] Kosorotov had given a speech that was anodyne in content but rabble-rousing in style. He had said it was time to replace the existing government with one chosen by the people, among whom, he said, there were people much more honorable, and wiser and better than the current government. But he punctuated the speech with calls for audience reaction, and the crowd responded with loud "hurrahs."[6] Despite the hurrahs, Maklakov noted, the indictment made no claim that Kosorotov had in any way invited lawless acts.[7] Though the courts convicted the two deputies, the trial judges chose *not* to bar them from the political process, a punishment the sentencing statutes put in their hands.

But a combination of statutes said that if a deputy was charged with a crime for which the judge had the *option* of imposing a loss of electoral rights and the deputy was "not acquitted," he was automatically excluded from the Duma, regardless of whether the judge actually imposed the loss of electoral rights.[8] But what did "acquitted" mean? The most obvious answer was "found not guilty." Maklakov countered that it made more sense to read the term to mean "not subjected by the court to loss of the specified rights." That reading preserved the long-standing Russian tradition of vesting courts with discretion over such a deprivation. Most important, he argued that his interpretation enhanced the independence of the representative branch of government by reducing Duma members' exposure to retaliatory removal via government prosecution: "For the renewal of Russia, we do not want a system under which people [read: the government] are free to remove their opponents from participation in the process."[9]

Maklakov lost this gambit, but the loss is not surprising. Context, and a vision of a wholesome polity, supported him, but his reading wasn't linguistically obvious, perhaps not even plausible. In the end, the Duma accepted the broad reading of the statutes and voted to exclude both deputies.[10]

Second, the use, let alone abuse, of the extraordinary security laws of 1881 threatened the rule of law. These laws enabled officials to exile citizens for up to five years, to imprison them for up to three months, and to impose potentially ruinous fines, with no check from the judiciary or indeed from any force outside the government itself.[11] And despite the principle that the executive could only act pursuant to duly adopted law, and the Duma's having not affirmatively renewed the laws after the lapse of their one-year term, the Kadet effort to stop their application (described in chapter 5) failed. The government continued to apply them.

Although Maklakov didn't participate in the Duma debate challenging the legality of the continued application of the extraordinary security laws, he inveighed frequently against the government's use of them, often citing absurd applications. His specific targets were usually the ministry of internal affairs or a provincial governor. Internal affairs, he pointed out, had come to swallow up the other parts of governance, so much so that before the creation of a (moderately) centralized cabinet under a premier in 1905, periods in Russian history had generally been known by the names of the minister of internal affairs—for example, Sipiagin, Plehve, Sviatopolk-Mirskii.[12] And provincial governors were the local representatives of the ministry.[13] So the ministry and the governors were, for the most part, interchangeable offenders.

Maklakov gave examples of how the ministry of internal affairs used the laws to punish the press and others for innocuous statements—such as reporting the opinion of a member of the State Council on the dissolution of the First Duma, discussing a congress of zemstvos, or identifying inadequate medical supervision at a hospital.[14] An especially silly action was an order by the governor general of Ekaterinoslav requiring that any building in which a bomb was found must be blown up; on top of that, in a case where the building's owner clearly could not have known of the bomb, he was fined 3,000 rubles and sentenced to prison for three months.[15] Another example was the authorities' use of the laws to exile an Old Believer bishop, one John Kartushin, because he wanted to register with the police as a bishop rather than, as the police preferred, as a "*meshchanin*" (roughly, "petty bourgeois").[16] The government used the laws to close eighty-one labor unions, thus short-circuiting the natural give-and-take between labor and capital, and tending to substitute the government for employers as the natural object of the employees' wrath.[17] And the ministry of internal affairs routinely banned or closed public meetings without regard to its own March 4, 1906, rules allowing such meetings (subject to conditions). In one case, the mayor of St. Petersburg banned a meeting simply on the ground that it was public—precisely the characteristic for meetings singled out by the rules as *allowed*.[18]

In his characteristic way of trying to point a path to a more cooperative future, Maklakov argued that, while in the old days before the October Manifesto it might have been necessary for the regime to use force to preserve itself, now, with a representative body, the government could develop communications with the people—certainly with the strata represented under the modified electoral laws—and could enlist their interest in solving the country's problems. He envisaged the country, thanks to the October Manifesto, no longer ruled by a single will from St. Petersburg but rather collectively engaged in creating a new life, with many issues resolved by voluntary agreement.[19] He also suggested a practical if partial explanation for official lawlessness—the officials' low pay.[20]

Maklakov often taunted the government for its vague but unfulfilled expressions that the country should be done with the extraordinary security laws, either immediately or as conditions warranted. In 1910, three years after the convulsions of the 1905 Revolution had ended, all was calm, but the government *boasted* that it had reduced orders of administrative exile from 10,000 a year to 2,000. If the secret police could find 2,000 to exile in such conditions, he asked rhetorically, what stopped them from finding 10,000?[21] Year in and year out, no matter how calm the country was, the government somehow never found the moment apt for a repeal.[22]

A third subject of Maklakov's attacks was the government's aggressive use of undercover agents. Regimes threatened by sedition must deploy undercover agents and tsarist Russia was no exception. But there are limits. Maklakov highlighted practical absurdities and moral corruption.

On the practical level, he pointed to what seemed to be innumerable cases where the seditious activity depended entirely, or almost entirely, on activities of the secret agents of the secret police. In a trial for bank robbery, it came out that the secret police had supplied the weapons. A military court found that a group of secret agents had shipped a vast supply of subversive literature across the border by bribing border guards, turning them into criminals. The investigating judges found that the agents' purpose was to press the contraband into the hands of naïve radicals and thus incriminate them.[23] His Duma speeches are chock full of episodes of this sort.

Maklakov of course recognized the need for some undercover work, as did Stolypin. At least for public consumption, Stolypin drew a line between initiating a crime, which he saw as excessive, and merely reporting or helping a crime's commission, which he regarded as permissible. Maklakov took a more restrictive view, arguing that even *helping* the commission of a crime was wrong.[24] I've found no place where he specified just how much help would qualify (surely not merely giving a perpetrator an easily ascertainable address or handing him a pencil for which the perpetrator could easily find substitutes?), but in the accounts of government behavior that he gave on the Duma floor, the help in question seems to have been robust, energetic, and almost certainly essential. That said, it would be nice to see an astute lawyer such as Maklakov drawing careful lines and more emphatically acknowledging the need for protection from subversion.

On the ethical issue, Maklakov argued that, in reality, revolution and provocation shared a similar contempt for morality and ethics: They are "both born of one faith, one outlook, one cult of force, one spirit of legal and moral abandon. On one side the government's lack of principle is manifested in provocation, on the other the revolutionary lack of discrimination is manifested in revolutionary terror. It is like the government in the way that a negative matches a photograph. The revolutionary terrorists laugh at the stories of peaceful struggle, of using cultured methods, at respect for the law." The revolutionaries' laughter, he thought, was echoed on the government side in a phrase coined by arch-reactionary Markov II for any kind of ethical restraint on the government's part: "sniveling humanism."[25]

Nor was Maklakov ready to accept the government position that most or all of the agents' excesses were just the activity of rogue subordinates. What was crucial was the attitude at the top: in practice, those at the top rewarded or winked at those involved in committing excesses of entrapment and punished those who exposed the wrongdoing. The most notorious case was that of Alexei Lopukhin, a police official (for a time head of the department) who publicly exposed Evgenii Azef, a secret police double agent. Azef had played a lead role in two of the era's most extreme acts of terrorism, the assassinations of Minister of Internal Affairs V. K. Plehve and of Grand Duke Sergei Alexandrovich. Lopukhin's reward was to be himself charged with treason for giving up state secrets, and to be found guilty of a different crime—participation in a terrorist society—in a trial that Maklakov viewed as rife with procedural violations.[26]

Maklakov also argued that the government's overuse of undercover agents and their entrapping practices fomented sedition, or at least the appearance of sedition, and thus created excuses for further delay in reforms. "When we hear that the government will support reform when sedition comes to an end, and yet the government is stirring up and sowing sedition, the contradiction forces us to doubt its claims."[27] Again, he linked the abuse of undercover agents to the government's failure to seek popular support:

> Our government, which grew up in the struggle with sedition, now cannot live without sedition; without it, it doesn't know what to do, how to use its army of functionaries. It occupied itself with suppression of sedition, when there was none; it seeks it out where it cannot be found; it creates it, it revolutionizes whole regions hitherto quiet; it turns loyal citizens into enemies; and it does this because it justifies not only its conduct but its existence. In the struggle with this imaginary danger it doesn't notice the real danger, the great danger of our time, which consists of the collapse of the popular spirit and the universal dissatisfaction in the country.[28]

It cannot be said that this despairing cry produced any change in government conduct.

Did the replacement of Alexander Makarov with Nikolai Maklakov as minister of internal affairs in late 1912, soon after the start of the Fourth Duma, have any effect on Vasily Maklakov's barrage of attacks on the ministry's lawlessness? Nikolai had been considered for the position after the 1911 assassination of Stolypin, who had been both premier and minister of internal affairs. The appointment in fact went to Makarov, largely, it appears, through the intervention of Count Kokovtsov, the new premier. But in little more than a year Makarov lost the tsarina's favor, evidently because of his decision to forward her letters to Rasputin to the tsar, or his inability or unwillingness to stifle criticism of Rasputin. Nicholas II had previously formed a favorable impression of Nikolai Maklakov, apparently based on his enthusiasm for the idea of a "strong tsar." Makarov's fall opened the way for Nikolai's rise.[29] So far as I can make out, the change produced no slackening in Vasily Maklakov's attacks on the ministry's arbitrariness.

One of Vasily Maklakov's first attacks on the new ministry had a nice irony. His immediate target was an edict stretching the extraordinary security laws beyond their supposed goal of controlling sedition; this one would allow internal affairs officials to imprison "hooligans" for up to three months. By coincidence, Maklakov had been mugged shortly before on the streets of St. Petersburg, where the new program was being launched; Pyotr Novitskii, a rightist defender of the new approach, seemed to think that as a victim Maklakov should be the first to embrace the new policy. Maklakov answered that opponents of the rule were perfectly happy with strong measures against hooliganism; they were just against ones that violated the principles of the October Manifesto. He compared the policy to the provision allowing land captains to jail a peasant for hooliganism for three days, saying that the new policy extended that approach to *any* citizen, and for three months. Novitskii interrupted, "Not citizens, hooligans," reflecting the regime's characteristic assumption that officials would never err in labeling someone a malefactor.[30]

A fourth target of Maklakov's attention was Article 87, which as we've seen allowed the government, while the Duma was not in session, to issue a law on its own—though only with temporary effect. Maklakov attacked Stolypin's use of the article to give

Russia's western provinces the institution of the zemstvo (local self-government in rural areas). The episode is usually seen as a case of Stolypin's overreaching against the tsar and the latter's right-wing allies. But for Maklakov, the key issue was Stolypin's abuse of Article 87, and more specifically a lack of the good faith that he saw as required for a constitution's proper functioning.

Stolypin's proposal was to bring the zemstvo to Russia's nine western provinces. But to counteract the electoral influence of the many aristocratic Polish landowners there, the bill would give a stronger voice in zemstvo elections to local peasants (of whom a majority were Ukrainian or Belorussian, but Orthodox and viewed by Russian nationalists as Russian and reliable) than the zemstvo laws gave peasants in the other regions of Russia. Three of the original nine provinces were soon dropped, essentially because the Russian landowners there were too outnumbered to secure control under any plausible scheme.[31]

The measure passed the Duma but was then rejected by the State Council; Stolypin saw in the rejection the treacherous hand of the tsar. Two members of the Council, Pyotr N. Durnovo and Vladimir Trepov, appeared to have acted as the tsar's cat's-paws. In tumultuous exchanges involving threats of resignation and interventions by the dowager empress, Stolypin demanded of the tsar, and got, an order temporarily banishing them from the capital and a grant of authority to issue his bill on the zemstvos by a decree under Article 87. To meet Article 87's threshold condition that the Duma be out of session, Stolypin prorogued both legislatures for a three-day recess and then adopted the law as a decree.

Article 87, of course, gave the government the choice of letting the "emergency" measure expire after two months from the opening of the legislature (by not introducing it as proposed legislation), or of introducing equivalent legislation in the Duma, with the risk of its being killed by either the Duma or State Council. But before the two months ran out, State Council and Duma members launched an array of "interpellations" assailing the premier. In his speech Maklakov expressed indifference as to whether the use of

Article 87 was technically legal. It seems reasonable to assume that Stolypin's move presented no such illegality. In failing to define the "extraordinary circumstances" that entitled the government to action, the article seemed to leave the existence of such circumstances to the government's political discretion. This is not to say that the article lacked *any* legal constraint on its exercise: its limits on how long such a decree could remain in effect seem to offer the kind of clarity needed for legal enforcement.[32] But Maklakov disputed the political propriety of the regime's actions. He quoted Bismarck, this time for the idea that good will and loyalty were necessary in the application of law.[33] He saw neither in this case. The claim of emergency was laughable, especially in light of Stolypin's casual dropping of three of the affected provinces. And could it be seriously argued that the few weeks between Stolypin's chosen proroguing date and the legislature's regular vacation were of any consequence?[34]

Maklakov also rejected Stolypin's claim that failure to use Article 87 would increase the State Council's readiness to veto Duma-approved bills, which Stolypin argued would confirm the public perception of the legislative bodies' stagnation and triviality.[35] Again he quoted Bismarck, this time for the thought that the essence of constitutionalism is compromise. Applying that concept, he said that a brief retreat in the face of the State Council's rejection would have been sure to work; with a little patience on the premier's part, the upper house could be mollified. He reasoned, as he was later to write when analyzing the Fundamental Laws in his historical writings, that in all countries the upper house must ultimately retreat before the opinion of the country and the lower house. But for Stolypin, he said, a defeat was so extraordinary that he took it as a social calamity.[36]

Maklakov closed by noting that, although the premier had finally won a great victory in the State Council, it would likely cost him dearly:

> For government officials of this type, who with excessive faith in their own infallibility and excessive disdain for the opinions of others place their own will above the law, the Russian language

has a characteristically expressive term, "minion" (*vremenchik*). Their time has come and gone. The premier may yet remain in power: fear of a revolution that his own agents are creating preserves him (*Count V.A. Bobrinskii, from his seat: "Shameful!" Uproar*), as does the danger of creating a precedent.[37] You may look on his agony with varying feelings, but I will say in the words of the premier himself, "In politics there is no revenge, but there are consequences." They have come, and you cannot now escape them. (*Applause from the left and cries of "bravo"; rustling from the right.*)[38]

Stolypin lost the vote on the interpellations decisively, but as a legislative matter the loss had no impact. As he had not resubmitted the bill to the Duma and State Council after the recess, it would have expired sixty days after the Duma reassembled. On May 13, 1911, one day before that deadline, he prorogued it again. When the Duma reassembled yet again, the two bodies passed the measure handily. Stolypin, however, could not enjoy the triumph. He had been shot on September 1 by Dmitri Bogrov, an anarchist revolutionary who also collected intelligence for the secret police. Four days later he died of the gunshot wounds.[39]

The debate over the western zemstvo bill was the third and last oratorical duel between Stolypin and Maklakov.[40] On no other occasion did Maklakov's rhetoric have so personal an edge. Had he known that Stolypin would be assassinated just four months later, or had he even been aware of the tsar's growing readiness to dismiss Stolypin, he surely would have tempered his barbs. He later wrote a friend that, at the time of the speech, he thought Stolypin was at the apogee of his power but "now I realize he was beaten prostrate. I feel ashamed of that speech."[41]

CHAPTER 9

Religious Liberty

RELIGIOUS LIBERTY did not flourish in tsarist Russia. The most well-known restrictions are the government's array of anti-Semitic policies: limits on Jewish opportunities in education and the professions and on their place of residence—the Pale of Settlement confined them to specific areas in the western regions of the empire. But there were also restrictions on non-Orthodox Christians, principally the Old Believers, a group that had split off from Orthodoxy in the seventeenth century. As a Duma member, Maklakov advocated elimination of the Pale and a lightening of the restrictions on the Old Believers. As an advocate, he was one of the three defense attorneys instrumental in securing the acquittal of Menahem Mendel Beilis, a Jew charged with the "ritual murder" of a young boy (supposedly to secure Christian blood to use in baking matzos). He published (and voiced in the Duma) an explanation of why the regime had pursued the Beilis case despite a complete lack of evidence, a puzzle that still interests historians. For this offending publication, Maklakov was sentenced to—but never served—three months in prison.

In the Duma, Maklakov advocated religious liberty not only

as desirable in itself but also as necessary to prevent government arbitrariness. His principal focus was a series of bills easing limits on Old Believers and repealing the Pale of Settlement.

The Old Believers had enjoyed a considerable degree of toleration since an April 17, 1905, decree of the tsar, which had been further implemented with an October 1906 decree under Article 87.[1] The government itself introduced a bill in conformity with the 1906 law, and the Duma committee on Old Believers expanded its reach. With the committee's amendments, the bill would allow Old Believers the right not merely to confess their faith but to proselytize, and would give Old Believer communities a right to automatic registration as such.[2]

Maklakov staunchly supported the committee's amendments. He argued that they were not really amendments, but simply precautions against the destruction and perversion of the tsar's April 17 manifesto through the arbitrariness of administrators and police. The purposes of the manifesto and the law would be "undercut by casuistry," as Old Believers and the authorities fought over the line between confession of faith (perfectly permissible) and preaching or advocacy of faith (illegal in the absence of the committee amendments). He cited a specific case of an Old Believer who came to a factory in Kaluga and was drawn into a religious dispute and mocked by Orthodox believers. He had hotly defended his position, for which he was charged and condemned for preaching his non-Orthodox faith. Without the committee's amendment allowing proselytizing, Maklakov argued, the bill would leave matters in the hands of the police, who would always be influenced by the Orthodox establishment's ubiquitous representatives.[3]

Even with the amendment, the bill would not entirely eradicate the potential for official abuse. In supporting it, Maklakov sought to assuage Orthodox anxiety by reminding them that the laws against blasphemy would remain in place. An Old Believer who preached but failed to show respect for faith could still be punished.[4] But "respect for faith" was itself a fuzzy distinction. Maklakov, if challenged on the point, could fairly have replied that a line drawn between blasphemy and preaching would engender far fewer cases than one between confession of faith and preaching, if only because blasphemy would presumably occur far less often than simple preaching. Also, the line between preaching and blasphemy might be drawn more easily than that between preaching and confession of faith.

Maklakov also invoked standard religious freedom arguments, for example, that Orthodoxy itself would benefit from having to win people's allegiance in free debate.[5]

Alternative amendments were offered, such as one allowing preaching but only in the Old Believers' own religious establishments. Just as hypocrisy is the homage that vice pays to virtue, the proffer of useless substitutes was a kind of backhanded acknowledgment of the difficulty in answering Maklakov's case. The Duma saw through the ruse and voted the proposals down.[6]

Advocating an amendment that gave Old Believer congregations a clear entitlement to registration, Maklakov again stressed the risk of arbitrary enforcement. (Why should there have been registration at all? Presumably because of the regime's deep suspicion of every association of citizens that might prove a site for seditious plotting—even when there was no reason to suspect the association's members of such plotting.) Among other things, the amendment removed a qualification of the Old Believers' rights, one that allowed registration only when their activities were "not dangerous for social peace." Maklakov called these "sacred words"—sacred to the police because it allowed them infinite discretion in enforcement. The exile of the Old Believer bishop for refusing to register as a petty bourgeois, mentioned in the last chapter, also showed the great potential for police arbitrariness, given the slightest chance. Maklakov ended by again pressing the idea that the amendments were only "a logical conclusion from the manifesto [of April 17, 1905]; without them the manifesto may be destroyed. The law will be law only at the pleasure of the authorities. . . . (*Prolonged applause from center and left.*)"[7]

The Duma approved the amended bill, but the State Council declined to accept the language emerging from the Duma. A reconciliation committee was formed (with Maklakov among its members), but reached no agreement.[8]

Another religious issue, a chance to repeal the Pale of Settlement, drew Maklakov's ardent advocacy. Putting aside a patchwork of exceptions, the Pale confined Jews to a large western strip of the empire. It dated from a decree of 1791, reflecting the great increase in Russia's Jewish population as a result of the successive partitions of Poland between Russia, Austria, and Prussia, together with a mélange of anti-Semitic and protectionist arguments.[9] In calling for repeal of the Pale, Maklakov laid the groundwork by pointing to the proliferating self-contradictions in Russian policy. While the state purported to protect the Russian people from Jewish "oppression," it retreated, he said, before the most powerful of the potential oppressors—presumably an allusion to the organizers of pogroms—and instead set out to oppress the most defenseless. It faulted Jews for not working the land but excluded them from the countryside. It gathered them into one place where there was not enough demand for their skills. It forced them into the lowest work and reproached them for being in that work. It drove them into conditions of poverty so extreme that official reports declared them worse off than peasants, and then reproached them for the filth of their conditions. Its injustice drove Jews to hate Russian authorities, and the state then found in that hatred a justification for its own anti-Semitism.[10]

Maklakov also suggested that recent economic changes had exacerbated the policy's inherent cruelty and made it more costly for everyone. In the twentieth century, he observed, when state authority collects everything it can from its subjects in money and services, where people seek their livelihood under unbridled competition, using all the advances that modern civilization has to offer (railroads, mail, telephone), the government artificially locked Russian Jewry away in a defined territory.[11] Further, to the extent the policy was driven by fear of Jewish competition, it had backfired: in the Pale, non-Jews were subject to exceptionally intense competition from Jews, stirring up hatred against them.[12] And on the other side, its anti-competitive features injured non-Jews: "When the question comes up of uprooting the Jews, you have requests from the rest of the Russian population about leaving Jews in place, about how their industry and economic strength are so useful. The Jews and the traits that distinguish them—energy, enterprise, willingness to put up with little—are a boon in economic life, especially necessary for us, in vast but sleepy Russia. . . . In short the state has contrived to make these traits a source of unhappiness for the western part of the country and their absence a source of great deprivation for the rest."[13]

Maklakov then catalogued some of the absurdities produced by the policy itself. The English minister of post and telephone had been unable to get a visa for Russia and so had been excluded. Even as the debate on repeal unfolded, there was a dispute pending in the Senate over evicting *one-year-olds* to the Pale, even though their parents had permission to live outside it. What is more strange, he asked, than for Russian soldiers who fought in the war with Japan and were taken to Moscow for an operation to be then sent out of Moscow immediately after the operation? What is more strange than that Jewish children, born of artisan parents living lawfully outside the Pale, should be sent off to the Pale when they reached their twenty-first birthday? Holidays also caused a problem. The law said that Jewish artisans could live outside the Pale only so long as they were working in their craft: so if the police came on Saturday, when they weren't working, they would be subject to eviction. And trade definitions could be treacherous. A Jewish watchmaker who made and sold watch chains had thereby gone beyond the precise definition of his trade (watchmaker), and was subject to eviction if the police took a narrow view of the permissible trade.[14]

By colliding with both economic reality and elementary fairness, the Pale's rules sparked government arbitrariness. "One might even say that the essence of the law is to increase police rewards," that is, bribes. Jews outside the Pale under a legal dispensation had to buy from the police the right that they had by law, because they knew that otherwise the lawless authorities would evict them. If a Jew violated the law by giving the bribes, Maklakov argued, he could not justly be blamed; the blame lay with the authorities who pressured him to pay, who corrupted him, but even more with the law that created the authorities' opportunity.[15]

Maklakov concluded:

> The Pale has been with us more than 100 years . . . , but again and again new questions arise, and again and again the questions appear unforeseen. . . . Time after time imperial decrees have issued that gave someone who has been living illegally the right to stay. There have appeared new interpretations, new permissions making new breaches in the law. Why? Because never, not once, not in any matter, has a state combined such an extraordinarily cavalier attitude toward feelings of humanity or of lawfulness with simultaneous reluctance to make decisions [presumably ones dispensing with the Pale itself]. . . . Those same authorities that have recognized that equal rights are the ideal toward which we should move and are moving, those same authorities about which the premier [Stolypin] said that if you don't believe in the strength of a rule-of-law state[16] you must not legislate, those authorities have not believed in their own strength and have retreated before anti-Semitic prejudice. . . . As was said 100 years ago [by the Abbé Sieyès], 'Those who don't know how to be just cannot be free.'[17] . . . The Jewish question is really the broader question of whether law and right can triumph in Russia.[18]

The debate ended with a 208 to 137 majority sending the matter to the committee on inviolability of the person (encompassing roughly what today we might call civil rights and civil liberties) under a one-month deadline.[19] But when the time was up, the committee chair reported to the Duma that it couldn't meet the deadline because of the volume of materials;[20] zeal for the matter seems then to have petered out without a vote.

Maklakov also confronted the state's anti-Semitism as defense counsel in the Beilis case. In a sense the prosecution was just a case of outrageous prosecutorial overreaching. But since it was driven forward by support at the highest levels (the tsar, Minister of Justice Shcheglovitov, and two ministers of internal affairs, Alexander Makarov and his successor, Vasily Maklakov's brother Nikolai), it was also a scandal of statecraft. (Stolypin, though minister of internal affairs as well as premier at the outset, appears not to have been involved in the shady work of skewing the investigation and was assassinated soon after the affair's start.)

In March 1911, a group of children found the body of 13-year-old Andrei Yushchinskii in a cave in Kiev. Almost from the outset there was evidence suggesting that a criminal gang, led by one Vera Cheberiak, had killed him because of suspicion that Andrei, a friend of Cheberiak's son Zhenia, knew too much about the gang's operations. But the local investigators initially fastened on the mistaken idea that Andrei's mother and stepfather were the culprits. Recognition that this was questionable created a kind of vacuum, into which right-wing anti-Semites plunged. They concocted the idea that the case was one of ritual murder, and specifically suggested Beilis as the murderer. His closest link seems to have been that he been a clerk at a brick factory near where Andrei's body was found; the factory was owned by a Jew, Jacob Zaitsev, who had used his brick factory profits to found a hospital open free of charge to indigent patients of all faiths.[21]

It seems to have been an accepted notion of such a murder (presumably propagated by those who invented the idea) that the blood should be drawn while the victim was still alive; but an autopsy found nothing to show that that had been true for Andrei.[22] Soon after Andrei's death, two of Vera Cheberiak's children died: first, Andrei's friend Zhenia Cheberiak, and a few days later a sister. Given that the two were quite likely to have had evidence about the real murderer of Andrei, there were suspicions that Vera might have killed them to forestall their possible testimony. In fact a pathologist's report showed that they died of dysentery, and the Beilis defense, though generally eager to point to Vera and her gang, explicitly declined to pin the deaths on her.[23]

Under the influence and pressure of local anti-Semites, of the nationwide Union of the Russian People, and of a high St. Petersburg police official, Alexander Liadov, who was sent to Kiev by Shcheglovitov, the Kiev prosecutor cast aside the primary initial investigator, Nikolai Krasovskii, and worked to develop the ritual murder theory. Beilis was arrested and imprisoned in July 1911 and indicted in January 1912 (he remained in prison till his acquittal in the fall of 1913). Both imprisonment and indictment preceded the day in December 1912 on which Nikolai Maklakov took charge of the ministry of internal affairs, so he cannot be blamed for those two milestones. But he was obviously aware of a privately organized and widely credited report published in May 1912 exonerating Beilis, and he acknowledged in private before the trial that a conviction of Beilis was out of the question. By the time he became minister, the government's focus had turned almost entirely to proving the general idea that Jews engaged in ritual murder, with the trial of Beilis serving mainly as a vehicle for that demonstration. Apart from helping to run the prosecution of a man whose innocence he pretty much accepted, Nikolai ordered surveillance of the jury through government agents in the guise of court officers. The results cannot have been heartening for the prosecution: one report said the jurors were wondering, "How can we convict Beilis if nothing is said about him at trial."[24]

Vasily Maklakov was one of the three primary defense counsel, the others also being nationally famous defense lawyers—Nikolai Karabchevskii and Oscar Gruzenberg. Involved on the government's side, though nominally appearing on behalf of the victim's family as "civil plaintiffs," was Georgii Zamyslovskii, one of Vasily Maklakov's fellow deputies in the Duma and a rabid anti-Semite. Zamyslovskii was being surreptitiously paid a generous 2,500-ruble stipend by the government, but his speeches suggest that he found ample compensation in the sheer joy of ranting against Jews. (After the trial, Zamyslovskii suggested that the government pay him 25,000 rubles for publishing an account of the trial, a payment that

Minister of Internal Affairs Maklakov arranged out of secret funds under the tsar's control.)[25]

Vasily Maklakov's main role was in summation. He addressed the jurors in a conversational tone, speaking throughout in simple words and starting: "They say, gentlemen of the jury, that the whole world is watching this trial, but I would like to forget about that, and would like it if no one was watching, and to talk only with you, gentlemen of the jury." He then proceeded to review the evidence, or its absence, in the same matter-of-fact manner, with an eloquent closing that urged the jurors to focus on Beilis and not on the irrelevant and dubious attacks on Jews.[26]

The jury found Beilis not guilty. The vote was not recorded, but tsarist rules treated a verdict as an acquittal if there was either a majority for acquittal or a six-six split. It's widely stated that the vote was six-six, an idea that appears to have originated with the right-wing paper *Novoe Vremia* (New times); its editors perhaps chose the six-six split because that was a vote consistent with the outcome but having the *least* tendency to show jury rejection of the state's case.[27] After more than two years in prison, Beilis at last won his release.

But in an unusual procedure, the court submitted another question to the jury. Though not specifically asking about ritual or religious purposes, the question was laden with religious/racial detail roughly tracking the evidence: had Andrei, in the brick factory associated with the Jewish hospital, had wounds inflicted on him "resulting in the almost complete loss of blood and in his death"? A yes answer would suggest a killing with intent to extract blood and thus probably a ritual murder. The jurors answered with a yes.[28]

A reporter who later talked with the jurors about the trial quoted one as saying: "Karabchevskii—we didn't understand; Gruzenberg—we didn't trust; Maklakov—he hit the nail on the head."[29] In fairness to Maklakov's co-counsel, we should remember that at trial and in the media frenzy, the prosecution's focus was on the canard of Jewish ritual murder, not poor Beilis himself, the main subject of Maklakov's summation. If the jury verdict on ritual murder reflects a degree of anti-Semitism, that may also account in part for the jurors' apparent distrust of Gruzenberg, who was Jewish.

Because the fiction of Jewish ritual murder seems so nonsensical, observers have wondered what might have possessed those at the political apex of the Russian Empire to pursue a case founded on that fiction, and to pursue it at such a cost—inflicting injury on an innocent citizen and exposing the regime to mockery and contempt among its Entente allies in Europe. Maklakov was among those weighing in on the subject, publishing articles in the newspaper *Russkie Vedomosti* and the journal *Russkaia Mysl* (Russian thought) in 1913. He explained the government's behavior as a response to political pressure from its allies on the right, sacrificing justice to politics.[30]

The most interesting effort to refute Maklakov comes from the scholar Hans Rogger. He rejects the idea of political pressure, in large part on the ground that the right at that stage was not all that powerful. And the government, before it was embarrassed by the Lena Goldfields massacre in April 1912 (a shooting of several hundred workers who were peacefully protesting their living conditions), had no special need to shore up its right flank. In fact the dependence ran the other way. While the government doled out massive secret subsidies to the Union of the Russian People and others on the far right from 1905 to 1917, mainly to subsidize their presses, its officials recognized that the subsidized papers had very low circulation; the regime got very little bang for its ruble. Those favoring continued subsidies were reduced to the argument that without the government aid the papers would collapse, and that, even though small, they were an answer to the "leftwing and Jewish" press.[31] Makarov, the minister of internal affairs immediately preceding Nikolai Maklakov, was planning, just before his replacement, to cut the subsidies off, but whatever chance of success that plan might have had, it came to an end with Nikolai Maklakov's ascension.

Given the lack of government dependence on the right, Rogger suggests that the pursuit of Beilis and ritual murder represented "a search for a principle, for a common belief that would rally and bind together the disheartened forces of unthinking monarchism," or "a conscious effort to supply ingredients for a missing faith."[32] In reaching this conclusion, Rogger offers some thoughts on Nikolai Maklakov: He notes Nikolai's full awareness of the hard right's weakness as a political force, characterizes him as "unstable and shallow," and endorses a suggestion that his activity was in significant part due to the "hypnotic sway" held over him by Shcheglovitov.[33]

Rogger's theory is enticing, but it doesn't really answer the question why high officials would embrace as a rallying principle a completely spurious claim—that Jews indulge in ritual murder. To be sure, one could take Rogger a step further and argue that it was precisely the lunacy of the thesis that gave it value: as in submission to fraternity hazing and thousands of other social practices, the more absurd and costly the behavior (and the cost can be intellectual or social embarrassment), the more a person's participation demonstrates his devotion to the cause or institution.

Both Maklakov and Rogger seem to me to overlook a simpler explanation—that people living in a milieu where a strong ideological proposition holds sway (here, the presumptive evil of Jews) are likely to accept without much independent evaluation claims that sustain the basic faith. On that view, the impulses of Nicholas II seem to be just a matter of doing what comes naturally, and the activities of Shcheglovitov and Nikolai Maklakov likely a combination of the same ideological inclination (perhaps chilled in Shcheglovitov's case by his undoubted intelligence) and an effort to please their imperial master.

Whatever the merits of Maklakov's analysis, he did not express it without cost. He and the editors of the paper and journal with his article were accused of distribution in print of "deceitful and shameful" information about officials. At about the same time, the government brought a similar charge against Vasily Shulgin, editor of a Kiev newspaper, the *Kievlianin* (Kiev citizen), for publishing an article exonerating Beilis. Shulgin's article had been especially startling, as he was persistently and openly anti-Semitic. But in this instance, at least, he looked at the facts. Maklakov testified in the Shulgin trial, but Shulgin was convicted and sentenced to three months' imprisonment. His term didn't start immediately, however, and when World War I began he was allowed instead to join the military service; after he was wounded, the government was ashamed to put him in prison and pardoned him. The trial of Maklakov and the editors was delayed, but in due course he and the editors were found guilty. They appealed, but the appeal was for some reason never heard. Maklakov encountered the sentencing judge during the February Revolution, when their power relationship was reversed (Maklakov now on top, the other powerless), but Maklakov refrained from reacting at all.[34]

Given the bloodshed of the civil war and the Bolshevik regime, many of the figures in this book necessarily came to untimely, dramatic ends. Among these were Shcheglovitov and Nikolai Maklakov, both executed by the Bolsheviks on December 5, 1918, the first day of the Red Terror, without, of course, the government's incurring the inconvenience of a trial. Menahem Mendel Beilis's life after the trial was financially harsh, as he was dependent at the end on selling his account of the trial from door to door in New York. But throughout he preserved his honor (rejecting offers to exploit his fame), and he died peacefully in 1934.[35] One is tempted to see a little poetic justice in this. But one should resist the temptation: however reprehensible the actions of Shcheglovitov and Nikolai Maklakov, their deaths in a massive Bolshevik bloodletting cannot be thought of as justice of any kind.

In light of Maklakov's advocacy against the Pale and for Beilis, it seems odd to find suggestions that Maklakov was anti-Semitic. There is a more nuanced and compelling suggestion that he was *not* philo-Semitic.[36] In any event, he himself observed in correspondence with Shulgin that he had a kind of "zoological" anti-Semitism—he claimed he had never seen a Jewish face that he found attractive. But he went on in the same paragraph to say that many people having this aesthetic impulse let it corrupt their thinking. Such a person "stubbornly stands on his convictions, insists on any rubbish, and an argument with such a person is obviously useless."[37] However Maklakov may have arrived at his negative aesthetic judgment, it seems not to have spilled over into his life as an advocate or, indeed, as a citizen and political figure.

An item of evidence that has been used against Maklakov is a January 27, 1916, entry in the diary of his good friend and fellow Kadet moderate, Ariadne Tyrkova-Williams: "Maklakov, always playful and joking, said, 'It's a big secret. I'm a good Kadet. Only I don't favor compulsory alienation of land, equal rights for Jews, and universal suffrage.'"[38] In a sense it's clear that Maklakov was joking, for his rejection of the party line on the first and third items, which were regular Kadet themes and which he did in fact reject, surely rendered him a dubious Kadet rather than a "good" one. But why would he have added the reference to "equal rights for Jews"? A conceivable explanation is that Tyrkova-Williams misunderstood his position on the bill expanding peasant rights, which he guided through the Duma in June 1916. In that context (as we'll see in chapter 12) he did reject an attempted expansion of the pending bill to embrace equal rights for Jews—the proposed change would have doomed the bill, injuring peasants and not helping Jews in the slightest. (His draft, by clarifying a provision that had been mistakenly read to the disadvantage of Jews, rendered the provision harmless.) But the Duma activity on peasant rights took place in June 1916, and he became reporter for the committee producing the bill only in March 1916, not in time for Tyrkova's January 1916 diary entry. Conceivably he foresaw the peasant rights issue as the next occasion for Duma action on equal rights, and his thoughts may have jumped ahead to that context. Whether it was a silly joke or an anticipation of the peasant-rights controversy, the remark (if correctly recorded) seems not to have reflected any genuine impulse to deny Jews equal rights.

A Soviet historian has hinted that one argument by Maklakov

in the debate on the Pale reflects anti-Semitism. Maklakov drew a distinction between individual anti-Semitism, both in business and even in culture (referring as an example to people who refuse to listen to pianist Arthur Rubinstein). He suggested that private anti-Semitism was each person's right, whereas state discrimination was inconsistent with the state's duty to its subjects. Then he went on to link the two as a way of supporting repeal of the Pale: "I would say to the anti-Semites that they ought first to insist on recognition of equal treatment of Jews by the state so as to have a better moral right to their personal anti-Semitism."[39] His purpose, plainly, was to turn what was likely a personal attitude of many Duma members, perhaps a majority, into an affirmative reason for ending the Pale. By opposing a grievous, large-scale wrong inflicted by Russia on its Jewish subjects, they would acknowledge a line that even their anti-Semitism would not cross. Whatever the abstract merits of a state ban on private discrimination might be, the argument made complete sense in context and may well have pulled some deputies into the repeal column.

In view of the Tyrkova-Williams diary entry, it seems worthwhile to recount briefly some of Maklakov's other advocacy for the fair treatment of Jews. During the war the government had the gall—at a time when it was engaged in an ethnic cleansing of Jews from a broad zone near the front—to issue circulars accusing Jews of, first, being part of a German-inspired plot to burn crops, exacerbate the food crisis, and generally foment revolution; and, second, of hoarding goods and money, and thereby promoting dissatisfaction and insurrection. Maklakov joined with Miliukov and other Kadet and non-Kadet leaders in seeking an interpellation in the Duma. The move was defeated, with Kadet agreement, out of fear that it would be voted down under Octobrist pressure.[40]

In the course of a Duma speech generally indicting the government's conduct of the war, Maklakov singled out the way in which a government circular had scapegoated the Jews for inflation (fictive explanations of inflation, disregarding increases in the money supply, are legion around the world!). He had some fun with the passage, saying that it went so far as to explain inflation as a Jewish scheme to end the Pale of Settlement. He noted instead the more obvious (and economically coherent) attribution of inflation to the government's issuance of paper money.[41]

In a Kadet party congress during the war, Maklakov opposed a resolution relating to government treatment of the Jews in Galicia, but only because he doubted it would have the slightest effect. He observed that anti-Semitism was "colossal" in the army there. Although no one thought that all Jews were spies, they generally thought all spies were Jews. Given the way Jews were being treated, they would have been morally justified in becoming spies, he thought, but he had no reason to think that many of them were. In any event, no facts about Jewish espionage would justify the way they were treated. What the party had to fight was the mistaken set of notions about the supposed link between Jews and espionage. "And there is only one means of doing so—with facts."[42]

A couple of other points in this vein: First, as we'll see in the next chapter's discussion of Maklakov's hostility to the tsarist regime's stumble-footed Russification programs, he drew a careful distinction between a healthy nationalism and a bullying nationalism. The principle accords with his work opposing restrictions on Jews. Second, during the Russian civil war, he exercised what influence he had, as the defunct Provisional Government's chosen representative to France, to lean on the White forces to behave better toward Jews in areas under their control. Strategic considerations, to be sure, called for such a policy to attract support from Russia's former allies, but his work there also tracks his record in the pre-Revolutionary years.

In short, Maklakov's eloquent efforts from 1905 to 1917 to curb the regime's religious discrimination show no sign of being infected by his aesthetic views, however puzzling we may find them. If the regime had followed his advice, the Jews and Old Believers at the receiving end of discrimination would have had far less reason to abandon it in 1917. So in all likelihood would other Russians who valued a state that respected its people.

CHAPTER 10

National Minorities

In Russia's multi-ethnic empire, two ethnic groups, the Poles and the Finns, had prior histories as nations. These survived into the pre-revolutionary era as the Kingdom of Poland and the Grand Duchy of Finland, both subject to Russian sovereignty. There was tension (to put it very mildly) between Russia's interests in being a nation itself, or at least a polity meaningfully unified under the monarchy, and the subject populations' interests in control over their own national life. Maklakov generally saw Russia's national interest as lying in respect for the interests and historic cultures of the Poles and Finns.

A useful starting point is a report that he prepared on the third session of the Third Duma (1909–1910), which he initially delivered as a speech to his constituents and then published as an article in the journal *Russkaia Mysl* in 1911.[1] To put this in perspective, imagine a member of the House or Senate publishing a report to his constituents in *Foreign Affairs* or perhaps *The New York Review of Books*; the American legislator of the last half-century whom one can most easily imagine doing so is Daniel Patrick Moynihan. Maklakov distinguished between several varieties of nationalism.

On the one hand, he recognized a kind of innocent or benign nationalism: "a burst of national feeling . . . an expression of joy and pleasure that ordinarily coincides with revolution. Take the Great Revolution: who could be more nationalist than the Girondists and Danton?" More broadly, this good nationalism arose in eras when the state began to "correspond more closely with popular trust and expectations." Nationalism—of the right type—is "firm toward the powerful, magnanimous to the weak. French nationalists dared to fight all Europe, but they voluntarily gave equal rights to the Jews."[2]

But the nationalism that Maklakov saw prevailing in Russia was utterly different. It was only "so-called nationalism," "a forgery and imposture"—and among the forgeries and impostures that distort the meaning of words, he said he knew of none more shameful than the forgery committed with nationalism. "Our nationalism is born of reaction, not revolution. It marks a moment of breakdown, not rise, in the public mood." It was born when "reaction prevailed and the frightened enemies of revolution came on the scene. . . . Reaction called all revolutionaries foreigners, and vented all its fear and weakness on them." From this sort of nationalism—the government's—he expected no good. Contrasting it with yet a third nationalism, that of the oppressed, he said, "What is forgivable in the weak can be repellent in the strong."[3] He pointed to the example of French teachers who shunned Germans after the Franco-Prussian war; as the reactions of the citizens of a defeated power toward those of the conqueror, their actions seemed at least excusable. Comparable actions by Russia toward its subject peoples were not.

Having set up this typology of nationalism, he used it to chide the Octobrists. If the government's policy, this forgery of nationalism, was the work of reaction, of hostility to aligning the state with the expectations of the people, then why on earth were the Octobrists, conceived in the name of the October Manifesto, giving it their support?

Maklakov's liberal positions on the nations within Russia may seem at odds with his rather nationalistic stance on the international scene (see chapter 14). But at least in one respect the two sets of ideas mesh, as Maklakov explained from time to time. For Russia to withstand international geopolitical competition, it required internal cohesion, which in turn required some degree of loyalty from its subject nationalities. Beating up on them was not the best way to win their loyalty.

In later life, Maklakov wrote a rather touching account of two fellow soldiers in the struggle for reform, Fyodor Rodichev and Alexander Lednitskii, a Pole, whom we've already met as Maklakov's chosen—but in fact unused—legal mentor (see chapter 2). The piece includes an episode that obviously made a strong impression on him, and may partly account for his sympathies for Russia's subject peoples. Maklakov was a member of a 1905 all-Russian congress to form a Lawyer's Union, gathering in response to the tsar's February 1905 decree calling on people to offer proposals for reform. The Polish lawyers announced in advance that they would participate only if the congress recognized the Poles' right to autonomy—evidently both as a general principle and within the lawyers' conference (that is, an understanding that the conference as a whole could adopt a position only if both Polish and Russian memberships approved). The Russians were unprepared, and disliked the pressure of such an ultimatum. Rodichev saved the day with a speech, the first of his that Maklakov had ever heard, that raised the matter to such a level "that any opposition would seem shameful," and the Poles' claims were promptly approved by all.[4]

At a slightly later zemstvo congress, Polish autonomy was again debated. Maklakov was not a participant but followed the proceedings closely, and was persuaded that the debate exposed the "deceit" in the principle of mere "equal rights," that is, simply extending the type of democracy advocated in the Kadet platform throughout the empire—a polity of strikingly varied histories and cultures—but without the kind of allowance for variation implicit in a federal structure. That principle ignored the facts and the distinctiveness of Polish culture, the Polish past, the not-yet-forgotten former Polish state, and even currently separate Polish legislation (a residue of its having formerly had an independent legislature). To ignore all this in the name of equality, to consider Russia a unitary state despite the obviousness of these problems was, he wrote, as doctrinaire as the demands for a constituent assembly and for universal and equal suffrage. The idea of Polish autonomy—popularized at meetings organized by Lednitskii—was, he said, as statesmanlike an idea as Russian society was ready to grasp at the time.[5]

In public discussion Maklakov attacked the government on two quite specific issues relating to the Poles: first, its plans for creating zemstvos in Russia's western provinces but with a franchise skewed to assure Russian dominance; and second, its carving a new province out of Congress Poland.

We saw in chapter 8 Stolypin's use of Article 87 in 1911 to overcome the State Council's resistance to the western zemstvo scheme, but the scheme had been in the works since May 1909. It started simply with a reactionary editor's idea of adjusting the franchise in the western provinces in order to have more Russians among the members of the State Council elected from that area than would be likely under the general franchise law. But Stolypin had the idea of marrying that goal with a policy of extending the zemstvo—the institutional route for selection of State Council members in the rest of Russia—to the western provinces. The standard zemstvo franchise rules, however, tilted heavily toward landowner interests, and would not produce the desired results in a region dominated by Polish landowners and Russian, or at any rate Orthodox, peasants. Accordingly the usual provisions had to be manipulated. The government devised an extremely complex set of electoral rules—even to the point of imposing limits on the number of peasants who might be elected as a result of the bill's weakening the usual tilt in favor of the gentry.[6]

But the principal target of Maklakov's account in *Russkaia Mysl* was the scheme's use of nationally based curiae, Polish and Russian, which could each vote *only* for its own nationality. This was, he pointed out, the antithesis of the government's whole nationality policy, under which it *forbade* voluntary and professional organizations that limited admission to those of a particular national group. "The government, which forbade associations defined on a basis of nationality for fear of separatism, itself unites the Poles of a whole region, gives them authority, making them representatives of a whole people, and sets them up in opposition to the Russians. It's hard to imagine a greater self-contradiction, a greater want of principle." This was, he thought, a sin against the idea of the state, "which ought to unite and not separate . . . all the peoples of a single state."[7]

He then turned to the scheme's sins against the zemstvo principle. There were three. First, it betrayed the idea of the zemstvo by subordinating it to an interest other than local popular authority, namely the goal of changing the composition of the upper house. Second, since the success of the zemstvo enterprise depended on the quality of the people chosen to exercise responsibility, constraining choice by an irrelevant consideration (the obligation of each curia to choose only "its own" nationality) would limit the group who could be chosen and thus degrade overall quality. "Russia is not so rich in cultivated local people not to fear the results of such a constraint." Third, the zemstvo is aimed at local self-government, at giving rights to local people, to whom local interests are near and dear. The bill's artificial support for the Russian landowner element, after the measures aimed at Russification of the area, would turn zemstvo matters not into the hands of the local people, but into the hands of bureaucrats who had obtained estates in the western provinces on easy terms and, living in St. Petersburg, were unaware of local needs. In short, the scheme made no sense in terms of Russia's nationality problems, and at the same time jeopardized local self-government. Maklakov again upbraided the Octobrists for renouncing their promises, for ignoring the zemstvo ideal and the constitution.[8]

In the Duma a little later, Maklakov attacked a bill that aimed to carve a new province, Kholm (Chelm), out of two existing provinces in Congress Poland. He argued that the bill made promises to the Russian (or Ukrainian) population that would not be kept, and threatened and insulted the Poles with no offsetting benefit. It was a lose-lose proposition.

Technically, he observed, all the bill did was to create a new province out of parts of two preexisting ones; but the new province would be the domain of the minister of internal affairs, and, just as before, the region would be governed from St. Petersburg. The excuse given for the bill was that it would protect the ethnic Russians from the consequences of city and rural self-government likely to be dominated by non-Russians once self-government was established. But the need for protection seemed fanciful. There was already urban self-government, and with the system of voting by curiae it posed no threat to the Russians. As to rural self-government, there was no way of figuring out what might be needed for such protection until the details of this as-yet hypothetical self-government were known. He argued that the "protection" excuse was given only to quiet the conscience of those who would not agree to the bill if it were recognized as simply an act of hostility to Poland.[9]

While he clearly would have no truck with forceful Russification, Maklakov saw a legitimate Russian concern over the likely "Polonization" of the area's Russian population. He identified three potential sources of Polonization, but doubted whether the bill would affect any of them: the Russian peasants' economic dependence on Polish landowners; the dominance of the Catholic Church; and the existence of schools, including private ones, that taught in Polish and reflected Polish sympathies and interests. Not only did the bill not address any of these issues, but Maklakov found it hard to see any decent way of doing so. The government could, of course, close Polish schools, forbid private schools, and encroach on the right of the population to learn the mother tongue, but he plainly regarded such measures as unthinkably drastic. So too with the influence of the Poles as landowners: nationalizing their land might solve that problem, but the bill certainly didn't propose it.[10] The bill would thus wholly fail to achieve its stated aims, at the cost of increasing alienation among the Poles.

Maklakov agreed in a qualified sense with the argument of Count Bobrinskii, one of the bill's proponents, that the administration in Kholm had been drawn from the dregs of Russia's administration. In Maklakov's view, Kholm had been run by "administrative careerists who have not understood—as they have not understood in Russia itself—that a population is a living organism, not scaffolding that is constructed around a building." He regarded Russia, with its clumsy efforts to support the Russian population, as acting like a "rhinoceros in a china shop."[11]

He then turned to an argument advanced by another supporter, Bishop Evlogi, who had said that the bill was needed to raise the spirits of the Russian population. He responded that it was trying to do it by means of show rather than substance, and in that respect the means were extremely "*ne-gosudarstvennyi*," an untranslatable phrase meaning, roughly, "destructive to a healthy state." The bill was also ne-gosudarstvennyi in that it tended to destroy the idea of Slavic unity. It would, for the sake of symbolic legislation, push the Poles toward Germany and would cost Russia our "dear and reliable friends." In the same passage he referred to the Germans as "our immemorial enemies," which was accurate in one sense but at the cost of neglecting other immemorial enemies such as the Poles and Lithuanians.[12] His choice of language was clearly driven by the increasing tension between Germany and France, Britain, and Russia.

Maklakov characterized the proponents' claims as demagoguery, as offering up a resounding and grand formula to raise the mood of the Russian population, but one so vague that a listener could fill it with whatever content he liked.

> You tell the Russian population that they will become *khoziains* in their country. [*Khoziain* is another untranslatable word, here suggesting "boss."] But did you tell them that they will be khoziains only in the sense that a Moscow or Tula peasant is a

> khoziain, someone who will be ordered around by every lower official of the Russian administration, that when famine comes Russian authority will obstruct the collection of relief funds? (*Prolonged applause from the left: shouts from the right and center: "Demagogue, shameful!"*) The Russian peasant, who suffers from dependence on Polish bread, will doubtless think that when he becomes a khoziain, as you have promised him, he'll no longer feel this economic dependence.[13]

The allusion to bureaucratic obstruction of famine relief of course echoed his own experience in the famine of 1891.

With the Octobrists' support, the Duma approved the Kholm bill and the tsar ultimately signed it. Maklakov's *Russkaia Mysl* article reflects his disappointment with the Octobrists, whom rightly he calls "the center": "And here is the center, which has followed along, which hasn't understood, in its naiveté, or perhaps in its hypocrisy, what sort of road it is pursuing."[14]

In the war, Maklakov gave several speeches directed to the government's bungling of the war effort, but in one he particularly focused on its relations with the Poles. "Poland for a long time has been a private preserve of the functionaries of Russification. In fighting Polonization they protected the Germans in Poland." And he examined the two-faced character of Russian statements on Poland's future. Grand Duke Nikolai Nikolaevich (Nicholas II's first cousin once removed), the commander of Russian armies in the west, had issued a proclamation in August 1914 suggesting that the regime would agree to autonomy for Poland after the war. But the authorities in St. Petersburg, behind his back, told the press that autonomy must not even be discussed. They explained to Russian functionaries that any autonomy for Poland would not involve Russian (as opposed to Austrian or German) Poles.[15] The tsar issued no declaration paralleling the Grand Duke's, a gap noted by the Poles.[16]

Maklakov later, in a speech celebrating Russian culture, identified Russia's role in the partition of Poland as a great sin, for which he thought Russia was still paying.[17] That position seems completely in accord with his positions on the western zemstvos and the creation of Kholm province.

In the case of the Finns, the government proposed legislation that seemed to Maklakov even more egregious than the western zemstvos and the Kholm carve-out: it violated solemn obligations Russia had made to Finland, obligations that he regarded as having constitutional status.

The government proposed its Finnish legislation to address the anomaly between Finland's status as part of the Russian empire and longstanding provisions that guaranteed Finland and its Diet authority over its internal affairs. Article 2 of the Fundamental Laws, for example, provided that Finland should be governed "in its internal affairs by special provisions on the basis of special legislation." A similar line was drawn in the 1869 legislation reorganizing the Finnish Diet and saying that the provision was Finland's fundamental law and could be changed only by the joint decision of the Diet and the monarch (that is, the tsar in his capacity as Grand Duke of Finland). That in turn drew on Alexander I's declaration to the Finnish people and the Diet assembled at Porvoo (or Borgo) on March 27, 1809 (after Alexander's conquest of Finland from Sweden), recognizing Finland as a separate political unit, "retaining its fundamental rights and the constitution it had hitherto possessed, to be maintained in force, intact and unchanged."[18]

The reservation of "*internal* affairs" to Finland implicitly left some matters outside that reservation, matters that the Russians came to call issues of "imperial concern."[19] Yet the line between these categories had never been clearly drawn. In a proposal precipitated by interpellations in the Duma by Octobrists and rightists questioning the status of Finland, Stolypin created a special committee of five Finns and six Russians (including the chair, Russian State Comptroller P. A. Kharitonov) to identify issues of "imperial concern" and the procedure by which legislation addressing such issues should be passed. On a predictable 6–5 vote, the committee proposed not only a virtually all-encompassing definition of matters of imperial concern, including, for example, education, but also a simple if rather brutal means of implementation: ordinary Russian legislative provisions would suffice, though the Diet would be invited to send a number of deputies to the Duma and State Council and would be asked for its (nonbinding) opinion on bills. The government introduced legislation embodying these ideas.[20]

Maklakov accepted a key premise of the legislation, namely that the existing situation was anomalous. He even went so far as to suggest that in extremis it might justify action in violation of the various constitutional commitments that he had identified. His theory here seems to be a variation on his basic view of coups d'état: they are bad, but sometimes the alternative is so much worse as to justify a coup. But here, he argued, Russia and Finland were by no means at such a point—there was considerable goodwill among the Finns despite highhanded Russian behavior, and the matter could be resolved in negotiations with the Diet.[21]

Although winning a significant number of Octobrist votes was probably hopeless, Maklakov aimed his speech especially at them. If they failed to insist that the state observe the constitution vis-à-vis Finland, how could they expect to demand that the state do so for Russia itself? Whereas members of the government might hate the October Manifesto and its ideal of constitutionalism, the Duma's Octobrist "center" had no reason to endorse such a breach.[22]

Rightists and Octobrists for the most part ignored Maklakov's constitutional arguments. They said that the Finns had been ingrates for various financial benefits supplied by Russia, including defense expenses (though they omitted any discussion of exactly what threat the Finns might have faced independently of Russia). More on point, but hardly compelling, were arguments by rightist N. E. Markov (Markov II), saying that, although Nicholas I spoke of the need to observe promises, he must have meant something different since he himself had deprived Congress Poland of the constitution promised by Alexander I. Markov also claimed that Alexander II's emancipation of the serfs violated promises to preserve serfdom, allegedly made to the serf-owners (technically, the *dvorianstvo*) by several tsars (Catherine II, Peter III, and Paul I).[23] These claims seem to belong in the basement of the argumentative arsenal, along with "so's your old man" and "two wrongs make a right."

Maklakov's efforts were to no avail. The bill whisked through all three readings in the Duma in less than a week; it was adopted by a Duma vote of 164 to 23, then by the State Council, and became law on June 17, 1910.[24]

A last and curious episode involving national minorities suggests Maklakov's rare spot on the palette of viewpoints in late imperial Russia. At the Kadets' June 7, 1915, party congress, one Nikolai Vasilenko, a delegate from Kiev, said that Maklakov had claimed in a press interview that the Ukrainian national movement was based on German money. Delegates cited similar statements, seemingly hostile to Ukrainian interests, by his fellow Kadet Pyotr Struve. (Maklakov himself in correspondence after the revolution called Struve a "Ukrainophobe.") Another delegate from Ukraine, M. K. Imshenetskii from Chernigov, reported that dissatisfaction with the Kadets was growing among the democratic intelligentsia in Ukraine, mainly because of the speeches by Struve and Maklakov. He wanted the party to clearly disavow their positions. Miliukov proposed a resolution explicitly saying that the opinion of the party was not the opinion expressed by those two. Whereupon another member, V. V. Lashkevich, asked for a word of personal privilege. He used it to say that Maklakov had authorized him to say that he (Maklakov) had given no interview at all on the subject of Ukraine and had never uttered the words ascribed to him. So far as the party congress's reproving Maklakov was concerned, this pricked the bubble.[25]

As we'll see in chapter 14, Maklakov took a rather nationalistic stance in the international maneuvering that culminated in the outbreak of World War I. In that project he was closely associated with Struve, who was with him at the intellectual core of the short-lived newspaper *Russkaia Molva* [Russia speaks]. Many public figures holding such viewpoints were also nationalistic vis-à-vis Russia's subject peoples: take the Octobrists generally and Struve himself. But Maklakov and Struve were hardly ideological twins. The delegates' readiness to believe that Maklakov had made the statement attributed to him seems likely to have stemmed in part from a notion that since he and Struve thought alike on many issues, including their nationalism abroad, they would share similar viewpoints on Ukraine. But things that often go together do not always go together. As we've seen, Maklakov didn't let his nationalistic views spill over into scorn for Russia's national minorities or a will to dominate them.

Maklakov's position on Russia's subject nationalities seems based on a full recognition of the political realities. It had a crucial gap, however. While recognizing the interests of both the Poles and Russians (or other Orthodox) intermingled in western Russia, and properly blasting the ineptitude of the government's solutions, he didn't affirmatively offer a solution of his own. In fairness, of course, no good solution was readily available. It's not clear even now whether any solution was available. The intermingling has now largely ended, but only through the massive ethnic cleansings that preceded, accompanied, and followed World War II. It's hard to dub those a "solution," much less a good one.

Despite this shortcoming, a little attention by the regime to Maklakov's position might have secured it a degree of loyalty and trust when the stresses of war and Russia's faltering military position inspired its national minorities to think of escape.

CHAPTER 11

Judicial Reform, Citizen Remedies

We saw in chapter 8 Maklakov's concerns with the government's persistent arbitrariness, especially its reliance on the extraordinary security laws and its use of agents provocateurs. He viewed the judiciary as a potential remedy. He often praised an independent judiciary as the hallmark of desirable governance, and when court findings exposed and recorded government malfeasance, he liked to treat their findings as the gold standard, conclusively establishing the facts. But he knew quite well that, despite Alexander II's nominal establishment of judicial independence in 1864, judges were incessantly subject to executive pressure, were selected for a variety of reasons that did *not* include their intellectual independence, and worked in a culture that placed a high value on congruence with government attitudes, if not downright submissiveness. His gold standard claim still held; findings or judgments *against* the government were most unlikely to be due to a lack of judicial independence.

Maklakov worked on three fronts to make the courts a serious barrier to executive arbitrariness: first, spotlighting the facts of judicial dependency and its sources; second, pushing for structural reforms to enhance judicial independence and otherwise extend the rule of law; and third, developing judicial remedies against official lawlessness. (Because the devil is as always in the details, some of the following discussion is quite technical, though not, I hope, legalistic.)

Because of the tenure rules of the 1864 reforms, which provided that judges were neither removable or even movable (from court to court) without their consent, government abuses of judicial independence tended to be secretive. But Maklakov identified plenty of signs. Direct threats were the government's most obvious means. The head of the Tiflis court, for example, told its judges that any judge who issued an acquittal with which the appellate branch disagreed would be subject to disciplinary measures. If this threat appeared to be an idle one, because such discipline would be unlawful, Maklakov reminded the Duma that the authorities could easily cover such a move with a fig leaf of legitimacy, citing examples of disciplinary proceedings that seemed to follow right after acquittals.[1] He also pinpointed government threats to a judge who had exposed a use of agents provocateurs. He contrasted this with the words of a French judge who had told the authorities there that they should "expect judgments from [the courts], not services."[2]

Of course the government could use carrots as well as sticks. Right after the Beilis trial, for example, all those in the judiciary and the procuracy who participated on the anti-Beilis side received special awards. And the government used sticks to beat those who did their jobs impartially. Investigator Nikolai Krasovskii, who had persisted in the search for truth, was fired and prosecuted for some supposed prior offense (he managed to win acquittal).[3]

If the judges could not be successfully pressured, the government could thwart the enforcement of their decisions. Maklakov pointed to a land dispute involving the prominent Stroganov family, in which a provincial governor, with the help or at least the indifference of the ministries of internal affairs and justice, had helped the losing parties defy a ruling of the Senate (Russia's highest court).[4]

Maklakov's recognition of executive domination of the judiciary was confirmed by investigations conducted later by the Extraordinary Investigative Commission set up by the Provisional Government in the wake of the tsar's abdication. Ivan Shcheglovitov, minister of justice for more than nine of the pre-revolutionary years (April 1906 to June 1915), coyly testified to the commission that it was "possible" that he had issued instructions calling for deliberate severity on the part of judges in choosing punishments for political crimes. And, though recognizing that by law a judge could not be removed or reassigned without his consent, he said "that there had been exceptional cases where it was necessary, as it were, by personal conversations, to bend (*skloniat*) a judge or two to accept a change in his position." The "bending" had apparently occurred in response to reviews of case outcomes that Shcheglovitov's assistants conducted at his request.[5]

What made such executive interference possible in a state that had supposedly adopted the principle of judicial independence? I've seen no systematic treatment of that question by Maklakov, but he did point to two types of explanations—a general attitude or culture, and the rules and practice of judicial selection.

High officials openly expressed their expectation that judges would act as part of a government team. In a speech responding to criticism from Maklakov, Stolypin hinted that the government might be contemplating measures to explicitly modify the tenure principle embodied in the 1864 reform. Stolypin cited France, a paragon of western European liberalism, as having recognized exceptions to the principle of irremovability.[6] (Indeed it had. In the Act of August 30, 1883, supporters of the relatively new Third Republic, in order to consolidate their victory, had suspended the principle and conducted a purge to remove judges hostile to the new regime.)

Maklakov, an ardent Francophile, was perhaps especially stung by having French practice thrown in his face, and took to the floor. Using his typically admiring language for the judges, he asked, "Can you speak this way of those who observe and guard the laws?" He claimed that there was "one fateful obstacle that causes them to make mistakes for which we reproach them—and that is the insufficiency of their independence." Their tenure (*nesmeniaemost*), he said, needed reinforcement, not dilution.[7]

Maklakov linked the issue to broader themes, trying to both shame and tempt the government. He shamed it by invoking the October Manifesto, which explicitly purported to establish "an unbreakable rule" that a law could become effective only with the approval of the Duma. Assaults on judicial independence would indirectly break that promise; if the courts could be swayed from adherence to the law as written, then the "law" would not truly bind the government. But he also pointed to potential political advantages for the government if it were to embrace rule-of-law reforms. Bismarck, he said, had observed that the strength of a revolutionary movement lay not in its leaders' ideas, but in the moderate demands that had not been satisfied in a timely way. Here the moderate demands and the government's own past promises were in agreement, as indeed were their interests. Honoring these promises, he argued, would sap the revolutionaries' strength.[8]

Minister of Justice Shcheglovitov was a frequent opponent of Maklakov on this topic. He was crudely dismissive of judicial independence, remarking in the Duma that the courts must be constrained by "an iron discipline." Maklakov responded that the minister seemed not to notice that with such a claim he was destroying the courts' position in the state. As a result of such a practice and attitude, he said, "the judgments of courts are no longer believed." Interrupting, Markov II shouted from the floor, "They don't believe this Jewish nonsense."[9] (Interjections from the floor were common in Duma debates, though rarely at such a low level.) Later, on the eve of World War I, Shcheglovitov suggested in the Duma that even in western Europe faith in constitutional guarantees was falling lower day by day.[10] In reply, Maklakov pointed out what a radical backsliding Shcheglovitov's view was from Stolypin's commitments in the Second Duma to create a rule-of-law state.[11]

Of course executive impatience with the judiciary is not confined to moribund autocracies. Jefferson, having instigated the treason case against Aaron Burr and meddled in its prosecution, and being disappointed at Burr's acquittal in a trial presided over by Chief Justice John Marshall, wrote to friends complaining about what he saw as the folly of the Constitution's having given judges life tenure. But at least in the United States the principle of judicial independence was well enough established that Jefferson didn't go public with his ideas.[12]

Nothing in the power or practice of judicial selection in imperial Russia tended to fill courts with people who were likely to withstand government pressure—or even interested in resisting. The appointments were up to the tsar or his subordinates in the ministry of justice, so there was no incentive to consider opposing points of view, other than the tsar's grasp of the long-run advantages of doing so—always a thin reed. When Shcheglovitov was asked by the Provisional Government's investigative commission how he went about choosing judges for the civil courts, he said he sought "the firmest people, of the most monarchist disposition, who would be guardians of the existing order."[13] Maklakov noted that Shcheglovitov had been a judge before becoming a minister, and expressed doubt whether the attributes he displayed as a minister—here Maklakov's examples all ran to Shcheglovitov's tendency to make choices likely to please his master, the tsar—would make a good judge.[14] Shcheglovitov's career path illustrated another pattern not conducive to judicial independence: continuous alternation between posts as procurator (virtually equivalent to a prosecutor) and as judge. For Shcheglovitov the sequence had been deputy procurator, then judge, then three (steadily rising) posts as procurator, judge again, ministry of justice official, procurator again, then two posts as a ministry of justice official, and finally minister of justice. Such a scramble of executive and judicial posts seems unlikely to foster a sense of the responsibilities unique to judges.

Discussing the Senate itself (specifically its "first" department, which dealt with appeals concerning government conduct), Maklakov argued that the ministry of justice's apparent preferences in exercising its appointment authority were first, for people who had left government service whom the government didn't know what to do with, and second, for people who had spent their whole lives "fighting the law."[15] The result was senators who, even if they were at all disposed to uphold the law, were outclassed by the skills and experience of the chancellery and procuracy. Maklakov drew a thumbnail sketch of what happened when a private person filed an appeal against a governor: "The senator, a former governor, says, 'The governor is probably right, write a decision in his favor,' and the chancellery carries it out."[16] Maklakov also lamented that the Senate had become "a place to which disgraced functionaries are sent."[17] He may have had a specific appointment in mind. Pyotr Durnovo, whom we've already met a number of times, was for a time police chief for the empire and in that role had used police officers to search the office of a diplomat who was his rival for the affections of a particular lady. For this misuse of government personnel, he was sent to the Senate's first department as "punishment."[18]

Maklakov sought where possible to nudge the system toward changes that would enhance judicial independence. The most critical opportunity was the government's proposal in 1909 to drop the township (*volost*) courts (that is, courts for the regional units of government just above the village) in favor of an expansion of jurisdiction for justices of the peace (the *mirovoi sud*). The proposal was a reversal of an 1889 policy change. Until 1889, the two systems had coexisted: the justices of the peace, which originated with the 1864 reform, and the township courts, which were created in 1861, when the emancipation of the serfs eliminated the political basis for having local landowners adjudicate peasant disputes. In 1889 the government largely eliminated the justices of the peace in rural Russia.[19]

There is some dispute over whether that abolition was simply another instance of the many reactionary changes of that year, the counter-reform apogee of the reign of Alexander III, or whether it was a sensible response to deep incongruities between the justices of the peace and peasant culture. The case for deep incongruities seems to rest largely on the justices' excessive reliance on written evidence. That created slowdowns in the administration of justice (to which the government responded by imposing additional burdens on the justices), and generated peasant complaints that the formal procedures enabled the "kulaks and miroedy" to rob them through the law. "Kulaks" and "miroedy," literally translated, mean "fist" and "village eater" respectively, and are both rather elastic terms of abuse used by peasants to stigmatize other peasants deemed to have grown prosperous by unfair means. Another peasant complaint was even more conclusory—that "the justices of the peace have nothing to do with justice."[20]

These complaints seem an odd basis for shelving a judicial system rather than reforming it. A more apt remedy might have been elimination of the procedural characteristics of the justices of the peace that led to the complaints—most obviously to correct the undue reliance on documents and to create a rule of "harmless error," so that trivial procedural errors would not require reversal. The same scholar who reported these complaints also summarized the government's basic theory as being that "separation of administrative and judicial authority at the borough level as well as the zemstvo election of justices of the peace were the fundamental obstacles to rural law and order and public respect for the government."[21] In this passage the author seems to be saying that the government's precise aim in removing the justices of the peace from the countryside was to curtail judicial independence.

In fact a major difference between the township courts and the justices of the peace was that administrators—that is, officials directly responsible to the government's political hierarchy—were involved in the township courts at key stages: appeal and judicial selection. Appeal from the township courts ran straight to the land captains, who were officials in the ministry of internal affairs. By contrast, an appeal from the justices of the peace would take a case through the usual judicial system, with decisions by judges whose tenure was protected by the 1864 reforms.[22] To the extent that rulings developed informal power as precedents (under civil law principles they would not have had binding precedential force), the adjudications could advance people's understanding of legal norms and allow them to form expectations about their rights and duties.

Similarly for the process of judicial selection. Judges of the township courts, a single-estate institution, were nominated by the estate in question, the peasants, but the nominations could be rejected by the local land captains.[23] In contrast, the justices of the peace were elected by the all-estate zemstvo assembly, which was itself elected, though to be sure in a system slanted to landowner dominance. The difference between the systems is capsulized in the rule barring persons serving as justices of the peace from holding other offices at the same time;[24] the land captains exercised their powers over the township courts as *part* of their administrative functions.

The government's 1909 bill, besides abolishing the township courts, restored the justices of the peace to their pre-1889 role in rural Russia, along with election by the zemstvo as in the pre-1889 era.[25]

But two subsidiary features of the bill posed risks of executive encroachment and drew interventions by Maklakov. First, the bill included property qualifications for the justices of the peace; and, for those exempt from that qualification because they had received a higher education, there was a requirement of birth in the locality where they were to serve.[26] These requirements led indirectly to an opportunity for control by the ministry of justice. If there were extended vacancies, the ministry was empowered to fill the gaps. And if the property qualifications sharply narrowed the zemstvo assembly's range of plausible choice—Maklakov offered figures suggesting that they would do so[27]—the resulting delays would widen the ministry's chances of selecting judges itself. Couple that with the three-year term for which judges were to serve,[28] and the risk to judicial independence was plain:

> If our ministry were occupied with matters of justice, and not politics, I would favor appointed judges, but in our times if you give the ministry of justice the right to name judges, how will it name them? The judges are not irremovable, but are chosen only for three years, and the minister of justice will plant his subordinates there for three years, people full of his viewpoints, who will judge on the basis of considerations satisfying to the people standing over them.[29]

Because the property requirements had no useful function—they didn't assure independence, as the property might well be recreational and produce no income (as Maklakov knew well from his own ownership of rural property), and they were unneeded to assure attachment to local interests, as the electing zemstvo assembly could judge that attachment itself, directly[30]—he saw no justification for them and their resulting impact on judicial independence. The Duma ultimately compromised, accepting property requirements, but at lower levels than originally proposed, and removing the special birthplace requirement.[31]

A second threat to judicial independence was the bill's provision on the selection of the heads of assemblies of justices of the peace. The committee bill had proposed that heads be named by the Ministry of Justice,[32] but Maklakov proposed election by the judicial assemblies themselves.[33] The committee report on the bill said that these heads were not to be "bosses" (*nachalniki*), but merely primus inter pares.[34] But it seems far more likely, in a society with hierarchical practices as entrenched as in Russia, that these court chiefs would have served as transmission belts for regime influence. Since these assemblies operated as courts of appeal over the individual justices, their power as collective entities was critical; they were not just social gatherings. Recall the chief of the Tiflis courts mentioned earlier in the chapter, who warned the other judges of the region that acquittals not confirmed on appeal would trigger disciplinary action.[35] Maklakov's amendment prevailed here, too.[36]

Insofar as the Duma's goal was complete *replacement* of the township courts, its work was in vain. In the State Council, Stolypin, possibly acting under pressure from the United Nobility, a group organized to advance landowner interests, dropped the bill that his own administration had proposed and instead championed retention of the township courts. But the State Council's changes, ultimately adopted by both legislative houses in 1912, were still a genuine reform. Although the ultimate bill preserved the township courts, it removed the land captains from their roles in appeals and in the selection of judges, thus addressing the two features that most obviously undermined their independence. Appeals would henceforth go to a special new appellate body, consisting of a justice of the peace and two township court judges, and its decisions could in turn be appealed to the assemblies of the justices of the peace. Land captains also lost their role in the selection of judges: the peasants would elect them, subject to confirmation by the assemblies of the justices of the peace. The bill thus discarded any role for executive officials in the selection of township court judges.[37]

Moreover, the 1912 reform retained the Duma's provision for the reestablishment of the justices of the peace in the countryside. The final bill kept a property ownership requirement for justices of the peace, though only at the level required for entitlement to vote for zemstvo chairman, a reduction of the 1864 requirement by half. But it reversed Maklakov's earlier success in the Duma on the selection of the heads of assemblies of justices of the peace, giving the power (as in the original ministry of justice bill) to the ministry rather the justices themselves.[38] Appeals from a single justice ran to these assemblies, and from them (in cases involving more than 100 rubles) to the cassation (appeal) department of the Senate. There was also provision for "oversight" (*nadzor*), which ran to the empire's regular appellate courts (the *sudebnaia palata* and the Senate) and the ministry of justice. Although this oversight authority appears directed exclusively at management issues, Maklakov was alarmed that it might put the courts' independence at risk.[39]

By creating overlapping jurisdiction, the 1912 statute provided an opportunity for competition between the two court systems. It gave the justices of the peace authority over cases up to a value of 1,000 rubles, as against a ceiling of 100 rubles for the township courts.[40] The township courts dealt only with disputes between peasants. But the overlap created a realm within which peasant plaintiffs could choose. Had the 1912 changes had time to be applied and tested, they might have yielded interesting evidence of peasant preference.

The dispute over the township courts and the justices of the peace of course involved more than degrees of judicial independence. Considering all the implications, Maklakov was of two minds about the choice. He fully recognized peasant attachment to the township courts. In a friendly exchange between Maklakov and a peasant on the floor of the Duma, the peasant said of the court, "Perhaps it's bad, but it's our court."[41] Maklakov echoed the idea in his *Russkaia Mysl* report to his constituents, insisting that any replacement court must have the qualities that made peasants value the township court—that it was "theirs, accessible and cheap."[42] On that account he fought to keep the jurisdiction of the justices of the peace relatively modest. An excessive jurisdictional load, he thought, would make that court an unsatisfactory substitute for the township court in the peasants' eyes; small-scale litigation, the sort typical for peasants, was just the sort that the justice of the peace courts might be tempted to slight.[43]

As to the quality of the township courts, modern scholarly opinion finds them to have provided fair and peaceful resolution of quarrels, despite uncertainty created by the courts' unclear mandate as to when to apply custom and when statute, not to mention land captain influence.[44] Except for attacks on the role of the township courts' clerks, whom he regarded as commonly corrupt and able to manipulate the judges,[45] Maklakov seems to have accepted their general fairness. But institutions can be generally fair but fall far short of rule-of-law ideals by failing to apply principles that people might rely on and by failing to articulate such principles for the future. Maklakov was distressed by the reliance of the township courts on unarticulated opinion and murkily established custom.[46] Moreover, if peasants were to be acculturated to the rule of law and truly integrated into the broader economy and society, as liberal democracy would ultimately require, a single-estate court could not survive—especially if, as was true of the township court from 1889 to 1912, it lay outside the reach of Russia's system for the application and interpretation of national law. As we'll see in the next chapter, Maklakov viewed the isolation of the peasants as one of the most troubling of Russia's political woes.

Another occasion for considering the status, role, and character of judges was a government bill purportedly reforming the Senate, whose cassation department was the highest court for criminal and civil appeals, and whose first department had jurisdiction over administrative issues (that is, questions concerning the acts of ministries and other government agencies). The senators of this first department, which obviously had potential for becoming a real court of administrative review, lacked any guarantee of tenure.[47]

Maklakov regarded the government proposals as mildly useful but as not going to the essence of the problem.[48] He noted that the government had contemplated schemes for serious reform from time to time, especially in 1906, but official interest had waned as soon as the crisis subsided.[49] On the specifics of the bill, he argued that it did little to address what he saw as the central problem of the Senate's first (administrative) department; given the government's bases of selection, its judges lacked the background and quality necessary to implement the rule of law. As a result the department served as little more than a screen for the lawlessness of executive officials.[50]

Maklakov proposed no basic overhaul of the bill. He faulted the government for not proposing serious reforms and argued that the area was too complex for drafting in the Duma.[51] And he kept returning to the government's lack of good faith.[52] "With the exception of those who build their privileges on the lawlessness and misfortune of Russia, we in the Duma all want renewal [of the country] on the basis of the October Manifesto. If the authorities shared that view, not in words but in deeds, there would be a working majority for it in the Duma and there would be results. (*Stormy applause from the left and center.*)"[53]

The speeches of Shcheglovitov before and after Maklakov's main speech exposed the government's vision of the first department's proper role. First, it was in this context that Shcheglovitov had disparaged the Duma on the ground that it was trying to imitate Western European ideas. He explained that in Russia, by contrast, the "basis of the rule of law is the free expression of the tsar's will." As the paper *Russkie Vedomosti* summarized his views, he appeared to see the Senate's first department as existing in order to fill in gaps in legislation and to help the government "get ahead of" legislation. After Maklakov's speech, Shcheglovitov said that the Duma's discussion of Senate reform had turned into a "continuous defamation of the authorities." Even the nationalist press decried Shcheglovitov's second speech.[54]

Maklakov offered some amendments, which on the whole were accepted, though he would have been the first to acknowledge their ultimate insignificance. All related to the Senate's authority to deny publication to various legal instruments, a legal prerequisite to their taking effect. The available grounds for such a denial seemed as sweeping as those that animate constitutional review in the United States.[55] So this power represented the germ of a system that would allow courts to weigh not only the validity of executive actions by reference to the supposedly supporting legislation, but also to weigh both legislation and executive actions against the Fundamental Laws, and to render inoperative any legislation or actions that failed to measure up. If the Senate had in practice exercised such authority, one of Maklakov's amendments, extending the Senate's power to imperial ukases and decrees,[56] would have been a game changer. But in fact the Senate never engaged in such a practice. So changes widening its scope were of little moment.[57]

Indeed, the easy passage of Maklakov's amendments and the virtual absence of debate seem to confirm his view that the Senate's review authority was a paper tiger, ineffective at holding government action accountable to legislation and to the Fundamental Laws. Had he been closely quizzed on the subject, my guess is that he would have recognized that Russia was unripe for a court exercising genuine constitutional review. Civil society and the balance between contending interests were not yet mature enough to provide the basis for a court to play the role of constitutional arbiter—to act as a constitutional gyroscope, to stabilize the political system, and to protect liberty.

In addition to an independent, conscientious, and efficient judiciary, Russia needed a set of judicial remedies for the victims of government lawlessness. (By the same token, such remedies would be useless, or nearly so, in the absence of an adequate judiciary.)[58] These might take criminal and civil forms. Criminal responsibility for the lawless officials would not directly benefit the victims but it would give officials an incentive to obey the law. Civil responsibility, in the form of rights for the victims to compensation, payable out of the pockets of the officials, the government, or both, would provide incentives to officials and reimbursement to victims. Maklakov worked on both the criminal and civil paths.[59]

Before turning to the issues, a note on the thinking of Vasily's brother Nikolai draws a revealing contrast: At the time of the main debates in which Vasily advanced his rule-of-law positions on remedies against officials, Nikolai was still a provincial governor and played no role. But later, after he served as minister of internal affairs and was dismissed from that post in the summer of 1915 as a sop to liberal and popular opposition, he was named a member of the State Council and spoke up on these issues. When a reform bill was introduced there in February 1916, Nikolai opposed it, denouncing liberals as believing that any administrative authority was bad and that such authority must be completely deactivated. But the State Council was far from uniform on the subject and certainly didn't paint the opposition with such a broad brush. State Council member E. N. Trubetskoi, for example, wanted to have officials generally subject to judicial responsibility and pinpointed the unique character of Russia's officials. Nowhere in Europe, he said, had officials as a class been so discredited as in Russia, so much so that the Russian word *chinovnik* (bureaucrat or official) had no real equivalent in any other language.[60] This was obviously much more in tune with Vasily than with Nikolai Maklakov.

A bill presented by the ministry of justice gave Vasily an opening on criminal responsibility. He saw the bill as a government response to the popularity of the idea of making officials answerable, but a response more for show than substance. The government was, he said, on "the path of recognizing the issue fully in words and keeping everything as before in reality. . . . A virtuoso performance of what in gymnastics is called running in place" (a phrase widely picked up by the press).[61] The existing rule was that an official could not be pursued criminally for illegal official acts unless his superior cut him loose, repudiating his behavior[62]—a repudiation that was highly unlikely in light of the solidarity among officials. The ministry bill purported to solve that by providing that, in the event of a split between the procuracy and the official's own ministry or department, the procurator could appeal to a special panel to resolve the split.[63] Maklakov thought this proposal wouldn't do the job, because the procuracy's position was inherently weaker than that of the executive agency. Quite apart from the general dominance of the executive department over the courts (to which the procuracy was appended), the procuracy would have far less information about the episode than the ministry. He proposed a rule *requiring* the procuracy to investigate when a complaint was filed, effectively forcing it to achieve at least a closer approximation of informational parity with the ministry.[64] The Duma voted it down, 147 to 118.[65]

Though aimed in the right direction, Maklakov's change seems unlikely to have been enough to turn officials' potential criminal responsibility into a powerful sanction. Yes, the procurators were attached to the courts, but they were appointed by the government, and their functions were classically executive: initiating investigations and cases on behalf of the state. So solidarity among officials, arising from a similarity in viewpoint, seems likely to have stretched across the divide between procurators and other state officials. Inclusion of the procuracy in the courts (an aspect of Russia's adoption of civil as opposed to common-law traditions) obscured rather than altered the affinity between the procuracy and the rest of the executive.

Another ministry bill, this time dealing with court authority to award compensation, gave Maklakov a more promising opening. Here he regarded the committee bill as merely saying that the Duma was convinced that everything was fine on the subject. In fact, he showed, available remedies were very limited. Although the Third Duma had adopted a law obliging the state to award compensation for injuries inflicted by *revolutionaries*, a Senate ruling had almost wholly sheltered the treasury from liability for the unlawful acts of *officials*.[66] Maklakov also pointed out that the system had an internally inconsistent system for answering the question of whether an official was truly acting for the state. If a citizen forcefully resisted an official's unlawful act, the state (via the courts) did not "withdraw its protective arms" from the official, but regarded the resisting citizen as a criminal, the official as supreme. Yet if the official's illegal act inflicted damages on the citizen and the citizen sought relief against the state, the state flipped, viewing the official as just a private citizen, so that his conduct was no responsibility of the government.[67]

And in cases involving complaints directly against government officials, remedies were at best spotty. In many cases the law called for some sort of mixed tribunal, as if judges could not, without the help of specialists, figure out if the conduct in question was lawful. Worse, the Senate had begun to systematically take the view that the courts lacked competence to decide a case whenever it posed issues of state security—an elastic concept that could easily encompass a broad range of cases. Apart from those problems, there were a host of complexities in identifying the correct defendant, with a great risk that the statute of limitations would run while the plaintiff struggled to find him. Maklakov suggested that Russia should instead follow the model of Congress Poland, which enjoyed a special institution for compensation out of treasury funds for those injured by the state, thereby alleviating the plaintiff's problems of identifying a particular offender and being able to collect on a judgment. (The Polish provision was a residue of the era when Poland had an independent legislature, and Maklakov's citation was a rare instance of a Russian political figure holding up Polish practice as a model.) Alternatively, he suggested, the Duma might adopt a rule that the statute of limitations should be tolled (that is, not run) when suit was filed against the wrong defendant.[68]

Maklakov proposed that the Duma adopt a resolution to conclude the then-current discussion (in Russian legislative parlance, such a closing resolution was called a "formula of transition" or *formula perekhoda*) with a direction to the judicial reform committee to develop a bill on official liability addressing the problems he had identified: establish treasury responsibility, solve the problem of the plaintiff who has difficulty identifying the right official to sue, and assure that the cases are resolved by a real court. But the vote was deferred until after the debate on specific articles and apparently never taken.[69] So the reform effort lapsed.

Would better judicial remedies for administrative lawlessness really have helped matters? Dominic Lieven expresses doubt about the usefulness of giving people rights against the police in late imperial Russia, arguing that controlling the "unimpressive lower ranks of the police force" would be impossible if they were "threatened with legal responsibility for their activities, protected by laws or regulations behind which they could find excuses for inaction, or confused by any but a simple line of command to their ministerial chief." The argument appears to be that they were of such low quality that they could not have handled the conflicting demands of the law and of their superiors. In a slightly more extreme formulation, he suggested that by the twentieth century it was impossible to "subdue the revolutionary movement by wholly legal means."[70]

Lieven's premise appears to be that reformers sought a system in which the line officers (the "unimpressive lower ranks") would take the fall for illegalities even when they acted under orders from their superiors. But a scheme of government liability would not necessarily subject the individual policeman to liability under those circumstances. Liability of the state would presumably lead to consequences for individuals in the executive (reprimands, pay cuts, loss of promotional opportunities, and so on), but at least in a well-designed system those consequences would fall on the parties responsible—the lower ranks where they exceeded their superiors' instructions or established norms, the higher levels when their orders were unlawful. Of course still higher officials might be tempted to cut their subordinates some slack, but a steady rain of adverse judgments would surely give the upper echelons incentives to assure a reduction in unlawful orders and to provide training to get the best out of all ranks. Orson Welles once observed, "Only in a police state is the job of a policeman easy," and any kind of accountability would make their lives harder. But the price seems reasonable—unless Russia had really come to such a pass that only the lawlessness of a police state could have saved it from the lawlessness of revolutionary terrorism.

Indeed, genuine assurance that state power would be applied to citizens only through the screen of a neutral, educated, independent judiciary, empowered to order reimbursement for victims of lawlessness, would at least have given citizens the sense that the state had concern for their welfare. Or so it would seem, unless persistent government lawlessness was truly the only way forward for Russia.

Peasant Rights

In the early twentieth century about 90 percent of the Russian people were peasants. Thanks to the long history of serfdom and the incompleteness of emancipation in 1861, they lived in legal, political, and social isolation. Their rights in the land they tilled were different from the property rights of any other citizens. And their relationship to provision of basic government services was special: they performed, without payment, all the physical work needed to produce and maintain local rural roads and other public goods—the benefits of which were shared by all rural residents—and had almost no voice in the decision-making. A serious reform of the Russian state would have to change all this, and change it radically. Maklakov saw the peasants as the "national wealth," and argued later that one of the monarchy's two great sins was its failure to foster that wealth.[1]

The property rights issue was, of course, critical in the Second Duma (see chapter 7), where the split between Stolypin and the Kadets explains the Duma's dissolution and the June 3 coup d'état. Those two events enabled the government to implement the Stolypin reform without Duma interference. Maklakov, not sharing the Kadet party's policy, made very few public statements on the subject. The statements he did make reflect much of his usual acuity, but can't be said to offer either a nuanced critique of the Stolypin program or a full assessment of the Kadet proposal—his assessment, if it were candid, would have been scathing. (As he wrote later while an émigré, he thought the Kadet idea would reinforce the principle of dividing the population into estates, a principle the Kadets normally and rightly opposed; only gentry would have property confiscated and only peasants would receive any rights. And it would violate property rights, one of the basic rights requiring protection in a rule-of-law state, to which the Kadets claimed to be committed.)[2] We'll look at the public statements that he made on the subject before the Bolshevik Revolution, but they are disappointingly few and brief, considering the issue's importance and the passions it aroused.

On the broader issue of peasants in local government and provision of local public services, however, Maklakov played quite a serious role. In the period between the dissolution of the First Duma and the assembly of the Second (a legally productive period, thanks to Article 87 and Stolypin's energy), the government issued not only its property-rights reform but also an October 5, 1906, decree eliminating or ameliorating some of the special rules that made the peasants a separate caste. In 1916 the government proposed a bill to turn the October 1906 decree into a regular statute. As a member of the Duma committee on judicial reform, Maklakov was assigned to be reporter (*dokladchik*) for the bill and prepared a comprehensive report. His recommendations included a revised bill, somewhat expanding the equalization measures of the original decree and of the government bill. Above all, his report recognized that the peasants' status as a separate estate was the keystone of an elaborate but decayed edifice. It could be removed; but its removal, unless accompanied by a host of other changes, would leave only a pile of rubble. His true accomplishment in 1916 was to put the task of replacing the obsolete estate system on the agenda—an agenda, to be sure, that was likely to move slowly because of the regime's foot-dragging and the war. The replacement would have to transform the nature of local government. The estate concept, itself a legacy of serfdom, would have to go, and with it the practice of requiring peasants to provide local services (roads, bridges, police, and so on) without pay. A new system, necessarily an all-estate system, would have to be created, a system in which peasants had a voice and financing depended not on "free" work but on revenues collected from all.

As to property rights, the Stolypin reform of 1906 had set Russia on a course toward private ownership, a somewhat rickety course, to be sure.[3] An understanding of the issue starts with the meaning of the term "allotment land." This refers to the land allotted to peasants in the course of emancipation, carved out of the land formerly owned by the serfs' owners. Peasants had had the legal right to acquire ordinary, non-allotment land since 1848, and when they did so they held it under the same rules that applied to anyone else.[4] They had increasingly taken advantage of that right over the years, but even by 1910 the overwhelming bulk of their interests in land continued to be allotment land. Stolypin's reform sought to transform this situation, enabling peasants to opt out of the commune's de facto collective ownership and into individual control.

In his 1910 report to his constituents in *Russkaia Mysl*, Maklakov explained that he hadn't had much to say on the property-rights issue, not only because of disagreement with his party but also because his own views on the subject weren't firm.[5] Indeed, his article didn't develop any strong position. His statements reflect some sympathy for both sides. That balance seems typically Maklakovian, but on this subject it was rather shapeless. He contrasted the Kadet "desire to take from the rich and give to the weak," with the government's desire "to take from those who cannot or do not want to farm their allotment land successfully, or don't use it, those who wasted or ruined it, and give it to the 'stronger peasants.'" He put "stronger peasants" in quotes because the phrase was an allusion to Stolypin's explanation—he had said his proposal was a "wager on the strong." Maklakov's wording in his *Russkaia Mysl* article implicitly recognized that by "strong" Stolypin meant those who, if given independent control over their land, could and would farm it successfully, or at least were likely to do so, *not* peasants who were already well off. His wording also implicitly recognized the force of one of Stolypin's basic policy judgments—that it was generally desirable for productive resources to flow into the hands of those most likely to enhance their productivity (as resources would in a well-functioning market economy).

But Maklakov's 1910 discussion also used some of the rhetoric of Stolypin's most vituperative critics, suggesting that the reform would "take" from one set of peasants and "give" to another. In fact, although the reform was more advantageous for some peasants than for others (as would be true of any adjustment in legal rights), it didn't "take" land from or "give" land to anyone—except to the extent that it shifted rights *within* a given peasant family. That shift represented the reformers' replacement of family ownership, which had governed allotment land, with individual ownership.

That adjustment was the subject of Maklakov's severest criticism in his 1910 article. Formerly, if we put aside the uber-ownership of the commune (with its power to control the timing and character of cultivation, and periodically to redistribute the parcels so that each peasant family's land would be roughly proportional to its supply of labor), the nearest thing to an "owner" of allotment land would have been an extended family unit. That meant that any decision to transfer land (itself difficult at best under commune conditions) would have involved all members of a multigenerational group. Under the Stolypin reform, ownership was reallocated to the oldest male of the family. The change had obvious potential for unfairness to the other members of the family.

Maklakov gave the example of a man with six children, whose father (the grandfather of the six) received the family's land under the reform's rule of giving the land to the senior male; he had then sold it, leaving the man and his six children poverty-stricken. Of course this is a risk in any economy with individual ownership (though it is sometimes qualified by rules like dower to protect widows or minimum shares for children at an owner's death); we depend for the most part on ordinary decency and parental affection and loyalty to keep the risk relatively low. A system that gives every family member the right to veto a sale tends to tie up resources inefficiently, but an abrupt shift to individual ownership can do violence to expectations. Maklakov believed that the reform hadn't adequately addressed the ill effects.

His concern was doubtless genuine. He elaborated on the problems in two extensive lectures that he delivered in December 1916.[6] (When the Rasputin assassins explained to him that they had the night of December 16–17 in mind for the deed and wanted him available to give legal advice in its wake, he told them his commitment to give these lectures in Moscow that very evening made it impossible; see chapter 16.) The lectures gave an elaborate account of the differences between the social premises of general civil law relating to inheritance of land (where the blood relationship tended to be key) and those of the peasants in regard to allotment land (where work, such as that of sons-in-law who labored with the family, gave rise to entitlements). Maklakov, being staunchly committed to ending the artificial division of the population into estates, clearly could not propose a reliance on the estate concept to protect peasant expectations. Instead he proposed that a special set of rights should apply to allotment land itself: although his proposal would not disturb the Stolypin reform's provision allowing a family to withdraw its property from control by the commune, it would, for that land, reestablish the intra-family property rights that had been applicable before the reform. Gradually, he proposed, blocks of land would be released from the intra-family ownership system and converted to the rules governing property rights in all other land. But he gave no details on this process of gradual release, did not address the problems of conflicting interests in getting consent to the release of a block (assuming it was to be consensual), and never confronted the costs in lost productivity for land tied up in familial ownership.

Maklakov's last intervention on property rights before the Bolshevik Revolution was a speech to the Kadets' Eighth Party Congress in May 1917.[7] He advanced a decidedly less intrusive approach than that of his party: a progressive land tax that would favor small farms but would not at one blow break up the larger, more productive properties. It may seem surprising for Maklakov to have even attempted offering a proposal at such variance with the party line, but circumstances in the spring of 1917 may have given him hope for a respectful hearing. He could reasonably have thought that wartime exigencies had softened the party's insistence on its program of massive compulsory redistribution, which, whatever one thought of its ultimate merits, was certain in the short run to upend the cyclical work of planting and harvesting. Moreover, his proposal favored small-scale over large-scale agriculture, and thus peasants over gentry, so it would have advanced oft-stated Kadet goals.

Maklakov characterized the Kadets' policy of compulsory redistribution as merely a means to the end of supporting small-scale agriculture, especially farms worked entirely by the owners and their families. This was quite an incomplete statement of the party's goals, as Maklakov well knew. After all, Miliukov and other party members actually looked forward to nationalization of the land, and for that reason opposed creating *genuine* property rights in the peasants who were to be the nominal recipients of the redistributed land.[8] Indeed Miliukov had scoffed at the idea that individual ownership was either a Russian dream or a Russian reality.[9] But Kadet orators had spoken warmly of small, family-worked farms, so it was only fair to take them at their word and offer policies that matched the rhetoric. Enough Kadet representatives might have placed that goal above compulsory confiscation to produce a majority for a policy that helped small, family-operated farms without disruptive effect.

Maklakov laid the groundwork for his proposal by referring

to the accepted understanding that small-scale Russian agriculture was considerably less efficient than medium- and large-scale production. Indeed, not only did larger tracts have higher productivity, but their productivity edge had been steadily and markedly increasing from 1861 through 1910.[10] Pointing to the wartime need for agricultural produce (the Provisional Government, as desperate for grain as its tsarist predecessor, had imitated the latter in forcing peasants to supply grain at government-fixed, below-market prices) and the long-run need for productivity imposed by international competition, he urged that it was folly to break up large agricultural holdings. The superior productivity of the large farms was not axiomatic, he said, just a function of current Russian conditions, so the government could reverse it over time, with policies helping small-scale producers to catch up. He also addressed the enthusiasts for breaking up "latifundia" who had argued that the large tracts broken up for purposes of redistribution could then be reunited for purposes of cultivation through cooperatives. Maklakov replied with the rhetorical question—did it make sense to artificially break them into pieces and then have to put them together again?

His solution was a land-tax with progressive rates, higher for large holdings, lower for smaller ones. Maklakov argued that such a tax would push the owners of large tracts either to enhance productivity, or, failing that, to sell them off into smaller parcels (for which buyers would be ready to pay more because of the lower taxes). As Maklakov saw it, this would nudge the country "painlessly and smoothly" toward both high productivity and the flourishing of small farms.

Maklakov's analysis received support from Rodichev and a few other Kadets, but not from the bulk of party representatives. Although a modern economist could poke a number of holes in his argument, that was not the ground of Kadet opposition. The party reporter for its position on agricultural policy, N. N. Chernenkov, swept Maklakov's analysis aside, saying that his and Rodichev's arguments were "so far from the basic party line that discussion of the differences of opinion would be completely fruitless."[11] The conference proceeded to adopt the standard Kadet nostrum, explicitly rejecting an amendment under which the peasant recipients would receive the land as private property.[12]

In this May 1917 speech Maklakov made no mention of the deprived heirs, even though the subject had been central to his *Russkaia Mysl* discussion of agricultural policy and his 1916 lectures. Of course by May 1917 there was no point in criticizing Stolypin, who had been assassinated in 1911, and in the Provisional Government's perilous situation it made sense to focus on reconciling Kadet attitudes with the need to produce adequate food supplies. The problem of intra-family claims made a brief appearance in an analysis he published in 1923 in a British scholarly journal, but there he passed rather quickly over to "the infinitely greater difficulties" connected with general governance issues in the countryside.[13] And in a 1927 preface to the French edition of the stenographic minutes of the Provisional Government's investigative commission, which he used as an opportunity to analyze the old regime's collapse, he seemed to give Stolypin his full due. Speaking of the agrarian reform, he didn't allude to the occasional child who lost out to the rapacity or self-indulgence or incompetence of an ancestor. Rather, he spoke of the "remarkable audacity and energy [with which Stolypin] cut the Gordian knot" and contrasted Stolypin's approach favorably with the policies and attitudes of his Kadet brethren.[14]

In a letter to Maklakov in 1944, his old friend and ally Ariadne Tyrkova-Williams criticized him for coming to his understanding of the peasant problem late in the day.[15] Her letter didn't say just when she thought he really got a handle on it: my guess is that she would have seen such an understanding in his shepherding the rights-equalization bill through the Duma in June 1916 (our next topic). But that was indeed late in the day. The Stolypin reform had been a central political issue since no later than November 1906. Four years later Maklakov tackled it, but concentrated on what he later (1923) acknowledged was a peripheral issue, perhaps in part because of a desire to agree with at least a sliver of his party's viewpoint. But from November 1906 onward, Maklakov's intellect and eloquence could have enriched the debate on the reform and perhaps led to important improvements, especially in 1910 when the Third Duma debated the reform and enacted it, somewhat amended, into a regular law. Tyrkova-Williams's rebuke seems just.

We now turn to the issue of Maklakov's work on the equalization of peasant rights and responsibilities. In the spring of 1916 Maklakov took up this issue, together with the closely related challenge of integrating peasants into local government. On March 2 he received the assignment to be reporter for the government's bill turning the October 5, 1906, equalization decree into a real statute. On April 4 he completed the committee's comprehensive report,[16] which included a revised bill, somewhat expanding the equalizations of the original decree and of the government bill. As Maklakov frequently acknowledged, in the report and on the Duma floor, the measure left a great deal to be done, even with the committee's enhancements.

Maklakov's work on the bill seems to have deepened his appreciation of how radically the Russian state was askew and how much it reflected the selfish interests of the landowner class. Observations of this sort appear constantly in his personal correspondence after the revolution. In a letter to Boris Bakhmetev, the Provisional Government's ambassador to the United States, for example, he wrote of how a moment can come in a society when a minority in a country begins to be "a burden and a cage preventing the country's development," and cites a passage in *Anna Karenina* for its "sharp observation about how hard it is for a person to condemn a situation that is personally advantageous for him." In the passage, Kitty's father observes that his son-in-law, Stiva Oblonsky (the husband of Dolly), has acquired a "post as member of a committee of a commission and whatever else, I don't remember. Only there's nothing to do there—what, Dolly, it's not a secret—and the salary's eight thousand. Try asking him whether his work is useful and he'll prove to you that it's very much needed. And he's a truthful man. But then it's impossible not to believe in the usefulness of eight thousand."[17]

The bill largely absorbed the Duma's calendar through the first half of June, taking seven days of debate. Throughout the discussion Maklakov was master of the Duma. The beginning was stormy. His initial explanation—the speech that his Bolshevik friend Alexandra Kollontai said was "very powerful, exact and successful"[18]—drove the Duma's fringes into a frenzy. Monarchists to right of him, revolutionaries to left of him, volleyed and thundered. But unlike the unfortunate six hundred in the charge of the Light Brigade, Maklakov rode not into the valley of Death but into a thorough vindication. Every amendment he opposed fell, every amendment he supported passed. After he had guided his sections through (a different reporter handled some special provisions relating to the Baltics), there was a call to recognize his accomplishment, leading to "prolonged applause for the reporter for the committee on judicial reform, Duma member Maklakov."[19]

The rules governing the continued survival of a decree under Article 87 meant that maneuvering such a bill through the Duma was a game of legislative chicken. The government's decision to offer the bill showed that it wanted the 1906 reform's continuation, but obviously it would never countenance reforms that radically transformed Russia's social system. Deputy Minister of Internal Affairs Aleksei Aleksandrovich Bobrinskii went out of his way to say that the bill did not dissolve the peasant estate and that the government had no intention of doing so.[20] As Maklakov saw it, the strategic context imposed two limits on how much the bill could add to the 1906 decree. First, the bill could not address problems whose solution would require additional, highly complex new legislation;[21] this meant that the most vitally needed change—creation of a new, all-estate system of village governance—was off the table. Second, the bill should adopt only extensions that both fitted the 1906 decree's basic concept (namely a reduction in the adverse effects of peasants' status as a separate estate) and that fitted the concept so well that the government would be embarrassed to reject the bill or have the State Council reject it. Rejection would deny peasants rights they had enjoyed for a decade unless remedied by the government's reissuance of the decree under Article 87. As for amendments that didn't fit the principle of the original decree, Maklakov tagged them "drive-by legislation."[22]

Before we look at the intense conflicts those constraints produced, we should consider Maklakov's basic pitch for the bill and its key provisions. His report included a lengthy passage from Ivan Strakhovskii's *Peasant Law and Institutions* (*Krestianskie prava i uchrezhdeniia*),[23] arguing that among all the special rules relating to peasants there was but a single right—the right, supplied by the state through its rules on allotments and periodic redistributions, to a sufficiency of land.[24] The entire system of caste isolation and the legal limits imposed by the peasants' estate status, argued Strakhovskii, fostered peasant consciousness of this claim to land and made it the central feature of their relationship with the state.[25] Isolation led to enmity; exclusive obligations gave rise to thoughts of exclusive rights; and life outside lawful norms stifled respect for others' rights.[26] Treated as wards of the state rather than as citizens, peasants were likely to focus on the entitlement they enjoyed through the allotment and redistribution activities that the state performed in its role as guardian—and guardian not of rights but of advantages provided in its discretion. It was natural for them to think that the solution to at least some of their problems lay in government decrees finishing what the emancipation in 1861 had begun: transferring *all* of a landowner's land to his former serfs (or their successors).

Always sensitive to the way economic change necessitated legal change, Maklakov pointed out that peasants had taken great steps since emancipation toward integration with the rest of society. Many had left the village and moved to the city, and yet retained ties to the village. Treating them as a separate group, assigned to performing a set of tasks under the direction of others, was a legacy of serfdom, under which the serf owners decided what work was to be done, and the serfs did it. Such a scheme was at war with current reality.[27]

The 1906 decree and the pending bill enabled peasants to *combine* receipt of a higher education or holding an official position with retention of membership in a village society, which would include retaining an interest in allotment land as well as retaining a voice in collective decisions made by the peasants they had left behind.[28] These reforms also ended the land captains' powers to arrest peasants for noncriminal behavior and to impose administrative penalties without having to justify their actions in formal proceedings. These key measures would obviously reduce peasants' isolation and could play a role in facilitating their evolution into citizens enjoying the same sort of rights as any other.

In an argument aimed at attracting a little right-wing support, Maklakov argued that even those who didn't care at all for equal rights should see the value of ending peasant isolation—a reduction of their interest in more government-ordered land transfers.[29] This brought on a rage from Alexander Kerensky, who offered a snide rephrasing of the committee's argument. In effect, he claimed, it told the peasants, "You're free of the land captains' power of arrest, so forget about your right to an adequate supply of land."[30] But Maklakov was not suggesting any sort of quid pro quo. He was arguing for movement toward a Russia where everyone could properly conceive of himself as a rights-bearing citizen, where peasants would see themselves and others in that light, and where they would both enjoy property rights as citizens in such a community and have reason to respect such rights in others.

It was obvious that curtailing the land captains' discretionary power to inflict penalties on peasants would facilitate the peasants' development as full citizens. For the provisions allowing peasants to secure a higher education or state office, even to become "gentry," yet to remain members of their village society, the theory was less obvious. The change meant that peasants with drive and ambition would continue to belong to their societies, instead of being cut off as before 1906. Peasants as a whole would benefit from the continued involvement of such people in the village society.

As a result of the 1906 decree, every village society ceased to be a purely estate institution, even if peasants were a majority of its members.[31] This change sharpened the question of equalization of rights. By introducing people from privileged orders into the estate that was assigned all the dirty work, it posed a choice for the decree's drafters (and for those drafting the bill in 1916): one could equalize rights and duties in village societies, and thus require peasants who were educated or in state service or otherwise had achieved higher status to bear the in-kind obligations of the peasantry (all the local scut work needed for public goods such as roads), or one could release such privileged peasants from these obligations and thus introduce a flagrant inequality among members of village societies. The change to a multi-estate village society not only made inequality among those living in the village obvious but also deprived that inequality of any rationale whatever; its prior rationale had really been little more than the fact that that was the way things had worked under serfdom.[32] The decree and the government bill had resolved the question in favor of the privileged peasants, enlarging their privileges to include relief from these burdens. The committee bill, taking advantage of a 1904 Senate ruling that had authorized persons subject to the burdens to get others to perform them by agreement (compare, for example, a U.S. Civil War draftee's right to hire a substitute), changed the government draft and provided instead that all members of a village society be treated alike (though free, of course, to exercise the options provided by the 1904 ruling).[33]

Anomalies in the burdens on village society members who had gone on to state service or higher education were, for Maklakov, a vivid example of a more basic anomaly: that one estate provided most of the local public services all on its own, without compensation, while everyone else enjoyed the benefits scot-free. It underscored the urgency of creating a suitable unit of local self-government, presumably some sort of all-estate township.[34] His Report's introductory words quoted the language of Stolypin in introducing the decree of October 5, 1906, reasoning that relief of the peasants from their special burdens required reform of local government.[35]

Indeed, in the years between the initial decree and Maklakov's efforts in June 1916, there had been ongoing efforts to implement the basic idea of an all-estate township government. These had generally been stymied by the clash between landowner desires for overwhelming voting advantages and strong bureaucratic powers of supervision over the actions of the local government, on the one hand, and the Kadet preference for a more democratic franchise and less state supervision, on the other. Negotiations on the subject continued under Stolypin, and a compromise bill passed the Duma in May 1911. Reform efforts continued after his assassination, in the period when Makarov was minister of internal affairs, but ground to a halt when Nikolai Maklakov assumed that post in December 1912. In 1914 a State Council committee amended the Duma bill to make it less reformist, but the State Council itself, presumably in part because of Nikolai Maklakov's lack of enthusiasm, refused by a narrow vote even to discuss the bill.[36] In August 1915, two months after Nikolai's dismissal as minister, the Kadets reintroduced the bill that had earlier passed the Duma. It was referred to the committee on local self-government, where it languished.[37]

The bill pending in June 1916 could not—without stepping out of the framework created by Article 87 and losing any serious prospect of approval by the State Council—attempt to create an all-estate government. But Maklakov plainly saw the Duma's consideration of the bill as a preface to genuine political integration of peasants and privileged. But for the preoccupation with the war, his advocacy of such a local government might have led to productive legislation.

Much of the Duma debate arose out of the clash between the limits on how far the Duma could go in extending the 1906 decree (*not* extensions requiring significant new legislation, and *not* extensions stepping out of the decree's basic concept, that is, not "drive-by legislation"), as Maklakov saw those limits, and the desire of Duma members to use the occasion to end restrictions imposed on Jews and others classified as "non-Russians" (*inorodtsy*). Maklakov believed that one couldn't seriously claim that amendments eliminating restrictions on "non-Russians" belonged to the decree's concept of relieving peasants of estate-based restrictions.

But he and the committee could, and did, amend language in the original decree that by a misunderstanding had adversely affected Jews. The Senate had mistakenly read a misplaced phrase, "except non-Russians," as requiring that Jews be denied passports of indefinite length.[38] The Duma's more unhinged anti-Semites took this correction (or pretended to take it) as a full-scale removal of all restrictions on Jews; by the same token, the left lambasted Maklakov and the bill for failing to do what the anti-Semites pretended the bill did.

The left, most ardently and frequently represented by Kerensky, never responded directly to Maklakov's strategic argument for not including full Jewish emancipation. Instead, Kerensky claimed that a failure to emancipate Jews would "set the oppressed against each other."[39] His tag-team partner, Akakii Chkhenkeli, a Menshevik, made a comparable fact-free argument—that the inequality of rights for Jews was based on inequality of rights for peasants.[40] He didn't explain how or in what sense this might be true. Maklakov responded, "Yes, it is our shame that non-Russians do not enjoy the right of state service, our sin, but if you would relieve our non-Russians of this, why would you not lift it from our peasants who have so long borne it? And if we are relieving the peasantry of it, why do you say we are doing nothing?"[41] He also turned the strange Kerensky-Chkhenkeli argument around, arguing that relief of the peasants would only strengthen the argument for relief of Jews: "When there are no longer 80,000,000 [peasants] deprived of rights in Russia, then no one will dare say that we must impose limits on 7,000,000 people of another faith. (*Applause from the left and center.*)"[42]

The rightist opponents offered equally curious arguments. The ever reliable Markov II proposed several times that the solution to the peasant problem was to give them the land belonging to Russia's German, Austrian, and Turkish citizens.[43] After proposing this giveaway of others' rights, he said, "You're rushing to allow Jews into the peasant village society, but the peasants themselves won't allow it, because they understand that you want to destroy the peasant estate, destroy Russia, and subject it to Jewish capital."[44] Markov's performance included a nice, if backhanded compliment for Maklakov. After lumping Kerensky and Maklakov together as "bowing before Great Jewry," he implicitly acknowledged Maklakov as far more deft than Kerensky at advancing the cause of Jewish emancipation, declaring, "I must say, I don't fear Kerensky, but Maklakov."[45]

One of the ways that the 1916 bill went beyond the 1906 decree casts an interesting light on rule-of-law reform. Existing law gave a village society the power (subject to confirmation by officials of the Ministry of Internal Affairs) to expel a member for behavior that was "harmful or depraved"—but not criminal.[46] Expulsion itself seems bad enough; it turned the victim into a kind of vagrant. But expulsion also typically entailed exile to Siberia.[47] Driven mainly by concerns over the effect on Siberia of an influx of rejects from European Russia—including these peasant expellees but also, in much greater numbers, criminals (mostly nonpolitical) and other administrative exiles—the government had in June 1900 adopted a law giving the Ministry more leeway in handling those driven from their villages, allowing it to settle them in places other than Siberia. It also cut out the ability of societies of petty bourgeois (*meshchane*) to order these expulsions at all. But it left the expulsion power of peasant village societies in place.[48] Maklakov's bill took the step of denying village societies that power.

The right wing attacked the change, claiming to speak for the interests of the peasantry and exalting peasant judgment on expulsions. (As Rodichev pointed out, when it came to matters of peasant voting rights, the right was not so sure of peasant judgment.)[49] Maklakov responded that other estates had their troublemakers, but no one saw that as justifying a rule that would allow them to drive the miscreants to Siberia without a trial, without a conviction, without evidence.[50] He noted that Stolypin had promised repeal of administrative exile altogether, and he would have loved to have included such a repeal in the bill; but since it was well outside the scope of the 1906 decree, the main effect of doing so would be to give the bill's opponents an excuse to oppose it altogether. Thus he had confined the measure to excising this special device for treating peasants lawlessly.[51]

But Maklakov didn't rest his attack on this element of the exile system on the goal of equality between estates. First, he argued, since exile required confirmation by non-peasant authorities, including the land captains, in effect the system enabled the peasants to exile only those whom the authorities wanted to exile. Second, responding to a claim that removing the power of expulsion would stimulate vigilante justice, he argued that in fact the power represented precisely the sort of arbitrariness that would inspire additional vigilantism. It gave peasants a right to denounce each other; it set them at odds with each other; and it enabled the authorities to disclaim responsibility for disorder in the countryside.[52]

The debate illustrates a complexity of rule-of-law reforms. It is nice to think that the opponents of rule-of-law reform would be only members of the elite who are typically in the best position to brush the law aside. But peasants were on both sides of this dispute. There were many peasants whose safety or quiet had been disturbed by offenders removed under this power, offenders whose behavior was not criminal or who for any of a number of reasons could not be successfully prosecuted.[53] But exposing people to the risk of such expulsion and exile was hardly consistent with the rule of law. It was plain to Maklakov that progress toward a constitutional regime required protection against government arbitrariness even when it might superficially appear to enhance social peace and to protect good citizens from nasty ones.

In the end, the bill was never presented to the State Council, and thus never took effect. In his writings in emigration, Maklakov analyzed the workings of Article 87 and argued that, in cases where the Duma wanted to add improvements to a decree in the course of its conversion into a statute, it had an advantage: the State Council would be reluctant to reject the amended law and thereby to shoulder responsibility for destruction of the benefits introduced by the decree under Article 87.[54] True enough; this was indeed the basis for Maklakov's addition of improvements to the bill. But his analysis disregarded the simple device by which the State Council could escape the bind, as it did in this very case: inaction, neither accepting nor rejecting the amended bill. This left the original decree in place, without the Duma's improvements.

So far this chapter has addressed mainly the substance of the 1906 decree and the 1916 bill, and the strategic bind faced by Duma members supporting further improvement. But the debate also provided a platform for Kerensky, who in March 1917 would become the Provisional Government's first minister of justice, and soon thereafter its "Minister-President," the government's dominant official. His performance in the debate may be instructive as to what lay ahead for the Russian people.

Kerensky in fact supported what the bill did.[55] To be sure, as we saw in relation to equal rights for Jews, he thought it did not go far enough. Fair enough—to a modest extent his comments in the debate argued the merits of various extensions. But the bulk of his eloquence was devoted to other matters: the unalloyed evil of Stolypin and of the United Nobility; the wondrous quality of the First Duma in comparison to the defects of a Duma elected on the franchise law adopted in the coup of June 3, 1907; and the dereliction of the committee reporter (Maklakov) in failing to recognize these truths.

In all this Kerensky displayed an indifference to facts and a lack of focus. On the issue of extending equalization to Jews, he argued that the idea of *not* addressing solutions for Jews and other non-Russians dated back to Stolypin, insinuating that Maklakov was somehow Stolypin incarnate.[56] Expatiating on the wickedness of Stolypin (and by association, Maklakov) naturally took him to a discussion of the field courts martial,[57] in which he overlooked the fact that Maklakov had led the attacks on that now long-dead institution. (The modern reader, plowing through all this, enjoys a shiver of delight when a voice pops up from the right, shouting, "It's boring, all this old stuff.")[58]

Kerensky offered no clue as to how that sin of Stolypin had any bearing on the Duma's turning his October 5, 1906, decree into law, which Kerensky recognized was a good thing to do. The whole effort to tar Maklakov with a Stolypin brush was odd. As Maklakov replied, he had been a determined foe of Stolypin, but felt the need to recognize his service when he accomplished something valuable, such as the October 1906 decree. "For me, to recognize when my opponent is right, to recognize the deserts of my political foe, is a duty of political honor and I have here fulfilled it."[59]

Although Maklakov had consistently downplayed the significance of the 1906 decree, and even more the bill (whose main effect was to change the legal status of the decree's rules), Kerensky suggested that Maklakov had claimed that the decree had repealed the estate condition of the peasantry, a claim Maklakov had never made.[60] Kerensky also seemed to feel it useful to insult those supporting the decree and the bill (even though he was actually among them), saying that "if you cared about justice, you would start, as did the First Duma, with repeal of the privileges of the gentry."[61] What useful purpose could he have expected to achieve with the implication that the active proponents of the bill didn't care about justice? And Kerensky's comparison to the First Duma was way off. As Maklakov pointed out, it had done nothing like repeal of the gentry's privileges, though it had entertained and sent to committee any number of general proposals to be developed into bills.[62] Finally, it was absurd of Kerensky to pretend that he favored complete removal of all distinctions: if that occurred, peasant allotment land would, like ordinary property, be fully marketable to non-peasants as well as peasants, while in fact Kerensky and his fellow travelers staunchly opposed full marketability, believing it would lead to peasants' selling off their land and falling into penury.[63]

Two nonsubstantive aspects of Kerensky's speeches are striking. First, he often gives a slanted version of a supposed quotation from Maklakov (from either the Report or his speeches in the Duma), and when called on the distortion produces a bowdlerized version of the initial statement in defense. Maklakov was probably foolish to call him on any of these, but one can understand his irritation. Second, while his own speeches were wall-to-wall ad hominem arguments, he reacted with high dudgeon to the slightest criticism of himself. A thin skin doesn't look well on a bully.

Maklakov's wind-up on June 9 is worth quoting:

> Between Kerensky and his fellow travelers and me there is no common language. And the reason is quite clear. We have completely different tactical positions. Mine is to advance this law, not to make beautiful speeches. And to advance it means to keep it within its boundaries and to remove all that would likely destroy it. While we live in a constitutional order we must know that constitutional life requires compromise. Kerensky has a different position. He would be glad if the Duma rejected the law, and threw off the mask, as they like to say. This would expose the illusion and show that it's impossible to hope for peaceful legislation in a June 3 Duma. Of course in truth the peasants would gain nothing, but then they could read his attractive, beautiful speech. . . .
>
> Sometimes I listen with great surprise to the praise of the First Duma that comes from the benches of the extreme left. The position that its fellow travelers had taken at the time was that their task was to discredit the Duma, and they couldn't find enough swear words to reproach it for its timidity, its pliability, its backwardness. And when the party to which I belong proposed a law requiring that public meetings be allowed without the government's permission, the left called this a prison law. Perhaps if enough time passes you will have a kind word to say about the decree of October 5.

> And I don't doubt that you, Alexander Fedorovich Kerensky, will enjoy cheap laurels, but laurels all the same. You will have success for a day. But the main thing is that it is easier to give the most eloquent speech than to resolve even the smallest question in peasant legislation. (*Applause from left, center, and the left part of the right.*) But woe to the popular legislature that believed that by such acts of legislation [the sort of broad proclamation favored by Kerensky] one could resolve the peasant question, woe to the country that, sympathizing with you, failed to understand that by such measures freedom cannot be obtained: freedom isn't easily secured—by these measures you might win a battle, but you would always lose the campaign. (*Stormy and prolonged applause from left, right, and center.*)[64]

Typically Maklakov received applause from the left and perhaps the center, plus, rarely, from "scattered benches" on the right. Here his speech seems to have resonated across the spectrum.

One cannot reach a final judgment on a political figure simply from his performance in a single two-week debate. Certainly I don't want to suggest that Maklakov would have been able to succeed where Kerensky so obviously failed—in leading the Provisional Government to a just peace and a stable, liberal form of government. But it was members of the Fourth Duma, most of them likely present for large portions of the June 1916 debate, who chose the Provisional Government's first cabinet. What could they have been thinking?

CHAPTER 13

Reforms and Reform

An Appraisal

MAKLAKOV WAS IN THE DUMA from 1907 to 1917. Did he and the Duma accomplish much by way of reforms, and, more subtly, did the Duma gradually mature as a legislative body? On the first question, the record of real accomplishment is painfully skimpy.

First, did Maklakov's and others' work spotlighting misbehavior by the regime actually change that behavior? With a minor and debatable exception, the answer appears to be no. The exception is the possibility, suggested in chapter 7, that Maklakov's depiction of the field courts martial as a state-destroying rather than a state-saving institution might have led the government to taper off its use more quickly than in the absense of his speech. But the case for any such link is highly speculative. The trend of its use was already down sharply, and we don't know either the government's earlier plans or the severity of the crimes allegedly involved (which might tell us whether Stolypin carried through on his apparent commitment, on the floor of the Duma, to limit its use to the worst offenses).

As to reliance on the extraordinary security laws and agents provocateurs, the most that could be said is that regime misconduct may have declined roughly in step with the decline in anti-regime violence; but recall Maklakov's wonder at how the ministry of internal affairs managed to find 2,000 people worthy of exile per year as of 1910, when the 1905 Revolution's unrest had largely abated. And there appears to be no trend line in the executive's practices of muscling the judiciary and appointing tractable people, forms of misbehavior that would be hard to detect or to measure objectively. The use of Article 87—which was in any event relatively unimportant, because its own rules severely limited the life span of Article 87 decrees that the Duma really disliked—was too episodic to create any kind of meaningful pattern. And Maklakov failed in his effort to limit the executive's ability to remove troublesome deputies through a narrow interpretation of the rules on exclusion of Duma members convicted of crimes.

What of actual reform legislation? The only realm where we can identify real success is the judiciary, where the reform finally enacted in 1912 advanced judicial independence and law-based adjudication: the justices of the peace were restored to the countryside under terms that (thanks in part to Maklakov) were more protective of judicial independence than in the government's bill, and the role of the ministry of internal affairs in control of the township courts (in both selection of judges and appeal) was extinguished. And the newly restored rural justices of the peace were free of such interference. Both systems were integrated with higher-level courts that were potentially capable of developing legal norms. These aren't trivial accomplishments, but they occurred so late in the day that they had little chance, before Russia's entry into the war, to sink roots in the countryside or inspire the Duma to enact follow-on reforms.

As to the rest, there were three different stages at which Maklakov and the views he propounded might fail: rejection in the Duma; succumbing to Duma inertia; or acceptance in the Duma followed by rejection or inertia in the State Council. He experienced each kind. His efforts to protect national minorities—by thwarting government efforts to undermine Finnish legislative independence and the status of Poles—were rejected in the most emphatic way: the Duma voted up the very legislation he attacked. On two very big issues, ending the Pale of Settlement and improving the meager remedies available against lawless officials, his advocacy failed to carry the bills through to Duma approval. Finally, the bill on Old Believer freedom passed the Duma but failed to overcome resistance in the State Council.

In the middle of the Third Duma's life span, Maklakov himself offered an appraisal on a par with this lugubrious report card. In his report to his constituents that was later published in *Russkaia Mysl*, he noted that interest in the Duma had fallen. He attributed this to various unidentified "scandals," but dismissed them as optical illusions and unimportant for the working of the Duma as a legislature. He relayed some then-current (1910) opinion on the Duma, including the accusation that it accomplished nothing. "It improved nothing, it made nothing worse. It vindicated neither the hopes nor the fears held for it." But he argued that, in fact, in its 3rd Session the Duma had failed to meet even that low standard: "The session wasn't fruitless; it made matters worse."[1] His main examples were its actions on the Finnish and Polish nationality issues, where, as we've seen, it didn't merely fail to adopt reforms but affirmatively approved the government's nationalistic proposals.[2]

Every so often Maklakov used the Duma itself to deliver similarly gloomy ratings. In December 1908, for example, he expressed his frustration with its inability to push the government toward observance of the spirit of the October Manifesto.

> If [the government] has turned its back on the October Manifesto, that's the matter of its opinions, its conscience. But we know that the country is losing its trust in the Duma, because it thinks either that the Duma is powerless in failing to implement the principles of the manifesto, or that the Duma no longer believes in those principles. This loss of the Duma's authority flows

> from the anti-Duma, anti-Octobrist policy that the government follows and that it offers the Duma, which discredits the Duma and by which it seeks to finish off the Duma in public opinion.[3]

More optimistically, he went on to suggest that, although there was now every reason to have lost faith in the government, there was enough of a gap between the government and the Duma majority to retain some hope for the Duma.[4]

Then again, in May 1914, he gave a speech using the Beilis case as an illustration of the government's utter lawlessness. In closing, he alluded to the words of the tsar at the opening of the First Duma, when he had said he hoped "to see Russia prosperous, comfortable, content." But "these people" (unidentified public figures, perhaps the so-called court camarilla or body of reactionaries with easy access to Nicholas II, whom Maklakov saw as guiding government policy), on whom the realization of that dream depended, were either unable or unwilling to realize it. Then, in a phrase probably reflecting the Lena Goldfields massacre of 1912 but also foreshadowing war and revolution, "We already feel what before we only foresaw, we see fields of grief, tears and, perhaps, blood."[5] His peroration tried to prod both Duma and government with expressions of near despair about the absence of reform:

> We must understand that if this movement [popular impatience with the government's policy of repression without reform] passes us by, passes by the Duma, the movement which was basically lawful, but can no longer live lawfully, if this movement turns to unlawful means, working not through us but around us, that is the beginning of the end. . . . And therefore we have to understand what the historical moment we're living through demands of us—not us the opposition, but the Duma—as the symbol of the peaceful life of our country. From you [the Octobrists] who seven years ago stood in the name of order on the side of the authorities, the historical moment demands that you show the country that you understand what is happening . . . , that at this moment, as a wise French writer [Berryer] said,

> "There is only one way to stop a revolution, and that is to make a revolution." You cannot allow the country to become convinced that the Duma doesn't count. And if you then stood on the side of the authorities in the name of order, now you must stand against the authorities in the name of order, and if they, madmen, do not understand what they are doing, you must accept the first blows of the enemy. (*Prolonged applause from the left and the left part of the center.*)[6]

In his public writings and his correspondence after the revolution, Maklakov offered a somewhat different assessment of the Third and Fourth Dumas (the "June 3 Dumas," to use the left's punchy label for them). In these writings his language suggests that the Duma was maturing, and that, over time and with a little luck, it could have developed into an effective force for reform and become the core political organ of a liberal democratic state. In *State and Society*, he referred to 1907–1914 as a kind of healthy corrective to the immediately preceding "fast jump." The period was, he said, "a quieting and sobering up," but not reaction. "It strengthened the existing popular representative body, it enabled the reforms of 1905 to succeed. The people who dreamed of a restoration of autocracy became fewer in those years, so it was not a real period of reaction."[7] A little later in the same book he contrasted the post–June 3 Dumas favorably with their predecessors: "For the real growth of society dramatic episodes aren't needed. Thus it was in the gray epoch of the Third and Fourth Dumas, not in the stormy 73 days of the First Duma, that a constitutional order sank roots into Russia. The ordinary citizen felt the defects of our system."[8] I take the last sentence, about the defects felt by the ordinary citizen, to refer to citizens' increasingly sophisticated grasp of what reforms were needed.

In his 1927 preface to the minutes of the Provisional Government's commission investigating the old regime, he responded to the dismissal of the Third and Fourth Dumas by "liberal opinion," a dismissal that sounds very like his own words in 1914, by pointing to specific, if low-level, contributions:

> The country saw only one thing, that it was not moving forward. And this time it blamed not only the government, as was its habit, but the Duma itself. Liberal opinion was unjust. It was unwilling to acknowledge even the Duma's serious merits: the careful examination of the budget, services rendered on its own initiative to national defense, the introduction of control even into the territory of the enemy—i.e., control over the acts of the all-powerful bureaucracy, etc. These successes, to be sure not brilliant, but real, were unappreciated. Public opinion was interested in the dramatic side of political life, scenes of conflict between the Duma and the authorities, in ringing discourses, and was deceived by the too prosaic attitude of the Duma.[9]

He then went on to argue that, as the country focused on dramatic conflicts between government and Duma, the revolutionaries and Duma opposition (mostly the Kadets) "rose in popularity as the Duma sank."[10]

The proposition that the Duma (and perhaps the politically alert more generally) were maturing is in essence an argument that its members were actually learning something valuable. Maklakov makes that argument, perhaps obliquely, in correspondence in 1923. He addressed the claim, central to the iconography of the First Duma, that the Duma needed more power. No, he said. Most of the Duma's conflicts with the government were a tempest in a teapot. And more power for the Duma would not have produced solutions: "It [the First Duma] didn't understand the main question."[11] Here, Tyrkova-Williams's reproach to him for his lateness in grasping the peasant question seems relevant. If it took even a level-headed and rather discerning deputy such as Maklakov till 1916 to see the scope of the peasant issue, then it seems reasonable to suppose that time could have advanced the thinking of most politically alert citizens, especially time in which an elected national legislative body openly wrestled with public issues. Citizens and deputies alike would presumably become more sophisticated on the issues and the need for compromise, and deputies would improve their technical skills in such tasks as drafting legislation. Maklakov himself, though already a skilled lawyer, seems to have benefitted from his legislative experience. In his memoirs, discussing his shepherding the bill on equalization of peasant rights through the Duma, he reports repeated meetings with the peasant deputies and assistance from them, and conveys an image of mutually beneficial exchange.[12] He thus seems to have exemplified the process.

But Maklakov's shift from dim appraisals of the Duma during its life to cautious postmortem praise cries out for explanation. Two possibilities come to mind. Possibly the full horror of the Bolshevik revolution made the regime's 1907–1917 recalcitrance and reaction seem less offensive than they had at the time, and therefore his own philippics against that regime (and the Duma's seeming acquiescence) a bit overdone. (I have found no explicit acknowledgment of any such reappraisal.) Or he may have known perfectly well at the time of delivery that his philippics were overstated but felt they were justified by the need to stir the Duma to more independence and the regime to more flexibility. The two possibilities are by no means mutually exclusive.

Whether the Duma and politically conscious society were evolving in a constructive direction seems impossible to assess. Perhaps a sophisticated computer analysis of deputies' words in the Duma, or of public intellectuals' writings in Russia's early-twentieth-century equivalent of today's Op Ed columns, could detect trends in the use of invective versus serious policy arguments. Absent such analysis, we have to accept the fact that the Duma's accomplishments were few and its maturation at best uncertain.

There remains the question of whether two of the great flaws that the left espied in the Fundamental Laws—Article 87 and the need for State Council approval for passage of a law—were of much consequence. As to Article 87, the answer seems fairly easy. There was no law enacted as a decree under Article 87 that survived for long in the face of genuine Duma opposition. The two decrees of consequence were the October 5, 1906, decree on the equalization of peasant rights and the November 9, 1906, decree on property rights in allotment land. As we saw, the Duma, including even its left, affirmatively embraced the first, though arguing (along with Maklakov) that it didn't go far enough. As to the second, it was plainly in jeopardy in the Second Duma, and thus would likely not have survived in the absence of the June 3, 1907, coup d'état. But it was the coup d'état, *not* Article 87, that preserved Stolypin's property rights measure.

What of the need for State Council approval for a bill to become law? There is no doubt that the State Council caused the death of the Duma-approved reductions in burdens on the Old Believers. But apart from that, its role was in practice modest. The bill ending the Pale of Settlement died (or at least went into a coma) in a Duma committee, so the views of the State Council were of no consequence. The government's legislation against the Finnish and Polish national minorities passed the Duma itself; again, the State Council caused no additional trouble.

On judicial reform, the State Council preserved the township court—thus reversing the Duma, whose bill would have discarded it—and watered down some of the Duma's provisions giving independence to the restored rural justices of the peace (for example, the ones relating to property qualifications and choice of the head of an assembly of justices of the peace). But in saving the township courts, the State Council cut out some of their most troublesome features—the role of the land captains in selecting the peasant judges and in appeals. The result was a restoration of something like the rural justice system before 1889, with two courts (township and justices of the peace) with partially overlapping jurisdictions and thus with a measure of competition between them. The competition provided a chance for comparison and thus perhaps a better basis for future legislative choices. So the State Council intervention here was by no means a total defeat for reform.

The reforms proposed for suits challenging official lawlessness died without help from the State Council: Maklakov's amendment on criminal suits was defeated in the Duma, and his effort to direct a committee to come up with proposals to improve civil remedies never secured a Duma vote. Again, the State Council was inconsequential.

Finally, the bill to replace the decree equalizing peasant rights passed the Duma but was never presented to the State Council. This seems like a death wound from the latter. But, as Maklakov repeatedly stressed, the most important aspect of the bill was to put the broader issues of peasant rights and their role in local self-government on the agenda. The fact that reformers achieved neither goal—enactment of the bill into law and a serious tackling of local self-government—may be due more to the war than to State Council recalcitrance.

In short, then, the State Council clearly had some capacity to thwart reform, but in practice seems to have played but a modest role from 1907 to 1917.

That judgment, however, depends on the comparatively conservative character of the Third and Fourth Dumas. Had the pre–June 3 franchise survived, clashes between the two legislative bodies would have obviously been more frequent and severe. If we accept the idea that the Duma in its 1907–1917 form was learning to be an effective legislature, we must qualify the idea—an effective legislature, yes, but one with little appetite for liberal reform.

But time and circumstances might have nudged it into becoming a transformative legislature. Consider the nineteenth-century British Parliament, which effected not only substantive reform (for example, repeal of the Corn Laws) but changes in the franchise that constantly increased the proportion of Britons having a say in government. Russian civil society was burgeoning during the Third and Fourth Dumas.[13] Had it been allowed to pursue a peaceful course, it seems likely to have become ever more willing and able to press for changes that corresponded to the needs of an open society.

Instead, of course, Russia's entry into World War I radically altered matters. War is hardly a favorable incubator of liberal democracy. Its exigencies tend to make societies more tolerant of government arbitrariness, even to the point of welcoming it, and the case for the rule of law correspondingly weakens. Brandishing violence becomes the state's primary activity. And although that violence is subject to certain regularities (for example, rules of thumb that help predict the outcome of a battle), these regularities are radically different from the norm-infused principles of law that Maklakov had sought to promote in the decade before the Great War. Although the conduct of war encourages a kind of pulling together against the external foe, it also involves government cultivation of venom, hatred, and paranoia toward that foe and internal ones, real or imagined.[14] Such passions seem likely to still or even anaesthetize the spirit of compromise that Maklakov stressed, time and again, was the essence of constitutionalism.

IV. The Slide toward Revolution

CHAPTER 14

National Liberals

MAKLAKOV NEVER TRIED ANY of the drastic remedies available for the divergence between his views and the Kadets'—switching to another party, founding a new one, or trying to engineer a takeover of the Kadets. But in a kind of halfway move, he became identified with a group of moderate Kadets, left Octobrists, and some Progressives, known collectively as "national liberals." A major strand in their thinking relates to foreign policy (an issue so far neglected here); the national liberals favored a relatively confrontational approach, above all toward Austria, Russia's rival for influence in the Balkans. Related activities of the national liberals include the founding of a national liberal newspaper, *Russkaia Molva* (loosely, *Russia Speaks*), which published a daily paper for about eight months in 1912–13; the efforts of many political figures, including Maklakov, to form a centrist legislative bloc; and relatively open disputes between Maklakov (and like-minded Kadets) and his party. Finally, we consider why Maklakov never went into open rebellion against the Kadet leadership.

In chapter 10 we saw how two of Maklakov's persistent concerns, the rule of law and respect for the distinct cultures in the Russian empire, led him to be quite supportive of Russia's national minorities, especially the Finns and the Poles. One might expect that someone who thought Russia should not push her domestic minorities around would, in a parallel spirit, favor a policy of avoiding confrontation with Russia's neighbors. Maklakov evidently did not see it that way.

His views surfaced clearly when Austria annexed Bosnia-Herzegovina in 1908. The Congress of Berlin in 1878 had approved Austrian occupation of the area but left its ultimate fate unresolved and presumably subject to future agreement of the great powers. In October 1908, Austria unilaterally annexed the region. Annexation didn't add to Austrian control, which was already total. But the formal shift, changing Austria's claim from indefinite to permanent tenure, set off an international crisis. In late October, Maklakov delivered a speech entitled "Serbia and the Slav Culture." The forum was the Society for Slav Culture, of which he was one of the founders. The moving spirits behind the Society, especially Dmitri Shipov (who had dropped out of the Octobrist party because of its acquiescence in the field courts martial and had formed the Party of Peaceful Renewal), had intended the society to reach across all parties and be based on interest and competency in matters Slav. The group that originally agreed to participate met that standard (it included Miliukov, for example). But in fact the group selected to run the society consisted almost entirely of Octobrists—Maklakov was the only representative of any party to their left.[1]

Maklakov's speech on the Bosnian crisis was rather vehement.[2] He called the annexation "an international crime against Bosnia and against Serbia." He called the German settlements in Russia, presumably including those made at the invitation of Catherine the Great, "colonization," and he imputed a "sinister character" to them. He specifically attacked the idea that Slav interests (Polish,

Czech, or Balkan) could be fulfilled within the Austro-Hungarian Empire. Not explaining why the dual empire of Austria-Hungary might not mutate into a triple empire by changing the status of its Slav regions, he declared that the position of the Austrian Slavs could be resolved only by a "victory outside of Austria."

Further, he attacked the left-wing idea that a nationalistic policy abroad would be a distraction from internal reform. He suggested, to the contrary, that a rebirth of national feeling would be good for reform: "Isn't a people's national feeling the same as an individual's personal feeling of worthiness?" In a slight variation on the types of nationalism that he invoked in discussing national minorities, he decried a "bad" kind of nationalism, which compensated for national abasement (of an unspecified kind) with actions against Finns, Poles, Jews, and Ukrainians, and saw in those actions a satisfaction of national feeling. At this point in the talk, according to the newspaper account, there was a prolonged outburst of applause (presumably based on audience dislike of the bad kind of nationalism). At that, a policeman broke up the meeting. Maklakov got out a few last words, "Our nationalism is not like that."

The newspaper account of the speech went on to say, "The lecturer would have said, if he could have gone on: That from the point of view of the progressive parties we should rejoice that in the lawful feeling of national rebirth there is a worthy content, that seeks the defense of the weak, defense of Slav nationalities against their oppressors, that acts in the name of the idea of freedom and equality."

Thus the message seemed to be that Slavs should cast their lot with the Russians (and the converse), and should abjure any possible future with the Austrians. Why? Later Maklakov speeches contained standard allusions to "our Slav brothers," but here he invokes a variant of Russian nationalism that "acts in the name of the idea of freedom and equality." At the time it was hardly obvious that those ideas would flourish better under Russian than Austrian influence. Austria's record included its 1867 self-transformation into the Austro-Hungarian Empire, based on a rough equality between those two national components. And whatever the potential of the October Manifesto and the Fundamental Laws of 1906, Russia's record left it, as Maklakov well knew, woefully short of freedom or equality. Given the weakness of these implied arguments, Slav brotherhood seemed to have a lot of work to do to justify sacrifices on either side. And what was this brotherhood, anyway? A similarity in language, and whatever experience people of long-past generations must have shared that gave rise to the linguistic similarity. Of course, another argument might be raw great-power rivalry—unmentioned by Maklakov.

The contrast with the Maklakov of domestic policy could hardly be starker. Gone are the nuances, the ability to see the other side, the search for win-win solutions. His arguments show a certain rhetorical ingenuity, as in the effort to elide nationalism and individual self-respect, but such ingenuity, untethered to an analysis of the real values at stake, seems more a deception than an example of Maklakov's characteristic rhetoric—an evocation of feelings, links, and intuitions that the listeners had long sensed but never heard so well expressed.

Dominic Lieven imputes Machiavellian *domestic* purposes to the national liberals such as Maklakov and Struve, for whom he uses a blunter term, "liberal imperialists." The less plausible the claim to idealistic purposes, the stronger the case is for Lieven's view. Nationalism had always been the regime's "great prop," he observes, and the positions taken by liberal imperialists meant competition on the same ground: "In seizing this ideal for themselves the liberals would take from the government's hands 'this flag, its only psychological resource.' "[3]

The real value of seizing a political weapon may naturally prove very different from its apparent value. On this purely empirical question—whether pursuit of a forward policy in the Balkans would actually *advance* reform—the conservative Pyotr Durnovo surely had the better argument. In a February 1914 memo to the tsar, he predicted that a general European war would tear Russia's government and society apart, probably bring on collapse of the imperial regime, and, given the lack of real authority in Russia's legislative institutions and political parties, plunge Russia into anarchy. Except for not specifying that the anarchy would end in Bolshevism, he came remarkably close to perfect foresight. With this vision of the effects of war, he advocated reconciliation with Germany, the opposite of the course implied by the national liberals' enthusiasm for Russia's Slav brothers in the Balkans.[4]

Maklakov seems not to have spoken much on these foreign policy issues. An important and telling exception is a speech in the Duma on December 7, 1912, about two and a half months after the start of the Balkan Wars of 1912–13 (September 25, 1912–July 5, 1913). In the first of these wars, Greece, Serbia, and Bulgaria succeeded in collectively conquering most of the Ottoman Empire's remaining Balkan territory. In the second, the erstwhile allies battled one another over the spoils. At the time of Maklakov's speech, the first war had ended in sweeping allied victories over the Ottomans, and negotiations over the necessary boundary adjustments were proceeding at a conference in London that included ambassadors of the six great powers that had been present at the Congress of Berlin.

Maklakov's speech was almost entirely on domestic matters; it was a vintage display of his ability to lampoon government follies and simultaneously paint an appealing picture, even for the government itself, of pursuing constitutionalism. Making what looks like a last-minute adjustment to his speech, he started by saying that he didn't want to go into detail on foreign policy, *but*, "at this critical moment when a page is being turned in world history closely linked to our national honor and our interests, we can't say that Russia speaks a language worthy of her." He went on to fault the government "for failing to say clearly that although Russia does not want war, does not want anything for herself, she knows what her merit lies in, her historic duty, and if she doesn't seek complications, at the same time she doesn't fear them." Russia, he said, had spoken in a "meek" language, not that of a great state. He closed this detour into foreign policy by expressing the hope that Russia would "not fall to the temptation to lower Russia in the eyes of Europe and give a cruel disappointment to our younger Slav brothers."[5]

What had the Russian government said that Maklakov found so "meek" and unsuitable for a great power? He doesn't specify, but, given the date, the trigger seems to have been Prime Minister Kokovtsov's speech in the Duma on December 5. Kokovtsov's speech was primarily on domestic matters, but had a brief discussion of the situation in the Balkans. He made the customary bow to Slav brotherhood, expressing "the warmest sympathy in all Russian hearts" for our friends and fellow Orthodox and for their "attainment of their vital interests." But the emphasis seemed to be much more on the government's hope of "remov[ing] for the future any expectation of new complications, which are always dangerous for European peace," suggesting that he found European peace a lot more important than the Serbs' territorial ambitions.[6] Notice that Maklakov echoed the word "complications" but gave it almost the opposite spin: in his view, Russia should say that while she "doesn't seek complications, at the same time she doesn't fear them."

In fact, unbeknownst to Maklakov or the public, Russia had acquiesced in Austria's insistence on establishing Albania with borders drawn so as to prevent Serbia from having direct access to the Adriatic (though the agreement also provided for Serbian access to the sea through an international railroad). In fact the population of Albania was not Slavic at all, so to the extent that concern for Russia's "Slav brothers" meant helping Slavs to join each other in a Slavic nation, that impulse provided no basis for objecting to the Austrian proposal. Indeed, from that perspective, the Austrian position might have been faulted for allowing Serbia to keep Kosovo, which was also ethnically non-Slav. But when Russian acquiescence in the establishment of Albania became public, the press was outraged, as it was toward Russia's generally unwarlike stance throughout the Balkan wars of 1912–13. Of the major papers, only *Rech* (*Speech*), which was controlled by Miliukov, advocated a calmer view.[7] Maklakov's nationalism seems to have been in tune with Russian sentiment—or, more precisely, the vocal element of that sentiment.

In intra-Kadet battles over foreign policy, Maklakov sounded similar themes. The battles differed from the usual ones in that on the Balkan issues it was Miliukov rather than Maklakov who was relatively isolated. Some of the party members' criticism of Miliukov suggests a curious political immaturity. At an October 12, 1912, meeting of the St. Petersburg central committee members, for instance, one of Miliukov's critics described an article by him as having more the "tone of a diplomat, a responsible minister of foreign affairs, than of a leader of the opposition."[8] In a normal moral universe, one might have thought that the highest praise. At a meeting of the Moscow branch of the central committee ten days later, Maklakov called for "preparedness," in itself not necessarily a warlike stance, but, when coupled with the general mood of zest and sympathy for Russia's fellow Slavs, and stripped of the sort of cautions that Kokovtsov stressed, it had an aggressive flavor.[9] Despite the criticism, Miliukov continued to oppose Russia's tying itself to Serb interests right up to the Austrian declaration of war on Serbia, whereupon he more or less reversed himself, becoming an ardent advocate of Russian pursuit of ambitious war aims, such as control of the Dardanelles.[10]

Maklakov's stance in 1912 (and in the whole period running up to Sarajevo) is a world apart from his views of the Russo-Japanese war in August 1904. At that time, in a speech at Beseda, he seemed to see the war mainly as an opportunity for scoring points against the regime, tying the regime to the war—which no longer presented any hope for a quick, decisive victory. More important, he disparaged the idea that a great power's loss of real estate, and thus of prestige, was of much importance: "Great powers have suffered losses and remained great. France lost Canada (and Alsace-Lorraine), England lost the United States. And for us it would not be dangerous to lose Manchuria."[11] He then returned to domestic political implications: "And even if we remain in the minority in our approach to peace, that in itself is not a problem; the agitation can still play a useful role."[12] One can argue that the Balkans were more important to Russia than the Far East, but even assuming that, the shift in tone over these eight years is striking. Whereas in 1904 Maklakov treated Russia's national prestige and great power status rather casually, in 1912 he saw them as critical.

Maklakov seems to have held to his pro-Serb position sincerely enough to have contemplated going to join the Slav brothers' fight. Lucy Bresser, soon after the start of the first Balkan war and obviously responding to a letter from him, implores him not to go, speaking with her characteristically breathless punctuation: "Darling—I can't let you go to the war—it would not be the wisest thing to do—you must remain to direct even though it seems simpler to go to the front & fight."[13] In the end he didn't go, so the impulse is incomplete evidence of his sincerity.

How could Maklakov have come to a foreign policy perspective so at odds with his position on domestic issues? We can only speculate, but a few stabs at it seem worthwhile. First, he was vastly more familiar with Russia's domestic problems. He had spent his career working on and in Russia's system of domestic institutions and law; he was perfectly situated from experience to propose remedies. Second, France had never ceased to be his great love abroad from the time of his initial visit in 1889. Given the Austrian-German alliance dating from 1879 and Franco-German hostility due to Germany's annexation of Alsace-Lorraine, a love of France lined up neatly with a readiness to confront Austria in the Balkans. Third, Fyodor Tiutchev, one of Russia's indisputably great poets, combined ardent pan-Slavism with enthusiasm for Alexander II's great reforms. To Maklakov, steeped in Russian poetry, the Tiutchev precedent may have seemed a worthy lineage for this intellectual combination. Similar elements may have been at work for Maklakov's fellow Kadets, most acutely the ties to France; after all, many educated Russians spoke French in their families and with their Russian peers. These general points are true of Miliukov as well, to be sure, but he was not only very well traveled but had long been interested in foreign affairs and was well connected abroad.

A final irony provides a fitting close to our consideration of Maklakov's Balkan imperialism. Although he was able to produce an apt Bismarck quotation for many an occasion, he seems to have completely forgotten one of the most famous: "The whole of the Balkans is not worth the bones of a single Pomeranian grenadier."

Maklakov and his imperialist advocacy became associated with national liberalism. This "ism" was never a political party but more a movement based on an amorphous set of shared political impulses. The main linking ideas were a lack of any apparent enthusiasm either for immediate universal franchise on the one hand or for the interests of the landowning gentry on the other; nationalism in foreign policy; and a belief in protective tariffs. Maklakov was a suitable adherent in terms of all but the last—a subject on which I've encountered no speech or article by him at all. National liberalism can be seen as bringing together politicians of several parties who were, roughly, middle of the road (that is, neither revolutionary nor devoted to autocracy); the movement thus served as a precursor of the Progressive Bloc that formed in 1915; otherwise it was not of great importance. But it did give birth to the newspaper *Russkaia Molva*, whose brief existence sheds light on the relation between the Kadets and Maklakov (and party members sharing his outlook).

The overall tone of *Russkaia Molva* on foreign policy is captured in a phrase in the publisher's statement of the new paper's outlook, stated in its first issue: "Russian power abroad is not a vain whim of the bureaucracy, it is *our* strength and joy."[14] *Russkaia Molva* also followed up Maklakov's Duma reference to Russia's "meekness" with a demand that the government confront Austria with an ultimatum. However one might evaluate the proposal's details, its overall tone was chauvinist, proposing that Russia say it would not permit Austria to advance "one step further" on the Balkan peninsula.[15]

Russkaia Molva was short-lived, lasting only a little over eight months, from December 9, 1912, to August 20, 1913. It evidently never won much of a place among Russian newspapers (even though it sought to lure readers with occasional pieces by major literary figures such as Alexander Blok and Ivan Bunin). In a letter written in mid-February 1913, about two months after its launch, Dmitri Shipov reported that he had heard the paper had fewer than four hundred subscribers and "negligible" newsstand sales.[16] Yet despite the paper's short lifespan and apparently slight impact, the Kadet hierarchy paid it remarkable attention—an entire central committee meeting on the day before the first issue appeared, and an extensive discussion at a party conference seven months after the paper's demise.

Miliukov introduced the subject at the December 8, 1912, central committee meeting, characterizing the paper's imminent launch as "the decision of some central committee members to publish their own newspaper," and noting that it reflected existing disagreements in the central committee. He thought the central committee should wait for a bit and then discuss the points of disagreement so as to avoid bringing central committee quarrels into the upcoming meeting of the "fraction"—the party conference scheduled for February 2–3, 1913.[17] Andrei Shingarev gave a response that seemed mildly sympathetic to the renegade central committee members (who, as everyone presumably knew, were Maklakov, Struve, and Tyrkova-Williams). The plan had been developing over two years, he said, and they had asked him to participate. He thought the paper simply grew out of their "dissatisfaction with the course of *Rech* and their desire to speak independently."[18]

Others cast the development in a more sinister light. Miliukov said that once central committee members "unite with Progressives and a group of industrialists and adopt 'non-party' as a slogan, that by itself is a major issue for the party."[19] Many of those present expressly assumed that the paper was funded by Alexander Konovalov, a leading Progressive and scion of a family of textile entrepreneurs. A. M. Koliubakin said, "The Konovalovs don't give money free," and predicted that they would want to see support for the ideas of "trade-industrial circles" (with no mention of what those ideas might be and how they might overlap with or offend Kadet principles). A. A. Kornilov thought the paper prefigured a new direction for the central committee, some sort of drawing together with the Progressives (a party dominated by figures from trade and industry), and that the new paper would be "an organ not of the Kadet party but of the Progressives and a few members of the central committee." These references to trade, industry, and "the Konovalovs" seem imbued with condescension. In his efforts at forging a liberal-commercial coalition, Maklakov saw—or believed he saw—exactly such condescension. He wrote later of how, "In the period of the Duma, a rapprochement of the intelligentsia and capital started in the famous evenings at [Paul] Riabushinskii's and Konovalov's. It was a first step, and it's curious that the intelligentsia looked on capital as from on high, adding it to its political struggle for power, to its political wishes, but as before remaining extremely negative to capital's economic desires."[20] It may seem "curious," as Maklakov thought, to find the intelligentsia acting this way, especially as the participants gathered to forge an alliance; whether it is rare is another matter.

Even Shingarev found some fault with *Russkaia Molva*'s founders. Though he thought there would be no surprise to anyone in a revelation of either Maklakov's opposition to a universal franchise or Struve's support of protective tariffs, he said, "We might have hoped that the initiators of this would have discussed the matter with their colleagues in the central committee."[21] Tyrkova-Williams, the only rebel on hand, stepped into action. First, she expressed astonishment at the speakers' confidence that the paper was funded by Progressives and industrialists, and was to be an enterprise of monied bosses. In fact, its founders were herself and

Dmitri Protopopov (a Kadet member of the First Duma, coauthor of the Kadet agrarian redistribution plan, and a signer of the Vyborg Manifesto), and the funds invested were more from Kadets than other sources. She could see how, if the Kadet party had its own journal, the *Russkaia Molva* founders might be criticized for starting their own paper without advance discussion, but *Rech* was *not* a party paper. It was a paper run by central committee members yet not responsible to the party; but no one in the central committee had criticized it on that account. And on what basis, she asked, did people claim that we of *Russkaia Molva* were Progressives? In fact, Duma and central committee members must know that the present Progressives are "a formless body." While *Russkaia Molva* wouldn't be an organ for the ideas of Struve, "he will find a place in its pages when *Rech* dogmatically limits free expression of ideas." "Must the Russian opposition have only one paper?"[22]

Ivan Petrunkevich, as chair of the meeting, precipitated its end by asking if the committee should address the question about how necessary it was to respond to *Russkaia Molva* in cases where it expressed negative views of the party or the central committee. Miliukov answered that he thought it was better not to prejudge the issue. Those present agreed to aim at a meeting with *Russkaia Molva*'s founders in January (it's not clear if that ever occurred).[23]

As it turned out, *Rech* evidently withheld its direct fire on *Russkaia Molva* for some time, but ultimately anathematized the figures behind the paper as "unKadet," a word with a rhetorical intention similar to that behind the modern "RINO"—Republican in name only. (Like all such epithets, they resound only among those who attach a lot of value to the label the criticized person is implicitly unfit to bear.) In March 1914, six months after the demise of *Russkaia Molva*, a party conference was enlivened by a brief exchange over the issue. Nikolai Gredeskul, a central committee member who was beginning to see merit in trying to work out alliances with Progressives and left Octobrists, deplored the angry mood toward *Russkaia Molva* and specifically attacked the "unKadet" label as demagoguery against mavericks. Miliukov responded that it was only when *Russkaia Molva* started "open talk against us" that he considered he had the right to attack them and to stigmatize them as "unKadet." This was somewhat disingenuous on Miliukov's part. As another central committee member had said in the meeting on the eve of *Russkaia Molva*'s appearance, an article in *Rech* had described Maklakov as the "darling" of the Octobrists, obviously intending it as a slur. The remarks of some supporters of the Kadet establishment seem a little unhinged. One speaker mentioned with horror that a Duma speech by Maklakov had received applause from the right; the speaker provided no clue as to the *content* of the speech, evidently viewing an enthusiastic response from the right, regardless of Maklakov's content and of who else was applauding, as an ample basis for condemnation.[24]

———•◆•———

A periodic bone of dissension was the issue of steps the party might take in the interest of legislative cooperation with other parties. Maklakov touched on the issue indirectly in an account he gave the central committee of why he had largely ceased to attend its meetings. In general terms, he said, he had become convinced that he offered the Kadet fraction nothing useful, and it offered him nothing useful. He then turned to three specific issues. First, in its attacks on the government's arbitrariness in the election campaign for the Fourth Duma, the party had ruined the project by using "urgent" questions (questions to the government given priority over other business by majority vote) rather than by calling for a special committee to investigate the matter systematically, as the widespread but complex abuses required. As to the party's proposal of universal suffrage, the party's basic position couldn't attract support. Finally, he thought it was pointless to insist, as a condition of Kadet participation on the Duma's military affairs committee, that leftists be appointed to the committee—a reference to a dispute over whether the party would honor the wish of Mikhail Chelnokov to serve on that committee. The reader may recall Chelnokov as one of the four Kadets who visited Stolypin on the eve of the

June 3, 1907, coup. Chelnokov made complaints parallel to Maklakov's—that the Kadets kept running after the left, for which it got only a spoke in its own wheels. He favored a tighter relation, be it with the Social Democrats or the Octobrists, in the interest of advancing real reforms.[25]

The issue of Kadet participation in the Duma committee on defense deserves a little detour. Chelnokov was very interested in defense and sought to serve on the committee. Miliukov had decreed that Kadets could not serve on it until the committee, which like the Duma generally was dominated by Octobrists, ceased to exclude deputies from the left-wing parties (presumably for security reasons). Chelnokov made it clear that the Progressives were ready to welcome him, and that if the Kadets barred him from the committee he would nonetheless accept the offer as a nominee of the Progressives. Despite intervention by the Moscow central committee on Chelnokov's behalf, Miliukov pulled what was probably a stunt, issuing a threat to resign if his will were not accepted. Chelnokov acquiesced for a time, but left the Kadet party in the fall of 1914.[26] Just what Miliukov's purposes were is unclear. But suppose the Duma leadership's exclusion of the left from the military affairs committee was based on a reasonable distrust; however admirable socialist internationalism may be in some respects, treatment of Russia's pursuit of its national interests as a nasty excrescence of capitalism might understandably inspire distrust. Critics may accordingly have traced Miliukov's action here to simple pacifism and then used that characterization as a basis for condemning his views on Balkan affairs. Although not a strict analogy, there is a parallel in the way that Churchill's zealous opposition to Indian independence in the 1930s undermined his warnings about Nazism.

On the broad strategy issues posed by Maklakov and Chelnokov, Miliukov's response is telling. He sneered at Maklakov for using (he said) possible "success" as a criterion for efforts in the Duma. The party couldn't follow Maklakov in that direction without ceasing to be the Kadet party. The party consciously made efforts "not for the Duma but for the country." And the Kadets had to court the left because they were competing with it for the support of the peasants.[27] (He never made clear just how he thought the Kadets could prevail in that competition—especially if Russia were to adopt a universal franchise—unless they matched the left's opening bid: redistribution of gentry land with *no* compensation at all.) In short, Miliukov made clear that he had a good deal of disdain not only for legislative accomplishment itself, but more corrosively for the very process of compromise, which Maklakov saw as fundamental to liberal democracy.

The December 1912 dispute in the central committee was the prelude to a more extended battle in the February 2–3, 1913, party conference. Though the printed conference records contain no speech by Maklakov, others pressed themes similar to his familiar ones. Gredeskul in particular lamented the obsessive focus on Miliukov's three "locks" (that is, the elements of Russian political life that locked out the pure parliamentary democracy that he treated as essential—the absence of a universal franchise, the State Council's veto power, and the absence of government responsibility to the Duma), problems that however you viewed them could not be quickly overcome in the absence of revolution. He deplored the absence from Miliukov's presentation of any sketch of a path forward for the country. He saw the elections to the Fourth Duma as having brought on board a group of Octobrists who were considerably more independent than those of the Third Duma; this would enhance possibilities of partnership. The argument that the three "locks" utterly doomed practical reform and thus must be overcome in advance was incomprehensible to him, a completely roundabout tactic, an abandonment of the direct path, a hiding of one's head in the sand. He wanted instead fulfillment of the October Manifesto, which, he pointed out, the Octobrist Mikhail Rodzianko had pressed in his opening speech as chairman of the Fourth Duma. Although he didn't go into detail on what fulfillment of the manifesto involved, he did specify remedying the regime's arbitrariness, which succinctly captured both the core of the manifesto and Maklakov's overall agenda. Chelnokov backed Gredeskul, opposing any limits on practical agreement with moderate elements.[28]

Miliukov made no apologies for the priority he attached to the three locks. He credited the Kadets' tactical success to his persistence on the subject, and seemed to have a genuine fear that without constant reiteration they would be forgotten—he felt obliged to deny that "every schoolboy" knew of them. And without even discussing the (concededly modest) accomplishments of the Third Duma, he insisted that no step forward was possible without overcoming the three locks. His strategy, he said, still left the party open to cooperation with others on specific issues.[29]

In the end, the conference approved a resolution that slightly modified the one proposed by the central committee in the direction of cooperation. Here is the original resolution, with the language that the conference forced on Miliukov in italics:

> Achievement of these conditions [elimination of the three locks] must be the basic task of the Kadets, and scheduled legislative activity with *other groups of* more moderate elements of the opposition and center *must be employed but* must not get in the way of these basic tasks.[30]

Thus even the amended version preserved Miliukov's priority.

Curiously, Miliukov never explained just how actual legislative accomplishment could "get in the way of" his famous priorities. It is quite easy to see the opposite—how continual Kadet flogging of the three locks might have thwarted reform. Non-Kadet deputies who were interested in real reform might be cautious about even ad hoc alliances with a party obsessed by a decade-old idée fixe, especially when at least one of the three elements (universal suffrage) was clearly unattainable without revolution.

Yet specific accomplishment—perhaps achieved by a focused negotiation and even horse-trading with potential allies in other parties—might have nudged Russia nearer to the rule of law and made it better able to avert chaos in the face of wartime stress and disaster. Reforms themselves could give citizens some sense that their lives were not subject to the whims of a free-range bureaucracy. Even more importantly, the very process could have helped the Duma develop into an institution capable of taking charge later, when army mutinies precipitated the tsar's abdication and the anarchy that Durnovo had predicted.

Despite Miliukov's priorities, a number of politicians made tries at legislative coordination among the relatively moderate parties. Maklakov was among them. Shipov recounts an attempt as early as the spring of 1908, originated by the editor of *Slovo* (Word), a paper closely attached to the leaders of the Party of Peaceful Renewal. The original invitation went to three members of that party (including Shipov and the editor of *Slovo*), three Kadets (including Maklakov and Struve), and three Octobrists. All agreed to the idea of coordination in principle. But the three Octobrists soon cooled, saying that they needed to consult the Octobrist fraction and that further efforts should be put off till the fall. The representatives of the Party of Peaceful Renewal took the message as a device to back out without doing so explicitly. Shipov chalked the failure up to party antagonisms and a failure to recognize the need for agreements in the interest of advancing shared goals of reform.[31]

A similarly fruitless effort occurred in January–March of 1914, bringing together Kadets such as Maklakov and Chelnokov, Progressives like Konovalov and Riabushinskii, some left Octobrists, some non-party intellectuals, and even a Bolshevik (I. I. Skvortsov-Stepanov). The first meeting, in Konovalov's St. Petersburg apartment, was aimed largely at legislative cooperation. But despite Kadet and Progressive readiness to compromise on local self-government reforms (rural and urban), the effort apparently foundered on Octobrist resistance to the very idea of creating an opposition center in the Duma. The second set of meetings, in Konovalov's and Riabushinskii's Moscow apartments, looked toward mobilizing pressure outside the Duma, pressure that was seen as being broad in scope (workers, peasants, bourgeois), but of somewhat unclear methods. Again the Octobrist leadership resisted, arguing that the rise of political strikes suggested a risk of return to the upheavals of 1905–1907.[32]

Miliukov's insistence on pure democracy (the universal franchise) and pure parliamentarianism was clearly not the sole cause of the opposition's remaining splintered, perhaps not even a principal cause. As Shipov remarked, the moderates lacked an urgent sense of the need for unity in pursuit of feasible reform. Ben Franklin's caution, "We must all hang together, or most assuredly we shall all hang separately," was not for them. Though not the whole reason for the moderates' failure to coalesce, Miliukov's devotion to the unattainable surely played a role.[33]

Explicit alliances with other parties might have been a palliative for Maklakov's frustration with his own, but such alliances failed to develop (until the formation of the Progressive Bloc in 1915, discussed in the next chapter). What of an effort to capture the leadership of the Kadets, to found a new party, or to bolt to an existing alternative? That Maklakov was restless is perfectly clear. In a conversation in 1908 with a political admirer, Evgenii Efimovskii, he said, "I don't understand you, why do you stay with this political rot?" The context made the site of the "rot" ambiguous, but it proved that Maklakov was referring to the Kadet party. He went on: "You're young. You have a right to a good career. You can't have it in the Kadet party. We're too full of old maids." Efimovskii turned the question around, "Why do you, one of the leaders of the party, give me this advice?" Maklakov: "Me—I'm another matter. I need credentials. I have them in the Kadet party." But Efimovskii believed that by not founding a party Maklakov had failed to seize his chance to be "a political eagle," and lived instead in a political "desert" where he could not fulfil himself.[34]

As to seizing the leadership of the Kadets, the numbers simply weren't there. In February 1914 an article in *Rech* sneered at Maklakov explicitly "for his very small group of supporters, having no influence over the party or the Duma fraction."[35] While the language was in part an effort to cow the opposition ("mau-mauing," to use Tom Wolfe's phrase), a reader of the reports of either central committee meetings or party conferences comes away convinced of Miliukov's domination.

And Maklakov's personality may not have fitted him for party leadership in any event. A diary entry of his good friend and ally Tyrkova-Williams for June 19, 1915, starts with her listening to Miliukov deliver a rehearsal of his forthcoming speech to the Duma and continues:

> Cold. A lot of trivial, old empty phrases. Shingarev, Maklakov and many others had to remind him that he needed to welcome the army. ("I implied it," he said.) . . .
>
> Maklakov, agitated . . . told how he'd spent the whole day "energizing" Rodzianko. Evidently he directly wrote a speech for him.
>
> "That's what I'd like to be tomorrow, chairman of the Duma, to be able to say all that needs to be said. Miliukov's speech won't do the job."
>
> "Right, it's bad. Only you could give a good speech, but you sold your place for a mess of pottage."
>
> "You want me to become leader?"
>
> "No, I don't. You're too flip. To me it's a shame that your talent goes to waste and Miliukov doesn't have any."[36]

Despite her admiration for him, she clearly saw his personality, encapsuled in the idea of having a tendency to be "flip," as making a bad fit with party leadership. And whatever the allusion in her mess-of-pottage line, it surely suggests a susceptibility to letting his energies be diverted, and perhaps a leaning to the role of maverick.

Some other remarks of Tyrkova-Williams hint at additional characteristics militating against him as a party founder. In a letter she observed that his popularity in widely different circles enabled him to see aspects of government policy that other Kadets were unaware of. That of course seems natural in someone who manifested, as Miliukov put it, the lawyer's tendency to see "a share of truth on the opposite side, and a share of error on his own." And her diary quotes Nikolai Nekrasov (a Kadet closely aligned with Miliukov) as saying that Maklakov never told the leadership in advance what he would be speaking about, "so I don't consider his speeches to be ones of our fraction."[37] Of course a wide acquaintance and an ability to get along with people of diverse views are great assets in a politician. But those admirable qualities, when combined with his being so independent that he didn't even alert fellow Kadets about his speaking intentions, evoke the image of a gadfly, and a gadfly who revels in his status as such. Not for him the tedious work of herding cats.

What of joining another party? Maklakov implicitly addressed the subject in an October 30, 1912, letter about the Octobrists, who had just suffered severe reverses in the elections to the Fourth Duma; indeed, the Octobrist party leader, Guchkov, had been unseated in Moscow by a Kadet. Maklakov wrote that he had often thought and occasionally observed in print that "Octobrism, as a form of liberalism distinct from Kadet radicalism and democracy, was a necessary condition for successful development of a constitution. Guchkov, as an opposition leader, is more impressive than Miliukov, and the interests of political liberalism demand that he not be cut off at the knees right now. I tried as much as I could to point our electoral campaign in that direction, and if it proved impossible it was not only because of the opposition of the party leadership but much more because of the complete lack of sympathy on the part of the voting masses."[38]

If a jump to the Octobrists was unpromising on the grounds of electoral math, what of the Progressives? I've encountered nothing on that specifically. But consider Maklakov's letter to Tyrkova-Williams in 1943:

> I could have jumped parties, but there was nowhere for me to go. There was not a single party in which I would have felt at home. . . . To do what was often suggested to me, to start a new

> party, would have been to rebuke my old comrades. I didn't like our party leaders, but the rank-and-file Kadets, the ordinary voters, whom I met in electoral meetings and with whom I often spoke, were familiar and close to me. But they themselves didn't like the leaders. I made peace with those who had support among these ordinary voters (especially in Moscow)—but to quarrel with the party leadership seemed useless and uninteresting. . . . And it wouldn't have made any difference. "It's not easy to correct the work of centuries."[39]

In the end, Maklakov's intuitive Burkean conservatism may have persuaded him to stick with the imperfect institution that he knew, and to work against the odds for its amelioration, rather than to migrate to another one, also surely imperfect.

CHAPTER 15

War—and the Mad Chauffeur

IN THE SUMMER OF 1914 Europe marched off to war. In Russian historiography, it's a hotly contested issue whether "the Revolution"—that is, a revolution roughly equivalent to that of 1917, including not only the collapse of tsarism in February but also the Bolshevik seizure of power in October—would have occurred if Russia had stayed out. For what it's worth, a couple of highly placed regime insiders, both of whom we already know, predicted that war would spell revolution: the first is Pyotr Durnovo, whom we first saw telling Maklakov's father that punishments of students for trivial matters would dissuade them from fooling around; the second is Vasily's brother Nikolai, minister of internal affairs. Durnovo wrote a lengthy memorandum to the tsar in February 1914 predicting that war would bring revolution—not a liberal but a socialist revolution. Nikolai Maklakov, shortly after the fateful cabinet meeting that sealed Russia's entry into the war, warned General Sergei Dobrorolskii, head of the General Staff's Mobilization Section, that the revolutionaries would welcome war, but he added sadly, "One cannot escape one's fate." Had he spoken up in the cabinet meeting, he would likely have been brushed aside.[1] Stolypin, who had been minister of internal affairs as well as prime minister and thus held direct responsibility for possible internal threats, might well, if he had lived, have had the same insight and been able to put up an effective fight.

Wherever the truth may lie, the war plainly created its own set of social tensions.[2] Maklakov's activity, from the start of the war until his setting out for Paris to assume his ambassadorship in October 1917, manifested an increasing readiness for risky actions in pursuit of two partially contradictory goals, victory in war and avoidance of revolution. His actions included speeches vividly decrying the government's increasing detachment from all levels of society, publication of an allegory that some of his contemporaries read as calling for a coup d'état, participation in plots to effect a coup, and entanglement in the assassination of Rasputin.

In his correspondence after the revolution he more than once expressed the view that without the war there would have been no revolution.[3] But he seems not to have explored the thought in his public writings. Simple embarrassment may explain the silence. If he thought that the war helped bring on the revolution, he would surely have to proceed to the implications: that he had been part of a nationalistic chorus, that the chorus's activity likely increased the risk of Russia's going to war, and that he had thus helped trigger conditions that brought to power the most extreme of the revolutionaries and cost Russia most of what he held dear.

Regardless of the war's role, no one should think that pre-war Russia was on a smooth course toward political reform. In April 1912 soldiers had intervened unnecessarily in a gold miners' strike near the Lena River in Siberia. After the government arrested the strike leaders, the miners marched toward the mining company offices to deliver a protest. Soldiers blocked their path and then shot into the crowd, killing between 150 and 300 miners. A judge, noting that scarcely any miners had been shot in the front, observed archly that the miners had "attacked the soldiers with their backs."[4] In the Duma, Maklakov pilloried the government for interfering in labor-management relations, for failing to fulfill the October Manifesto, and for failing to protect the weak. In such a case "the first duty of an honorable and conscientious government . . . is repentance." Instead, the government had tried to cover up its responsibility, to characterize the strike as political rather than economic (thus using the familiar scare tactic of waving the red banner of revolution), and to induce drafters of an official report to bend the truth.[5] It was the sort of episode that a sound system of judicially enforced remedies against official misconduct might have prevented or (partially) redressed.

At the end of January 1914, Nicholas II had fired Prime Minister Kokovtsov and replaced him with Stolypin's predecessor, Goremykin. Though Kokovtsov had hardly been a dynamic leader in the Stolypin mold, that deficiency was not the reason for his dismissal. Kokovtsov himself speculated that it was because of the empress's antipathy, which he saw as arising from his failure to stifle criticism of Rasputin in the press and the Duma.[6] Other explanations are available, including hostility of his fellow ministers to his insistence on government thrift, his heavy reliance on revenue from the vodka monopoly, and the tsar's false friends' exhortations to him to reassert his power over his officials.[7] Still worse, why did the tsar once more choose Goremykin? The reader may recollect his disastrous handling of the First Duma and Kokovtsov's devastating enumeration of his inadequacies just before his first appointment as prime minister, coupled with the tsar's apparent agreement with Kokovtsov and his explanation that, having offered Goremykin the appointment, he must follow through on it (chapter 5). Even Goremykin seemed to view himself as unsuitable. On his second appointment as premier, he spoke of himself as being "pulled like a winter coat out of mothballs."[8]

The tsar's uninspired selection of a prime minister matched a sense of ennui prevailing in the Duma. The Soviet historian A. Ia. Avrekh quotes a number of private letters exchanged in mid-January, even before the cashiering of Kokovtsov and resurrection of Goremykin, awash in language of fatalism and dismay. A deputy writes: "The Duma opened [after Christmas break] with half its numbers on hand, like a dead fly. They gossip, discontent, and they split apart. No one believes in the future. In a word, tedious, gray and wretched. About a hundred deputies have taken leave already, for two-to-four weeks. Many want to leave the Duma. Paralysis in the government, paralysis in the Duma, paralysis in the zemstvos. . . . Even the proverbial 'discontent' is somehow non-partisan, impersonal, mediocre. Not 'divine discontent,' but 'Katzenjammer.'"[9] Maklakov appears to have shared this somber mood. As we've seen, his Duma speech on the Beilis trial in the spring of 1914 sounded a newly despairing note: "We already feel what before we only foresaw, we see fields of grief, tears and, perhaps, blood."[10]

The onset of war produced a momentary surge of patriotic fervor, at least among the groups well represented in the Duma. Miliukov switched position radically, now championing the so-called *union sacrée* in support of the war effort. This patriotic spirit even reached into portions of the opposition extreme enough to be in exile. The return of one exile, Vladimir Burtsev, precipitated yet another clash between the Maklakov brothers.

Several years before the war, while in exile in Paris, Burtsev had met Maklakov and had spoken of his intention to return to Russia. Maklakov had tried to talk him out of it, but promised to defend him if he did come home. When he returned at the outbreak of war, the council of ministers debated whether he should be arrested. Sazonov, the foreign minister, opposed arrest; Nikolai Maklakov favored it, and prevailed. Burtsev turned for help to Maklakov, who promptly visited him in prison. Burtsev said, "Vasily Alekseevich, I've kept my promise to return to Russia." Maklakov replied, "I've kept mine, and have come to defend you."

Burtsev was convicted, largely because he refused to repudiate his earlier attacks on tsarist policy, and despite Maklakov's reminding the judge that the tsar himself had said at the outbreak of war that it was time to forget past disagreements. After the conviction, the executive-branch fight over Burtsev resumed. The prime minister urged the tsar to release him, but again Nikolai Maklakov, seconded by Shcheglovitov, had his way. Months of Siberian exile followed, ending only when Russia's allies convinced the tsar to let him go. Burtsev wrote of his experiences in "Arrest under the Tsar and Arrest under Lenin"[11]—a title many of Maklakov's clients could probably have used, especially if "Lenin" had been broadened to "Lenin/Stalin." The *union sacrée* seems to have been something of a one-way bargain.

The tsar called the Duma into session rarely during the war, generally for brief votes on funding. In the gaps, the government could adopt laws under Article 87. At the start of the war, then, the Duma failed to operate either as a catalyst or as a safety valve for public opinion. In the session of January 27–29, 1915, for example, it passed the budget on the second day and on the third was prorogued until November. There ensued a number of repressive acts that the government had evidently deferred until the Duma had come and gone: Nikolai Maklakov took steps to rein in the press, especially the liberal *Russkie Vedomosti*. Five Bolshevik Duma deputies were convicted and exiled, and Vasily Maklakov, Vasily Shulgin, and Pyotr Struve each received a three-month sentence—for writing (Maklakov and Shulgin) and publishing (Struve) analyses of the Beilis trial.[12]

Russia's military fortunes ebbed and flowed, with successes helping the regime and reverses emboldening the opposition. In mid-April 1915 the Central Powers launched an offensive that rolled back nine months of comparative Russian success; by September they had captured all of Poland.[13] The Russian debacle was in part the result of failures in munitions supply, which was more easily traceable to civilian government incompetence than defects of tactics or strategy would have been. This produced a spirit of compromise in the regime. As Maklakov put it in his later summary account of the regime's fall, "Everywhere people called for [the Duma's] convocation. The tsar didn't dare resist. The Duma was convoked; as a preliminary, some of the most unpopular ministers were removed and replaced by others in whom public opinion had confidence."[14] The lead "unpopular minister," not identified in Vasily's account, was Nikolai Maklakov, fired on June 5. Sukhomlinov (war minister) followed on the 11th, and Shcheglovitov (justice) and V.K. Sabler (procurator of the holy synod) on the 12th. The dismissals left Goremykin as the cabinet's only reactionary. The day before the tsar started this purge, a group of liberals including Vasily Maklakov and Struve had gathered to discuss who could be sent to ask the tsar for Nikolai Maklakov's removal. For once, their hopes were more than realized.[15]

But these moves by the tsar proved not to introduce a period of reconciliation. On August 1 and 8, 1915, Maklakov lambasted the government for allowing a split between the ministers of war and trade to paralyze government policy on fuel supply.[16] On the 28th, he execrated the old (pre-June) government but argued that its replacement had failed to improve the situation. "We know that [the old government] was a government of ill will, blind and foolish, which could be tolerated only because its ill will was paralyzed by its lack of gifts and intelligence. But then we saw a new government and we were willing to trust it. A month after it came in we held back from any word of criticism. Now, with a new government we refrain from any criticism, but two months have passed, and we can ask whether it has justified our expectations. It is a government of good intentions but of no strength. It reminds one of a debtor who runs away from a creditor, hoping that the creditor will forget him."[17]

Between the first and last of these August speeches, two critical events occurred—formation of the "Progressive Bloc" and the tsar's move to staff headquarters, to take (nominal) charge of Russia's military effort.

Consisting of Kadets, Octobrists, and Progressives, the Progressive Bloc came together in part at the initiative of Maklakov,[18] the culmination of his and others' longtime efforts to form a political center in the Duma. (Like-minded members of the State Council formed a similar bloc there.) What made it possible for a center at last to jell? The war plainly helped create a sense of urgency. A specific manifestation of this was Miliukov's retreat from his usual insistence on solutions to the "three locks." Indeed, the demands for a universal franchise and removal of the State Council seem to have disappeared altogether, leaving only his requirement of a ministry responsible to the Duma. Even this proviso faded a bit. In the Kadets' June 1915 party conference, Miliukov—over the opposition of the party's left—now favored a ministry of "public confidence," that is, a ministry tied to the legislative majority more vaguely than in the standard parliamentary regime. The war effort required subordination of all other goals. Maklakov offered a slightly different formula, a ministry of "national defense," but at the party conference Kokoshkin—probably correctly—denied any contradiction between the two formulae. The resolution adopted by the conference seemed even more general, asking for creation of a cabinet to secure "a proper organization of the home front, maintenance of internal peace, and close cooperation between government and society."[19]

But the Miliukov-Maklakov harmony did not bring the whole Kadet party together. Kokoshkin reported to a Kadet central committee meeting on August 19 (after the Progressive Bloc was formed, on August 11–12) that at a meeting of Kadets, Octobrists, and Progressives Maklakov had argued that a ministry of "public figures" would be dangerous because it would be considered "a signal for action in the streets, outside legal institutions"; he preferred that Krivoshein be the premier. Though only minister of agriculture, Krivoshein was a longtime state official who was widely seen as effective. According to Kokoshkin, the gathering responded to Maklakov with irritation.[20]

In any event, no matter the hurdles that had been overcome in negotiating the bloc into existence, the timing undermined its usefulness. As Maklakov said later, "There ought to have been a Progressive Bloc under Stolypin, but when Stolypin sought it there was no Progressive Bloc. When there was a Progressive Bloc in 1915, there was no Stolypin."[21] After negotiations between the Progressive Bloc and a deputation of ministers, a majority of the cabinet voted in late August to recommend to Nicholas that he replace the present cabinet with one having the confidence of the Duma. The cabinet majority also expressed its opposition to Nicholas's decision to relocate to the front and take command of Russian forces. The reason they gave the tsar for resisting the move (a reason they genuinely believed) was that he would thereby be assuming responsibility for any military reversals. Among themselves they also expressed another reason—fear that the move would increase Rasputin's influence in the capital. Prime Minister Goremykin emphatically disagreed with his cabinet colleagues on both the proposed cabinet changes and the tsar's relocation to the front. Immediately after the cabinet vote in favor of a ministry with the support of the Duma, he went to staff headquarters to exhort the tsar to reject both of the cabinet's ideas and instead to prorogue the Duma. The tsar agreed, moved by various factors, evidently including improvements in the military situation, expressions of support from his conservative base, and the advice of Nikolai Maklakov, who on the occasion of his discharge had told Nicholas that the slightest concession to liberals would only lead to further demands.

Soon after the tsar's relocation to the front, Maklakov published in *Russkie Vedomosti* an allegorical fable expressing the dilemma that the government's halting and seemingly inept war management posed for any Russian who hoped that the country might emerge relatively well—possibly with "victory" or at least without calamity beyond the war itself.

A Tragic Situation

> . . . Imagine that you are driving in an automobile on a steep and narrow road. One wrong turn of the steering-wheel and you are irretrievably lost. Your dear ones, your beloved mother, are with you in the car.
>
> Suddenly you realize that your chauffeur is unable to drive. Either he is incapable of controlling the car on a steep gradient, or he is overtired and no longer understands what he is doing, so

> that his driving spells doom for himself and for you; should you continue in this way, you face inescapable destruction.
>
> Fortunately there are people in the automobile who can drive, and they should take over the wheel as soon as possible. But it is a difficult and dangerous task to change places with the driver while moving. One second without control and the automobile will crash into the abyss.
>
> There is no choice, however, and you make up your mind; but the chauffeur refuses to give way . . . he is clinging to the steering-wheel and will not give way to anybody. . . . Can one force him? This could easily be done in normal times with an ordinary horse-drawn peasant cart at low speed on level ground. Then it could mean salvation. But can this be done on the steep mountain path? However skillful you are, however strong, the wheel is actually in his hands—he is steering the car, and one error in taking a turn, or an awkward movement of his hand, and the car is lost. You know that, and he knows it as well. And he mocks your anxiety and your helplessness: "You will not dare to touch me!"
>
> He is right. You will not dare to touch him . . . for even if you might risk your own life, you are travelling with your mother, and you will not dare to endanger your life for fear she too might be killed. . . . So you will leave the steering-wheel in the hands of the chauffeur. Moreover, you will try not to hinder him—you will even help him with advice, warning and assistance. And you will be right, for this is what has to be done.
>
> But how will you feel when you realize that your self-restraint might still be of no avail, and that even with your help the chauffeur will be unable to cope? How will you feel when your mother, having sensed the danger, begs you for help, and, misunderstanding your conduct, accuses you of inaction and indifference?[22]

The reference to the observer's "beloved mother" is, naturally, to the "motherland."

To let the mad chauffeur continue at the wheel seemed to assure disaster. But to grab the wheel—to oust the tsar, or at least the tsarina, whose meddling was notorious, simple-minded, and incompetent—risked outcomes quite possibly as bad. Successor authorities might prove no more competent, and seizing authority could unleash revolution, with a certainty of violence and a risk of disaster.

Scholars have reached quite different conclusions as to the meaning of Maklakov's fable; many refuse to read it as simply stating a dilemma. One (Pearson) dismisses the article as "a striking metaphorical apologia for the weakness of Octobrist policy." (In the author's account, "Octobrist policy" encompasses the approach of all the relatively moderate political figures, a group that at this stage included many Kadets, such as both Miliukov and Maklakov.)[23] Another (Katkov) seems to see it as a virtual incitement to revolution; he says that press stories about the article communicated "the seething atmosphere of the Moscow [party] congresses of September 1915 . . . to wide circles of the newspaper-reading public in Russia."[24] What of Maklakov himself? In a letter to him long afterwards, his friend Tyrkova-Williams mentioned that she read his fable to mean that he was uncertain which course was riskier;[25] his letters in response do not refer to that interpretation. His failure to correct her (as he often does on other matters), the fable's careful balancing of hazards on either side, and his later ruminations on the revolution suggest that she was right. But whatever the fable's "true" message, it was a bold move to suggest—even through allegory—that the disruptive effects of ousting the tsar were the main, perhaps the sole, reason not to oust him.

About the time of the Mad Chauffeur article, the tsar, at the urging of Alexandra, not only prorogued the Duma but also dismissed two liberal ministers (September 26) and then Krivoshein (October 26). These maneuvers launched what came to be called "ministerial leapfrog"—a phrase coined by Duma deputy Vladimir Purishkevich (of whom more shortly). Between September 1915 and February 1917, the leapfrog game gave Russia four prime ministers, five ministers of internal affairs, three ministers of foreign affairs, three ministers of war, three ministers of justice, and four ministers of agriculture. Finally, the tsar allowed Rasputin to return to the capital, enabling him to become (or at least be generally thought to become) the ringmaster of the ministerial leapfrog. Before these steps by Nicholas, the stars had come as close to an alignment in favor of a reconciliation between society and the regime as they had ever been or were ever to be—but obviously not close enough.[26]

The Progressive Bloc struggled on, rent by divisions. Miliukov, supported by Maklakov, continued to beat down the left-wing Kadets' demands for a more aggressive policy toward the government. Some of the moderates' specific hesitations may have been ill conceived. But later scholars' denunciations of their strategy, calling it "craven" and a form of "sedation of all opposition inside and outside the Duma,"[27] overlook the mad chauffeur dilemma. Calling "the street" into play, either directly or by actions likely to have that effect, would risk defeating the moderates' hope of bringing the war to a nondisastrous end. That hope may been naïve or ill-considered on a wide variety of grounds, but for politicians preserving that hope, it made sense to continue a moderate line.

Nonetheless, on November 1 and 3, 1916, Miliukov and Maklakov successively delivered dramatic anti-regime speeches in the Duma. Miliukov's was both savage and unfair. He pilloried now–prime minister Boris Stürmer, successor of the luckless Goremykin, for allegedly contemplating a separate peace. Paragraph by paragraph he pointed to real or alleged mistakes by the regime, closing each paragraph with the rhetorical question "Is it stupidity or is it treason?" Given the widespread though totally unfounded rumors that Alexandra was a German agent, or at any rate rooting for Germany (she was, by birth, a German princess), the speech played to the mob's most paranoid impulses. Miliukov also attacked the recent appointment of Alexander Protopopov as acting minister of interior, an anomalous attack in view of his relatively liberal disposition and close association with the Duma leadership. A plausible explanation for the attack is liberal concern that the tsar was coopting the Progressive Bloc's supposed dedication to appointment of a ministry of public confidence: if the tsar himself started choosing exemplary ministers of this sort, it would cut off the bloc's power to do so.[28]

Maklakov's speech, two days later, made no accusation of treason but was still incendiary.[29] He suggested that Russia's military leaders were beginning to panic. "Why is there panic among the warriors? There's only one reason—they have stopped believing in their leaders. They feel that the dispositions of the authorities are muddle-headed and harmful, that they aren't taking care of things. The fearful cry, 'They're betraying us,' has stolen up on them, and when the thought of the general welfare is lost, the readiness to obey is lost. Each begins to think of how to save himself, sauve qui peut, and then panic is on us." Echoing the "leapfrog" epithet, he spoke of a "ministerial kaleidoscope, where we don't even succeed in seeing the faces of ministers who fall." He charged the regime with choosing appointees on the basis of their "ability not to be excited, to be quiet," their connections, and their devotion to the regime rather than to the country. Posing the question of how this situation could persist, his answer at times sounded like a call for revolution:

> I ask why does Russia stick to this government which is destroying Russia? Is it accident? No, gentlemen, it is not accident, it is the system. It is not accident when we know that among us the trust of the country undermines a ministry, that the country's hatred strengthens it. . . . No, it is not an accident, it is the regime, this cursed, old regime that has outlived its time but is still alive, that is the basic cause of everything. (*Voice from the left, "Bravo, right."*).

Again hitting the theme that the regime chose officials not for competence or devotion to the country but for being good toadies, he quoted a line of Pushkin from the 1830s: "Woe to the country where only slaves and flatterers can approach the throne."

Rejecting the idea (shouted from the rightist benches) that he was calling for revolution, he said, "Russia will not answer you with an uprising, I hope." Rather, he thought, Russia might settle for "a shameful peace, peace to a draw." But the country would know "that if that happens, Germany will not have defeated us, rather it will be this cursed regime, whose representatives constantly exchange ministerial places with each other, that has defeated us. And when Russia calls them all to account, it will give mercy to no one, I repeat, no one. (*Prolonged applause from center, left, and right; voice, 'Bravo.'*)"

He closed in somewhat Manichean language:

> If the authorities embark on escapades that lead us to catastrophe, the Duma may still be needed. It may in the future be the sole support of authority, the sole bulwark of order. But for it to be able to play that role, it will have to have the right to look the country in the eye without blushing. And for that we must say to the authorities, it's either us or them. Our life together is impossible. *(Prolonged and stormy applause from center, left, and right; a voice, "Bravo.")*

However we view this rhetoric (the Kadet party loved it, and distributed millions of copies of Maklakov's and Miliukov's speeches),[30] two features seem far outside the familiar Maklakov of moderation. First, equating "peace to a draw" with a "shameful peace" was an indulgence in precisely the rhetoric that makes useless bloodletting hard to stop. As the death toll mounts, so does the passion to redeem those deaths—with further bloodshed spilled in the hope of gains that would justify all the past losses. At about the same time as Maklakov was scoffing at "peace to a draw," that is, peace without serious territorial acquisitions for Russia, the Germans were proposing a peace under which Germany would in effect occupy Belgium.[31] As long as both sides define "peace to a draw" as "shameful," the slaughter must continue. The speech's focus on "honor" rather than results sets up (or reflects) a wall between sides, a way of thinking completely at odds with Maklakov's usual tendency to see "a share of truth on the opposite side, and a share of error on his own."

Second, though the passage saying that the regime had "outlived its time" might be ingeniously reconstructed as merely a call for the tsar to compromise on the membership of the cabinet (that is, accept something like the Progressive Bloc's proposal of August 1915), it certainly didn't sound that way.

In fact, Maklakov was at work on another mode of regime change. His view of coups d'état was, as we saw in chapter 7, pragmatic. In a lecture given in 1909 he had described a successful coup d'état as a "mechanism by which a legally invalid act, being politically accepted, receives recognition and becomes the law." Citing the palace coup that brought Catherine the Great to power in place of her husband, the lawful tsar, he said, "Catherine triumphed. An uprising turned into a state coup, and the criminal—became empress."[32] Thus it is hardly startling to find him involved in the coup plots that swirled around St. Petersburg and Moscow in late 1916 and early 1917. The clearest evidence of his participation is a December 29, 1916, letter to Konovalov, a key center of coup planning,[33] reporting on his efforts to scout out the views of another political figure.

The letter survives only in the form of a copy made by the secret police, who often opened letters in the mail, copied them, and sent on the originals. The letter leaves the exact nature of the plan unclear and never identifies Maklakov's interlocutor, whom Maklakov seems to be assessing for some future action. The target expressed full agreement with the "program" but was cautious. As Maklakov confides to Konovalov, "You yourself know that he's an unstable person and it's hard to assess his mood. He agreed with me on everything, but he left me with an anxious feeling that he agreed so readily because he was afraid. In my view he's deathly afraid that that he'll be called on to do something illegal, unconstitutional. At the start of the conversation he often bristled. But when he understood there was no question of that, he quickly relaxed and agreed to everything. So his agreement is unreliable."

(Was the "no question of that" line inserted as protection against liability for treason?) Maklakov then wrote that nothing was going on in St. Petersburg, and "unless you have something else for me I'll return to Moscow. . . . One more impression: things are going much slower than it had seemed to us."[34] The scouting seems not to have been a one-off event for Maklakov.[35] We'll return in chapter 17 to the tricky relationship between coups d'état, the pressure leading to Nicholas II's abdication, and the February Revolution itself.

CHAPTER 16

The Killing of Rasputin

BETWEEN THE FIERY Kadet speeches of early November 1916 and the February Revolution came the killing of Rasputin in the night of December 16–17. Surprisingly, Maklakov had a hand in the assassination—a relatively remote hand, but close enough, as he acknowledged, to have entailed criminal responsibility as an accessory or abettor. In 1932 he published a detailed account of his role in an illustrated weekly that was popular with Russian émigrés in France,[1] from which the next few pages are largely drawn. Before turning to his account, we should glance at the Rasputin story, a context that his readers knew well and of which many Americans have a general idea.

First, of course, is the louche figure of Rasputin himself. A kind of religious faith healer unattached to any congregation, he appeared able, perhaps by hypnotism, to relieve Alexei, heir to the throne, of the agonies of hemophilia. This service wins him the devotion of the tsarina, which enables him to hobnob with the mighty and exercise his hypnotic powers over elite ladies of the capital. Many Americans may know that he also played a king-maker's role, or at least seemed to do so, advancing and retarding careers at the apex of Russian political power through his influence over the tsarina and hers over the tsar, in effect overseeing the "ministerial leapfrog." In due course eminent figures close to the throne come to believe that his influence and his conduct cry out for remedy, and that the best remedy would be assassination. They embark on the project. If the conspirators' poison were as genuine as they thought, its administration to Rasputin proves him to be almost supernaturally tough, and a hail of bullets is needed to finish him off. The conspirators then dump his body into the freezing Neva River. Without weights attached, the body resurfaces, and Russia's educated elite soon know the general outline of the entire story. At least in part because the conspirators include the tsar's relatives (Prince Felix Yusupov, married to the tsar's only niece and thus his nephew-in-law, and Grand Duke Dmitri Pavlovich, the tsar's cousin), none of them is ever prosecuted. The regime continues to lurch along until it is swept aside in the February Revolution.

This biography of Maklakov doesn't directly modify that account. But it does add a surprising figure to the list of conspirators—an eminent lawyer, legislator, and sincere avatar of the rule of law. The relatively well-known conspirators, Yusupov and Purishkevich (whom we encountered before as coiner of the phrase "ministerial leapfrog"), published accounts that contained a role for Maklakov, but some of the conduct imputed to him—above all, supplying a possible but unlikely murder weapon—seems so bizarre as to strain credulity. Nonetheless, Maklakov's 1932 account in broad outline confirms their stories. Maklakov is at pains to correct some of their details, and argues that his recollection is likely to be better because his link consisted solely of his conversations with them, whereas they were involved in all aspects of the plot. His argument seems persuasive. Rather than specify their disagreements and justify my crediting of him, I simply draw on his account and refer interested readers to theirs.[2]

Maklakov fixes the time of his first meeting with Yusupov by its relation to memorable political news. Around November 6 or

7, 1916, he learned of the imminent dismissal of Prime Minister Stürmer; the rumor also held that Protopopov, depicted as a villain in Miliukov's "stupidity or treason" speech, would soon get the axe. These removals seemed to Maklakov not only a great Duma victory but also a "pledge" of further successes. They put Duma members in an optimistic mood. At about the same time, a Yusupov employee asked Maklakov when he could see the prince, with whom he had no prior acquaintance. He named that same evening.

They met, and Yusupov presented his ideas. He argued that Rasputin was the *cause* of Russia's political chaos, not just a symptom of the tsar's ineffectiveness, as Maklakov believed. Yusupov said he had read Maklakov's Duma speeches and those of his friends, but he was disappointed in what he viewed as Maklakov's serious misunderstanding of Rasputin's role. Based on his knowledge of the tsar's court, he regarded Rasputin as all-powerful. "While Rasputin lives, you'll get nowhere." He gave examples that he thought showed Rasputin's power over the tsar, but Maklakov thought them exaggerated. Maklakov maintained that Yusupov underestimated the Duma's influence, citing in support of his contention the departure of Stürmer and the imminent departure of Protopopov as evidence. Yusupov explained that Stürmer was dismissed because he'd kept the empress waiting for four hours, and he assured Maklakov—correctly, as it proved—that Protopopov would stay. (Protopopov lasted right up to the February Revolution.)

Yusupov went on to argue that the only solutions were either to buy Rasputin off or to kill him. Maklakov said he thought that buying him would involve the buyer with unreliable intermediaries, and that there was a much richer buyer in the market for Rasputin's allegiance—he was alluding to rumors that Rasputin was in league with the Germans. Yusupov insisted that apart from buying or killing him, there was no way out. Maklakov argued that even if Yusupov were correct about Rasputin's influence, the fault lay with the regime; if they killed Rasputin, others would appear to replace him. Yusupov responded, "You talk this way because you have no idea of his supernatural magnetism. I'm very familiar with this, and I assure you one meets such strength only once in a hundred years. . . . If he's killed today, within two weeks the empress will have to go to a place for the mentally ill. Her mental balance depends entirely on Rasputin. As soon as he's not there, she'll fall apart. And when the tsar is freed of Rasputin, everything will change; he'll become a good constitutional monarch."

Judging Yusupov to have made up his mind, Maklakov asked if he'd considered the dangers for himself personally. "You have a lot to lose." (This comment may have been partly an allusion to Yusupov's being one of the richest men in Russia—indeed, in the world.) Yusupov explained that he was planning to have it done by others. Who was he counting on? Yusupov answered as if it were obvious: revolutionaries. Maklakov was shocked by the naiveté, since in his view the revolutionaries viewed Rasputin as their best friend; no one else's existence and activities so undercut the monarchy's prestige. (Maklakov speculated that Yusupov had come to him as an entrée to revolutionaries, thinking that revolutionaries and the liberal opposition were all pretty much the same. This inability of Russia's contending forces to see vital distinctions among their adversaries was of course a longtime Maklakovian theme.) Yusupov then proposed an alternative—to hire killers. "I'm ready to give all that's needed." This suggestion irritated Maklakov in a different way. "I asked him rather sharply, 'Why have you turned to me? Do you think I run an office for assassins?'

"The conversation became unpleasant for me. Yusupov sensed it, and we started to say goodbye. I was troubled by his inexperience. I imagined the danger he would run with his proposed plan. As we said goodbye, I said: 'Now that you've turned to me and placed confidence in me, let me respond with some good advice. If you find someone who agrees to kill for money, run away from him. Only rascals will kill for money, and any one of them will figure out that it's easier to blackmail you than to kill Rasputin. But if you stand by your decision and want to do it yourself, feel free to come to me and I can perhaps warn you away from unnecessary errors.'" Then they parted.

Maklakov's account pauses to note the political events of the moment. Protopopov did not resign; Prince Yusupov was right. A wave of bitterness replaced the Duma's optimism. Then, on November 19, in a full assembly of the Duma, with a new cabinet on hand headed by Alexander Trepov (he lasted only a few weeks; the leapfrog pace was accelerating), Purishkevich gave a speech denouncing Rasputin. About a week later he met Maklakov in the Duma's Catherine Hall, and Purishkevich asked him if he had seen Yusupov. Maklakov answered that he had seen him once. Purishkevich, in the midst of a throng of public figures: "So you know, now it's been decided to kill Rasputin." Maklakov feigned not to understand. Purishkevich pressed on, "I know all, how Yusupov talked with you and what he told you." Maklakov drew him aside, and they sat on a bench under a bust of Alexander II. Although they remained in everyone's sight, at least they could not be heard. Maklakov's Russian readers would have recognized in Purishkevich's conduct one of his signature traits, complete lack of discretion; even for them it may have seemed extreme. As it proved, an outburst by Purishkevich directly after the assassination first alerted the police—though the scheme was so loosely strung together that they would have discovered it before long anyway.

Once the two sat down, according to Maklakov, "Purishkevich as usual didn't give me a chance to open my mouth." He said, "I know everything you've talked about with Yusupov." Maklakov countered, "If you know all, you know how I answered him." Purishkevich answered that Yusupov agreed with him, and they weren't going to hire an assassin; only "intelligent people" would participate. Maklakov especially remembered (and marveled at) Purishkevich's contrast between hired people and intelligent people. As Maklakov earned his living by his wits, he doubtless saw no conflict. Purishkevich named the other participants and told him the assassination was to take place on the night of December 16–17. As we know from chapter 12, Maklakov was committed to give a talk to the Moscow Juridical Society on peasant rights that same evening. He told Purishkevich of his prior commitment and asked why he was telling him all this. Purishkevich answered that he was acting at the request of Yusupov, who wanted to know whether, now that Maklakov knew who was going to join, he would help. Maklakov writes, "I was already bound by my proposal to Yusupov"—presumably the agreement to give advance advice—"and gave my agreement." This was November 28.

There follows a passage in which Maklakov corrects various parts of Purishkevich's account of the conversation, particularly his saying that Maklakov offered to help with legal advice and act as their defense counsel. In reality, Maklakov notes, it should have been clear that his sole goal was to make sure, through advance advice, that any such trial would be unnecessary and, indeed, impossible.

A second visit from Yusupov followed, occurring just as Yusupov recounted in his memoirs. Maklakov reproached him for inviting Purishkevich into the plot, saying he was completely unsuitable. Yusupov defended his decision, saying he turned to Purishkevich after his speech in the Duma attacking Rasputin, and had found a kindred spirit, ready to act. He trusted in his patriotism; in that, writes Maklakov, he was not mistaken. He met with Yusupov several more times.

Maklakov then seeks to explain his conduct. As before, he writes, he didn't expect the assassination to bring about Russia's salvation. But he realized the plot wasn't idle chatter, as he had thought at first. Yusupov revealed persistence and decisiveness and, finally, was not alone. No matter what Maklakov's relation to the assassination, it would take place. "I couldn't prevent the assassination, and I did not want to assist it. . . . But I wanted to warn them off steps that might deprive the action even of the purpose that Yusupov saw in it." His view of the assassination was like that of Macbeth before the murder of Duncan, with a slight edit: "If it were done when 'tis done, then 'twere well it were done well."

But was Maklakov correct in his understanding that he could

not prevent the assassination? Nothing counters his assessment that he couldn't dissuade Yusupov. Still, he could have brought the plot to the attention of the police. Why not do so? He never discusses it, but one can see potential problems. First, they might not believe him: his word against that of the tsar's nephew-in-law? Or they might believe him and prefer not to act. Second, if the police did take action, revelation of a plot within the Russian elite would likely generate a prolonged public wrangle. It would expose and aggravate fault lines within the elite (the empress against much of society) and within the country as a whole (the anti-Rasputin elite against millions of ordinary people), perhaps precipitating a struggle to seize control—a struggle that could drive Russia over the cliff with the mad chauffeur still clinging to the wheel. An assassination in which the actors remained anonymous might pose less of a threat to stability. It seems likely that Maklakov harbored such concerns. Later in the account he explains why he wholeheartedly shared Yusupov's hope that the assassins would not be revealed: a trial, especially in time of war, would stir up passions so much that assassination might prove a prologue to revolution. It was critical that the assassins not be found. But could the assassination be so well choreographed as to fulfill Maklakov's hopes that they would remain unknown? The belief that it could strikes me as naïve; there, it seems to me, is where Maklakov's reasoning is most vulnerable—even if we put aside the ethics of participating in a murder.

In one of his consultations with Maklakov, Yusupov said that the idea was for Purishkevich to take Rasputin's body to the front when he himself went there by train, and somehow hide it there. Maklakov threw cold water on that idea, saying that having the indisputable body of Rasputin was essential to the empress's believing in his death. Also, without the body, people would arise claiming to act in his name. Though the conspirators obviously abandoned the plan of taking the body to the front, the decision to drop it into the Neva seems at odds with Maklakov's advice.

A few days before the assassination, Purishkevich blabbed

again. A journalist at the Duma named Baker (probably George Barr Baker, later associated with Herbert Hoover in American relief activities) told Maklakov of how Purishkevich had come into a room full of journalists and said that Rasputin would soon be assassinated. Maklakov asked Baker when this had happened. Baker said only that Purishkevich entered and began to talk of the war and such, and that when someone expressed doubt that it could be won under Rasputin (Maklakov quotes Baker as using the Russian preposition *pri*, meaning "under" in a political context, as in "*pri* Alexander I" or "*pri* Stalin"), he told them not to worry: Rasputin would soon be killed. The journalists laughed and didn't believe him. Purishkevich began to get angry and finally blurted out, "It's not just idle talk. I'm in the plot myself, with Yusupov and Grand Duke Dmitri Pavlovich. The killing will be December 17." Maklakov told Baker, "He was kidding you. If it were true, obviously he wouldn't have started to talk about it."

Maklakov reported the conversation to Yusupov, who seemed overcome by his confederates' hopeless inadequacy. He asked Maklakov, for the first time, if he could be in St. Petersburg on the scheduled night: "Things may take a turn such that I'll need good advice. You alone could give it to me. . . . I don't ask you to participate, just be near enough so that I could talk with you if necessary." Yusupov specifically asked Maklakov to be present in Yusupov's house on the night.

Again Maklakov felt he was being dragged steadily into a project in which he had no confidence and of which he didn't approve. But, he reports, he felt that to refuse Yusupov now, when he had already taken part so much, would seem to show fear for his own personal responsibility. And he did think that conspirators like these might well commit an irreparable mistake at the most decisive moment. But he reminded Yusupov of his commitment to speak at the Moscow Juridical Society and consented to be on hand only if it agreed to postpone the meeting.

Maklakov then turns to the subject of a curious rubber truncheon that he had given to Yusupov. By the latter's account, Maklakov had handed it to him on his own initiative, saying, "Just in case." Maklakov makes a subtle correction to that account, fitting it into his persistent effort to persuade Yusupov that Rasputin should be killed (if at all) without noise and leaving as little evidence against the assassins as possible. With that in mind, he suggested killing him with a sharp blow. It would then be possible to carry the corpse off to a park by car, and to make the death appear to be some sort of accident. Talking with Yusupov of this on one occasion, he pointed as an example to an object lying on his desk, a kind of truncheon or bludgeon with an encased lead sphere at either end. (The 1932 article contains a picture of an item said to be like this object.) He had bought it abroad, and it always lay on his desk, partly for use as a paperweight and partly for self-defense if need be.

As Yusupov was leaving, he asked for the truncheon. Maklakov said no. His resistance, he claims, was not out of concern over criminal responsibility. Regardless of the truncheon, he was in the plot deeply enough to be guilty as an accomplice or abettor. But that sort of truncheon could not be found in Russia, and he wanted to keep it. Yusupov insisted, however, and Maklakov yielded. He explains why he bothered to correct Yusupov's version: that version, he thought, made him sound like a silent provoker. Yusupov, in his own account of the murder, gives the truncheon a surprising role. He describes using it to beat the body of Rasputin, lying on a stairway landing in the Yusupov mansion, apparently already dead or at least dying from bullet wounds.[3]

Following up on the "silent provoker" theme, Maklakov mentions that Purishkevich went even further, asserting that Maklakov had given Yusupov potassium cyanide. In his introduction to Purishkevich's account, Maklakov had fairly handily dispatched it, at least as to Purishkevich's dealings with him, noting that although Purishkevich's text was presented as a "diary," its dates were jumbled. Regarding his supplying Yusupov with poison, he had written, "It was not I who gave Yusupov potassium cyanide, or more precisely, what to Yusupov passed for potassium cyanide—had it been genuine, no amount of hardiness on Rasputin's part would have saved him."[4] Maklakov's skepticism about the supposed poison seems justified. An autopsy performed soon after the slaying reported no trace of poison. Apparently by coincidence, the autopsy was prepared by Professor Dmitri Kosorotov, who had testified for the prosecution in the Beilis trial. There he claimed that the victim's wounds manifested the killers' intent to extract the maximum amount of blood (thus supporting the "blood ritual" theory), a notion persuasively countered by the defense experts. In exchange for his Beilis trial testimony, Kosorotov received 4,000 rubles, arranged through then–Minister of Internal Affairs Nikolai Maklakov and paid out of 10 million rubles at the disposition of the tsar for off-the-books expenses.[5] Despite Kosorotov's shabby behavior in the Beilis trial, his autopsy on Rasputin seems to have held up.

As of the evening of December 15 Maklakov still had not heard from the organizers of the Moscow meeting whether it could be postponed. But at the Duma meeting that night Purishkevich approached him and said that Yusupov no longer insisted on his being available, and explained that Grand Duke Dmitri Pavlovich had objected to the previous plan. He didn't want a Kadet to appear to be involved: let the assassination be done only by true and dedicated monarchists. Maklakov never checked as to whether the grand duke actually said this, but it seemed sound. "As I said goodbye to Purishkevich I asked him to send me a telegram when it was all done. . . . That is the end of what I know about the killing as a participant."

In closing the account, Maklakov observes that Yusupov's hopes of a serious change proved unjustified. The assassination left the empress even more embittered against Rasputin's enemies and all who had condemned him, and the tsar absorbed her views. There was a sharp political tilt to the right.

Maklakov's account includes a report by a "worldly" St. Petersburg lady who was visiting a hospital at the time, evidently as a volunteer. Feeling joyful about Rasputin's death, she told the soldiers of it. They responded with a gloomy silence. Thinking they didn't understand, she repeated the news. They continued to be silent until finally one of them spoke up, "Yes, one of us [peasants], just one, gets close to the tsar, and the lords kill him." The others agreed. Maurice Paléologue, the French ambassador, picked up similar stories in the wake of the assassination—that Rasputin's murder by aristocrats was turning him into a martyr among the peasants.[6]

Maklakov's evaluation of the political impact is succinct. "The killing, carried out by circles surrounding the throne, the impunity of the killers despite their being perfectly well known, the unconcealed grief of the emperor and empress, together with the obvious delight of Russian society, revealed with unusual clarity the deep, age-old split at the heart of the Russian state. The highest authority was clearly and hopelessly divided from Russian society. It appeared that no force could reconcile them. All now awaited some event, some with terror, others with hope." His words capture the problem exactly—*except* that he fails to note the chasm between society and the masses, so well illustrated by the hospital story.

In the end I find no sure explanation for Maklakov's conduct. Although Maklakov himself believed the project hopeless in terms of saving Russia, the civic zeal that moved the most honorable of Caesar's assassins may have played a role. He allowed himself to become entangled in the criminal enterprise, and perhaps the momentum, and a misplaced sense of honor, overcame his judgment. And perhaps he had not fully internalized the advice that Kapnist gave him after the Chernyshevskii episode: "You need to think first, and then act. Learn to rule yourself before you may have to rule others."

CHAPTER 17

February 1917

John Reed called the Bolsheviks' October 1917 revolution "Ten Days That Shook the World." But the "February Revolution"—starting on February 23 and culminating on March 3 with the tsar's abdication, his brother Mikhail's rejection of the crown, and the Romanovs' replacement by a "Provisional Government" and the Petrograd Soviet of workers, peasants, and soldiers—was itself pretty earth-shaking. It brought down a three-hundred-year-old dynasty, replaced it with an awkward system of dual power, and paved the way for October. Not bad for nine days.

The revolution appears to have been largely spontaneous and its success more a result of regime confusion, hesitancy, and disorganization than of the rebels' inherent power. It—or at least the preliminary convulsions—began February 23 with the celebration of International Women's Day. Despite a wartime lapse of celebrations in western Europe, Russian socialists had kept the day alive, if barely so. In February 1917, despite revolutionary leaders' coolness (ranging from exhortation *against* action to provision of some inflammatory leaflets), strike meetings of women factory workers snowballed into mass action. Whatever their political grievances, their immediate cry was for bread. Many had had to stand in line for hours to get a single loaf. The first strikers moved into factories not yet on strike, called on workers to join them, and, in many cases, swept through factories and herded workers into the streets. Strikers vandalized and robbed stores and robbed a bank of 35,000 rubles. Ominously for the regime and heartening for the strikers, Cossack officers responded sluggishly to orders even for nonlethal crowd-control measures. Their commander defended this reluctance. Among other arguments, he asked how they could control demonstrators if they had not been supplied with *nagaikas*—sticks with a leather thong ending in a knot that enclosed lead, reputed to enable a skilled Cossack to "brush a fly from one's face without touching the skin, or . . . maim one for life."[1]

The strikers' number and activity expanded rapidly. Their behavior must have reminded many educated Russians of a famous line from Pushkin: "God forbid we should see a Russian revolt, senseless and savage." Looting was rife, and looters threw parties with the loot. Soldiers often resisted their officers' commands and defected in increasing numbers to the side of revolution, ultimately turning their weapons on their officers. Workers seized weapons and munitions from arsenals and arms factories. Soldiers assailed prisons, disarming the guards and releasing thousands of prisoners (and not only "politicals"). Official resistance was plagued by backtracking and uncertainty. By the end of February 27, unrest had become revolution; "insurrection had triumphed in Petrograd."[2]

During the first four days (Thursday the 23rd through Sunday the 26th), Maklakov devoted himself to two salient challenges: the crisis in grain supply and the need for broad political compromise. In the Duma meeting of February 23, the grain supply issue exposed the liberals' lack of preparedness—perhaps even of good sense. Shingarev, soon to become minister of agriculture in the Provisional Government, scoffed at the idea that the grain shortage could be due to the low ceiling on prices paid to the peasants; rather, it was the government's lack of a "plan." Later in the debate he argued for "governmental intelligence" as a corrective to the spontaneous outbreaks. As historian Tsuyoshi Hasegawa observes, in the midst of this turmoil the liberals "had no answer except to plead to the government to have more intelligence."[3]

Maklakov, quite apart from having a better grasp of economics than most of his liberal colleagues, thought to consult with the peasant deputies who had joined him in the spring of 1916 to prepare, and get through the Duma, his bill codifying the peasant equalization decree of 1906 (chapter 12). They assured him that the low ceiling prices were indeed the key. They also told him of various local officials' foolish activities, stories he thought should be brought to the attention of Alexander Rittikh, the minister of agriculture. Maklakov arranged for a meeting between them and Rittikh. The Duma chairman, Rodzianko, got word of the scheduled gathering. Seeing it as an intrigue of the minister to seek agreements with parties behind his back, he reached representatives of the peasant group and told them to cancel the meeting. They reported this development to Maklakov, who called Rodzianko and pacified him. The meeting went ahead, and the peasant deputies later told Maklakov that they had found it useful.[4]

Maklakov next visited Rittikh to get his opinion of the meeting. Rittikh also expressed satisfaction but then, reports Maklakov, burst out crying like a child. He had reported to the Duma the government's decision to turn local control of grain distribution over to the Petrograd city duma—a policy change that liberals had demanded. (He did not mention grain prices; evidently the cabinet viewed the price ceiling as a defensible form of thrift.) But the Duma liberals reacted with horror, considering the action a ploy, even though it was exactly what they had been demanding. Rittikh told Maklakov, "Yesterday we got approval from the cabinet, with difficulty, for all that the Duma wanted, and it curses us for it. It's impossible to govern this way." Maklakov calmed him down, arguing that the Duma didn't distrust him but that it would never trust the government while it still contained Protopopov.[5] In fact, the cabinet met late on the 25th and voted overwhelmingly to seek negotiations with the Duma; it assigned the negotiations to Rittikh and the foreign minister, Nikolai Pokrovskii.[6]

The next morning (Sunday, February 26), Maklakov unexpectedly received a call from Pokrovskii asking him to meet and to name the hour. Maklakov proposed noon. Before seeing Pokrovskii, he talked with Struve and Shulgin about what to say. Shulgin's memoirs discuss the meeting, including a brief encounter with Kerensky. The latter, according to Shulgin, said that no new government should include any "bureaucrats." Maklakov asked, "Why not?," pointing out that sensible, honest bureaucrats existed and that "we" (the politicians) had no experience running a state. Another deputy, Mikhail Tereshchenko, an ally of the Progressives, turned up and went with him to Pokrovskii's office.[7]

En route, evidently in Pokrovskii's anteroom, they met the French ambassador, Maurice Paléologue, who asked, "Why are you here?" Maklakov answered, "I don't know. I was summoned by the minister." Paléologue responded, "Ah, it's high time"[8]— to engage the Duma and especially Duma moderates.

In Pokrovskii's office Maklakov found Rittikh. Other Duma representatives besides himself and Tereshchenko apparently were there, but Maklakov doesn't mention them.[9] Pokrovskii promptly expressed the government's great concern over the situation as well as its belief that the Duma and government could accomplish nothing unless they worked together. Maklakov reformulated the statement: "You want to know under what conditions the Duma will help," and went on to acknowledge that he spoke only for himself and a few close friends. He also said that what he was going to advise might be good only for that day—the next might be too late. "Tomorrow the Duma itself may lay down other conditions. You've got to anticipate them. Seize the initiative. Give the Duma as an accomplished fact something that it can accept."[10]

He then presented his idea. The entire cabinet, not simply a few ministers, should resign; a new premier should be appointed, with the freedom to pick a cabinet. Pokrovskii and Rittikh asked for thoughts about the new premier. Maklakov rejected the option of a Duma member or bureaucrat or ordinary public figure. "Choose a person who will be a symbol of a new ministry. It should be a ministry of war, war to the end. Pick as premier a popular general. You have one—Alekseev [Mikhail Alekseev, then chief of the general staff and in effect commander of all Russia's armies]. The Duma and the country will trust him." He urged that the new premier include in the cabinet bureaucrats with whom good relationships were possible, and recall to office ministers who had been recently thrown out under Rasputin's influence, naming among others Kokovtsov and Sergei Sazonov (Pokrovskii's predecessor as foreign minister, if we disregard the four-month interregnum of Rasputin's puppet, Stürmer). Maklakov urged that the new ministry go before the Duma with a brief but well-defined program, "entirely for the war, but including everything necessary for the war, without exception. Let it announce that it will rely on the Duma, let it announce a stringent program, calling for sacrifices, but only for the war. The Duma couldn't refuse such a ministry and such a program. But lose no time; it's the last chance." He especially urged them to act, not to ask the Duma. It would answer by demanding too much.[11]

Pokrovskii and Rittikh talked with each other. After a while Pokrovskii told Maklakov the program was acceptable to them, and they hoped to get the tsar's agreement. Again Maklakov stressed the need for speed; they should act before the Duma resumed. He agreed to do what he could to delay that resumption.[12] Whether any efforts at delay were necessary is not clear, as the tsar prorogued the Duma on the 26th; at least as an institution, it shrank from defying the order to dissolve.[13] (As we'll see, it created a Provisional Government indirectly, through the decisions of members acting unofficially and through a "Council of Elders").

Whatever the prospects for Maklakov's plan, a seeming ebb in the insurrection doomed it at the cabinet meeting late in the night of Sunday the 26th. That day had proved to be the one day that regime forces successfully controlled the crowds; special detachments of guards regiments—units to train selected soldiers to become noncommissioned officers—obeyed orders to fire on crowds that refused to disperse. Some appearance of order was restored. One unit, the Fourth Company of the Pavlovskii Regiment, mutinied, but the government didn't read the mutiny as a strong signal. The cabinet listened "with boredom" to the report of Pokrovskii and Rittikh on their negotiations; it dismissed the possibility of further talks.[14] As if this rejection were not enough, the cabinet decided to prorogue the Duma, over the objections of both men.

Maklakov was wakened early the next morning (Monday the 27th) by a call from the deputy chairman of the Duma, Nekrasov, who told him of the proroguing and also of a mutiny by the Volynskii Regiment, which had killed its officers and gone out into the streets. Once arrived at the Duma, Maklakov phoned Pokrovskii, who confirmed the proroguing of the Duma: "One of your wishes has been fulfilled. Duma deliberations are suspended." He evidently regarded the regime's insulting dismissal of the Duma as equivalent to a voluntary pause to give the government time to present an overture. Then he said, "As to the rest [Maklakov's proposal], we'll discuss it Wednesday." Maklakov then asked him, "You know what's happening?" "What?" "The military have rebelled." "I've heard nothing of that." Maklakov replied, "Then I've nothing more to discuss with you," and hung up.[15]

Reflecting on these efforts later, Maklakov thought the plan might have satisfied the Duma, though he had doubts—after all, the liberals in 1905 had rejected a ministry headed by Shipov. But, he thought, such a ministry would have provided far more hope for success in the struggle against the Bolsheviks and the Germans than did the "idealistic" cabinet of the Provisional Government—"idealistic" doubtless referring to the ministers' complete lack of experience in guiding a state, much less guiding one through revolutionary chaos. He concluded that the exchange at least showed where responsibility lay:

> Characteristically, in this last hour of the old regime, a plan to escape from revolution was thwarted not by the extreme left,

> not by Kadet society, but by the authorities themselves. It was as if it wanted to preserve all responsibility for the Revolution to itself.[16]

How realistic was Maklakov's proposal? The idea of a focus on the war, led by a widely respected figure, had a kind of merit: individuals and peoples can perform amazing tasks when put to a deadly challenge. And it would have brought the regime and the Duma together. But by this stage, how many ordinary Russians cared in the slightest about achieving Russia's war aims, such as securing the Turkish straits and, with them, access to the Mediterranean? We return again and again to the gap between the masses and the elite. As we'll see, Maklakov came to doubt the wisdom of a full-throttled pursuit of the war earlier than his Kadet colleagues—but late in the game and certainly not by February.

With the failure of any effort at reconciliation, the Duma confronted its official suspension. What to do? One possibility was obviously to proceed in defiance of the proroguing order. The historical model (probably familiar to most deputies) was the Third Estate's defiance of Louis XVI's lockout in June 1789, its swearing of the Tennis Court Oath, and its self-transformation into a national assembly. Rodzianko was firmly against such an extreme measure. But under pressure he agreed to a meeting of Duma members as private citizens, and to a summoning of the Duma's "Council of Elders,"[17] an institution created under Article 12 of the Duma's legal constitution[18] for addressing issues arising in the work of the Duma; all parties were represented in the council (large ones with two representatives, small ones with one), and it acted by consensus. The council and some other members in their unofficial capacities (about a third of the full Duma membership) met, apparently off and on, over the afternoon of Monday, February 27. Between them, they established a committee, usually called the Duma Committee,[19] though formally labeled the "Provisional Committee of Members of the State Duma for the Restoration of Order in the Capital and Establishment of Relations with Public

Organizations and Institutions"—"a name itself redolent of indecision," as Melissa Stockdale writes.[20] Soon thereafter the committee in turn gave birth to the Provisional Government.

Scholars have criticized the Duma's failure to assert legal authority directly. Leonard Schapiro, for instance: "The Duma itself, by its pusillanimous and indecisive lack of action, lost the opportunity, which would never recur, of taking over power with a semblance of legitimacy."[21] We'll return to this issue when we have the other elements of regime collapse in place.

With two exceptions, the Duma Committee was composed of members of the Progressive Bloc; the exceptions were Kerensky, a Trudovik, and Nikolai Chkheidze, a Menshevik. The committee asserted authority promptly and aggressively. On the morning of February 28 it took over management of the state railways from the tsarist ministry; the railways' new director sent a telegram to all railway stations announcing that the old regime had fallen and that the Duma had formed a new government. This was of course an exaggeration, but it created its own reality. By the morning of February 28 the Duma Committee had appointed twenty-four "commissars" to assume authority in the existing ministries. For the ministry of justice the commissars were Maklakov and V. P. Basakov, a centrist deputy. Formal appointment of Maklakov's friend Moses Adzhemov, also a Kadet deputy, followed on March 1.[22] The Duma Committee also reached out to the military, enlisting influential Duma members to rally important units; Maklakov addressed the Volynskii guards.[23]

The ministry of justice commissars were among the first into action, with Maklakov and Basakov appearing at the ministry on February 28 itself.[24] On arrival, Maklakov sought to get the ministry moving again. But he didn't want to appear to be giving the functionaries orders. The revolt might fail, and those who listened to him might pay dearly for it. He called a meeting of the top officials and other ministry personnel. Great numbers arrived. Ironically, the first was D. D. Ivanov, who as judge had but two years earlier condemned him to prison for his article on the Beilis case.

Maklakov resisted the temptation to settle accounts with him, but he saw him as the very emblem of the judges who, out of servility, had created the Beilis affair. The ministry officials came forward with proposals for advancing the revolutionary agenda. The most significant one was to telegraph an order for release of Social Democratic deputies who had recently been arrested and sent to Siberia. The commissars also ordered an amnesty for political prisoners and removal of the ban on enrolling Jewish lawyers as "sworn attorneys." In the event of counterrevolution, the telegraphed order of release would have irrevocably compromised its sender. But the officials seemed eager to embrace the new regime, and Maklakov saw that embrace as reflecting the public-spirited officials' conscience and complete loss of confidence in the regime.[25]

The two elements of the future system of dual power—the Provisional Government and the Petrograd Soviet—took shape virtually simultaneously. (In the provinces, the balance of dual power shifted rapidly toward local majorities more in tune with the Soviet than the Provisional Government, and commonly under the influence of the most impassioned orators.)[26] The Soviet's "Executive Committee" formed itself on February 27. Oddly, the Soviet itself, of which the Executive Committee was in principle the delegate, did not meet until the next day. On March 1, Miliukov, as the most politically astute member of the Duma Committee and its de facto leader, composed a list of ministers for the Provisional Government. Although Rodzianko as chairman of the Duma was a natural for head of the government, Miliukov selected Prince George Lvov, who had been head of the Union of Zemstvos and a leader in Zemgor (a union of the Union of Zemstvos and the Union of Towns), which had supplemented the government as providers of military supplies. Richard Pipes's characterization of him may be unusually vivid but is far from extreme: "A less suitable individual to direct Russia's affairs in this turbulent era would be hard to conceive. Lvov not only had no experience in public administration, but he professed an extreme form of Populism rooted in an unbounded faith in the sagacity and goodwill of the 'people.' He considered central government an unmitigated evil. . . . Vladimir Nabokov, the cabinet secretary, writes: 'I do not remember a single occasion on which [Lvov] used a tone of authority or spoke out decisively and definitively . . . he was the embodiment of passivity.' " As these defects seem to have surprised no one, Pipes speculates that Miliukov chose him "because, aspiring to leadership in the government himself, he saw in Lvov a convenient figurehead."[27] It appears, however, that by the time of the February Revolution Lvov had so successfully maneuvered among the key elites that his selection as prime minister was virtually inevitable regardless of Miliukov's preferences.[28] Indeed, the tsar at about the same time was authorizing Prince Lvov to form a government, evidently on the understanding that that choice fulfilled the Duma's wishes.[29] Miliukov named himself foreign minister.

Maklakov was widely expected to be named minister of justice. He appears to have been on most of the "short lists" for the post, along (sometimes) with Nabokov.[30] Miliukov in fact chose Kerensky. There were important political reasons for doing so: Miliukov and others of the Duma Committee recognized that the new government needed a link to the Petrograd Soviet and the forces it represented. Of the two leftist members of the Duma Committee, Chkheidze did not want to be a minister, and Kerensky did. As for which post, Kerensky's reputation as defense counsel for victims of political prosecution made justice suitable. Shulgin (a member of the Duma Committee) argued that the "post has no importance," which in his view made it a suitable spot for the committee's opening to the left.[31] Maklakov seems never to have expressed resentment at having been passed over, though he told friends that no one had offered him a position.[32]

But Kerensky's selection by the Duma Committee was not enough to secure him the post. On the very day of that selection, the Executive Committee voted that no socialist should take part in the government—a decision, of course, that fit the standard Marxist doctrine that a bourgeois revolution should precede a socialist one. But Kerensky recognized that the Executive Committee's ban, to be final, had to be ratified by the Soviet itself, scheduled to meet on March 2. He accepted the post, counting on his ability to sway the Soviet. And so he did. In an impassioned speech, he justified accepting appointment to the Provisional Government without the Soviet's approval by falsely saying that he'd been allowed only five minutes to decide (actually, he had had overnight). Then he asserted that immediately on becoming minister of justice he had ordered political prisoners released—thus claiming credit for himself for what Maklakov and his active fellow commissars had done before Kerensky was even offered the ministry. Next he turned to the Executive Committee's rule against socialists' being members of the Provisional Government: "I resign from the duties of vice-chairman of the Soviet. But I am ready to accept that title from you again if you acknowledge the necessity of it." The crowd roared, "We do, we do." So, with no formal vote, Kerensky manipulated the Soviet to reverse the Executive Committee's decision.[33] In his account of the prisoner release, Maklakov makes no mention of Kerensky's spurious claim of credit.

The choice of Kerensky as the Provisional Government's bridge to the Soviet seems an unforced error. In chapter 12, on peasant rights, we saw the generally demagogic character of his oratory. His maneuvers to secure his role as the bridge do nothing to boost our confidence in his character. And, as we'll see in the next chapter, once he became head of the Provisional Government his character flaws precipitated a convulsion that sealed the government's fate. Surely the Duma Committee could have found a sturdier bridge.

Kerensky's position, straddling the Provisional Government and the Soviet, nicely symbolizes the awkwardness of the emerging structure. The bourgeois representatives—the Duma Committee and the Provisional Government—fearing the insurgent masses and intent on a restoration of order, desperately sought approval of the Executive Committee and the Soviet. Neither of the latter was in a position to assume power. Only the Executive Committee was small enough to exert itself continuously. And its, or the Soviet's, assumption of power would likely have precipitated a counter-revolution by military officers. (Indeed, after the revolution Maklakov contemplated the alternative scenario of the liberals' refusing to form a government; he speculated that the military would then have stepped forward to scatter the Soviet.)[34] So the Executive Committee relatively easily worked out an accord with the Duma Committee: the latter agreed to various policy commitments by the Provisional Government (most of which were already part of the Duma Committee's plans) in exchange for the Executive Committee's agreement to have the Soviet issue a proclamation (in fact drafted by Miliukov) calling on the masses to support the new government.

But the Executive Committee proved unable to deliver. First, the Soviet itself issued Order No. 1, which radically altered the country's military structure. Though it did not literally call for election of officers, it came close. The order provided for election of soldiers' committees in military units and for control of weapons by company and battalion committees. Plainly the Soviet didn't contemplate the army as an instrument of the new state in any traditional sense. Second, when the Soviet came to express its position on the Provisional Government, it didn't use the words negotiated with Miliukov but issued only a "half-hearted, wishy-washy endorsement, which fostered suspicion rather than trust among the masses for the Provisional Government." The Executive Committee was simply not in a position to control either the insurgents or the Soviet. Hasegawa again: "It would not be unreasonable to assume that the leaders of the Executive Committee found it more comfortable to talk with the representatives of the Duma Committee than to deliver speeches in front of the masses in the general sessions of the Soviet."[35]

Also aggravating the new regime's hazards was Nicholas II's decision to abdicate in favor of his brother rather than his son. Initially he signed a document abdicating in favor of 12-year-old Aleksei, for whom Nicholas's younger brother Grand Duke Mikhail would have been regent. Before the abdication could be issued, he had second thoughts. As the new regime would not welcome him in the vicinity of the throne, he recognized that if he issued the first draft he would likely never see his son again. So instead, at 11 p.m. on March 2, he signed an abdication purporting to name Mikhail his successor. (It was backdated to 3 p.m., to avoid the impression that it was a response to pressure from Duma representatives Shulgin and Guchkov, who had arrived in the interim; in fact, it wasn't.) The purported transfer to Mikhail was of doubtful legality. Nicholas II was not the owner of Russia's throne, free to give it away as an ordinary person might give away a parcel of land. And transfer to Mikhail rather than Aleksei meant that the monarchy as an institution would forfeit whatever sympathy might have accompanied the accession of a child.

On March 3 members of the Provisional Government and the Duma Committee met to discuss whether Mikhail should abdicate or accept the throne. Kerensky strongly favored abdication; the others present agreed, except for Miliukov. (Maklakov was not present at this meeting or the later meetings with Mikhail himself.) Miliukov argued for the need of a unifying symbol that could attract the support of the masses, who he believed didn't share the Petrograd insurgents' radicalism. Miliukov's opposition at least persuaded the group to leave it up to Mikhail. So the same men met with Mikhail later in the morning, joined by Shulgin and Guchkov. In that conversation only Miliukov and Guchkov favored Mikhail's taking the throne.[36] Mikhail then had a few words alone with Lvov and Rodzianko, and Rodzianko made clear to him that the government could not assure his personal safety. (As we'll see, Rodzianko's advice was not disinterested.) Whether his warnings were decisive is contested,[37] but in any event Mikhail declined.

Mikhail accompanied his refusal of the throne with a manifesto drafted initially by Nekrasov but completed by Nabokov and Baron B. E. Nolde. Via this manifesto Mikhail accepted the throne only in the event of being asked to do so by a constituent assembly elected by "universal, direct, equal, and secret vote." He asked the people in the meantime to "submit" to the Provisional Government, declaring it to be "endowed with full authority" until the constituent assembly adopted an alternative form of government.[38]

According to Mark Vishniak, Maklakov's left-wing Kadet colleague, Maklakov had lost hope in the February Revolution by March 3.[39] Maklakov's later writings make apparent that the key issues were the failure to pressure Grand Duke Mikhail to accept the crown and the wording of his manifesto. The lack of a monarch pulled the legal rug out from under both the constitution and the Duma: "If a monarch remained, then a constitution survived—laws, institutions, a *legal* terrain for action; there would be no revolution. If by contrast there was no longer a monarch, then the two legislative bodies were by the same act dispossessed, the Duma included, having no legal existence apart from the monarch; there was then no longer a constitution."[40] Of course when Maklakov says that with preservation of the "legal terrain . . . there would be no revolution," he means that the immediate events of February 23 to March 3 would not themselves have constituted a revolution—only a coup d'état. But for him the distinction was critical: preservation of the old institutions would have improved the chances for a liberal outcome.

As to the grand duke's manifesto, Maklakov viewed it as compounding the destructive effects of his abdication. Mikhail had, on the advice of the Duma representatives,

> signed a strange and criminal manifesto, which even if he had been a monarch he would have no right to sign. Despite the Constitution, without the consent of the Duma, he declared the throne vacant until the calling of a constituent assembly. He established on his own authority the franchise for this assembly. And until its convocation, despite the Duma and the Constitution, he transferred absolute power, which he himself did not have, to a Provisional Government, which in his expression "was formed on the initiative of the Duma."[41]

The drafters indeed appear to have shown little or no interest in legal or institutional continuity, and thus in whatever order or legitimacy it might have supplied. In the grand duke's manifesto the Provisional Government springs out of the Duma but then miraculously receives "full authority" from the grand duke, and so it is no longer responsible to the Duma at all.[42] Or, as Maklakov put it elsewhere, "The government, having issued from the Duma, repudiated it and delivered itself disarmed to its adversaries"[43]—the radicals in the Soviet and their allies.

To constitute the Provisional Government without legal foundations was also to constitute it without legal limitations. Maklakov drew a contrast between these arrangements and the "despised" constitution of 1906 (the October Manifesto and its implementation through the Fundamental Laws). The latter, he wrote, "introduced into Russian life the idea of lawfulness and of the subjection of authority to law. This crashed in the February Revolution, which restored autocracy, first that of the Provisional Government, then that of the Communist party and its heads, Lenin and Stalin."[44]

It may seem extravagant to accuse the feeble Provisional Government of wielding "absolute power" and to analogize it to Lenin and Stalin, but Mikhail's abdication manifesto implicitly dismissed any notion of *legal* bounds on the new government's authority. It completed the process begun a few days earlier by the Duma's failure to claim authority as an institution: the new institutions were wholly untethered to the old.

Among the challenges facing the Provisional Government was the conflicting nature of its claims to legitimacy. On the one hand it arose from the revolution in the streets. On the other hand, it claimed title, as it were, from Nicholas II's abdication (under pressure from a despairing military leadership and virtually the entire political elite). Indeed, the Provisional Government's link to Nicholas was expressed in his abdication manifesto, which exhorted Grand Duke Mikhail Alexandrovich to act in accord with principles to be established by the representatives of the people.[45] And shortly before his abdication Nicholas had issued a manifesto—rendered moot by the abdication itself—agreeing to put in place the Kadet dream of a government responsible to the Duma.[46]

But the Provisional Government's two claims to legitimacy were anything but mutually reinforcing. As Hasegawa puts it, "The simultaneous pursuit of legitimacy from the revolution as well as from the old regime was logically as well as politically impossible and was doomed to fail."[47] Each source of legitimacy drew on a powerful social element that had as a major characteristic—perhaps its defining characteristic—a lack of experience and skill at working with the other element to negotiate a coherent national policy.

Personal power struggles among the liberals also affected the choices made in February. Rodzianko had a notion that the Duma Committee and the Duma would function (pending creation of a constituent assembly) as Russia's upper and lower legislative bodies, with the Provisional Government acting as a cabinet responsible to them.[48] He was chairman of both and apparently saw them as avenues to fulfillment of his own ambitions. Thus he could easily see a continuing monarchy as a potential threat to his position.[49] But Rodzianko's calculation seems a gross misreading of the nature of parliamentary government. Such regimes typically include a figure largely outside the political hurly-burly, a monarch or president, to symbolize national unity and to smooth transitions from one political coalition to another. Rodzianko's persuasiveness with Mikhail had eliminated that model, leaving the Duma institutionally orphaned.

In the early days after February, Guchkov sought to give the Duma a chance, politically, by correcting the taint of the shrunken franchise of June 3. His idea was for the Duma itself to elect new members, a procedure evidently sometimes used by zemstvos and city dumas. The Duma would add back in all available members of the prior Dumas, especially of course those of the first two, elected under a relatively broad franchise. He consulted various people, including members of the Duma Committee and Maklakov. But his proposal evidently received little or no support except from Maklakov and Rodzianko.[50] In April Rodzianko called Maklakov to discuss the possibility of reassembling the Duma. (In fact, informal gatherings of these deputies occurred several times during the brief life of the Provisional Government.) But as Mikhail's abdication had cast aside the Fundamental Laws, Maklakov mused, in whose name might such a summons go out? He noted the irony that in advising Mikhail to abdicate, Rodzianko had perhaps "saved the grand duke's life but sacrificed that of the Duma."[51]

In the course of these discussions Maklakov received a call from Kerensky, asking him whether he was "plotting" against the Provisional Government and saying that summoning the Duma would be an act of hostility; it would cause the Soviet to demand the Duma's immediate dissolution. Maklakov later argued that the Provisional Government could have used the Duma as a counterbalance to the Soviet. For Kerensky, of course, as the Soviet's man in the Provisional Government, this wasn't necessarily an advantage, but for the rest of the Provisional Government it could have been, and Maklakov was in retrospect astonished that its members opposed reassembly of the Duma.[52]

Were there realistic alternatives to the outcome in February? Did Maklakov's preferred outcome—preserving the Duma and the monarchy—have a chance? Maklakov makes a case that the Duma was in fact the focal point for opposition to the regime. It had defied the tsar at least by informally refusing to disperse. Its Council of Elders, plus members acting "unofficially," had formed the Duma Committee and thus the Provisional Government, and its president had signed the proclamation announcing that formation. Soldiers of the mutinous garrison had paraded before the Duma, with their flags and military music.[53] In addition (though not mentioned by Maklakov), the series of strikes occurring a week before the wave that started February 23 had been aimed in part to coincide with and celebrate the Duma's reopening.[54] And Vasily Shulgin reports that when he and Shingarev drove to the Duma on February 27, the young workers who were limiting access ("Take the car back! No passage!") cheerfully let them through when they said they were Duma members.[55] A historian writing recently, A. B. Nikolaev, stresses that at least one of the creators of the Duma Committee, the Council of Elders, was a legal organ, and that through the prompt activities of its commissars the Duma Committee had in important ways seized the reins of authority.[56]

Yet Maklakov's account slides over the point later made by Schapiro: it was not the Duma itself that formed the Duma Committee and thus the Provisional Government. That had been achieved by members meeting unofficially and the Council of Elders; even the latter, though created under the Duma's constitution, could hardly claim the Duma's own status for purposes of giving the seizure of power a stamp of political legitimacy. Nor does Maklakov reply to Miliukov's argument that the Duma's popularity was due less to its status or achievements than to its being the forum where a handful of speakers (most obviously himself and Maklakov) had voiced the public's unrest.

Maklakov himself recognized that the Duma's history had impaired its legitimacy. It owed its composition to the electoral law of June 3, 1907, which was both a sharp contraction of the prior franchise and an unlawful coup—hardly a solid foundation for a liberal democratic institution. In addition, the Duma had not warmly embraced the insurrection but instead had formed an alliance with it out of a kind of necessity: given the regime's intransigence, the Duma could not morally align itself with the regime against the mutineers.[57]

What of the monarchy? Even the Petrograd insurgents' loathing of Nicholas and Alexandra seems not to have fully enveloped the institution and the family. When Shulgin and Guchkov arrived back in Petrograd after having received Nicholas's abdication, both spoke to the crowd gathered at the railway station. Shulgin delivered a passionate speech calling for people to unite for the salvation of Russia, ending it, "Long live Emperor Mikhail II"; the crowds responded with hurrahs. Guchkov, in contrast, was received with great hostility—but hostility directed against the members of the Provisional Government, not the imperial family. A speaker asked the audience a rhetorical question: had they made their revolution in order "to install a prince [Lvov] and an owner of tens of sugar factories [Tereshchenko] into the revolutionary government?"[58]

Further, Russian hostility to the monarchy apparently was deeply confused. The British ambassador, George Buchanan, reported that in the early days of the revolution a soldier told him, "Yes, we need a republic, but at its head there should be a good Tsar."[59] Countless examples of such muddled thinking exist.[60] And though a multitude of tracts and flyers depicted Nicholas and Alexandra venomously, even in these texts the grand dukes, including Mikhail, appeared as "positive characters."[61] In short, the Provisional Government seems to have been more hasty than the people in tarring the entire monarchy with a brush fit for the departed monarchs.

However one assesses the choices made by the Duma Committee and the Provisional Government, it's hard not to be struck by the casualness with which the latter abandoned Russia's institutions. In the initial meeting to confront Nicholas's purported handover to Mikhail, only Miliukov spoke up for a serious effort to preserve the monarchy. And even he, though stressing the monarchy's symbolic role and sensibly aiming at Russian masses not caught up in Petrograd's revolutionary fervor, appears not to have fully developed the case for constitutional continuity—or, indeed, for constitutionalism itself.

Discussing these attitudes later, Maklakov attributed them to a general indifference about governmental structure, extreme confidence based on the public welcome of Duma members' speeches, and lack of concern about the possible menace from the far left. He perceived all those features as flowing from the liberals' years without practical political experience, itself the result of the autocracy's success in politically marginalizing almost the entire country. The liberals' prior activity had "presupposed the existence of a normal state of affairs, in which press, speech and the vote were the sole means of combat."[62] Invoking Stolypin's line (a Maklakov favorite), "In politics there is no revenge, but there are consequences," he viewed the unrealism of February's winners as the direct result of the old regime's stifling of political activity. "The attitude of the moderates was the first consequence of our past, the immensity of the disaster the second."[63]

Maklakov's concern for constitutionalism was grounded in recognition of the need for institutions that could bring together a working coalition. He envisaged that coalition as drawing from "the old force of the overthrown state, the army, and the popular leaders of opinion."[64] But could such a coalition, even if embodied in plausibly legitimate institutions, have enabled Russia to address its problems—above all, to maneuver through the war?

At the core of the February Revolution was a policy split between those who saw it as enabling Russia to fight the war more effectively and those who saw it as enabling the country to stop fighting altogether. Maklakov was remarkably inattentive to that clash and must in part be considered a creature of Russia's underdeveloped civil society. Unlike his liberal colleagues, he turned to the peasant deputies for assistance on the equalization of peasant rights and then on the government's grain policy. But these conversations evidently did not reach much beyond those immediate issues. What a missed opportunity! The bulk of the army's enlisted men were, after all, peasants. While the peasant deputies may not have perfectly represented peasant views, they surely were a potential source of information. But if Maklakov queried them on the war at all, he did not report his findings. To judge from an October 1916 report of the tsarist secret police, recounting the peasants' resentment against the government (and other social classes) and their complete lack of faith in a successful outcome for the war,[65] the secret police were more realistic about Russia's social divide than were the elite leaders of the February Revolution.

Maklakov's failure to fully grasp the depth of Russia's problem underscores the soundness of his basic thesis: that centuries of autocracy had stunted the growth of civil society. In the decades before the revolution, to be sure, economic forces were gradually breaking down the barriers of estates and distance and were fostering the growth of civil associations, many of which cut across classes and interest groups. These developments gave Russians opportunities to negotiate solutions for themselves, to build leaders, to learn the necessity and the art of compromise—in short, to create the building blocks of liberal democracy. But Russia was still far behind western Europe, and the government was energetically (if haphazardly) fighting the process with bans, fines, requirements of police "permission," and so on.[66] Again, one thinks of Maklakov's line from the poet Nekrasov: "It's not easy to correct the work of centuries."

All this is not to say that accidents of timing were not critical. We saw how the moment in February when the armed forces got the upper hand was brief, but just in time to scuttle an effort at cooperation between the government and the Duma. Another bit of bad timing—though perhaps a more fit characterization is liberal hesitancy—was the slow motion of the various coup plots preceding February. Had these plots promptly achieved their aim, liberalism might have set down roots strong enough to survive the chaos caused by the downturn in the war and February's grain supply crisis. Maklakov touched on this issue in a speech on May 4, 1917, before one of the assemblies of deputies from all four Dumas:

> But there came a moment when it became clear to all that it was impossible to carry the war through to the end, to prevail, under the old regime. And for those who believed that revolution was ruinous, for them the task arose of saving Russia from revolution from below by means of a coup from above. That was the task that lay before us and that we didn't fulfill. And if our posterity curses this revolution, then they will curse those who did not understand at the time by what means it could have been averted.[67]

The speech of course reflects the priority Maklakov gave to winning the war. But it also suggests the benefits of a timely coup, removing Nicholas and Alexandra and making way for a regime with less baggage and more competence. Delay in their removal meant that liberalism as represented in the Duma had no choice but to support the embryonic revolution in the streets—even with the recognition that without the Duma's support on February 27 the revolution could not have survived: "The Duma understood that its participation in the movement was a matter of honor [given the hopelessness of Nicholas and Alexandra]. It knew that it was taking a path leading to revolution and in the name of patriotism and the rescue of Russia it destroyed the old regime."[68] Having failed to coalesce around a reform program, the moderates and the monarchy left Russia to extreme alternatives—either a fairly brutal counterrevolution or the chaos and uncertainty of the Provisional Government and its replacement by the Bolsheviks in October.

In short, then, a timely coup might have spared the Duma its February dilemma: having to support an intolerable regime or to stand against the authorities and implicitly in favor of insurrection. But even the institutions emerging from a coup would have had to navigate the war. Could they have had the political capacity to forge a broadly acceptable policy?

CHAPTER 18

In the Maelstrom

The Liberals in Office

THE FEBRUARY REVOLUTION brought liberals into office; it didn't bring liberalism into practice. To be sure, the Provisional Government adopted measures that, at least on paper, halted much of the old regime's lawlessness. It did away with administrative deployment of criminal sanctions; it purported to abolish distinctions based on religion or estate; it adopted a principle of liberty of the press and assembly.[1] But while changes like these surely restrained the state's lawless use of violence, other actors took up violence on a large scale, and law did little to constrain them. Peasants seized land, workers took control of factories, and peasants and workers assaulted landowners, factory owners, and managers who stood in their way—sometimes with fatal results. Although the government did not authorize these acts, it either turned such a blind eye, enforced the law so irresolutely, or was so powerless that the actions became commonplace and the participants had little reason to think their behavior illegitimate.

A few examples suffice. The Provisional Government authorized establishment of local "land committees" for the purpose of gathering data for "reform" proposals. In many places, however, the committees embarked on a much broader program, imposing restrictions on rents and mortgages, on sharing of equipment and livestock, and on management of land that was "not being fully exploited" by its owners. Decisions reached by these committees could be appealed to commissions in Petrograd and were often reversed, but the local committees commonly plunged right ahead.[2] Committees in the factories, nominally elected by workers but in practice often dominated by politicized outsiders, exacted wage hikes and other changes in working conditions. These pressures forced many enterprises to close and reduced the "bulk" of them to operating at a deficit.[3] But spontaneous violence was not directed solely at institutions of contract and property. Anti-government violence also broke out—a problem that was largely of the government's own making. It continued the old regime's wartime assault on free contracting, ordering peasants to deliver their crops to the state at fixed prices (which were always out of date), minus a vaguely determined allowance for the producers' own consumption. Peasants naturally resisted the state collectors, often violently.[4]

On top of the violence from self-help "reform" and resistance to state seizures came the activity of soldiers (typically deserters). Many of these had participated in ethnic cleansing of Jews and German Russians near the front. Although the military leadership had approved this extralegal violence at a general level, many of the troops had added their own ruthlessness. Back home or on the way home, they applied the unspoken lesson more broadly, pillaging the citizenry at large.[5]

Thus, if one follows the classical definition of the state as the holder of a monopoly on the legitimate use of force, the era of the Provisional Government witnessed the Russian state's disintegration. Its monopoly on legitimate force broke down. Nonstate violence burgeoned—so little deterred (perhaps even countenanced) by the state that it qualified as at least quasi-legitimate.

Some of the chaos of March 1917 was due to a kind of spontaneous crumbling of the state, exemplified by the fading away of the ordinary police. But some was due to the new government's excesses of zeal, such as its immediate discharge of all governors and deputy governors, without having named replacements, and its dismissal of the secret police and the Corps of Gendarmes.[6] Of course replacement of the tsarist governors and reform of lower-level enforcement institutions were in order, but abruptly zeroing them out left a gap that Russian civil society was ill suited to fill.

Russians could not fall back on the instinctive order of people accustomed to working out their affairs through individual and negotiated exercise of property and contract rights. Property rights did not enjoy the mystique of association with freedom that they enjoyed in the West. Furthermore, Russians had little experience with the practical benefits of property rights as a foundation for individual decisions on production, or as starting points for mutually advantageous contracts. And emancipation of the serfs did little to recast property rights in a favorable light. While the peasants received interests in part of the land they had formerly worked as serfs, they received them as communal interests rather than as the sort of individual property rights common in the West. Until the Stolypin reforms (which were implemented only in small part by 1917), a farmer had no individual right to choose his own farming strategy and possessed only a limited ability to sell his interests. And though the zemstvos developed by Alexander II provided peasants with an opportunity to participate in rural self-government, the peasant influence was slight (as they were systematically underrepresented in the zemstvo councils), and the zemstvos' authority itself was subject to fairly arbitrary supervision by officials of the ministry of internal affairs.[7] In short, both in the private sphere and in politics peasants had little experience in acting as a free people, seeking improvement of their lives by acting independently and with others in a framework of clearly established rights.

Workers in the immediately prerevolutionary era, typically migrants from the countryside or their offspring, similarly lacked experience with the rule of law. Limits on strikes, combined with officials' random exercises of authority—usually on the side of employers—largely denied workers a chance to pursue improved conditions through negotiation between citizens under the law. In light of this experience, it seems quite natural that they had a jaundiced view of conventional private rights.

Symptomatic of the mindset prevailing in prerevolutionary Russia was the popular (and even elite) usage of the term "bourgeois." The word seems tailor-made for an entrepreneur dependent on property and contract rights for the development of his business. Thus it should have been seen as encompassing groups with the greatest concern for the rule of law. But in Russia after February it became a ubiquitous term of abuse, virtually a swear word, equivalent to "scoundrel" or "blackguard," applied indiscriminately to anyone with whom the speaker disagreed.[8]

Thus, in an instant Russia removed not simply a defective monarch but the monarchy itself and drastically cut back existing institutions of authority. It did so in a population long accustomed to overwhelming centralized authority, with civil society more than embryonic but less than robust. The upshot parallels the annual Tatiana Day at Moscow University, when the university's suspension of its normally rather oppressive rules produced a student bacchanal.

The war of course further dimmed the prospects for a liberal outcome. First, it drove politicians to defer the calling of the Constituent Assembly (conducting elections in war-ravaged Russia would have been daunting). This reluctance in turn thwarted the resolution of matters that plainly required a representative assembly, such as the peasants' long-standing demand for gentry land. Second, the war gave special urgency to the split mentioned earlier, between those who hoped Russia could pursue the war to victory and those who hoped the country could be done with the war at almost any cost. Russians had to adopt a strategy, promptly, or German arms would settle the matter for them. A symptom of the long shadow cast by the war is the priority it assumed in Maklakov's activities.

Though obviously deeply concerned by the disintegration of order—it's a major theme of his May 4 speech, in which he expressed remorse at liberal society's failure to circumvent the revolution with a coup against Nicholas II—Maklakov was not in much of a position to stop or even retard it. He held a number of positions under the Provisional Government, but none gave him leverage for transformative action. After initial activity as a commissar at the Ministry of Justice, he was a member of a commission producing rules for the election of the promised Constitutional Assembly, a commission fixing the financial position of the imperial house, the State Juridical Commission (which among other projects worked to improve the rules for transfer of property), and a Kadet committee to maintain liaison with party members in the cabinet. He was elected a member of the Constituent Assembly, but it assembled only after he had arrived in Paris, and the Bolsheviks then promptly and violently dispersed it. Offered the chairmanship of the commission to investigate crimes of former tsarist officials, he declined, regarding its mission as anomalous: he saw it as falling between two stools, constituted neither as a genuine pursuit of officials for actions that were crimes under the law applicable when performed, nor as an openly revolutionary body imposing "revolutionary justice."[9] (And he surely would have had to recuse himself from the inquiries into brother Nikolai.)

His deepest involvement in the formation of Provisional Government policy seems to have been related to war policy, where the government struggled with three fundamental issues. First was its position on peace terms. Miliukov, foreign minister at the start of the Provisional Government, took a line pursuing victory and the concomitant rewards promised by Russia's Entente allies—above all, Russian control of Constantinople and the straits between the Black Sea and the Aegean (that is, direct Russian access to the Mediterranean). The liberal establishment was generally in accord. Resistance from the Soviet led rather quickly to Miliukov's ouster and government adoption of a version of "Revolutionary Defensism," a pursuit of peace without annexations or reparations but qualified by rejection of a "separate peace." Given the lack of Allied readiness to jettison annexations and reparations, this strategy didn't promise a quick exit. Finally, Lenin and the Bolsheviks had no objection to a separate peace and were ready to accept whatever they could work out with the Germans. As the war dragged on, the Leninist position grew ever more appealing.[10]

The second issue was military policy itself, with the government having at least some choice between an aggressive and a relatively quiescent stance. A possible model for the latter would have been the approach of the French government, which responded to soldiers' mutinies in April through June 1917 by forbearing from offensive action while awaiting the arrival of American troops. The Provisional Government took an aggressive stance, launching the "June offensive." This effort started well, but after a brief period of triumph the troops—other than the Eighth Army—stopped dead, exercising what they saw as their democratic right to decide on strategy unit by unit. Soon the Eighth Army was isolated and the retreat became universal. The Russian forces ended up far east of their starting position.[11]

Finally, and deeply entangled in Russia's divisions over both foreign and domestic policy, was the "Kornilov affair" of August 1917. Lavr Kornilov was a Russian general who won the fervent loyalty of his troops and commanded them with success (thus the behavior of the Eighth Army in the June offensive); he was ultimately appointed the army's commander in chief. The alternative label sometimes used, the "Kornilov plot," assumes the existence of a plot by Kornilov, which is at best questionable. A neutral label would be the "Kornilov-Kerensky imbroglio," as the core of the episode was the relationship between the two and the question of forming a dictatorship (of undefined character) to improve Russia's chances in the war. More detailed discussion of the imbroglio will follow toward the end of this chapter, but for now it is enough to note that the events brought Kerensky's fear of a challenge from the right to the flashpoint and likely sealed the fate of the Provisional Government. Overreacting to this supposed threat, the Provisional Government rescinded orders restricting Bolshevik activity, freed several leaders (including Trotsky), and distributed forty thousand rifles and revolvers to Bolsheviks and their sympathizers. The government thereby provided leaders and weapons for the Bolshevik coup in October, and it mobilized the extreme left psychologically.[12] The episode revealed Kerensky, by then "minister-president" and the embodiment of the Provisional Government, as vacillating and dissembling, deserving the trust of neither left nor right.

Maklakov's positions on these issues can be quickly summarized. *Peace terms:* Originally obdurate in support of those hoping to secure for Russia the spoils of victory, he ultimately began to show more flexibility than most of his Kadet colleagues. *June offensive:* He neither favored nor opposed it, but he used rumors of a military initiative as the occasion for a speech that attempted to view Russia's foreign and domestic issues through a unifying perspective. *Kornilov:* He sought to dissuade Kornilov from action in defiance of the Provisional Government, but without success.

The June offensive was central to Russia's effort to formulate a stance toward the war. Two weeks earlier, speaking to a private gathering of deputies to the now defunct Fourth Duma, Maklakov discussed the conduct of the war and the evidently imminent offensive. Noting his past clashes with Kerensky, he said that the attack and the conduct of the war would, if successful, show the current regime to be worthy of ruling Russia, and Russia worthy of freedom. In the event of victory, even the current regime's most desperate opponents would have to salute it—"You have conquered, Galilean," quoting the (probably apocryphal) deathbed words of the emperor Julian the Apostate acknowledging that Christianity had triumphed. But Maklakov also considered the possibility of failure. He framed Russia's choice as lying between the obviously difficult path of pursuing the war, on the one hand, and, on the other hand, sliding toward Lenin's foreign policy ("disgracing ourselves like cheats and cowards who cover their cowardice with pretty words" and ending in submission to the Kaiser) and foundering on his domestic political action (where force is above the law).[13] Failure of the offensive would thus expose Russia's lack of a working state, and the disastrous implications of that lack.

Maklakov's effort to fuse foreign and domestic policy reflected his long-held conviction that liberty made sense—in fact, could meaningfully survive—only in conjunction with an effective state. The ongoing chaos throughout Russia, which was soon to be manifested in the troops' insistence that each unit decide its strategy by democratic vote, was neither liberty nor the rule of law. Though the June speech is fair in its implied rebuke to the Provisional Government for failing to bring popular violence under control, it seems to mistakenly focus too much on Lenin as a cause of the violence. He was in part a cause, surely, but in part only a symptom. The seemingly endless bloodletting, the chaos, the delay in constitutional and policy reform—all were bound to breed discontent and a thirst for desperate solutions.

On the issue of broad strategy, the case for Lenin's solution—accepting a German diktat—looks overwhelming in retrospect, as it enabled Lenin's domestic victory. But at the time the outcome was not clear. Russian military, economic, and political exhaustion had their parallels in Germany and Austria. And the war aims of the tsarist regime and its liberal successors were not as frivolous as they may seem today, when we measure them against the ensuing disaster. They were grounded in the long-running imperial rivalries that had precipitated the war and could reasonably be expected to persist in one form or another (as indeed they have persisted). And the slogan "peace without annexations or reparations" carried the germ of an idea that made the Leninist position seem especially threatening to conventional patriotic Russians. While technically the slogan seemed to propose only that both sides call it quits and go back to the status quo ante, a suitable end to a military stalemate, it morphed into the idea that imperialism was itself reprehensible, so that peace should accommodate self-determination. The idea had obvious appeal to Finns, Poles, and Ukrainians, and enjoyed Lenin's strong support.[14] So for the liberals it seemed to spell the end of even a liberal Russian empire (assuming that's not an oxymoron). And as it proved, Lenin's position had an unspoken caveat: though enthusiastic about self-determination vis-à-vis the

Russian empire, there was nothing to prevent him, once he controlled the Russian state, from reversing position and reacquiring Ukraine (as well as invading Poland all the way to Warsaw, albeit in response to Polish moves in Ukraine).

Even if serious national interests justified continuing the war, two points in the liberals' reasoning seem weak. First, their rhetoric invoked the idea that a compromise peace would somehow betray those already killed or maimed, that persistence was necessary to redeem those losses. This argument is a classic case of the sunk-cost fallacy—invoking resources that can never be recovered to justify expending more. What had to be compared were the slaughter that persistence would entail against its possible gains. Russia of course was not alone in this; leaders in all the belligerent powers made the same error, obstructing chances for peace. Second, the Russian liberals' apparent feeling that they owed it to the Entente to persist in the war seems ill founded and excessive. Could the liberals' status as Westernizers and their identification with the West have blinded them to the realpolitik guiding their allies?

In the end we have to judge statesmen primarily in terms of results, and by that measure the liberals' approach was (as was said of a decision by Napoleon) "worse than a crime, it was a blunder."

Maklakov's positions seem to have belonged squarely in the broad run of liberal viewpoint—until September 1917. The evidence of his change of mind—disappointingly late in the game—comes from two sources, Alexander Ivanovich Verkhovskii, a general who became minister of war on August 30, and Vladimir Nabokov, who was cabinet secretary of the Provisional Government. In his wartime memoir, Verkhovskii notes his conviction that the Russians' only hope for a successful outcome was to make an offer of peace "on democratic terms," meaning in the parlance of the time a peace without annexations or reparations and, implicitly, a peace separate from the Allies. If the Germans accepted the offer, there would be peace; if they rejected it, then ordinary Russians would be willing to fight—otherwise they would not.[15] Verkhovskii's account appears consistent with (though not identical to) Vladimir Nabokov's report of his stance at a meeting in Petrograd in early October.[16]

Verkhovskii's memoir reports that Maklakov was present at a September 27 meeting at "Stavka," Russian army headquarters in Mogilev, assembled to prepare the Russian side for a scheduled meeting in Paris with Russia's allies. Maklakov was there, Verkhovskii says, because he was about to go to France as Russian ambassador (as he did, two weeks later). Verkhovskii misidentifies Maklakov as the minister of internal affairs, an astonishing mistake for the minister of war; brother Nikolai had been dismissed as minister of internal affairs back in June 1915 and at the time of the Stavka meeting was in the dock, under investigation by the Provisional Government's extraordinary investigative commission. Vasily Maklakov was well acquainted with the high command; he had, for instance, visited General Brusilov at the front in July 1916 with Rodzianko and Tereshchenko, and in February 1917 Brusilov told Tereshchenko that he'd like a repeat visit, as he felt cut off from events in the capital.[17]

In any event, the Stavka meeting included a review of the numbers in Russia's army. Stavka's estimates had recently ranged from seven to twelve million—quite a range! But by the time of the meeting Verkhovskii was convinced that the right number was ten million, of whom only two million were actually at the front. Verkhovskii speaks of the remaining eight million as performing support tasks; it is not clear how he accounted for deserters, who were flooding Russia at the time.[18] He proposed to reduce the support numbers to four million (still a ratio of support to frontline troops far exceeding that of France), thereby releasing four million for productive work on the home front. The Stavka group rejected his proposal. Despite Maklakov's familiarity with and condemnation of the old regime's conduct of the war, he must have found this evidence of disarray rather daunting.[19] Verkhovskii's impressions of the Stavka meeting, which he almost certainly shared with Maklakov, may have provoked some rethinking on Maklakov's part.

Indeed, Nabokov's account of meetings in late September and early October suggests that Maklakov engaged in just such a reevaluation. Though Nabokov is not absolutely clear, Verkhovskii was present at one and Maklakov at another. Verkhovskii took a thoroughly defeatist stance. By this time Baron Nolde had also concluded that the war was hopeless. In a Kadet central committee meeting he put forward that case, but instead of supporting Verkhovskii's idea of a straightforward Russian proposal of a "democratic peace," he argued that Russia should try to persuade its allies of the need to open peace negotiations, evidently sharing Nabokov's assumption that "a separate peace was naturally out of the question."[20] In another meeting of liberals, at the home of Prince Grigorii Nikolaevich Trubetskoi, Nolde made a similar pitch. On this occasion Nabokov and the Progressive Konovalov supported Nolde. Nabokov had to leave the meeting early and thus missed speeches by Struve and Maklakov, but he notes that he was told later that "only the latter partly supported Nolde."[21] Though secondhand, Nabokov's report provides reason to believe that Maklakov had by then begun to doubt the merits of a full-fledged war effort.

Nabokov's account is somewhat confusing and is especially perplexing in his view of Verkhovskii. At one point Nabokov is quite venomous, speaking of Verkhovskii as "utterly bankrupt" and "a sort of psychopath undeserving of any trust."[22] Elsewhere, contrasting Verkhovskii's position with the warlike stance of Tereshchenko, Miliukov's successor as the Provisional Government's foreign minister, he says, "Alas, we must acknowledge that Verkhovskii was essentially correct."[23] He makes no effort to explain how this (morally?) bankrupt psychopath could have stumbled into a sound position on an issue on which the liberal magnates of the day were almost uniformly wrong. Nabokov never seems puzzled by the paradox. He also is tantalizing about the exact nature of Maklakov's "partly" supporting Nolde—which parts?

On October 20 Verkhovskii pressed his view of the necessity of immediate peace proposals before the defense and foreign policy committee of the Provisional Council of the Russian Republic, a broadly representative consultative conference created by the Provisional Government in September, perhaps in belated and partial recognition of the gap left by its discard of the monarchy and the Duma. But the council failed to support Verkhovskii.[24] Maklakov was a member of the council but had by this time left for Paris. October 20 was in any event extremely late in the scheme of things, five days before the Bolsheviks' coup. It is tempting to fantasize a brilliant Maklakov speech endorsing Verkhovskii and persuading the liberals to score an end run on Lenin. But the lateness of the proceedings and Maklakov's dedication to the Entente make the fantasy, even if he had been on hand, just that.

The Kornilov affair proved fatal to the Provisional Government and thus to any chance for liberalism in Russia. A liberal's conduct in the matter raises at least two issues. The first is whether a true liberal could support any move to more extreme, or draconian, exercises of government power. Maklakov undoubtedly favored action to check the prevailing chaos, on grounds of both foreign and domestic policy, a judgment seemingly rooted in a combination of wartime necessity and a broader belief that bolstering the "ordered" part of "ordered liberty" was necessary to prevent anarchy or civil war. A second, more pragmatic, question concerns his judgment. Because the ensuing debacle was a natural result of the mere *appearance* of a Kornilov coup attempt, any liberal who had an opportunity to prevent the appearance or reality of a Kornilov coup and failed to do so seems to have exercised poor judgment. Maklakov acquitted himself well on this score, trying to avert both the appearance and the reality of a coup, only to be thwarted by Kerensky's wiles and Kornilov's rashness. Since the first question is heavily entangled in imponderables, this text will focus on the second.

Kornilov himself has had the fate of becoming the subject of a witty phrase that is at best three-quarters correct—that he had "the heart of a lion and the brains of a sheep." No one questions his bravery, which was coupled with leadership skills and an ability to impart his courage to his troops. In the ill-fated June offensive only the Eighth Army—under Kornilov's command—performed well, and no one claims that this was coincidence.[25] His masterful leadership is hard to square with the brains of a sheep. His political judgment, however, was sketchy.

In part because of the Eighth Army's success, Kerensky appointed Kornilov commander in chief in July. Kornilov accepted the post, subject to Kerensky's meeting his demands for restoring military discipline, including making the death penalty applicable to troops in the rear. The demands became publicly known. On July 24, after various clarifications, Kerensky gave assurances that he would fulfill the demands, but he then embarked on a course of backing and filling, mixing deceit and irresolution.[26] The conflict was still unresolved at the time of the Moscow State Conference, August 12–15, summoned by the Provisional Government to gather representatives of the whole spectrum of Russian opinion. The conference did indeed bring disparate elements together in the same hall (the Bolshoi Theater), but it served mainly to display their mutual loathing. Speakers from the right received cheers from the like-minded and catcalls from the left, and vice versa.[27] Maklakov's talk pursued the theme he had developed in his speech to members of the Fourth Duma in June: success in the war depended on the discipline that only a strong state could provide, not a state in shambles, and military success therefore required an effort to strengthen the state.[28] Kerensky's speech closing the conference was true to form. Boris Savinkov, deputy minister of war (Kerensky being formally the minister), characterized it as "frenzied"; Miliukov pinpointed a special Kerensky stage affect, "a catch in his voice that fell from hysterical scream to stage whisper."[29]

The most notable event of the conference was the Kornilov moment, not for the content of his speech but for the theatrical effects and their apparent impact on Kerensky. Kornilov came to Moscow from the front, surrounded by his bodyguard of Tekke Turkomans dressed in red robes (he had learned various Turkic dialects while on assignment in Central Asia). His arrival at the Bolshoi and rather mundane speech received a tumultuous welcome (from the right). Kerensky later wrote that the conference persuaded him that the Provisional Government's next threat would come from the right (the Bolsheviks had unsuccessfully attempted a coup in July). Pipes argues that this vision of a possible right-wing coup lodged itself so firmly in Kerensky's thinking that it colored his interpretation of all later events.[30]

Kornilov's clash with Kerensky over the former's demands stirred rumors that Kornilov might attempt a coup. In a kind of sideshow to the Moscow State Conference, Kornilov and several of his representatives met a few leading Kadets (including Maklakov and Miliukov) and the Octobrist Rodzianko in the apartment of Nikolai Kishkin, a Kadet Central Committee member. Kornilov said that he would not submit to removal by the government; he would regard any removal as merely an intrigue by the Soviet. In that event he would attempt a coup, and he asked the assembled politicians if they would support him. By Maklakov's account, the assembled Kadets indicated that they would. Kornilov departed at some point, but a discussion ensued among the Kadets in the presence of Kornilov's representatives. Maklakov opposed such a coup—not, as he explained, because it was illegitimate but because he thought it would fail. (He appears to have regarded the whole issue of legitimacy as hopeless after Grand Duke Mikhail's purported handoff of power to the Provisional Government.[31]) Maklakov later pursued the issue with Leonid Novosiltsev, a Kadet who had been with Maklakov in the Fourth Duma and was now head of the Russian Officers' Union and among the Kornilov representatives, telling him he thought that the assurances of support were a "provocation" and that in the event of a coup attempt the Kadets would in fact take cover and provide no support.[32] (In Russian usage, "provocation" commonly means laying a trap.) The 1922 memoirs of Anton Denikin, a tsarist general who was soon to be among the leaders of the White forces in the civil war, confirm Maklakov's communication to Novosiltsev.[33]

Maklakov's second effort to avert a coup took place in what

is typically called a "telephone conversation," but the technology used was quite foreign to any phone we know. The parties used a "Hughes machine," a kind of printing telegraph. A person at one end dictates a communication to the telegraph operator, who types it in; a transcript arrives at the other end. Most critically, the persons at opposite ends of the line cannot hear each other's voice. The effect is thus a little like a modern email. One such conversation (between Kornilov and Kerensky) triggered the Kornilov affair. A second (between Maklakov and Savinkov in Petrograd and Kornilov at Stavka) uncovered Kerensky's misapprehension (or purported misapprehension). Both occurred during the night of August 26–27.

The Kornilov-Kerensky exchange was brought about by the activities of one of those officious intermeddlers who turn up from time to time to sow chaos. Vladimir N. Lvov (a man of "legendary stupidity," in Maklakov's estimation[34]) had been Procurator of the Holy Synod in the Provisional Government until July, when Kerensky removed him. On August 22 he met with Kerensky, claiming that several people—unidentified—asked him to pass on a message that the government needed to bring in some figures with good relations with the military. Kerensky seems not to have given the conversation another thought.

Lvov then went to Stavka and told Kornilov that Kerensky had asked him to seek out Kornilov's views on how to assure firm government in Russia. Lvov opined that there were three options, the third being that Kornilov would become dictator, with Kerensky and Savinkov holding ministerial portfolios—presumably subordinate. Interpreting Lvov's message as a proposal from Kerensky, Kornilov said he regarded that choice as best. Lvov then returned to Petrograd and spoke with Kerensky, claiming in essence that Kornilov was *demanding* to become dictator. Kerensky, at first amused but then alarmed, asked Lvov to put the "demands" in writing, which he did. Lvov also said (truthfully, it so happens) that Kornilov would like Kerensky to be at Stavka the next day. Kerensky scheduled a conversation with Kornilov over the Hughes machine, asking Lvov to be on hand at 8 p.m. Lvov was late, and Kerensky began the call at 8:30. At a critical moment he *impersonated* Lvov. The phone call would seem funny if it were not so tragic:

Kerensky: Prime Minister on the line. We are waiting for General Kornilov.

Kornilov: General Kornilov on the line.

Kerensky: How do you do, General. V. N. Lvov and Kerensky are on the line. We ask you to confirm that Kerensky can act in accordance with the information conveyed to him by Vladimir Nikolaevich.

Kornilov: How do you do, Aleksandr Fedorovich. How do you do, Vladimir Nikolaevich. To confirm once again the outline of the situation I believe the country and the army are in, an outline which I sketched out to Vladimir Nikolaevich with the request that he should report it to you, let me declare once more that the events of the last few days and those already in the offing make it imperative to reach a completely definite decision in the shortest possible time.

Kerensky [impersonating Lvov]: I, Vladimir Nikolaevich, am inquiring about this definite decision which has to be taken, of which you asked me to inform Aleksandr Fedorovich strictly in private. Without such confirmation from you personally, Aleksandr Fedorovich hesitates to trust me completely.

Kornilov: Yes, I confirm that I asked you to transmit my urgent request to Aleksandr Fedorovich to come to Mogilev.

Kerensky: I, Aleksandr Fedorovich, take your reply to confirm the words reported to me by Vladimir Nikolaevich. It is impossible for me to do that and leave here today, but I hope to leave tomorrow. Will Savinkov be needed?

Kornilov: I urgently request that Boris Viktorovich come along with you. What I said to Vladimir Nikolaevich applies equally to Boris Viktorovich. I would beg you most sincerely not to postpone your departure beyond tomorrow. . . .

Kerensky: Are we to come only if there are demonstrations, rumors of which are going around, or in any case?

Kornilov: In any case.
Kerensky: Goodbye. We shall meet soon.
Kornilov: Goodbye.

Kerensky's critical move, of course, is his pretense of being Lvov and his asking Kornilov to confirm that what Lvov has told Kerensky was correct. In "confirming," Kornilov signs a blank check, agreeing to a message that has never been specified. Interestingly, he is explicit only in "confirm[ing]" a very narrow proposition—that he would like Kerensky *to come to Mogilev*. Kornilov's behavior in this exchange supports the "brains of a sheep" hypothesis. Kerensky's impersonation of Lvov, and his failure to pick up on Kornilov's having been specific *only* about the invitation to Stavka, suggest that he was far more interested in getting the goods on Kornilov than in ascertaining his position. As we'll see, he almost immediately sent a telegram to Kornilov dismissing him.[35]

The part of the story that brings in Maklakov erases any doubt about Kerensky's manipulative intent. As Maklakov records in postwar correspondence, Kerensky called him to the Winter Palace that evening. Hearing Kerensky's account, Maklakov urged that the matter be disposed of without publicity and offered to go to Stavka to talk with Kornilov. Savinkov objected, accusing Kornilov of being two-faced and arguing for "merciless punishment." Rejecting the idea of Maklakov's going to Stavka, Kerensky proposed a Maklakov-Savinkov conversation with Kornilov by Hughes machine. Maklakov agreed.[36]

Boris Savinkov deserves a word before we turn to the phone conversation. Had he died before the February Revolution he would have gone down in history solely as a leading member of the Socialist Revolutionary Party's terrorist wing, its "Fighting Organization." In that role his signal achievements were the assassinations of V.K. Plehve, minister of internal affairs, and Grand Duke Sergei Alexandrovich, Nicholas II's uncle and, through his marriage to Alexandra's sister, also his brother-in-law. Arrested for these killings, he escaped to France and fought in the French army in World War I. After the February Revolution he returned to Russia to fight as a Russian and was appointed deputy minister of war, the position he held at the time of the phone call. He won the admiration of Winston Churchill, who gave him a chapter in his book *Great Contemporaries*, calling him a "terrorist for moderate aims."[37] Churchill may have been especially taken with him because of his military activities to overthrow the Bolsheviks after their October coup, which paralleled Churchill's own effort to "strangle Bolshevism in its cradle." Churchill's portrait quotes Sergei Sazonov, onetime tsarist minister of foreign affairs, reacting to a mention of Savinkov: "Savinkov. Ah, I did not expect we should work together." Maklakov may have had similar feelings, side by side with Savinkov at the Hughes machine.

The conversation has two segments.[38] In the first, Savinkov laid out several understandings (or misunderstandings). He claimed that he never proposed to Kornilov in the name of the Provisional Government any kind of political combination, and he could not have done so. (Maklakov reads this part of the pitch as Savinkov's effort to exonerate himself from culpability for any coup attempt.) He asked if Kornilov repudiated the "demands" that he had presented to the Provisional Government through Lvov—demands that we know Kornilov never made. He warned Kornilov against attempting to impose his will on the Russian people. He closed by inviting Kornilov to return to the Hughes machine at 4 a.m. with his responses.

Kornilov answered with quite a long discourse of his own, which ended at 5:50 a.m. (no record exists of when it began). He reminded Savinkov of the government's "firm" decision—which had in fact been passed on from Kerensky to Kornilov via Savinkov—for the transfer of a cavalry corps to Petrograd, to be completed when martial law was declared in Petrograd. (I take Kornilov to be making this point in order to remind Savinkov of the Kerensky-Kornilov cooperation in the interests of quelling unrest, and thus to undercut Savinkov's implicit accusations against him.) He emphatically denounced the government's vacillation in reference to the measures formerly agreed on by Kerensky, but he assured Savinkov that no matter what his opinion of Kerensky, he believed his continued participation in the government was "absolutely necessary." He gave a succinct version of his colloquy with Lvov, saying that Lvov had presented three alternatives, and that his deepest conviction was that the third—establishment of a dictatorship at the invitation of the current government and including "you both" (presumably Savinkov and Kerensky)—was "absolutely necessary."

At the end came Kornilov's stunner: During the break, he had received a telegram from Kerensky—"absolutely unexpected"—dismissing him from his position. Believing, he said, that such a dismissal could have come about only through the pressure of the Soviet, and that to leave his position under such pressure would amount to going over to the enemy, he said, "I will not leave my post." By issuing the dismissal order, while the conversation proceeded or even before, Kerensky acted as if he had no interest in clarifying Kornilov's intent, even though he himself had proposed the conversation.

Savinkov responded, confirming the intention that a cavalry corps should go to Petrograd to put down any attempts against the Provisional Government, "regardless of where they come from." He expressed himself against any kind of one-man rule, saying that if Kerensky announced himself dictator he "would find an enemy in me [Savinkov]. . . . "From your statement I see that Lvov has played a sad role—if not worse. . . . I fear that the misapprehension created by Lvov has played a fateful role for our country. . . . I've already said that it's not for me to quarrel with you, but Maklakov is here and would like to speak with you."

Maklakov tried to simmer down Kornilov:

> This is Maklakov at the apparatus. Good day, Lavr Georgievich. In the transmission of Lvov your proposal was understood here as a desire for a violent coup d'état. I'm very glad that this is evidently a misunderstanding. You are not adequately

> informed of the political mood. Such an attempt would be a disaster for Russia and would lead to destruction of the army, butchery of the officers, and victory for [Kaiser] William. It's essential to take all measures to liquidate this misunderstanding without hesitation and without publicity. You're not up to date about what's going on here. If I can be useful, I'm happy to go to Stavka.[39]

Though not backing off his intention to disregard the dismissal, Kornilov pronounced himself happy to meet at Stavka with Maklakov, Kerensky, and Savinkov. He said he thought that direct personal conversations could eliminate the misunderstanding, "only I must say that with this telegram of dismissal the grounds for a happy outcome are not favorable."

Rushing back to the prime minister's office to report on the conversation, Savinkov ran into Nikolai Nekrasov, a left-wing Kadet who in July had become not only minister of finance but also assistant to Kerensky. Nekrasov told Savinkov he'd sent the newspapers Kerensky's statement charging Kornilov with treason, claiming that Kornilov had "in a direct wire conversation" confirmed making a demand for dictatorial powers; the statement claimed cabinet authority to dismiss Kornilov. The latter exploded with rage at the accusation and dismissal; he issued a statement that actually was treasonous, or close to it. His rallying cry received friendly telegrams from fellow generals but no action, and the politicians, whether confused by Kerensky's disinformation or simply too cautious, did nothing (as predicted by Maklakov). The "rebellion" promptly petered out.[40] But by rousing the left with the specter of a right-wing coup—and indeed arming it with leaders and weapons—and by showing Kerensky as a man without clear convictions, the phony Kornilov "coup" eased the path for the real Bolshevik coup in late October. Maklakov had by then arrived in Paris to take up his ambassadorial post.

In his writings after the revolution, Maklakov argued that the fate of the Provisional Government showed what a mess the liberals would have made if Nicholas II had agreed to a Kadet cabinet in 1905.[41] Indeed, the liberals played their hand badly in 1917. They were quick to dismantle the old regime, even though, as shown by Maklakov's experience in the ministry of justice at the moment of transition, many in the bureaucracy were ready to apply liberal policies. They also—and here Maklakov himself was pushing the government toward danger—were remarkably single-minded in their war policy, closing their eyes to a host of factors: German peace offers (doubtless in part manipulative), the range of possible Russian bargaining policies, and military strategies less costly in Russian blood.

But in fairness the liberals were dealt a very bad hand in 1917. To their advantage, the period from 1905 to 1917 had produced modest development of Russia's institutions for self-government and its people's experience at conducting affairs on a basis of mutual respect for others' rights. But that progress was more than offset by the immediate effects of a staggeringly costly war, which by 1917 threatened the vivisection of the Russian empire, and whose conduct had inured millions of young men to indulging in almost random violence. Plus, the war plainly made it far more difficult to preserve the monarchy (and thus the constitutional structure). With all these weaknesses, and little experience in institutions for peaceful reconciliation of vehemently conflicting interests, it seems nearly inevitable that by late 1917 the choice would come down to which sort of dictatorship was least bad—right (Kornilov) or left (Bolshevik).

So 1917 does not seem a fair test for a hypothetical Kadet cabinet in 1905. At the same time, Russia's relatively slight experience with the underpinnings of liberal society made *any* sudden liberal accession to power extremely risky. Stolypin's remark, "Give Russia twenty years of internal and external peace and quiet, and it will change beyond recognition," was probably overoptimistic, but history denied Russia the chance to find out.

V. Postlude

CHAPTER 19

Exile

AMONG DISTINGUISHED political figures Maklakov proved unusual in the long gap between national prominence and death—a few months short of forty years. Quite naturally he saw the years in exile as a comedown. He agreed with the observation of his friend Boris Bakhmetev, the Provisional Government's ambassador to the United States and thus also a representative of a nonexistent country,[1] that for him, too, the years in emigration were much less interesting than his former life.[2] And he expressed the wish that anyone writing a biography of him cover only the years before October 1917.[3]

In fact, Maklakov's activities in exile were wide-ranging and intrinsically interesting. Consistent with having come to Paris as ambassador, he tried to protect Russia's geopolitical interests in the immediate postwar period despite Bolshevik rule. The Allies initially did not expect the Bolsheviks to hang on, and it was natural to think that their governments might take account of Russian interests, as perceived by non-Bolsheviks. He also pressed the White leaders in the Russian civil war to adopt inclusive policies, above all to take a resolute stand against the anti-Semitic pogroms that their troops allowed or even joined. And until his death in 1957, he continuously ran interference on behalf of the Russian émigrés in France (interrupted only by the Nazi occupation, including three months' imprisonment), helping them navigate bureaucratic and other hurdles. (The French government itself supported him in these efforts, giving him an official post through which to carry them out.)

These activities seem all too relevant today. Many high-level political exiles must make trade-offs between love for country and its citizens and loathing for the country's current rulers. Participants in civil wars have to tame the worst instincts of their partisans. Political refugees and their host countries face conflicts of interests similar to those of France and the Russian exiles. Maklakov appears to have pursued all these projects with his usual intelligence, eloquence, and diplomacy.

But as these activities are distinct from the topic that brought me to Maklakov—the question of how citizens can advance the cause of liberal democracy—I will cover them only briefly. Once in exile, Maklakov soon recognized that he and his fellow émigrés could do little to affect events in Russia. Because his thoughts on the limited role of émigrés were an outgrowth of his earlier strategies toward the imperial government, and because they led to his taking the most controversial step in his forty years of exile, I'll address them first and then turn briefly to the three projects—postwar diplomacy, advice to the Whites, and help for Russian refugees—before closing with a word about day-to-day life in Paris and Maklakov's last years.

Despite his efforts to counsel the White forces, Maklakov recognized, even before the end of the civil war, that he and his fellow exiles were virtually powerless. In an April 1920 letter to Bakhmetev (well before serious fighting ended with General Pyotr Wrangel's withdrawal of his forces from the Crimea in the fall of 1920), he wrote that he found an article by Miliukov "dishonest at the core" in its apparent assumptions about the émigré community's influence over Russian events. "What we can do from abroad comes down merely to giving explanations of what is happening in Russia, and holding foreign powers back from mistakes. We can do that, and, unfortunately, we do it inadequately. Anything more is pure illusion."[4]

His realism about émigré influence was coupled with a firm position on how any liberalization of Bolshevik rule might occur. His view not only parallels his approach in 1905–17 but also has been partially—if belatedly—vindicated. He staunchly opposed supporting terrorism or violent rebellion, such as the peasant revolts that Savinkov sought to stir up. Even if violence managed to overthrow the Bolsheviks, he thought, it would not produce a healthy state. Reform, when it came, would come from Bolsheviks who saw the need. "Only Bolshevism can save Bolshevism,"[5] he wrote, and "Salvation will come not from the emigrants but from the midst of the Bolsheviks."[6] History, in a sense, proved him correct. While the reforming zeal that swept the Soviet Union in the second half of the 1980s drew heavily on non-government, non-party figures, and on the sentiments of ordinary people, it also depended vitally on high officials such as Gorbachev, Shevardnadze, and Alexander Yakovlev, whose liberalizing convictions brought censorship virtually to an end and launched a brief era of truthful accounting for Soviet times.[7] Such a belated vindication may seem no vindication at all. It happened sixty-five years after Maklakov was writing, so much later that the label "Bolshevik" applies awkwardly to the reformers of the 1980s. But writing in 1920 and 1921 Maklakov could hardly have anticipated the extreme events that tended to delay any amelioration, such as Stalin's accession to power and World War II; with adjustments for those shocks, the prediction seems pretty good.

That said, his vision of Soviet developments was for a time blurred. In late 1944, for example, he included in a letter to his friend Ariadne Tyrkova-Williams the astonishing statement that the "USSR is developing into a rule-of-law state on new foundations."[8] Though the references to "developing" and "new foundations" serve as qualifications, it was sheer fantasy to suggest that late

Stalinism in any way approximated, or was progressing toward, the rule of law.

Maklakov wrote the letter during a relatively brief period in which he appears to have been carried away by his patriotic admiration for his countrymen, who had borne the brunt of Allied casualties in defeating the Nazis. Besides the scale of Russian sacrifices and the horror of Nazi rule, he noticed that to rouse the Russian people Stalin had had to start speaking of *Russia*,[9] invoking patriotism rather than socialism, "the revolution," or the party. Also, in language somewhat reminiscent of his speech just before the June 1917 offensive, saying that victory under the Provisional Government would vindicate the February Revolution, he appeared to see a comparable vindication for the Soviets in the victory over Hitler; at least they had been able to forge a state capable of defending the nation.[10] And his work on the problems of Russian refugees in France brought home to him the devastation inflicted on many of them through loss of the opportunity to practice their professions or earn a decent living; this recognition gave his hopes for improvement in Russia a special urgency. In a 1934 letter he had expressed his sickness at reading in the newspaper an endorsement of the thought that France should expel those "who violate the elementary rules of hospitality." For the French to impose restrictive work rules that drove willing workers into the streets and then call them "vagabonds" seemed monstrous—a "pitiless state's sacrifice to Moloch."[11] And of course he was familiar on a day-to-day basis with talented, well-educated émigrés scraping by as taxi drivers, doormen, and waiters. The situation led him to a belief that émigrés thwarted in France should be able, if they chose, to take the risks of returning to Russia.[12]

Maklakov's flirtation with the Soviets reached its zenith on February 12, 1945, when he led a delegation of Russian exiles to a meeting at the Soviet embassy (the same building at 79, rue de Grenelle, where he had served as quasi-ambassador until France's recognition of the Soviet Union in 1924). In the spring of 1944 he had organized a "Russian Émigré Action Group," aimed at expressing a centrist view among the émigrés; it would fall between the Union of Russian Patriots' unabashed Sovietophilia and the hopes of some, such as General Denikin, for violent overthrow of the regime.[13] After rejecting two invitations to the embassy by Alexander Bogomolov, the current ambassador, Maklakov finally accepted the third. He brought to the parlay eight others, ranging in pre-revolutionary political position from Right Kadet to Right Socialist Revolutionary.[14] Although the Soviets' choice of Maklakov over the Russian Patriot group outraged the latter, it seems obvious that Soviet propagandists would gain far more from a lukewarm recognition by Maklakov than an ardent embrace by apologists for Stalin.

The event featured speeches by Maklakov and Bogomolov and by the eight in Maklakov's group. Maklakov, after reviewing émigré attitudes toward Soviet Russia before and during Stalin's alliance with Hitler, turned to the period after Hitler's invasion. He spoke of how the émigrés then felt themselves "on the same side of the barricade" as the Soviets and how they recognized "Soviet power as a national power" (not just usurpers). Thus he saw an opportunity for reconciliation between the emigration and Soviet power. He included a seemingly favorable reference to the Stalin constitution of 1936 but followed it with a comment that Russia's evolution was "far from complete"; he didn't say what he thought was needed for the evolution to be completed.

After recounting the words of Bogomolov and of those accompanying him, Maklakov records, "The ambassador proposed a toast to 'the Soviet people, the Red army and Marshal Stalin,'" followed by toasts to the ambassador and to everyone present.[15]

The main historian of this reception calls it "the biggest sensation in 'Russia Abroad' since June 22, 1941"—Hitler's invasion of Russia.[16] This is surely an exaggeration, but word of the event did trigger powerful reactions. Kerensky was initially outraged but somehow became convinced that Maklakov had acted under orders from de Gaulle,[17] which seems an implausible scenario—Maklakov would almost certainly not have made a serious turn in his relationship with the Soviets at the behest of a foreign head of state, even of his host country. Vladimir Nabokov, the novelist and son of Maklakov's fellow Duma member and Kadet leader, wrote to a fellow émigré:

> I can understand denying one's principles in *one* exceptional case; if they told me that those closest to me would be tortured or spared according to my reply, I would immediately consent to anything, ideological treachery or foul deeds and would even apply myself lovingly to the parting on Stalin's backside. Was Maklakov placed in such a situation? Evidently not.

Nabokov went on to catalogue émigré attitudes toward Soviet Russia, starting with the "philistine majority, who dislike the Bolsheviks for taking from them their little bit of land or money," and running through "fools" and several other categories, finally reaching the group in which he presumably included himself—"decent freedom-loving people, the old guard of the Russian intelligentsia, who unshakably despise violence against language, against thought, against truth."[18] Doubtless because of the toasting outrage, Nabokov didn't recognize that Maklakov belonged in this last group. Evgenii Efimovskii, a friend and admirer of Maklakov, says in a memorial appreciation that Maklakov didn't touch the champagne poured for him.[19] Maklakov's own account suggests nothing of the kind, and such an excuse would make him out to be a bit of a weasel.

Plainly he was trapped. Confronted with a toast to the Soviet people and the Red Army, he could hardly interrupt to insist that it was the *Russian* army and people whom he toasted; nor could he join the toast with qualifications—"Yes, but not Marshal Stalin." Accepting the invitation at all was probably folly, as the prospects for honest or useful reconciliation were dim and the event surely included a risk of some sort of toast or equivalent embarrassment. But having come to the event, he had no way out of the toast that was consistent with his purpose in having come.

Nabokov's reaction may have been the most vividly expressed, but many others shared its basic impulse; and some had long memories. When émigrés joined to create a Russian archive in the United States (now the Bakhmetev Archive at Columbia University), to replace one previously established in Prague and rendered useless by the Communist coup d'état in 1948, several of the moving spirits objected to the inclusion of Maklakov on the committee, pointing to the embassy visit. Ariadne Tyrkova-Williams wrote an impassioned letter to Bakhmetev opposing Maklakov's exclusion. Though she was herself categorically against the visit, and acknowledged that he had made no public confession of error, she said that in private conversation he didn't deny that it had been a mistake. "And all this was six years ago." From the visit onward, and indeed before, he had done what he could for Russians, and done it honorably. To exclude him from a cultural initiative (which he'd already been asked to join) would be not only cruel but also impolitic from a Russian point of view: to leave out someone who was "one of the few remaining dazzling individuals among us," one who had made a great contribution to Russian scholarship and culture, would send a strange signal to other refugees, who ought to be taught to respect his talent, learning, and intellect. In the end the founders of the committee brought Maklakov on board.[20]

Maklakov's thinking behind the embassy visit was clearly wishful. He had powerful reasons to hope that Stalinist tyranny would abate. How wonderful if liberty and constitutionalism were to join Russian might! And in the broadest sense the visit was likely harmless, inconsequential in the long East-West battle for European hearts and minds. But if the visit's faux friendliness was pivotal in convincing any émigrés to return to the Soviet Union, then it inflicted high, indeed astronomic costs on those returners. According to a rumor that reached Russians living in New York, the Soviet embassy in Paris was reminding Russians who inquired about moving back that "Siberia was in the Soviet Union as well as Moscow and Leningrad"; indeed, most of the few thousands who did return ended up in Siberian prison camps along with forced repatriates.[21]

The "Stalin toast," though probably the most famous episode of Maklakov's forty-year exile, should not eclipse his productive work. These efforts started with his role as diplomat without portfolio. On arrival in Paris in 1917 he could not, given the overthrow of the Provisional Government, claim full diplomatic status. This situation deeply upset numerous Russian exiles, who felt that Russia deserved better at the hands of the Allies, in light of the country's extraordinary sacrifices in the war. Maklakov was philosophical about it, observing to a French journalist that he was "like a newspaper placed on a chair to show it was occupied."[22] In any event, he was quite successful in forming a unified non-Bolshevik effort to influence the Paris Peace Conference; it proved, perhaps unsurprisingly, that even with unity the non-Bolsheviks could accomplish little.

Rejecting the idea espoused by Kerensky and others that White elements should seek recognition for one of several White governments in Russia and then coalesce around that government, Maklakov argued for achieving diplomatic unity first and then working for recognition. He pointed out that picking one of the governments in advance would stir resentment from the others, as well as from national groups in the old Russian empire.[23] Prevailing on that argument, he and Bakhmetev took the lead in forming the Russian Political Conference, a group stretching from Savinkov (Socialist Revolutionary) to Sazonov (longtime tsarist foreign minister), which was formally constituted in January 1919.[24] A leadership group (the "Russian Political Delegation Abroad") was formed to respond to events quickly: it comprised a similarly broad range: George Lvov, Sazonov, Maklakov, and Nicholas Tchaikovsky—a socialist leader imprisoned for a time by the old regime, a member of the St. Petersburg Soviet, and in 1919 prime minister of the White government at Arkhangel. Savinkov was later added to the group. Lvov's title role was no more than that; Maklakov was the conference's "guiding spirit."[25]

One distinguished Russian diplomat did not join—Constantine Nabokov, the novelist's uncle and the Provisional Government's chargé d'affaires and de facto representative in London. His refusal seems to have been due partly to dislike of being subordinated to Maklakov and Sazonov, and partly to a serious policy objection: he thought the Russian Political Conference should accept nothing less than full representation at the peace conference. He regarded the role that it did accept, representing Russia only informally, as degrading: "sitting in the anteroom."[26] Despite declining to join the Russian Political Conference, he recognized Maklakov's role, saying in his memoirs that the "attitude of the French Government, especially in the first few months, appears to have been determined to a greater extent by the personal qualities of the Ambassador than by his official title."[27]

But obvious reasons of state pushed the non-Bolsheviks to the peace conference's periphery. The Bolsheviks might not last, but then again they might. If they did, they would not look kindly on the great powers' having treated their enemies as speaking for Russia. As Lloyd George put it in refuting a proposal to seat the Russian Political Conference, they "represent every opinion except the one prevalent in Russia."[28] The French suggested that any Russian representation be accompanied by an announcement that participation would act as waiver of Russia's rights under the secret treaties.[29]

On one specific issue the peace conference may have invited Maklakov to present the Russian point of view directly to the Big Four—Wilson, Lloyd George, Clemenceau, and Orlando. The question was whether the conference should recognize Romanian control of Bessarabia, which had been acquired by Russia in the nineteenth century and contained a mixed population of Russians and non-Russians. In terms of realpolitik, the issue was a conflict between Romania, a member of the victorious coalition (although it had made a separate peace with the Central Powers), and Russia—also an ally, but one that was now dissolved in civil war. Addressing the four in the summer of 1919, Maklakov asked only that a plebiscite be held; he both opened and closed his remarks with an acknowledgment of correlation of forces overshadowing his cause:

> Gentlemen: let us indulge in a dream. I imagine that before me are free people who can express their free opinion and take free decisions, and you imagine that you have before you an ambassador plenipotentiary of great Russia.

After making his case, he closed by combining an acknowledgment of their political constraints,

> the importance of which I do not dispute. And before you is a person with no office, an ambassador without official papers. But again I thank you for listening to the opinion of the representative of Russia that you have sought.

In trying to move the discussion to a broader frame, the remarks echo his summation defending the riotous Dolbenkov peasants. A witness reports that the eyes of the Big Four were wet. But the conference, after some delay, pronounced itself in favor of Bessarabia's union with Romania, with no plebiscite.[30]

The Russian Political Conference devoted considerable effort to promoting Western intervention in Russia (already proceeding in a lackluster fashion), but such a policy faced a serious obstacle: military reality. As one observer has put it, the West was ready to help the White forces if they secured control of more terrain, but they couldn't win more terrain without more Western help.[31] The Russian Political Conference did help persuade the peace conference to express formal support, a kind of quasi-recognition, for Admiral Alexander Kolchak, head of the White government in Siberia. This acknowledgment came in exchange for a proclamation by Kolchak that met the demands of the peace conference for commitment to a constituent assembly and guarantee of rights for peasants and workers. The proclamation paralleled what Maklakov had urged on the Kolchak foreign ministry—"positive and solemn declarations which indicate the true face of the Russia of the future."[32] While short of outright recognition, the conference's expression presumably gave Kolchak a boost in prestige—not enough, as it proved, to let his government survive.[33]

Besides exhorting White leaders to commit to general principles of liberal democracy, Maklakov pushed them specifically to pursue decent policies toward Jews—most importantly to rein in their troops' pogroms. Here much turned on the disposition of the commanders. He encountered a good deal of resistance from General Denikin. As he later reported, Denikin was not himself a "pogromist" but was slow to act because of concern over soldiers' anti-Semitism: serious punishment of pogromist troops would cause unrest. Denikin ultimately took action. In January 1920, after a series of reverses and shortly before his replacement by Wrangel, he issued an order requiring "severe measures, up to and including the death penalty, against those engaging in robbery and violence," regardless of rank.[34]

A related issue was accepting Jews as members of the armed forces. Denikin refused to do so, on the ground that the resulting attacks on them would have to be punished, thus propelling a cycle of hatred. Maklakov appears to have been equivocal on this point. He reportedly endorsed this reasoning at a meeting in Rostov in October 1919, but soon afterward, in a letter to the finance minister of Denikin's government, he argued that any such exclusion was simply a capitulation to anti-Semitism.[35] Even assuming the oral statement in Rostov was correctly heard and reported, his written position is more in tune with his general thinking and more likely to have had an effect. He also urged Denikin to appoint at least one Jew to the government, an idea Denikin dismissed as only "a demand of Parisian Jewry."[36]

Maklakov made more headway with Denikin's successor, Wrangel, who impressed him with his "temperament, pragmatism, and decisiveness." Most concretely, he wrote to Wrangel's prime minister, Krivoshein (longtime minister of agriculture in the tsarist regime), encouraging the Wrangel government to reenact (or, if it was still in effect, to start applying) an old provision of the tsarist penal code punishing civil disorders based on religious hatred. Use of the provision, he argued, would frame the issue as attacking pogroms "from the perspective of their danger to civil order." Krivoshein evidently responded favorably. He also sought to appoint a Jew as finance minister, and indeed extended offers to two Jews in succession, but both declined—it was late in the day for the White movement and no one wanted "to climb aboard a sinking ship."[37]

Maklakov's fall 1920 trip to the Crimea yielded dismaying evidence of resurgent anti-Semitism. At Wrangel's request, he spent an entire night and morning talking with Sergei Bulgakov, his old colleague in the Second Duma and one of the four who visited Stolypin on the eve of the June 3, 1907, coup d'état, the group who jokingly called themselves the Kadets' "black hundreds." Now it seemed less of a joke. Wrangel had asked Maklakov to speak with Bulgakov in order to get the more educated members of the Orthodox clergy (Bulgakov was now an Orthodox priest) to discourage the Orthodox from engaging in pogroms. As Maklakov reported to Bakhmetev (in obvious dismay at the evolution of his old friend's thinking), Bulgakov told him that he preferred Bolshevism to democracy (thinking it would lead to a rebirth of the spirit of Christianity), and that he opposed constitutional monarchy and would prefer a return to autocracy. Although Bulgakov seemed not to "personally" believe that the world was controlled by a single Jewish syndicate, "he has serious misgivings." When Maklakov asked Bulgakov to discourage the circulation of a leaflet that Wrangel thought likely to provoke pogroms, Bulgakov replied, "I wrote it myself."[38] In an interview with a *New York Times* correspondent, Maklakov said the principle of equal rights was "non-negotiable," but he pointed to several difficulties of putting it into practice. Many local people believed that most Bolsheviks were Jews (which was false, but even if it were true, was a bad reason for disliking Jews, much less for subjecting them to pogroms), and the Bolsheviks themselves had tried to "turn the population against Denikin by claiming he defended Jews." "[I]t takes time and an iron hand to control the unchained passions of a country which has been so stirred up."[39]

In his first years defending the interests of Russian refugees, Maklakov acted in his role as quasi-ambassador. In 1924 France brought that to an end by recognizing the Soviet Union, but it then created a substitute in the form of a Central Office on Russian Refugee Affairs (*Office Central des Réfugiés russes en France*), to be linked with an Emigrants Committee via a single head for the two. Though George Lvov laid claim to the office, both left and right in Russian émigré circles joined to support the candidacy of Maklakov. As Budnitskii explains, "Besides his political inclusiveness (rare for a Russian politician) and his reputation as a first-class jurist, the authority that he commanded among French authorities played a role." He thus continued to be the voice of émigré Russia in France, with a population in Paris alone of nearly one hundred thousand.[40]

Part of his work was simply enabling Russians to secure the right to stay in France, in part through identification papers that the committee was authorized to issue.[41] Even today these efforts give him a reputation among descendants of the beneficiaries. A recent novel by the nephew of a soldier from Wrangel's army, for whom he secured papers in 1922, gives Maklakov a cameo appearance.[42]

He also served on a League of Nations group developing an international convention on the treatment of refugees, adopted in 1933. It was in some respects more generous in spirit than a post–World War II version, but the French, at least for the pre-war Russian refugees, continued to apply the 1933 agreement.[43]

Some of his work was more exotic—smoothing over feelings aroused by the crimes of émigrés. Two extreme cases were assassinations. In May 1932 a deranged Russian named Paul Gorgulov fired fatal shots at Paul Doumer, the incumbent French president, as he was opening an exhibition devoted to great writers of World War I. It fell to Maklakov to apologize on behalf of France's Russian guests. In another case, the Russian community had to be calmed. In 1927 a Russian named Boris Koverda assassinated Pyotr Voikov, the Soviet ambassador to Poland, in a railroad station in Warsaw; Koverda apparently acted in revenge for Voikov's role in the killing of Nicholas II and his family. (Voikov's story still roils the waters, thanks to the Soviets' naming a Moscow subway station after him.) The Polish authorities assigned the case against Koverda to a military tribunal, an assignment that outraged the émigrés in France, who evidently thought this would mean the sort of rush to judgment familiar to them from the infamous field courts martial, or would at least make the death penalty possible (as it would have in tsarist Russia). Maklakov feared that the Russians' mood might lead to dangerous actions. By a lucky coincidence Vaclav Lednitskii, the son of his old colleague Alexander Lednitskii, was visiting Paris from Warsaw. He assured Maklakov, on the basis of high-level political gossip in Poland, that the shift to the military courts had been ordered by the Polish head of state, Józef Piłsudski, to be absolutely sure that he (Piłsudski) would be able to *prevent* imposition of the death penalty. With this information, Maklakov was able to calm a meeting of overwrought Russians, who had been on the verge of adopting an inflammatory resolution. In the end, Koverda was sentenced to a long prison term, which was soon commuted to a few months.[44]

The German occupation interrupted Maklakov's work. The Nazis promptly shut down both the Central Office on Russian Refugee Affairs and the Emigrants Committee (along with about eight hundred Russian organizations in France). On April 28, 1942, they arrested Maklakov and kept him in La Santé prison until July. The Nazis gave no reason, leaving their thinking to speculation, which has been abundant. In fact, the arrest seems, as social scientists say, "overdetermined." Among the obvious causes appear to be his leadership of the Emigrants Committee, his known liberalism, and his Russian patriotism. Some scholars have mentioned Maklakov's being a Mason, a fact occasionally invoked to explain aspects of his behavior (in my opinion quite unconvincingly). As a possible element in Nazi thinking, however, it seems plausible here—they would naturally have been anxious about any clandestine group. One writer has in part explained Maklakov's arrest by reference to the spirit of a pithy expression attributed to Goebbels: "When I hear the word culture, I reach for my revolver." Apparently the Germans didn't torture Maklakov, and he used his prison time to work out a mental map of what became his history of the Second Duma. The Germans conditioned his release on his going to the countryside; his old Kadet colleague Baron Nolde put him up, and there he wrote the book he had conceived in prison.[45]

He and like-minded Russians were in touch with the Resistance, working to counter pro-Hitler propaganda among the émigrés and in some cases sheltering Jews. At least one member of the group was arrested—Igor Krivoshein (son of the tsarist minister). Maklakov was on the Germans' list of people to be whisked away to Germany at the approach of Allied troops, but the Allies moved too fast for the Germans to carry out the plan.[46]

After the war, both the Emigrants Committee and the Central Office on Russian Refugee Affairs were reestablished. One might suppose that by this time the need for regularizing Russian émigrés' positions in France would have been fully satisfied. But problems with labor and residence permits continued. And Liberation created a whole new concern. As many Russians were staunchly anti-Communist, including émigrés who had unequivocally supported Russian victory over the Nazis, they were attractive targets for French Communists seeking to exploit the immediate postwar assault on collaborators, real and imagined, in some cases wanting to burnish their own anti-Fascist credentials. Maklakov's friend Nina Berberova was tied up and threatened with hanging by a Communist neighbor; in some instances such threats were carried out. Between Liberation and October 1946 Maklakov wrote more than four thousand letters interceding to prevent such miscarriages of justice. The earliest, sent to the Paris prefect of police on September 1, 1944, said that many Russian immigrants had been recently arrested and subjected to savage interrogation. While the Emigrants Committee would do nothing for those who had helped the enemy, they staunchly protested arrests simply on the basis of anonymous denunciations.[47]

Until his death Maklakov continued to head the committee and the office and to work on Russian refugee issues, but the burst of activity in 1944–46 may have been his last opportunity to engage intensively in a project critical to his compatriots. Up to the very end he retained both his mental acuity and his dazzling memory as well as his oratorical gifts. But to exercise these gifts he increasingly had to overcome deafness, which the hearing aids of the era couldn't completely correct. Through deafness, infirmity, and the death of old friends, loneliness stalked him; he mentions it quite mournfully in letters to Tyrkova-Williams.[48]

Still, even into extreme old age his joie de vivre and zest for sociability remained unabated. A film snippet that must date from very late in his life—it shows him somewhat infirm and wearing a hearing device—reveals him absorbed in vivacious conversation with Ivan Bunin. (At a Russian celebration of Bunin's receiving the Nobel Prize for literature in 1933, which may have been the last great gathering of the Russian emigration, Maklakov had been the sole speaker.) Seated with fellow émigrés around a table, he talked with the same animation as he had in the Duma. Typically a similarity between a public figure's speeches and dinner-table conversation would not augur well for the latter, but not so for Maklakov, given his engaging and conversational speaking style.[49]

Through all these years he was fortunate to have the companionship and assistance of his sister Mariia—a woman of enterprise and talent in her own right, cofounder in 1920 of a school in Paris for the children of émigrés. For about thirty years, starting shortly after his forced removal from the Russian embassy, she had served as his secretary and kept house for him in his modest apartment on the rue Péguy, which had long attracted the cream of the émigré community.[50]

Unluckily for him, she died before him. His young friend Lednitskii gives a vivid account of a visit in April 1957, just before Mariia's death and three months before Maklakov's. When Lednitskii phoned to propose coming by, Maklakov's hearing was so poor that he could barely determine who was calling. And when Lednitskii arrived, Maklakov offered him wine but apologized that he lacked the strength to pull the cork. The focus of the visit was his concern for Mariia, who was sick and in a clinic; Maklakov was terribly anxious, torn between her desire to return to the apartment and his hope that the clinic could cure her.

Her death left him distraught. His nephew Iury Nikolaevich Maklakov, son of Nikolai, Vasily's estranged brother whom the Bolsheviks had shot in 1918, reported Maklakov's reaction to a glowing obituary of Mariia published in a Russian newspaper. Paper in hand, he rushed into her old bedroom, saying, "Marusia, look at what they're writing about you." When Lednitskii visited again after Mariia's death, Maklakov was still more distracted; he had trouble getting to his feet and constantly said that he must get out of Paris.[51]

He succeeded. Somewhat anomalously for a man who had loved Paris ever since his visit as a college student in 1889, he died in Switzerland, on July 15, 1957, taking a cure not far from Zurich. With him was his nephew Iury—evidently these two branches of the Maklakov family had reconciled. Maklakov had brought along from Paris a copy of the New Testament. Grasping it in one hand and indicating it with his eyes, he said, speaking thickly, "*Vot*"—another untranslatable Russian word, in this case probably meaning "There it is—what people need to know."[52] Though religion was surely peripheral in Maklakov's life, his first Russian biographer, drawing on recollections of Maklakov's friends, summarizes their collective portrait as showing a person who "loved life, though not closing his eyes to its dark side," and was "grateful to his creator for the very fact of his existence."[53]

Though he died in Switzerland, Maklakov is buried in the cemetery of St. Geneviève des Bois just outside Paris, along with several thousand Russian émigrés, including many whose words or deeds have appeared in this story—Struve, S. N. Bulgakov, Kokovtsov, George Lvov, Yusupov, Bunin, Nekrasov.

For us the lessons of Maklakov's life and career lie in his struggle to reform Russia, mainly by enhancing the rule of law, hoping not only to avert violent revolution but also to bring Russians the political conditions needed for better, freer, more creative lives. Reflections on that challenge follow in the next chapter. But Russians may treasure other aspects more. One of his Russian biographers writes:

> Vasily Alekseevich was very old, so his death could hardly be thought unexpected. But he was clearly necessary to people, and his existence acted as a guaranty of continuity, as a pledge that the old Russia—or what was best in the old Russia—would continue. With his death something was torn away, and this feeling shone through in the memorials devoted to him.[54]

Russia found in Maklakov an articulate, scholarly, balanced rule-of-law advocate, concerned for genuine justice—and recognized him as, besides all that, deeply Russian.

CHAPTER 20

Coda: The Rule of Law as the Thin End of the Wedge

Whether Maklakov had a strategic design in his emphasis on building the rule of law is not clear. His experience as a lawyer and legislator directly exposed him to ubiquitous rule-of-law deficits in Russia and honed his skills for mending those deficits, both in detail and in broad political strategy. Further, the concept of the rule of law advanced his strongest political goals—to develop a state strong enough to protect individual rights from private assault and to carry out the other necessary functions of government, yet constrained from violating individual rights itself. In our political culture, this vision has been most logically and eloquently expressed by James Madison:

> If men were angels, no government would be necessary. If angels were to govern men, neither external nor internal controls on government would be necessary. In framing a government which is to be administered by men over men, the great difficulty lies in this: you must first enable the government to control the governed; and in the next place oblige it to control itself.[1]

The themes recurred endlessly in Maklakov's public life. Most of the time his focus was on "oblig[ing the state] to control itself." But at key points a parallel concern for state effectiveness was evident. It was on that account that he reminded the Kadets at the initial meeting in October 1905 that the party itself, once in office, wouldn't want the state to be thoroughly hamstrung. And in the June and August 1917 speeches discussed in chapter 18 he expressed his acute anxiety about the Provisional Government's inability to perform its basic functions. A term that Maklakov frequently used in his speeches and historical writings, *gosudarstvennost* (literally "stateness" but defying precise translation), captures this feature.

The rule of law has by now earned a clear place in Western aspirations for reform in authoritarian countries. Elections, even moderately open elections, are plainly not enough. Such elections occur with regularity in one of the two great post-Communist behemoths (Russia), and from time to time in much of the Middle East, but friends of liberal democracy take little comfort from these events. Without institutions to protect citizens from overbearing executive officials, elections count for little.

But should the rule of law enjoy a special priority as a *path* to reform rather than simply being an element of the hoped-for end state? One can rest a case for such priority on two intuitions: First, the rule of law benefits the governors as well as the governed, thus perhaps making it easier to secure than reforms that impinge more directly on the rulers' privileges. Second, it facilitates the compromise resolution of issues that might otherwise precipitate violence and even civil war.

I don't want to exaggerate the advantages of rule-of-law reforms. If these reforms were always clear win-win opportunities, they would be ubiquitous, which of course they are not. Moreover, the people whose action is needed to establish the rule of law—the people subject to lawless governments and the people running those governments—have their own priorities. Among citizens, for example, particular government offenses provide chances for mobilizing opposition; for them, the opportunities of the moment are much more vital than theories of reform. But while specific government outrages—a stolen election here, concealment of government malfeasance there, indifference to environmental calamity elsewhere—may rally popular support, there is nothing to prevent a two-track strategy: citizens can seize those protest opportunities and at the same time spotlight the lawlessness that is (commonly) a part of the government outrage. And rule-of-law concepts can figure among their proposed remedies.

I will not attempt to define the rule of law, but I do want to make clear that I have in mind only core characteristics: that the laws be reasonably coherent, clear, consistent, transparent and available, applied "without respect to persons,"[2] not allowing officials excessive discretion, not retroactive, applicable as much to officials as to citizens, and in fact applied by persons substantially independent of the other branches of government yet disciplined (largely self-disciplined) by serious craft values (for example, logic, analytical rigor, close reading of texts, tracing the path from facts and law to the outcome, addressing arguments posed by the ultimately losing party). This list is quite long. But it does not include everything good under the sun.[3] People defining and promoting the rule of law are likely to be seduced by the temptations of "persuasive definition"—the practice of advocates to take a concept with positive connotations and fill it with their preferred principles or goals.[4] The rule of law generally has positive connotations.[5] So it is unsurprising that we often find it broadly defined. Those who ardently favor government intervention to prevent various types of private discrimination, for example, may be tempted to envisage the rule of law as requiring such interventions.[6] My argument here doesn't share this sort of conceptual imperialism.

Nor do I understand the "rule of law" to require a system of "judicial review" in the sense of judicial scrutiny of legislation for compliance with a constitution. As a simple matter of history, countries with what we normally classify as rule-of-law regimes have often lacked such review—most obviously the British state from 1689 until its acceptance of the authority of the European Court of Justice and the European Court of Human Rights. Rule of law *with* constitutional review would likely have seemed to the tsarist regime more like a six-by-six timber than the thin end of the wedge. We saw in chapter 11 how a number of Maklakov's amendments to a judicial reform bill nominally increased the Senate's power to review executive acts for constitutionality. These alterations sailed through the Duma; had anyone thought that the Senate was about to exercise such a power, it seems safe to say that there would have been formidable resistance. Of course even without this sort of judicial review, courts can sometimes use their interpretive authority to nudge a regime toward a more humane order. In any event, the case for the rule of law should not rest on any notion that the human beings who populate the courts are systematically wiser or more humane than those of other branches. As the *Dred Scott* case suggests, history belies or at least seriously qualifies such a sunny view.

Let's first consider benefits and costs from the rule of law that we can ascribe specifically to the ruled and/or to the regime, then benefits and costs too diffuse for any such assignment.

For the ruled, the most obvious benefit is some degree of protection from officials' actions beyond the scope of their prescribed authority, the very core of the rule of law. This theme was central to Maklakov's legislative activity, starting with the memo on agrarian issues that launched him into politics. We see it in his inveighing against the regime's threats to judicial independence and in his advocacy of improving the remedies against executive officials' lawlessness. And for some types of laws, the field courts martial and the extraordinary security laws, he challenged both specific instances of misapplication (acts not conforming even to the broad statutes) and also the way in which broadly or badly drafted laws invited abuse by allowing officials to inflict punishments free of judicial check.

Citizens will also benefit from the *practice* of judicial restraint of officials' actions, its *in terrorem* effect. Hosts of cases will never arise because the pattern of litigation will change officials' incentives—from an attitude of indifference to law to anxiety about the consequences of violating it.

The benefits will in some cases be limited. In societies where the only "lawmaker" is the executive, or the executive operating through a puppet legislature, use of a *text* to constrain officials' actions may (apart from preventing what amounts to an ex post facto application of law) only delay the challenged official behavior until the lawmaker has an opportunity to change the text; until the October Manifesto and the Fundamental Laws such a system prevailed in Russia.[7] But the process of changing the law will entail some thinking at the highest levels of government, and the rethinking may be enough to persuade the rulers not to authorize the sort of official behavior found unlawful.

Of course where the laws are bad, insistence on legality won't produce appealing results. But even where the citizen's claim is rejected, the process itself can at least give the loser an opportunity to have his say and supply a focus for critique of the regime, directing public attention to absurdities, cruelties, or anomalies in existing law. And for an official on the verge of making an aggressive application of an unjust or outmoded law—the Pale of Settlement rules come to mind—merely the prospect of facing an independent tribunal may be enough to give pause.

The rule of law may occasionally even produce setbacks for the ruled. For example, when courts reject a challenge, the challengers' position is in one sense affirmatively weakened by the validation of the officials' action; at least it is weakened if the courts enjoy any prestige at all, which they must if the rule of law is to work. Similarly, officials who had been wary of such a challenge and had held back will now be emboldened.

More important, the "ruled" are never completely homogeneous, so an increase in the rule of law may in practice disadvantage many of them. We saw in chapter 12 how, right up to the February Revolution, Russian peasant communes could, with the consent of officials from the ministry of internal affairs, banish commune members for behavior that was "harmful or depraved" but not necessarily criminal, with the usual consequence being exile to Siberia. Maklakov and like-minded legislators sought to eliminate the power, arguing that while *non-peasants* also had their troublemakers, no one saw that as justifying a rule that would allow them to ship the offenders to Siberia with no consideration by an independent tribunal. This is a good rule-of-law argument, resting on the goal of protecting citizens from arbitrary government power. But of course there were many peasants, perhaps a majority, whose safety or quiet could be enhanced by use of this mechanism to remove offenders—ones whose behavior was not severe enough to be criminal or who could not be successfully prosecuted. Curtailment of government arbitrariness would have reduced the security of good citizens vis-à-vis thugs and would to a degree have imperiled social peace. Conflicts of interest such as these are surely one reason behind Tocqueville's warning, well known to Maklakov, that the most dangerous moment for a bad government is when it begins to reform.

What does the rule of law offer the rulers? Those at the very top, with authority to adopt regulations implementing statutory law, gain a monitoring mechanism. Even an authoritarian regime has incentives against creating rules of limitless breadth or vagueness. It wants to accomplish something, and licensing officials to randomly mistreat the population will rarely be to its advantage. Judicial review of administrative action can give those at the top more confidence that subordinates will carry out their decisions as intended, that they will be less prone to bureaucratic inertia and willfulness or to "policy drift."[8]

Institutions other than the judiciary can perform such supervision. Indeed, almost all bureaucracies have monitors of some kind, such as the inspectors general of the various departments of the United States executive branch. But the private lawsuit, brought by parties who have been injured or are about to be injured by official disregard of instructions, is a decentralized device that mobilizes citizens to act as the spark plug for a focused examination of official conduct. What is more, it seems relatively likely to yield attacks on the bureaucratic malfunctions that the population finds most irritating; this is especially true if a good balance is found between keeping the costs of litigation low and constraining frivolous suits. And if the judiciary emerges as a staunch defender of people and firms from bureaucratic excesses, its activities can add to the regime's legitimacy.

I have so far omitted a benefit that should loom large in any assessment but doesn't seem to belong exclusively to either the ruled or the regime. By protecting economic and commercial rights from arbitrary government agents, the rule of law enables potential entrepreneurs to engage in productive entrepreneurship. It diminishes or at times eliminates an entrepreneur's need to focus on meeting unpredictable (and perhaps insatiable) demands from authorities. The results could benefit society as consumers, as workers, and of course as potential entrepreneurs. The population's benefits from having economic activity driven by consumer desires rather than by government fiat (especially the fiats of random officials) would in turn redound to the regime's advantage in increased legitimacy, not to mention generating a broader basis for securing tax revenue.

But these economic benefits come with a downside from the perspective of some in the regime. Officials whose abuse of authority has taken the form of manipulating crony capitalists (or crony socialists, for that matter,[9] or even cronies with Chinese characteristics), extorting wealth by various carrots and sticks, would lose the opportunities afforded by untamed executive power and the crony relationship. From an abstract perspective one may think such losses thoroughly deserved, but the regime's chiefs may not be able to afford such an Olympian viewpoint. The officials who benefit from crony relationships are by definition likely to have political clout. Their hostility might well abort reforms that would undercut their power, and possibly topple would-be reformers. So rule-of-law reforms that penetrate the system deeply may face the classic dilemma identified by Mancur Olson: diffuse benefits and concentrated losses. Leaders contemplating such an extreme reform may well be daunted. As a result, the hardest element of rule-of-law reform may be protection of entrepreneurs from bureaucrats' arbitrary demands.

I have already mentioned regime legitimacy, and it too has something for both regime and ruled. For the regime the advantage is obvious. For the ruled, simply to say that the benefits deriving from the rule of law enhance regime legitimacy is to posit those very benefits—at least when we speak of legitimacy enhanced through rule-of-law improvements as opposed, for example, to military triumphs. But on the side of the ruled it is a double-edged sword. To the extent that the rule of law enhances legitimacy, it may retard the hoped-for erosion of the authoritarian system.[10] The rule of law has been found to be positively correlated with political stability, in both democracies and autocracies.[11] If so, then rule-of-law reform seems likely to extend the regime's longevity.

But it seems natural to suppose that increased stability, when associated with the rule of law, will entail the growth of civil society. This in turn suggests the possibility of a virtuous circle. If courts emerged as champions of the citizenry against rogue officials, news of their activity could (depending, of course, on the brutality and thoroughness in the regime's suppression of speech) further embolden citizens to resist excesses of authority. Courts alone are weak institutions; as Hamilton reminds us, they have "no influence over either the sword or the purse."[12] Popular support, manifested through a developing civil society (ideally amplified by an independent legislature and a free press, but we can't assume those), is likely to be essential to courts' effectiveness.[13] The relation of rule of law and civil society is one of symbiosis and overlap: enforcement of the rule of law tends to build up civil society, which in turn both reinforces the courts and acts as an independent constraint on executive malfeasance.

Civil society may also be an *indirect* by-product of rule-of-law improvement. Removing arbitrary lines in order to reduce the risks of arbitrary enforcement is likely to facilitate wholesome association. We saw in chapter 9 how Maklakov, in opposing restrictions on religious minorities, stressed the risks of arbitrariness and corruption in police enforcement. Religious restrictions of the sort he attacked tend to create (and aggravate) divisions between minorities and the majority, thus impeding growth of the kind of effective groups that make up a powerful civil society. An extreme example is the way in which the Pale of Settlement confined most Jews to a limited geographic area and allowed others beyond the Pale only to the extent that they engaged in specified occupations. Removing the barriers would have tended to nurture a rich mix of variegated, complex, interlocking civic bodies, such that people in one sphere would be more likely to be aware of the interests and values of those in another, and willing to exert influence on their behalf. But, as I warned in chapter 9, in a highly anti-Semitic society, enhancements of freedom for Jews will create new occasions for friction, somewhat offsetting the advantages.

Another indirect connection appears in Maklakov's critique of the estate-based limits on peasants. He argued that those limits deprived peasants of a vested interest in the idea of universal, legally protected rights; removal of the limits would give peasants a stake in that idea (chapter 12). Civil society and the idea of universal legal rights seem mutually reinforcing.

Rule-of-law reform enabling citizen suits against administrative agencies carries its own enhancements for civil society. Considering pending proposals for enhancing the feasibility of such suits in China, Neysun Mahboubi suggests three specific ways such litigation may help build civil society. It (1) regularizes contention between citizens and the state; (2) facilitates development of interest groups, and (3) generates public discourse about official accountability.[14] The first is obviously critical in a country where "harmony" is exalted as a social value.[15] The second is a sample building block of civil society, consisting of associations that arise from specific legal parties' shared needs (an aspect of the rule of law that was far less apparent in the era before the modern state's typically vast administrative system). The third involves creation and spread of a vocabulary for accountable governance, and an ability to deploy that vocabulary. Lawsuits in themselves are only a fraction of the discourse of accountability, but they can help propagate that discourse.

Rule-of-law reform also affects the nature of any succeeding regime. Tocqueville's *The Old Regime and the Revolution* is fundamentally an account of those characteristics of the old regime in France that doomed the country to illiberal successor regimes—the Directorate, Napoleon, the restored Bourbons, and Napoleon III. He focuses on the way in which the centralization of all decision-making in Paris stifled the development of local capacities for ordering life:

> When the Revolution happened, one would have to search most of France in vain for ten men who had the habit of acting in common in an orderly way, and taking care of their own defense themselves; only the central power was supposed to take care of it, so that the central power, fallen from the hands of the royal government into the hands of a sovereign and irresponsible assembly, and changed from good-natured to terrible, found nothing which could stop it, or even briefly slow it down.[16]

The polity Tocqueville depicts—its social groups splintered by a variety of government policies, its writers cowed by irritating but ineffective censorship, its potential leaders unpracticed at solving problems by negotiation within a clear framework of legal rights—is the antithesis of a powerful civil society and the rule of law. Indeed, it seems very like the polity inherited by the Provisional Government, which confronted acute social divisions and lacked institutions for resolving them in a framework of broadly respected rights. And the sequels in France and Russia seem quite similar.

So far, this discussion has disregarded the elephant in the room: the natural resistance of leaders at the very top to accept *any* institutional curtailment of *their* power. They may gain by institutions that provide remedies against their subordinates, but they are almost sure to want to cut the process off at the point where it would reach them—making sure, for example, that political adversaries are the sole targets of corruption charges. Some regimes explicitly privilege the elite; the Chinese Code of Conduct for judges, for example, requires them to "give priority to the cause of the Party." It lists other goals as well, but the Party is conspicuously first.[17] Such a system has been called "rule *by* law"—greater efficiency in control of the lower echelons, but with broad freedom of maneuver at the top. Where this system prevails, the hoped-for benefits will be truncated.

But another element may give the rule of law some appeal, even to those at the pinnacle of political power. Autocrats in the modern world must, as did their predecessors, keep an eye out for those who would overthrow them—either simple replacements (ones who hope to follow roughly the same business model but with a new CEO) or system changers, hoping to introduce a genuine innovation such as liberal democracy. Associated with the difference in any likely successor regime is the difference between what we may call a hard and a soft landing. A dictator at risk of losing all authority must be very interested in the transition. One who has reason to anticipate a bloodbath (think of the 1918 slaughter of Nicholas II and his family or the Christmas 1989 execution of Nicolae Ceausescu and his wife) might well be willing to lose considerable power to reduce that risk. He faces a range of possible outcomes, from ability to pass a comfortable national inheritance on to his favorite child, through forced retirement in some degree of honor and safety, and finally to execution (perhaps preceded by torture). He may choose to incur a loss in power in exchange for increasing the chances for the intermediate outcome over the last. While some rulers merely tighten the reins at the first sign of popular unrest, others offer concessions. (Nicholas II had an unfortunate habit of doing both simultaneously, the classic example being his actions on February 18, 1905, when he proposed broad reform, including a promise to institute a consultative assembly and an invitation to citizens to offer suggestions for improvement of Russia, but also called on "all true Russians" to rally round the tsar and protect "true autocracy."[18])

Of course the highest officials aren't the only people with a natural preference for peaceful evolution over violent change. Besides the healthy tendency to develop civil society, the rule of law represents a system for enforcement of bargains among competing elites. With such a system in place, parties are more likely to consider a bargain reliable. The rule of law also opens the door to a competitive electoral system, as incumbents will have assurance that if they lose office they will not lose their lives and property as well at the whim of the new authorities. Further, the rule of law is itself an institution, a practice, that exalts orderliness and regularity, values antithetical to violent revolution.

Rule-of-law reform here contrasts sharply with substantive reform such as the sudden shift in property rights advocated by the Kadets over the twelve key years of 1905–1917—confiscation of gentry land, with the owners to be only partially compensated. That proposal was charged with risk of violence. Landowners facing loss of their status and prosperity, and the existing regime (which was closely tied to those landowners), were unlikely ever to have gone gentle into the night of impoverishment. And with the Provisional Government's weakness, "moderate" politicians' support for confiscation naturally encouraged peasant self-help. The Kadets' zeal for a universal franchise and a government responsible to the Duma carried the same implications. A Duma so elected would have promptly adopted a compulsory land transfer, quite possibly more extreme than the Kadet proposal, and thus have triggered a violent clash. The sort of rule-of-law reforms pressed by Maklakov carried little danger of such earthquakes; indeed, they militated against them. Their embrace by the regime would have harmed only officials (and, marginally, some private persons accustomed to rely on lawless official assistance).

This point leads to the issue of mixed strategies among reformers. Those who focus entirely on the rule of law, and thus on pacific methods of protest, are unlikely to make the *threat* of a hard landing seem plausible. They might therefore benefit from the activity of violent resisters.[19] But the extra pressure on the regime comes at a cost. First, though such methods might give the regime an incentive to accept rule-of-law reforms, they might also, by fostering anxiety, make the regime unwilling to palliate its suppression techniques by upholding the rule of law.[20] Second, rule-of-law reformers may get tarred with a broad brush applied to "oppositionists" in general, both in exposure to suppression and in an extra harshness in the regime's assessment of rule-of-law proposals. In late tsarist Russia both of these side effects were present. In the face of extremist agitation the regime clung to the extraordinary security laws and viewed even moderates such as Vasily Maklakov with alarm—thus, as we saw in the Introduction, Nicholas II's writing off Maklakov as "theirs" in contrast to his reactionary brother, whom the tsar embraced as "ours." It's far from clear how rule-of-law reformers can achieve the right balance—provide enough support for revolutionaries ready to embrace violence to concentrate the authorities' minds, but not so much as to drive them into a cul-de-sac where they think the rule of law is too risky.

It is perhaps no surprise that any final tally on the utility of a rule-of-law strategy is inconclusive. If successful, it seems to carry benefits for virtually all concerned. But there is little assurance of success. The incumbent regime is almost always likely to be able to thwart such reform. The French and Russian stories suggest that authoritarian leaders may be more effective at resisting rule-of-law reform than in preventing their own ultimate overthrow, even though overthrow, when it comes, will follow a path as disastrous for them as for others.

Chronology

Except for dates after January 1, 1918, all dates are "old style," that is, by the Julian rather than the Gregorian calendar. In the twentieth century, these are thirteen days behind Western dates.

1869	May 10	Birth of Vasily Maklakov
1894	October 20	Accession of Nicholas II
1895	January	Nicholas's "senseless dreams" speech
	May 4	Death of Alexei Nikolaevich Maklakov, Vasily's father
1896	Spring	Vasily Maklakov completes legal studies and starts practice
1904	January	Start of Russo-Japanese War
1905	January 9	Bloody Sunday

	February 18	Nicholas II issues three proclamations, promising consultative assembly, inviting people to propose reforms, and asserting inviolability of the autocracy
	May 14–15	Russian fleet sunk in battle with Japanese in Straits of Tsushima
	August 6	Nicholas makes formal proposal of consultative parliament
	October 12–18	First Congress of Constitutional Democratic Party (Kadets)
	October 17	Nicholas II issues October Manifesto
	December 11	Electoral law issued
1906	February 20	Law governing new Duma and State Council issued
	March 4	Rules on public meetings issued
	April 23	Fundamental Laws issued
	April 27	Opening day of First Duma
	July 8	Tsar signs decree dissolving First Duma; Stolypin becomes prime minister
	July 9	Kadet and Trudovik deputies issue Vyborg Manifesto attacking dissolution of First Duma
	August 19	Government issues decree creating field courts martial
	October 5	Government issues decree advancing equal rights for peasants
	November 9	Government issues decree enabling peasants to convert their rights in land into approximation of full ownership

1907	February 20	Opening day of Second Duma
	June 3	Dissolution of Second Duma and issuance of decree modifying electoral law to limit franchise (the June 3 coup d'état)
	November 7	Opening day of Third Duma
1911	September 1	Stolypin assassinated (dies September 5); replaced by Kokovtsov
1912	June 9	Closing day of Third Duma
	November 15	Opening day of Fourth Duma
	December 16	Nikolai Maklakov becomes Minister of Internal Affairs
1913	October 28	Menachem Beilis acquitted
1915	Summer	Nikolai Maklakov and three other reactionary ministers are dismissed under liberal pressure
	Mid-August	Formation of the Progressive Bloc
1916	June	Maklakov secures Duma passage of bill expanding October 5, 1906, decree of peasant rights
	September 27	Maklakov's "Mad Chauffeur" allegory published in *Russkie Vedomosti*
	November 3	Maklakov's "we or they" speech in Duma
	December 16	Assassination of Rasputin
1917	February 23	Riots that launch February Revolution start
	February 27	Formation of Duma Committee (which forms Provisional Government), and of Executive Committee of Petrograd Soviet

	March 2, 11:40 p.m.	Tsar signs decree of abdication in favor of Grand Duke Mikhail
	March 3	Grand Duke Mikhail declines the throne and issues decree purporting to vest authority in Provisional Government
	October 12	Maklakov leaves Russia to assume post as ambassador to France
	October 25	Bolsheviks overthrow Provisional Government
1957	June 15	Maklakov dies in Switzerland

Abbreviations

Works and archives frequently cited in the Notes and Bibliography have been identified by the following short forms and abbreviations.

Bakhmetev-Maklakov Correspondence	*Sovershenno Lichno i doveritelno!: B.A. Bakhmetev—V.A. Maklakov, Perepiska, 1919–1951* [Strictly personal and confidential!: B. A. Bakhmetev and V. A. Maklakov, correspondence, 1919–1951], ed. Oleg Budnitskii, 3 vols. (Moscow and Stanford, CA: ROSSPEN and Hoover Institution Press, 2001–2002).
GARF	Gosudarstvennyi Arkhiv Rossiiskoi Federatsii [State Archive of the Russian Federation]
GDSO	Gosudarstvennoi Dumy, Stenograficheskii Otchet [State Duma, stenographic minutes]
GIM	Gosudarstvennyi Istoricheskii Muzei [State Historical Museum]
Hoover	Hoover Institution Library and Archives, Vasilii Maklakov Papers, 1881–1956. Collection no. 57005. Two-number citations indicate the box followed by the folder.

Maklakov, *La Chute*	V.A. Maklakov, preface to *La Chute du Régime Tsariste: Interrogatoires des Ministres, Conseillers, Généraux, Hauts Fonctionnaires de la Cour Impériale Russe par la Commission Extraordinaire du Gouvernement Provisoire de 1917* [The fall of the Tsarist regime: Interrogations of the ministers, counsellors, generals, high officials of the Imperial Russian Court by the Extraordinary Commission of the Provisional Government of 1917], French translation by J. and L. Polonsky (Paris: Payot, 1927), 7–87.
Padenie tsarskogo rezhima	*Padenie tsarskovo rezhima, stenograficheskie otchety doprosov i pokazaniia, dannikh v 1917 g. v Chrezvychainoi Sledstvennoi Komissii Vremennogo Pravitelstva* [Fall of the Tsarist regime: Stenographic records of interrogations and evidence taken in 1917 by the Extraordinary Investigative Commission of the Provisional Government] (Leningrad-Moscow: Gosudarstvennoe Izdatelstvo, 1925).
Protokoly	*Protokoly Tsentralnogo komiteta i zagranichnykh grupp Konstitutsionno-demokraticheskoi partii, 1905–seredina 1930-kh gg.* [Protocols of the Central Committee and Foreign Groups of the Constitutional Democratic Party, 1905–mid-1930s], compiled, with introduction and notes by Dmitrii Borisovich Pavlov (Moscow: ROSSPEN, 1998).
Sezdy i konferentsii	*Sezdy i konferentsii konstitutsionno-demokraticheskoi partii: 1905–1920 gg.* [Congresses and conferences of the Constitutional Democratic Party], 3 vols., ed. O.V. Volobuev (Moscow: ROSSPEN, 1997–2000).
Tyrkova-Williams Diary and Letters	*Nasledie Ariadny Vladimirovny Tyrkovoi: Dnevniki, Pisma* [The legacy of Ariadne Vladimirovna Tyrkova: Diary, letters], collected, with an introduction and commentary by N.I. Kanishchevas (Moscow: ROSSPEN, 2012).

Notes

INTRODUCTION: WHY MAKLAKOV?

1. A. Lunacharskii, K. Radek, and L. Trotskii, *Siluety: Politicheskie portrety* [Silhouettes: Political portraits] (Moscow: Izdatelstvo politicheskoi literatury, 1991), 240. Trotsky's comment originally appeared in an article entitled "Guchkov and Guchkovshchina" [Guchkov and the Guchkov Era], in the newspaper *Kievskaia mysl*, no. 276 (October 6, 1913).
2. See, for example, P. N. Miliukov, "Sud nad Kadetskim 'Liberalizmom,'" *Sovremennye Zapiski* 41 (1930): 347, 365, 368.
3. Quoted in Michael Karpovich, "Two Types of Russian Liberalism: Maklakov and Miliukov," in *Continuity and Change in Russian and Soviet Thought*, ed. Ernest J. Simmons, Joint Committee on Slavic Studies of the American Council of Learned Societies and the Social Science Research Council (New York: Russell and Russell, 1955, 1967), 129, 138 (citing Miliukov's remarks at Kadet party congress of October 12–18, 1905).
4. V. V. Shelokhaev, "Agrarnia programma kadetov v pervoi Russkoi revoliutsii" [Agricultural program of the Kadets in the first Russian revolution], *Istoricheskie Zapiski* 86 (1970), 172, 183, 192, 204–7. Peasant issues are discussed in various places, but especially in chapter 12.
5. V. A. Maklakov, *Iz Vospominanii* (New York: Chekhov Publishing House [Izdatelstvo imeni Chekhova], 1954), 146–48; see also I. P. Aleksinskii, "Pervye gody moego studentchestva (1889–1891)," in *Moskovskii universitet, 1755–1930* (Paris: Izdatelstvo "Sovremmenie Zapiski," 1930), 355, 363–65. S. V. Zavadskii, "Iz Zhizni Moskovskogo Univer-

siteta v XIX stoletii," in *Moskovskii universitet, 1755–1930* (Paris: Izdatelstvo "Sovremmenie Zapiski," 1930), 351–52, acknowledges Maklakov's eloquence but reports the student vote as coming out the other way.

6. Compare a recent argument that abolitionist zeal, particularly in opposing Lincoln's consideration of proposals to buy out the South's slaveholders, had the effect of drastically prolonging the Civil War, with its terrible loss of life and long-run setback for healthy political evolution in the South. Thomas Fleming, *A Disease in the Public Mind* (New York: Da Capo, 2013).
7. N.I. Dedkov, *Konservativnyi liberalizm Vasiliia Maklakova* (Moscow: AIRO-XX, 2005), 64–65.
8. I.I. Tolstoi, *Dnevnik, 1906–1916* [Diary, 1906–16] (St. Petersburg: Evropeiskii Dom, 1997), 469–70.
9. He was named acting minister on December 16, 1912; confirmed as minister on February 21, 1913; and relieved of the office on June 5, 1915.
10. Boris Efimov, *Desiat desiatiletii: O tom, chto videl, perezhil, zapomnil* [Ten decades: What I saw, survived, remembered] (Moscow: Vagrius, 2000), 204.
11. *Bolshaia Sovetskaia Entsiklopediia* (Moscow: 1926–47), 37:752.
12. Alexander Hamilton, *Federalist* No. 78.
13. Matthew Stephenson, "'When the Devil Turns . . .': The Political Foundations of Independent Judicial Review," *Journal of Legal Studies* 32 (2003), 59.
14. See chapter 12, discussing the June 1916 legislation and the disconnect between peasant life and the country's general laws.
15. See chapter 9.
16. Dominic Lieven, *Nicholas II: Twilight of the Empire* (New York: St. Martin's Press, 1993), see page 106 for the Pobedonostsev quotation.
17. Ibid.
18. Stephen F. Williams, *Liberal Reform in an Illiberal Regime: The Creation of Private Property in Russia, 1906–1915* (Stanford: Hoover Institution Press, 2006), 97.
19. For the absence of peasant rights, see Victor Leontovitsch, *The History of Liberalism in Russia*, trans. Parmen Leontovitsch, with a foreword by Aleksandr Solzhenitsyn (Pittsburgh: University of Pittsburgh Press, 2012). For peasant sayings about the law, see Boris Nikolayevich Mironov, with Ben Eklof, *A Social History of Imperial Russia, 1700–1917* (Boulder, CO: Westview Press, 1999–2000), 304–5.
20. Richard Wortman, "Property Rights, Populism, and the Russian Political Culture," in *Civil Rights in Imperial Russia*, ed. Olga Crisp and Linda Edmondson (Oxford: Oxford University Press, 1989), 13–32.
21. Bakhmetev-Maklakov Correspondence, 1:460 (Maklakov to Bakhmetev, August 30, 1921); ibid., 3:475 (Maklakov to Bakhmetev, April 1, 1930); Lieven, *Nicholas II*, 176–77.
22. Fred W. Carstensen and Gregory Guroff, "Economic Innovation in Imperial Russia and the Soviet Union: Observations," in *Entrepreneur-*

ship in Imperial Russia and the Soviet Union, ed. Gregory Guroff and Fred V. Carstensen (Princeton: Princeton University Press, 1983), 353.

23. Thomas C. Owen, *Russian Corporate Capitalism from Peter the Great to Perestroika* (New York: Oxford University Press, 1995), 187, and generally, 50–84, 115–38 [LR 246]; Thomas C. Owen, *Capitalism and Politics in Russia: A Social History of the Moscow Merchants, 1855–1905* (New York: Cambridge University Press, 1981); Thomas C. Owen, "The Russian Industrial Society and Tsarist Economic Policy, 1867–1905," *Journal of Economic History* 45, no. 3 (September 1985), 599–600.
24. See Jacob Walkin, "Government Controls over the Press," *Russian Review* 13 (1954), 203–9.
25. V. A. Maklakov, *Vlast i obshchestvennost na zakate staroi Rossii (Vospominaniia sovremenika)* [State and society in the twilight of old Russia (Recollections of a contemporary)] (Paris: Izdanie zhurnala "Illustrirovanaia Rossiia," 1936), 149–50, 161–62, 242–43.
26. Chapter 3 discusses Maklakov's relations with Tolstoy and includes Maklakov's analysis of the relation between Tolstoy's views and his actual conduct as a reforming public figure.
27. Kathleen Parthé, "Who Speaks the Truth? Writers vs. Lawyers," *Universals and Contrasts*, NY-St. Petersburg Institute of Linguistics, Cognition, and Culture, no. 1 (Spring 2012), 1.
28. Wayne Dowler, *Russia in 1913* (DeKalb: Northern Illinois University Press, 2012), 47, 58.
29. Douglas C. North, John Joseph Wallis, and Barry R. Weingast, *Violence and Social Orders: A Conceptual Framework for Interpreting Recorded Human History* (New York: Cambridge University Press, 2009); Francis Fukuyama, *The Origins of Political Order: From Prehuman Times to the French Revolution* (New York: Farrar, Straus and Giroux, 2011); Daron Acemoglu and James Robinson, *Why Nations Fail: The Origins of Power, Prosperity, and Poverty* (New York: Crown Business, 2012); Joel Mokyr, *The Enlightened Economy: An Economic History of Britain, 1700–1850* (New Haven: Yale University Press, 2012); Deirdre McCloskey, *The Bourgeois Virtues: Ethics for an Age of Commerce* (Chicago: University of Chicago Press, 2006); Deirdre McCloskey, *Bourgeois Dignity: Why Economics Can't Explain the Modern World* (Chicago: University of Chicago Press, 2011); Deirdre McCloskey, *Bourgeois Equality: How Ideas, Not Capital or Institutions, Enriched the World* (Chicago: University of Chicago Press, 2016).

CHAPTER 1: SCAPEGRACE AND SCHOLAR

1. V. A. Maklakov, *Iz Vospominanii* (New York: Chekhov Publishing House [Izdatelstvo imeni Chekhova], 1954), 25.
2. Ibid., 12.
3. N. G. Dumova, *Kadetskaia partiia v period pervoi mirovoi voiny i Fevralskoi revolutsii* [The Kadet party in the period of the First World War and

the February Revolution] (Moscow: Nauka, 1988), 130. See also William G. Rosenberg, *Liberals in the Russian Revolution: The Constitutional Democratic Party, 1917–1921* (Princeton, NJ: Princeton University Press, 1974), 23, saying that Maklakov came from one of "Russia's oldest families" and speaking of the "drawing rooms" of Maklakov and other Kadet leaders as "frequently the scenes of large social gatherings, in which guests opposing the party's political orientation often outnumbered Kadets."

4. So Maklakov said in his memoirs (see Maklakov, *Iz Vospominanii*, 329; see also 22, 280, for Zvenigorod connection). A Russian scholar reports that the Maklakov archives confirms that the Maklakov property was not income generating. N. I. Dedkov, *Konservativnyi liberalizm Vasiliia Maklakova* (Moscow: AIRO-XX, 2005), 22–23. On the subject of family wealth, Maklakov noted that Aunt Raisa's eighteen children (his first cousins once removed) all had to work for a living. Maklakov, *Iz Vospominanii*, 11–12. Of course, that would not be inconsistent with his mother's inheriting enough to live on without working, she being an only child.
5. Maklakov, *Iz Vospominanii*, 21–24.
6. Ibid., 14–17.
7. Ibid., 27–28.
8. V. A. Maklakov, *Vlast i obshchestvennost na zakate staroi Rossii (Vospominaniia sovremenika)* [State and society in the twilight of old Russia (Recollections of a contemporary)] (Paris: Izdanie zhurnala "Illustrirovanaia Rossiia," 1936), 32–38.
9. Ibid., 39–41.
10. Maklakov, *Iz Vospominanii*, 28–31, 301.
11. Ibid., 17–21.
12. Ibid., 32–41.
13. Marina Aleksandrovna Ivanova, "Rol V. A. Maklakova v Obshchestvenno-politicheskoi zhizni Rossii" [The role of V. A. Maklakov in the social-political life of Russia] (PhD thesis, Rossiiskii Universitet Druzhby Narodov, 1997), 141, citing GIM, fond 442, ll. 112–112ob.
14. Maklakov, *Iz Vospominanii*, 32–54; Maklakov, *Vlast i obshchestvennost*, 12–13.
15. Kornei Chukovsky, *Diary, 1901–1969*, ed. Victor Erlich, trans. Michael Henry Heim (New Haven and London: Yale University Press, 2005), 251–52.
16. Otdel Rukopisei, Rossiiskaia Gosudarstvennaia Biblioteka [Manuscript Department, Russian State Library], fond 131, papka 32, delo 62. November 18, 1892.
17. Maklakov, *Iz Vospominanii,* 122–28.
18. Maklakov, *Iz Vospominanii*, 121–22; Dedkov, *Konservativnyi liberalizm*, 26.
19. Maklakov, *Iz Vospominanii*, 54–56, 128–30, 136, 188–89; Dedkov, *Konservativnyi liberalizm*, 32.
20. V. A. Maklakov, "Vinogradov," *Slavonic and East European Review* 13,

no. 39 (1939), 633–40; Maklakov, *Iz Vospominanii*, 194, describing Vinogradov as a "European in the best sense of the word."

21. Maklakov, *Iz Vospominanii*, 192, 211–13.
22. Ibid., 62–64; Dedkov, *Konservativnyi liberalizm*, 34.
23. Maklakov, *Iz Vospominanii*, 63–67; Dedkov, *Konservativnyi liberalizm*, 34–35.
24. GDSO, Third Duma, 5th Sess., pt. 2, February 29, 1912, col. 3400.
25. Maklakov, *Iz Vospominanii*, 62; Maklakov, *Vlast i obshchestvennost*, 75.
26. Maklakov, *Iz Vospominanii*, 110–12; Dedkov, *Konservativnyi liberalizm*, 37.
27. Maklakov, *Iz Vospominanii*, 113.
28. Ibid., 110–15.
29. Ibid., 116–21.
30. "Prime minister" slightly oversimplifies. From 1903 to October 1905 he was chairman of the "committee" of ministers, and from then till his dismissal in April 1906, chairman of the "council" of ministers. The difference between committee and council is that, associated with that change in name, was a jump upward in the authority of the chairman to coordinate the cabinet.
31. Maklakov, *Iz Vospominanii*, 133–36; see also Jonathan Daly, "Political Crime in Late Imperial Russia," *Journal of Modern History* 74, no. 1 (March 2002), 62–100, 94n138.
32. Ivanova, "Rol V. A. Maklakova," 58, citing GIM, fond 442, ll. 112–112ob. Bogoslovskii identifies V. A. Dolgorukov as the crucial contact—mistakenly, so far as it appears.
33. Maklakov, *Iz Vospominanii*, 138.
34. Ibid., 72.
35. Dedkov, *Konservativnyi liberalizm*, 36.
36. Maklakov, *Iz Vospominanii*, 60, 88–90.
37. Ibid., 142–49.
38. Ibid., 148–49.
39. Ibid., 150–51.
40. Ibid., 78–80, 84–86.
41. Ibid., 90.
42. Ibid., 92, 97–99.
43. Ibid., 100–101; Bakhmetev-Maklakov Correspondence, 1:508 (citing Ariadne Tyrkova-Williams, "Russkii parlamentarii," *Novyi Zhurnal*, no. 52 [1958], 238).
44. Maklakov, *Iz Vospominanii*, 103–4.
45. Ibid., 108–10.
46. Ibid., 106, 136–38.
47. Ibid., 18–19, 163–64.
48. Ibid., 164–65; see also V. A. Maklakov, "Lev Tolstoi: Uchenie i Zhizn" [Leo Tolstoy: Teaching and life], in V. A. Maklakov, *O Lve Tolstom: Dve Rechi* [On Leo Tolstoy: Two speeches] (Paris: Annales contemporaines, 1929), 54–55.

49. Maklakov, *Iz Vospominanii*, 165. In his account of his student years, Maklakov seems to have placed the Singer event ahead of the relief efforts because it was a natural follow-up to his own obvious excitement at merely seeing Tolstoy.
50. Georgii Adamovich, *Vasilii Alekseevich Maklakov: Politik, Iurist, Chelovek* [Vasily Alekseevich Maklakov: Politician, jurist, human being] (Paris, 1959), 81; Dedkov, *Konservativnyi liberalizm*, 128.
51. Maklakov, *Iz Vospominanii*, 165–68.
52. V. A. Maklakov, "Lev Tolstoi kak obshchestvennyi deiatel" [Leo Tolstoy as a public figure], in *V. A. Maklakov, Rechi: Sudebniia, Dymskiia i Publichniia Lektsii, 1904–1926* [V. A. Maklakov, Speeches: Judicial, Duma and public lectures, 1904–1926] (Paris: Izdanie Iubileinogo Komiteta, 1869–1949), 142.
53. Maklakov, *Iz Vospominanii*, 181.
54. Ibid., 197–201.
55. Dedkov, *Konservativnyi liberalizm*, 51.
56. Maklakov, *Iz Vospominanii*, 203.
57. Ibid., 185–88.
58. Ibid., 213, 216–17.
59. Ibid., 218–19.
60. Ibid., 225–30. Apropos of exam preparation as a sporting achievement, Maklakov once said, in an homage to Vinogradov, "I felt an irresistible weakness for examinations as a kind of sport." Maklakov, "Vinogradov," 636.

CHAPTER 2: TRIAL LAWYER

1. William E. Pomeranz, *The Emergence and Development of the Russian Advokatura: 1864–1905* (PhD dissertation, University of London, 1990), 78–80, 84. The rules were somewhat relaxed in the period from 1896 to 1910 but were then restored in their full restrictive vigor. In chapter 17 we'll see Maklakov ending these restrictions in one of the first reforms of the February Revolution.
2. Ibid., 184.
3. V. A. Maklakov, *Iz Vospominanii* (New York: Chekhov Publishing House [Izdatelstvo imeni Chekhova], 1954), 231–34; V. A. Maklakov, "F. I. Rodichev i A. R. Lednitskii," *Novyi Zhurnal*, no. 16 (1947), 240, 244–45; Vaclav Lednitskii, "Vokrug V. A. Maklakova (lichnye vospominaniia)" [Around V. A. Maklakov (personal reminiscences)], *Novyi Zhurnal*, no. 56 (March 1959), 222–50.
4. Maklakov, "F. I. Rodichev i A. R. Lednitskii," 245.
5. Girish N. Bhat, "The Moralization of Guilt in Late Imperial Russian Trial by Jury: The Early Reform Era," *Law and History Review* 15, no. 1 (Spring 1997), 77–113; Samuel Kucherov, *Courts, Lawyers, and Trials under the Last Three Tsars* (New York: F. A. Praeger, 1953), 64–68.

6. Maklakov, *Iz Vospominanii*, 282–86.
7. Ibid., 235–38.
8. See Lev N. Tolstoi, *Polnoe Sobranie sochinenii* [Complete works], ed. G. Chertkov, 90 vols. (Moscow: Gos. izd-vo khudozh. lit-ry, 1928–58), 70:453–54; 73:287; 79–80:113, 163–64; 81:217–18, for letters from Tolstoy to Maklakov.
9. Maklakov, *Iz Vospominanii*, 238–47.
10. Ibid., 248–50.
11. Ibid., 250–56.
12. L. I. Goldman, *Politicheskie protsessy v Rossii, 1901–1917* (Moscow: 1932), 42, 45, 57, 76, 141–43, 146.
13. "Sudebnaia khronika," in *Russkie Vedomosti* (c. July 23, 1906), located in GIM, fond 31, delo 87, l. 235. For praise of Maklakov's eloquence in this summation by a fellow defense lawyer, see A. A. Goldenbeizer, "Vospominaniia o V. A. Maklakove," *Novoe Russkoe Slovo* (July 28, 1957), 2.
14. Kucherov, *Courts, Lawyers, and Trials*, 235–38; Maklakov, *Iz Vospominanii*, 275–77.
15. Maklakov, *Iz Vospominanii*, 276. The new code had been nominally adopted in 1903, but its provisions on political and religious crimes, the only ones finally approved, were put into effect in June 1904. Jonathan W. Daly, "Political Crime in Late Imperial Russia," *Journal of Modern History* 74, no. 1 (March 2002), 62, 71.
16. Maklakov, *Iz Vospominanii*, 264–67, 275–76.
17. Jonathan W. Daly, "On the Significance of Emergency Legislation in Late Imperial Russia," *Slavic Review* 54 (Autumn 1995), 602, 624.
18. Georgii Adamovich, *Vasilii Alekseevich Maklakov: Politik, Iurist, Chelovek* [Vasily Alekseevich Maklakov: Politician, jurist, human being] (Paris, 1959), 241n*.
19. M. L. Mandelshtam, *1905 god v politicheskikh protsessakh: Zapiski zashchitnika* [The year 1905 in political trials: Notes of a defense counsel] (Moscow: Izdatelstvo polikatorzhan, 1931), 101.
20. V. A. Maklakov, *Vlast i Obshchestvennost na zakate staroi Rossii (Vospominaniia sovremenika)* [State and society in the twilight of old Russia (Recollections of a contemporary)] (Paris: Izdanie zhurnala "Illustrirovanaia Rossiia," 1936), 170–73.
21. Ibid., 174.
22. Maklakov, *Iz Vospominanii*, 294; Marina Aleksandrovna Ivanova, "Rol V. A. Maklakova v Obshchestvenno-politicheskoi zhizni Rossii" [The role of V. A. Maklakov in the social-political life of Russia] (PhD thesis, Rossiiskii Universitet Druzhby Narodov, 1997), 95–97, citing GIM, fond 31, dela 92, 108, 110–12, 117, 122, 125–29, and 131–32.
23. Maklakov, *Iz Vospominanii*, 292–93.
24. A. Lunacharskii, K. Radek, and L. Trotskii, *Siluety: Politicheskie portrety* [Silhouettes: Political portraits] (Moscow: Izdatelstvo politicheskoi literatury, 1991), 237. Trotsky's comment originally appeared in an article

on Miliukov in the newspaper *Luch*, nos. 6–7 (September 22–23, 1912). See http://magister.msk.ru/library/trotsky/trotm193.htm.

25. N. I. Dedkov, *Konservativnyi liberalizm Vasiliia Maklakova* (Moscow: AIRO-XX, 2005), 113–14.
26. David Arwyn Davies, *V. A. Maklakov and the Problem of Russia's Westernization* (PhD thesis, University of Washington, 1967), 37 and n29. Davies learnt of the practice from M. Kantor, a close personal friend of Maklakov in his later years.
27. The Beilis trial illustrated a somewhat different procedure, in which a "civil plaintiff" appears in a criminal trial on behalf of a party claiming injury, there evidently the family of the murder victim. See chapter 9 for details in connection with Beilis.
28. V. A. Maklakov, "F. N. Plevako," in *V. A. Maklakov, Rechi: Sudebniia, Dymskiia i Publichniia Lektsii, 1904–1926* [V. A. Maklakov, Speeches: Judicial, Duma and public lectures, 1904–1926] (Paris: Izdanie Iubileinogo Komiteta, 1869–1949), 71, 72, 112.
29. Ibid., 75–85.
30. Iosif V. Gessen, *V Dvukh vekakh: Zhiznennyi otchet* [In two centuries: A life's account], *Arkhiv Russkoi Revoliutsii* 22 (1937), 170–71. Gessen was also a Kadet party leader, Duma member, and advocate.
31. Adamovich, *Vasilii Alekseevich Maklakov*, 68–69.
32. Lednitskii, "Vokrug V. A. Maklakova," 222, 235.
33. Ibid., 226.
34. Maklakov, "F. N. Plevako," 97–99, 101.
35. Ibid., 104, 104; Adamovich, *Vasilii Alekseevich Maklakov*, 60.
36. Maklakov, "F. N. Plevako," 100–101.
37. Ibid., 105–6.
38. Ibid., 112.
39. Maklakov, *Vlast i obshchestvennost*, 165–66; Pomeranz, *Emergence and Development*, 221.
40. Maklakov, *Vlast i obshchestvennost*, 167–68; Maklakov, *Iz Vospominaniia*, 348, and, speaking of citizens who went to electoral meetings in the same terms as he had used for jurors, 356–57.
41. Gessen, *V Dvukh vekakh*, 183. See Shmuel Galai, *The Liberation Movement in Russia, 1900–1905* (Cambridge: Cambridge University Press, 1973), 247, regarding Maklakov's leadership role.
42. Galai, *Liberation Movement*, 245–48. Though Galai identifies Maklakov as a leader of the union of lawyers on page 247, it is not clear if he exercised any of that leadership after the 1905 change described in the text.
43. This was technically the All-Russian Peasants Union. It had few peasant members and was really an extension of the union of agronomists and statisticians. See Galai, *Liberation Movement*, 253.
44. Maklakov, *Vlast i obshchestvennost*, 361–62, 365–68.
45. Bakhmetev-Maklakov Correspondence, 3:97–98 (Maklakov to Bakhmetev, November 23, 1923); Dmitrii Vladimirovich Aronov,

Pervyi spiker (Moscow: Iurist, 2006), 92–95; N. A. Kaklukov, "V Moskovskoi Iuridicheskom Obshchestve" [In the Moscow Juridical Society], in *Sergei Andreevich Muromtsev* (Moscow: Izd. M. i S. Sabashnikovykh, 1911), 134–40.

CHAPTER 3: FRIENDS AND LOVERS

1. GIM, fond 31, delo 69, l. 1 (letter of June 18, 1903, from Chekhov to Maklakov).
2. V. A. Maklakov, *Iz Vospominanii* (New York: Chekhov Publishing House, 1954), 174–75.
3. See Marina Aleksandrovna Ivanova, "Rol V. A. Maklakova v Obshchestvenno-politicheskoi zhizni Rossii" [The role of V. A. Maklakov in the social-political life of Russia] (PhD thesis, Rossiiskii Universitet Druzhby Narodov, 1997), 102, 217n46 (citing GIM, fond 31, delo 150) (letter to Maklakov acknowledging his role as a prototype).
4. GIM, fond 31, delo 110.
5. See I. Kashuk, "Poslednii god Shaliapina" [Chaliapin's last year], *Illiustrirovanniia Rossiia*, 684, no. 26 ([June 18], 1938), 3–5.
6. V. A. Maklakov, "Lev Tolstoi: Uchenie i Zhizn" [Leo Tolstoy: Teaching and life], in V. A. Maklakov, *O Lve Tolstom: Dve Rechi* [On Leo Tolstoy: Two speeches] (Paris: Annales contemporaines, 1929), 7–57.
7. See Tyrkova-Williams Diary and Letters, 1011–16 (Maklakov to Ariadne Tyrkova-Williams, October 12, 1955, and November 3, 1955).
8. Maklakov, "Lev Tolstoi: Uchenie i Zhizn," 10, 13.
9. Ibid., 20–24.
10. Maklakov, *Iz Vospominanii*, 169–70.
11. Maklakov, "Lev Tolstoi: Uchenie i Zhizn," 29–30.
12. Ibid., 31.
13. Maklakov, *Iz Vospominanii*, 170.
14. V. A. Maklakov, "Lev Tolstoi kak obshchestvennyi deiatel" [Leo Tolstoy as a public figure], in *V. A. Maklakov, Rechi: Sudebniia, Dumskiia i Publichniia Lektsii, 1904–1926* [V. A. Maklakov, Speeches: Judicial, Duma and public lectures, 1904–1926] (Paris: Izdanie Iubileinogo Komiteta, 1869–1949), 146–48.
15. Ibid., 153.
16. Maklakov, *Iz Vospominanii*, 173; "Lev Tolstoi: Uchenie i Zhizn," 49–50.
17. "Lev Tolstoi: Uchenie i Zhizn," 47–48. Maklakov also observed: "The degree of a person's religiosity is defined not so much by his views as by the seriousness for him of those questions and interests that religion answers." V. A. Maklakov, "Tolstoi—kak Mirovoe Yavlenie" ["Tolstoy as a world presence"], in V. A. Maklakov, *O Lve Tolstom: Dve Rechi* [On Leo Tolstoy: Two speeches] (Paris: Annales contemporaines, 1929), 71.
18. V. A. Maklakov, "Tolstoi i sud" [Tolstoy and the courts], in *V. A. Maklakov, Rechi: Sudebniia, Dumskiia i Publichniia Lektsii, 1904–1926*

[V. A. Maklakov, Speeches: Judicial, Duma and public lectures, 1904–1926] (Paris: Izdanie Iubileinogo Komiteta, 1869–1949), 168.
19. Ibid, 171.
20. Ibid., 173–74.
21. Ibid., 181.
22. Ibid., 189–90; Maklakov, *Iz Vospominanii*, 178–81.
23. Maklakov, "Tolstoi i sud," 192.
24. See chapter 2.
25. This is confirmed in many references to social events with "the Maklakovs" in *The Diaries of Sofia Tolstoy*, trans. Cathy Porter (New York: Harper Perennial, 2009), a group that clearly included his sister Mariia and brother Alexei.
26. Maklakov, *Iz Vospominanii*, 168.
27. Maklakov, "Lev Tolstoi: Uchenie i Zhizn," 52.
28. Ibid., 53.
29. Ibid., 56–57.
30. GDSO, Second Duma, March 12, 1907, Meeting 8, cols. 391–92.
31. See Ivanova, "Rol V. A. Maklakova," 187, 230n103 (citing GIM, fond 31, delo 1).
32. GIM, fond 31, opis: describing dela 5 (124), 6 (114), 11 (199), 12 (194), 54 (225), 78 (319), 79 (439), 80 (500), 81 (337), 82 (207), 83 (201). The correspondence amounts to eleven folders, each having no less than 124 pages and no more than 500.
33. GIM, fond 31, dela 11 and 12.
34. The Kollontai-Maklakov letters have been transcribed and posted on the Internet; see http://ru-lib.3dn.ru/publ/kollontaj_aleksandra_mikhajlovna_pisma_k_v_a_maklakovu/1-1-0-460.
35. Hoover, 1–3. The passage is part of a brief snippet on Maklakov in Rosa Vinaver's draft memoir of Paul Miliukov.
36. GIM, fond 31, delo 11, l. 1.
37. Ibid., l. 3.
38. Ibid., l. 6.
39. Ibid., ll. 14, 9.
40. Ibid., l. 15.
41. Kollontai-Maklakov Letters, Letter no. 14 (as numbered on website). The speeches on the peasant question seem necessarily to be those of June 1916, discussed in chapter 12, as those were the only ones where Maklakov focused on peasant issues. Kollontai's hesitancy about the "later ones" may be because they reflect his reluctance to try to extend the reform to achieve Jewish equality; as we'll see, he believed that such an extension would jeopardize passage of the peasant reform.
42. Barbara Evans Clements, *Bolshevik Feminist: The Life of Alexandra Kollontai* (Bloomington and London: Indiana University Press, 1979), 253.
43. Ibid., 183–99.
44. Ignazio Silone, *Emergency Exit* (London: Victor Gollanz, 1969), 68.

45. Kollontai-Maklakov Letters, letter nos. 9 and 13.
46. Ibid., letter no. 14.
47. Ibid., letter nos. 7 and 14.
48. Ibid., letter no. 10.

CHAPTER 4: INTO POLITICS

1. V. A. Maklakov, *Vlast i obshchestvennost na zakate staroi Rossii (Vospominaniia sovremenika)* [State and society in the twilight of old Russia (Recollections of a contemporary)] (Paris: Izdanie zhurnala "Illustrirovannaia Rossiia," 1936), 306–11; V. A. Maklakov, *Iz Vospominanii* (New York: Chekhov Publishing House, 1954), 328–32. Maklakov's view that the peasants' inability to develop reasoned solutions was due to lack of experience finds support in the finding that IQ has been steadily rising at a fairly steady pace around the globe, which is known after its discoverer as the "Flynn effect"; one of the explanatory theories for the effect is that modern life has increased the occasions calling on people to deploy analytic reasoning. Steven Pinker, *The Better Angels of Our Nature* (New York: Penguin, 2012), 650–57.
2. GIM, fond 31 (papers of V. A. Maklakov), delo 141, ll. 139–42 (both sides); Maklakov, *Iz Vospominanii*, 333; Maklakov, *Vlast i obshchestvennost*, 311–12. The memo is undated, but as the local committees started collecting evidence in August 1902 and reporting to St. Petersburg by the end of July 1903, those dates must frame the period of the memo's circulation; David A. J. Macey, *Government and Peasant in Russia, 1861–1906* (DeKalb: Northern Illinois University Press, 1987), 70.
3. Maklakov, *Iz Vospominanii*, 335–36.
4. Ibid., 336.
5. Shmuel Galai, *The Liberation Movement in Russia, 1900–1905* (Cambridge: Cambridge University Press, 1973), 47–52 (at 52 and 55 he uses the adjective "semi-conspiratorial"); Maklakov, I*z Vospominanii*, 336; Maklakov, *Vlast i obshchestvennost*, 291–94.
6. Galai, *Liberation Movement*, 52–56; Maklakov, *Vlast i obshchestvennost*, 293–94.
7. Maklakov, *Vlast i obshchestvennost*, 295.
8. Ibid., 294–95. This passage is also quoted in K. A. Soloviev, *Kruzhok "Beseda." V poiskakh novoi politicheskoi real'nosti 1899–1905* [The Beseda Circle: In search of a new political reality, 1899–1905] (Moscow: ROSSPEN, 2009), 231.
9. Abraham Ascher, *The Revolution of 1905*, 2 vols. (Stanford: Stanford University Press, 1992), 1:77–92.
10. I. A. Isakov, "Kak nachalos Krovavoe voskresenie [How Bloody Sunday happened]," *Voprosy istorii* [Historical questions] 4 (1996), 175.
11. See Maklakov, *Vlast i obshchestvennost*, 345–49; Ascher, *Revolution of 1905*, 1:90–95; Martha Bohachevsky-Chomiak, *Sergei N. Trubetskoi: An Intellectual among the Intelligentsia in Prerevolutionary Russia* (Belmont,

MA: Nordland Publishing, 1976), 140–41, citing *Sergei N. Trubetskoi, Sobranie Sochinenii kn. Sergeia Nikolaevicha Trubetskogo*, ed. L. M. Lopatin (Moscow, 1907–1912), 1:397–99, for the wording of the minority statement. Bohachevsky-Chomiak gives the vote as 219 to 147; Maklakov reports it as 219 to 153. Either way, the sum adds up to more than the total membership, so clearly some people voted for both the liberal and the conservative variants.

12. See, for example, Maklakov's caustic comments on E. de Roberti's saying that the destruction of five to twenty gentry estates had no meaning at all and expressing concern only for estates burned by the Black Hundreds. V. A. Maklakov, *Vtoraia Gosudarstvennaia Duma* [The Second State Duma] (Moscow: Tsentrpoligraf, 2006), 262.
13. See Soloviev, *Kruzhok "Beseda,"* 222, citing GIM, fond 31, delo 142, ll. 245 and 245ob; Marina Aleksandrovna Ivanova, "Rol V. A. Maklakova v Obshchestvenno-politicheskoi zhizni Rossii" [The role of V. A. Maklakov in the social-political life of Russia] (PhD thesis, Rossiiskii Universitet Druzhby Narodov, 1997), 109–10, citing the same pages but in delo 148.
14. Galai, *Liberation Movement*, 219.
15. Maklakov, *Vlast i obshchestvennost*, 509–10; Maklakov, *Iz Vospominanii*, 344–45.
16. Maklakov, *Vlast i obshchestvennost*, 480–81; Maklakov, *Iz Vospominanii*, 343–45. Neither the remark on possible future responsibility nor the talking-to that he gave the policeman is recorded in the formal minutes of the congress, but it is plain that those minutes are radically incomplete.
17. Maklakov, *Vlast i obshchestvennost*, 475; Maklakov, *Iz Vospominanii*, 340.
18. V. A. Maklakov, "F. N. Plevako," in *V. A. Maklakov, Rechi: Sudebniia, Dumskiia i Publichniia Lektsii, 1904–1926* [V. A. Maklakov, Speeches: Judicial, Duma and public lectures, 1904–1926] (Paris: Izdanie Iubileinogo Komiteta, 1869–1949), 102.
19. Ascher, *Revolution of 1905*, 1:228–29.
20. Ibid., 2:45.
21. A. A. Kizevetter, *Na rubezhe dvukh stoletii: Vospominaniia* [On the Border of Two Centuries: Memoirs] (Moscow: Iskusstvo, 1996), 391–92.
22. Maklakov, *Vlast i obshchestvennost*, 346; Paul Miliukov, *Political Memoirs*, 66; Paul Miliukov, *Vospominaniia* (Moscow: Sovremennik, 1990), 1:316. Although Miliukov expresses uncertainty over the wording of his reaction, he acknowledges expression of the general sentiment—we "mustn't leave our battle positions." See also Galai, *Liberation Movement*, 264.
23. V. V. Shelokhaev, ed., *Sezdy i konferentsii Konstitutsionno-demokraticheskoi partii* [Congresses and Conferences of the Constitutional Democratic Party] (Moscow: ROSSPEN, 1997), 1:31–33. See also Shmuel Galai, "Konstitutsionalisty-demokraty i ikh kritiki [The Constitutional Dem-

ocrats and their critics]," *Voprosy istorii* [Historical questions] no. 12 (1991), 3, 10, 13.

24. *Pravo* (*Law*), no. 44, November 13, 1905, 3619–20. The Congress adopted a resolution that included the "precious achievement" language, but that was considerably vaguer in its demands on the government. *Pravo* (*Law*), nos. 45/46, November 20, 1905, 3701–3.
25. Maklakov, *Vlast i obshchestvennost*, 434–35.
26. Ibid., 435.
27. Anthony Kroner, "The Debate between Miliukov and Maklakov on the Chances for Russian Liberalism," *Revolutionary Russia* 7, no. 2 (1994), 239, 253. Miliukov himself wrote that "the choice of Kokoshkin meant that the Bureau did not want compromise decisions." P. N. Miliukov, *Tri Popytki* [Three Attempts] (Paris: Presse Franco-Russe, 1921), 11; see also Maklakov, *Vlast i obshchestvennost*, 436–37.
28. Paul Miliukov, "Politika v 'Sovremennykh zapiskakh,'" [Politics in "Contemporary Notes"], *Poslednie Novosti* [Recent news], April 4, 1929, col. 6.
29. Geoffrey A. Hosking, *The Russian Constitutional Experiment: Government and Duma, 1907–1914* (Cambridge: Cambridge University Press, 1973), 16; Maklakov, *Vlast i obshchestvennost*, 437–39.
30. Maklakov, *Vlast i obshchestvennost*, 440–41 (quoting Miliukov's *Tri Popytki*); Hosking, *Russian Constitutional Experiment*, 17n16 (citing Witte's memoirs).
31. Miliukov, *Vospominaniia (1859–1917)* (New York: Chekhov Publishing House, 1955), 1:314–18, 328. Belgium and Bulgaria seem to have been the "go-to" countries for people in autocracies in search of a constitution; Iranian liberals turned to them in 1907. See Christopher de Bellaigue, *The Islamic Enlightenment: The Struggle between Faith and Reason, 1798 to Modern Times* (New York: Liveright Publishing, 2017), 241–43.
32. See chapter 12.
33. Maklakov, *Vlast i obshchestvennost*, 444–46.
34. Ascher, *Revolution of 1905*, 1:312.
35. M. L. Mandelshtam, *1905 god v politicheskikh protsessakh: Zapiski zashchitnika* [The year 1905 in political trials: Notes of a defense counsel] (Moscow: Izdatelstvo polikatorzhan, 1931), 327.
36. Maklakov, *Vlast i obshchestvennost*, 429.
37. Francis W. Wcislo, *Tales of Imperial Russia: The Life and Times of Sergei Witte, 1849–1915* (Oxford: Oxford University Press, 2011), 232–33.
38. Ivanova, "Rol V. A. Maklakova V. A. Maklakov," 121, 219n91 (citing GARF, fond 523, delo 261, l. 27). In a conversation with Stolypin during the First Duma, Miliukov evidently claimed that if a Kadet cabinet adopted its proposed reforms and the revolutionary left nonetheless sought to overthrow the government, Miliukov would shoot the revolutionaries down, "more freely than Stolypin himself." Stolypin claimed to have replied that, as a liberal humanitarian, having just abolished the death penalty and brought about a general amnesty, Miliukov

"could not use such energetic measures without completely discrediting himself and his party. Within a month he would be compelled to resign, and would disappear in a deluge of execration launched at him by his former admirers." Peter Enticott, *The Russian Liberals and the Revolution of 1905* (London and New York: Routledge, 2016), 129.

39. Bismarck's exact statement appears to have been less pithy: "An experienced constitutional statesman has said that all of constitutional life is one long series of compromises." Lothar Gall, ed., *Bismarck: Die grossen Reden*, 62–63, 66–76. "Clinton, Bush Share Laughs and Memories at Launch of Scholars Program," *Wall Street Journal*, September 9, 2014.
40. The Logan Act, 18 U.S.C. § 953.
41. See Olga Crisp, "The Russian Liberals and the 1906 Anglo-French Loan to Russia," *Slavonic and East European Review* 39, no. 93 (June 1961), 497–511; James William Long, "Organized Protest against the 1906 Russian Loan," *Cahiers du monde Russe et soviétique* 13, no. 1 (1972), 24–39.
42. Long, "Organized Protest," 28n5; compare Maklakov, *Iz Vospominanii*, 321, discussing his having started a practice of Christmas and Easter vacations in France in 1897. Long cites Miliukov's account, written in emigration, reporting that the Kadet central committee had been asked to consent to party leaders' joining the French campaign against the loan, a request the central committee rejected. Long thinks that "perhaps this is where [Maklakov] got the idea." Long, "Organized Protest," 28. In fact Maklakov and other Kadets in France did communicate a proposal of such involvement (which indeed the central committee rejected), but they made the proposal *after* Maklakov's anti-loan activities in Paris. The later events (the exchange on party involvement) could not have prompted the earlier ones (Maklakov's activities).
43. See Maklakov, *Iz Vospominanii*, 321, for his regular practice; Maklakov, *Vlast i obshchestvennost*, 529, for this specific occasion.
44. Long, "Organized Protest," 28–30; Maklakov, *Vlast i obshchestvennost*, 529.
45. Crisp, "The Russian Liberals," 508–11.
46. Maklakov, *Vlast i obshchestvennost*, 530.
47. Compare Crisp, "The Russian Liberals," 508n39, with Maklakov, *Vlast i obshchestvennost*, 531–32.
48. See Crisp, "The Russian Liberals," 509 (text of memo, emphasis added).
49. Ibid., 510–11.
50. Ibid., 510.
51. Ibid., 509.
52. Long, "Organized Protest," 25.
53. Maklakov, *Vlast i obshchestvennost*, 533–37.
54. Long states that the loan was actually signed April 16, two days before the apparent delivery of Maklakov's memo; Long, "Organized Protest," 25.

55. Maklakov, *Vlast i obshchestvennost*, 537–38.
56. Ibid., 541–42.
57. Ibid., 539–41.

CHAPTER 5: A CONSTITUTION FOR RUSSIA?

1. V.A. Maklakov, *Vlast i obshchestvennost na zakate staroi Rossii (Vospominaniia sovremenika)* [State and society in the twilight of old Russia (Recollections of a contemporary)] (Paris: Izdanie zhurnala "Illustrirovanaia Rossiia," 1936), 556–59.
2. For example, certain provisions of the International Emergency Economic Powers Act of 1977 and the USA PATRIOT Act give the president the authority to declare a national emergency and then to administer laws that would otherwise have lapsed, such as the export control regime. See 50 U.S.C. §§ 1701–1702.
3. Ben-Cion Pinchuk, *The Octobrists in the Third Duma, 1907–1912* (Seattle: University of Washington Press, 1974), 178–79; GDSO, Third Duma, 5th Sess., pt. 1, October 17, 1911, cols. 125–55, 185–90. For the 1903 change, see *Polnoe Sobranie Zakonov, III*, No. 23180 (June 20, 1903).
4. Maklakov, *State and Society*, 595–96. All translations of the Fundamental Laws are from Marc Szeftel, *The Russian Constitution of April 23, 1906* (Brussels: Librairie Encyclopédique, 1976), unless otherwise noted.
5. Ibid.
6. Maklakov mistakenly says that the laws had said that for 109 years. Ibid., 563–64. But they had only been promulgated in 1833. The reference may be to the accession to the throne in 1796 of the emperor Paul, an outspoken proponent of autocracy. See Abraham Ascher, *The Revolution of 1905*, 2 vols. (Stanford: Stanford University Press, 1992), 2:65n*.
7. Maklakov, *Vlast i obshchestvennost*, 567.
8. Szeftel, *The Russian Constitution*, 99.
9. Maklakov, *Vlast i obshchestvennost*, 575.
10. The western zemstvo legislation, discussed in chapter 8.
11. Maklakov, *Vlast i obshchestvennost*, 577–79 (N.A. Khomiakov's term).
12. Ibid., 579. The Second Duma did vote down a handful of provisions adopted in the lengthy period between the first two Dumas.
13. V.A. Maklakov, *Vtoraia Gosudarstvennaia Duma* [The Second State Duma] (Moscow: Tsentrpoligraf, 2006), 175.
14. See chapter 12.
15. Olga Crisp, "The Russian Liberals and the 1906 Anglo-French Loan to Russia," *Slavonic and East European Review* 39, no. 93 (June 1961), 497, 510.
16. Under Article 100 of the Fundamental Laws, he could not increase that share.
17. Maklakov, *Vlast i obshchestvennost*, 586–93; GDSO, Third Duma, 4th Sess., pt. 3, April 27, 1911, col. 2880. See also Tsuyoshi Hasegawa,

The February Revolution (Seattle and London: University of Washington Press, 1981), 149 (discussing Nicholas II's right-wing transformation of the State Council on January 1, 1917).

18. Maklakov, *Vlast i obshchestvennost*, 586–88; Abraham Ascher, *P.A. Stolypin: The Search for Stability in Late Imperial Russia* (Stanford: Stanford University Press, 2001), 281–90.
19. Maklakov, *Vlast i obshchestvennost*, 580–82.
20. Ibid., 582.
21. Ibid., 570–73.
22. *Uchrezhdenie Gosudarstvennoi Dumy* [Statute of the State Duma], Articles 55–57.
23. Peter Enticott, *The Russian Liberals and the Revolution of 1905* (London and New York: Routledge, 2016), 85, 116.
24. V.A. Maklakov, *Pervaia Gosudarstvennaia Duma* [The First State Duma] (Moscow: Tsentrpoligraf, 2006); Maklakov, "1905–1906 gody" [The years 1905–1906], in *Vinaver i russkaia obshchestvennost nachala XX veka; sbornik stateĭ* [Vinaver and Russian society at the start of the twentieth century: Collected articles] (Paris: Imp. Cooperative Étoile, 1937), 53–96.
25. Vladimir Kokovtsov, *Out of My Past* (Stanford: Stanford University Press, 1935), 126.
26. Enticott, *Russian Liberals*, 94.
27. Ascher, *The Revolution of 1905*, 2:64–69.
28. Maklakov, *Vlast i obshchestvennost*, 544–46.

CHAPTER 6: THE FIRST DUMA: TAKE-OFF AND CRASH LANDING

1. Abraham Ascher, *The Revolution of 1905*, 2 vols. (Stanford: Stanford University Press, 1992), 2:51, 77; Tyrkova-Williams Diary and Letters, 914 (Maklakov to Tyrkova-Williams, August 8, 1945).
2. V.A. Maklakov, *Pervaia Gosudarstvennaia Duma* [The First State Duma] (Moscow: Tsentrpoligraf, 2006), 127–28. GDSO, First Duma, Meeting 8, May 13, 1906, pp. 321–24 (government speech); ibid., Ukazatel, pp. 244–47 (listing ministry bills relating to these topics).
3. V.A. Maklakov, *Vlast i obshchestvennost na zakate staroi Rossii (Vospominaniia sovremenika)* [State and society in the twilight of old Russia (Recollections of a contemporary)] (Paris: Izdanie zhurnala "Illustrirovanaia Rossiia," 1936), 514–16; A. Ia. Avrekh, *Tsarizm i IV Duma, 1912–1914 gg.* [Tsarism and the Fourth Duma, 1912–1914] (Moscow: Izdaletsvo Nauka, 1981), 189; P.N. Miliukov, "V.A. Maklakov mezhdu 'obshchestvennostiu i vlastiu, II,'" *Poslednie Novosti* [Recent news], May 30, 1937.
4. See Steven Pinker, *The Better Angels of Our Nature* (New York: Penguin, 2012), 490–92.
5. See Francis W. Wcislo, *Tales of Imperial Russia: The Life and Times of Sergei Witte, 1849–1915* (Oxford: Oxford University Press, 2011), 234.

6. Maklakov, *Pervaia Gosudarstvennaia Duma*, 40–41.
7. Ibid., 41, citing V.N. Kokovtsov, *Iz Moego Proshlago* (The Hague and Paris: Mouton, 1969 [reprint of 1933 edition]), 1:168–69 (translated as Vladimir Kokovtsov, *Out of My Past* [Stanford: Stanford University Press, 1935], 126). In chapter 7 I discuss Maklakov's description of the treatment of agrarian issues in the Second Duma, from which he draws (possibly optimistic) inferences about the feasibility of progress even on divisive issues.
8. Duma Address to the Tsar, GDSO, First Duma, Meeting 5, May 5, 1906, pp. 239–41. The Duma's address did not explicitly call for four-tailed suffrage, but in the context of electoral laws that provided nearly universal male suffrage and the Kadet background on this, its literal call for "universal" suffrage was bound to be understood as demanding the familiar "four-tailed" version.
9. Maklakov, *Pervaia Gosudarstvennaia Duma*, 94–95.
10. Maklakov, *Vlast i obshchestvennost*, 555 (Miliukov at the April 1906 Kadet party congress); *Sezdy i konferentsii*, 1:349 (statement of third party congress, April 21–25, 1906).
11. Duma Address to the Tsar, First Duma, Meeting 5, May 5, 1906, 240. As a historian, Maklakov later wrote that at their January and April 1906 congresses the Kadets had adopted resolutions forbidding participation in legislative work until the constitution was reformed. Maklakov, *Pervaia Gosudarstvennaia Duma*, 59. Although there was clearly much sentiment to that effect, the congresses do not seem to have established such an absolute priority. See, for example, *Sezdy i konferentsii*, 1:116–17 (January), 246 (April).
12. Maklakov, *Pervaia Gosudarstvennaia Duma*, 237. Kizevetter was also struck by this episode. See A.A. Kizevetter, *Na rubezhe dvukh stoletii: Vospominaniia* [On the Border of Two Centuries: Memoirs] (Moscow: Iskusstvo, 1996), 432.
13. Maklakov, *Pervaia Gosudarstvennaia Duma*, 238.
14. Ibid., 138. GDSO, First Duma, Meeting 8, May 13, 1906, p. 326.
15. Dmitrii Vladimirovich Aronov, *Pervyi spiker* [First speaker] (Moscow: Iurist, 2006), 142–43; GDSO, First Duma, Meeting 1, April 27, 1906, p. 3.
16. For the way the extraordinary security laws enabled application of the death penalty, see William C. Fuller, "Civilians in Military Courts, 1881–1904," *Russian Review* 41, no. 3 (July 1982), 288, 292. Note that with such a transfer under the extraordinary security laws, the applicable law in the military courts was wartime law, with far more severe penalties than peacetime military law, including the death penalty in specific classes in cases.
17. GDSO, First Duma, Meeting 29, June 19, 1906, p. 1503.
18. Maklakov reviews this in "1905–1906 gody" [The years 1905–1906], in *Vinaver i russkaia obshchestvennost nachala XX veka; sbornik stateĭ* [Vinaver and Russian society at the start of the twentieth century: Collected articles] (Paris: Imp. Cooperative Étoile, 1937), 53, 84–88; and in *Per-*

vaia Gosudarstvennaia Duma, 196–202. Benjamin Beuerle, "A Step for 'The Whole Civilized World': The Debate over the Death Penalty in Russia,1905–1917," in *One Law for All?: Western Models and Local Practices in (Post-) Imperial Contexts*, ed. Stefan B. Kirmse (Frankfurt am Main, New York: Campus, 2012), 39–66, 50 and n.22.

19. Maklakov, *Pervaia Gosudarstvennaia Duma*, 88–89 (quoting Vinaver).
20. Duma Address to the Tsar, First Duma, Meeting 5, May 5, 1906, 241. See also Maklakov, *Pervaia Gosudarstvennaia Duma*, 90–91.
21. GDSO, First Duma, Meeting 8, May 13, 1906, p. 322.
22. Maklakov, *Pervaia Gosudarstvennaia Duma*, 284–85.
23. Ibid., 225–30; Maklakov, *La Chute*, 78; Shmuel Galai, "Kadet Domination of the First Duma and Its Limits," in *The Russian Revolution of 1905: Centenary Perspectives*, ed. Jonathan D. Smele and Anthony Heywood (London and New York: Routledge, 2005), 196, 204.
24. Abraham Ascher, *P.A. Stolypin: The Search for Stability in Late Imperial Russia* (Stanford: Stanford University Press, 2001), 138 (3,611 employees killed from October 1905 through September 1906); Ascher, *The Revolution of 1905*, 2:95 (mock letter to Rodichev); Maklakov, *Pervaia Gosudarstvennaia Duma*, 99–114; Shmuel Galai, "The Impact of the Vyborg Manifesto on the Fortunes of the Kadet Party," *Revolutionary Russia* 20, no. 2 (December 2007), 197, 216 (finding the Kadet position "neither very coherent nor persuasive").
25. Galai, "The Impact of the Vyborg Manifesto," 199.
26. Galai, "Kadet Domination," 205.
27. Maklakov, *Pervaia Gosudarstvennaia Duma*, 57–59.
28. Ibid., 321–23.
29. Ibid., 156–57. Stolypin, who had studied natural sciences at St. Petersburg University, may have gotten the idea from Robert G. Ingersoll (1833–1899), who had said, "There are in nature neither rewards nor punishments—there are only consequences."
30. Ibid., 155–59.
31. Ian D. Thatcher, "The First State Duma, 1906: The View from the Contemporary Pamphlet and Monograph Literature," *Canadian Journal of History* 46 (Winter 2011), 531–61, summarizes that literature as generally reflecting the Kadet perspective, along with Trudovik advocacy of greater militancy.
32. Ascher, *The Revolution of 1905*, 2:202–9; *Protokoly*, 1:12 (from "Tragediia kadetskoi (konstitutsionno-demokraticheskoi) partii" [The tragedy of the Kadet (Constitutional Democratic) Party], by the editorial board of the collection); Kizevetter, *Na rubezhe dvukh stoletii*, 435.
33. Aronov, *Pervyi spiker*, 168–74.
34. V.A. Maklakov, "Delo o Podpisavshikh Vyborgskoe Vozzvanie" [The case against the signers of the Vyborg Manifesto], in *V.A. Maklakov, Rechi: Sudebniia, Dymskiia i Publichniia Lektsii, 1904–1926* [V.A. Maklakov, Speeches: Judicial, Duma and public lectures, 1904–1926] (Paris: Izdanie Iubileinogo Komiteta, 1869–1949), 52–59.

35. Mandelshtam, *1905 god v politicheskikh protsessakh*, 357. The translation is mine, but has benefitted from that of Samuel Kucherov in his *Courts, Lawyers, and Trials under the Last Three Tsars* (New York: F. A. Praeger, 1953), 242. The word that I have translated as "rights" is ambiguous in Russian, and could mean "law." Mandelshtam's editor assumed it to be law, and then posed a question based on the assumption that law could be tsarist (bad) or proletarian (good). Maklakov noticed this, and, quoting the Mandelshtam passage and his editor's question in his memoirs, answered in terms imputing to Mandelshtam (and thus to himself) the "rights" meaning. V. A. Maklakov, *Iz Vospominanii* (New York: Chekhov Publishing House [Izdatelstvo imeni Chekhova], 1954), 279.
36. Aronov, *Pervyi spiker*, 174.
37. Maklakov, *Iz Vospominanii*, 361.

CHAPTER 7: THE SECOND DUMA: CHALLENGING STOLYPIN, ENGAGING STOLYPIN

1. A. A. Kizevetter, *Na rubezhe dvukh stoletii: Vospominaniia* [On the Border of Two Centuries: Memoirs] (Moscow: Iskusstvo, 1996), 455–56.
2. V. A. Maklakov, *Vtoraia Gosudarstvennaia Duma* [The Second State Duma] (Moscow: Tsentrpoligraf, 2006), 107–8.
3. Kizevetter, *Na rubezhe dvukh stoletii*, 446.
4. Maklakov, *Vtoraia Gosudarstvennaia Duma*, 75–79.
5. See Kroner, *The Debate Between Miliukov and Maklakov on the Chances for Russian Liberalism* (Amsterdam, 1998), 112–14; *Vestnik Partii Narodnoi Svobody* no. 1 (1907), 45, 46, 48.
6. S. V. Shelokhaev, *D. N. Shipov: Lichnost i obshchestvenno-politicheskaia deiatelnost* [D. N. Shipov: The Person and the public and political activity] (Moscow: ROSSPEN, 2010), 111–12.
7. Abraham Ascher, *The Revolution of 1905*, 2 vols. (Stanford: Stanford University Press, 1992), 2:51, 284; Don C. Rawson, *Russian Rightists and the Revolution of 1905* (New York: Cambridge University Press, 1995), 196–97. There are very small differences in classification between Ascher and Rawson.
8. J. W. Riddle to Secretary of State Elihu Root, March 15, 1907 (n.s.). Numerical and Minor Files of the Department of State, 1906–1910, National Archives Microfilm Publication no. M862, roll 20, case nos. 69/66–79/135, no. 15, images 712 ff., https://catalog.archives.gov/id/19106425.
9. Shmuel Galai, "The Jewish Question as a Russian Problem: The Debates in the First State Duma," *Revolutionary Russia* 17, no. 1 (June 2004), 31, 48–49.
10. Abraham Ascher, *P. A. Stolypin: The Search for Stability in Late Imperial Russia* (Stanford: Stanford University Press, 2001), 138–42; Maklakov, *Vtoraia Gosudarstvennaia Duma*, 27–28.

11. Melissa Kirschke Stockdale, *Paul Miliukov and the Quest for a Liberal Russia, 1880–1918* (Ithaca and London: Cornell University Press, 1996), 165.
12. *Sezdy i konferentsii*, 1:623 (Central Committee member N. A. Gredeskul is quoting Maklakov to that effect in an effort to resist claims that the Kadet faction should have been more aggressive).
13. Ascher, *P.A. Stolypin*, 187.
14. GDSO, Second Duma, Meeting 5, March 6, 1907, cols. 106–20. Duplicated in P. A. Stolypin, *Nam Nuzhna Velikaia Rossiia* [We need a great Russia] (Moscow: Molodaia Gvardiia, 1991), 50–62.
15. GDSO, Second Duma, Meeting 5, March 6, 1907, cols. 167–69. Duplicated in Stolypin, *Nam Nuzhna*, 64.
16. Maklakov, *Vtoraia Gosudarstvennaia Duma*, 123–24.
17. Ibid., 124.
18. Anna Geifman, *Thou Shalt Kill: Revolutionary Terrorism in Russia* (Princeton: Princeton University Press, 1993), 20–21.
19. Maklakov, *Vtoraia Gosudarstvennaia Duma*, 134–37.
20. GDSO, Second Duma, Meeting 8, March 12, 1907, col. 390.
21. Ibid., col. 392.
22. Ibid., Meeting 9, March 13, 1907, cols. 513–14.
23. GDSO, Second Duma, Meeting 9, March 13, 1907, col. 517.
24. See the discussion in Stephen F. Williams, "A Kadet's Critique of the Kadet Party: Vasily Maklakov," *Revolutionary Russia* 23 (2010), 29–65.
25. *Tovarishch* [Comrade], April 20, 1907, 3. This table excludes 42 death penalty verdicts in September from the "*voenno-morsk. polevykh sudov.*" The table also excludes figures from the ordinary military district courts (*voenno-okr*), and there are some discrepancies among the issues of *Tovarishch*. For example, the March 3, 1907 issue (p. 5) has February figures of 19 for the field courts martial and 22 for the military district courts. It may be that figures originally attributed to the military district courts were found later to be properly assignable to the field courts martial.
26. For perspective on the tsarist regime in relation to its successors, consider that in the relatively tranquil years from 1962 through 1990, the Soviet Union executed about 24,000 people, or an average of nearly 1,000 a year, with 3,000 executions in 1962 alone. Frances Nethercott, *Russian Legal Culture before and after Communism* (London and New York: Routledge, 2007), 135. Another point of comparison might be the toll from the shooting of hostages in one day after Fanny Kaplan's attempted assassination of Lenin. It's fair to estimate that the day's work exceeded eight months of the field courts martial, since 553 hostages were executed in Nizhny Novgorod and Petrograd alone, according to *Izvestiia*. Jonathan W. Daly, "Political Crime in Late Imperial Russia," *Journal of Modern History* 74, no. 1 (March 2002), 62, 100.
27. Bakhmetev-Maklakov Correspondence, 1:473 (Maklakov to Bakhmetev, August 30, 1921).
28. For Maklakov's Duma speeches on the subject, see the original attack

on the field courts martial, GDSO, Second Duma, Meeting 8, March 12, 1907, cols. 390–91; ibid., Meeting 21, April 3, 1907, cols. 1586–91; ibid., Meeting 30, April 30, 1907, cols. 2297–2305. Maklakov recounts the full story in *Vtoraia Gosudarstvennaia Duma*, 188–97.

29. GDSO, Second Duma, Meeting 49, May 28, 1907, cols. 1300–1305.
30. Maklakov, *Vtoraia Gosudarstvennaia Duma*, 274–75.
31. Ascher, *The Revolution of 1905*, 2:322–25; Maklakov, *Vtoraia Gosudarstvennaia Duma*, 262–85.
32. Geifman, *Thou Shalt Kill*, 217–20; see also Stockdale, *Paul Miliukov*, 165–67.
33. I'm using the Western term *village* not to mean a political entity but the economic and political unit technically called an *obshchina*, typically translated as "commune."
34. For some detail on the differences, see Stephen F. Williams, *Liberal Reform in an Illiberal Regime: The Creation of Private Property in Russia, 1906–1915* (Stanford: Hoover Institution Press, 2006), 216–17, 220–23.
35. V. Maklakov, "The Agrarian Problem in Russia before the Revolution," *Russian Review* 9, no. 1 (January 1950), 3, 13.
36. Ingeborg Fleischhauer, "The Agrarian Program of the Russian Constitutional Democrats," *Cahiers du Monde russe et soviétique* [Notes on the Russian and Soviet world] 20, no. 2 (1979), 173, 184–86; V. V. Shelokhaev, "Agrarnia programma kadetov v pervoi Russkoi revoliutsii" [Agricultural program of the Kadets in the first Russian revolution], *Istoricheskie Zapiski* [Historical notes] 86 (1970), 172, 204–7.
37. Fleischhauer, "The Agrarian Program," 186.
38. Leonard Schapiro, "The *Vekhi* Group and the Mystique of Revolution," *Slavonic and East European Review* 34, no. 82 (December 1955), 56, 67.
39. Maklakov, *Vtoraia Gosudarstvennaia Duma*, 173, 297–98.
40. Ibid., 291.
41. Ibid., 295; Tyrkova-Williams Diary and Letters, 875 (Maklakov to Ariadne Tyrkova-Williams, September 1, 1943).
42. Maklakov, *Vtoraia Gosudarstvennaia Duma*, 296.
43. Ibid., 297–98. Maklakov was convinced that the June 3 coup d'état would not have occurred if Stolypin had been sure that the law of November 9 would be accepted, albeit with major changes. See Bakhmetev-Maklakov Correspondence, 3:32 (Maklakov to Bakhmetev, July 4, 1923).
44. Maklakov, *Vtoraia Gosudarstvennaia Duma*, 297–99.
45. GDSO, Second Duma, Meeting 36, May 10, 1907, cols. 444–45; Maklakov, *Vtoraia Gosudarstvennaia Duma*, 301. The Stolypin speech is duplicated in Stolypin, *Nam Nuzhna*, 96.
46. Maklakov, *Vtoraia Gosudarstvennaia Duma*, 303.
47. Ibid.
48. Ibid., 304–9; Tyrkova-Williams Diary and Letters, 401 (Tyrkova-Williams to Maklakov, April 16, 1944).

49. Kizevetter, *Na rubezhe dvukh stoletii*, 463–64.
50. Maklakov, *Vtoraia Gosudarstvennaia Duma*, 314–15.
51. Ibid., 315.
52. P. A. Pozhigailo, ed., *P.A. Stolypin glazami sovremennikov* [P. A. Stolypin through his contemporaries' eyes] (Moscow: ROSSPEN, 2008), 118–19. See also what seems like a rather fanciful account by Vladimir Kokovtsov, *Out of My Past* (Stanford: Stanford University Press, 1935), 185.
53. Letter of Ambassador J. W. Riddle to Secretary of State Elihu Root, June 22, 1907 (n.s.). Numerical and Minor Files of the Department of State, 1906–1910, National Archives Microfilm Publication no. M862, roll 20, case nos. 69/66–79/135, no. 51, images 791 ff., https://catalog.archives.gov/id/19106425.
54. Richard Pipes, *Struve: Liberal on the Right, 1905–1944* (Cambridge: Harvard University Press, 1980), 63. Pipes generally draws his account from Maklakov's and tells us that Struve confirmed Maklakov's version. Ibid., 61n125.
55. Iosif V. Gessen, *V Dvukh vekakh: Zhiznennyi otchet* [In two centuries: A life's account], *Arkhiv Russkoi Revoliutsii* 22 (1937), 250. See also M. L. Mandelshtam, *1905 god v politicheskikh protsessakh: Zapiski zashchitnika* [The year 1905 in political trials: Notes of a defense counsel] (Moscow: Izdatelstvo polikatorzhan, 1931), 360–63.
56. Maklakov, *Vtoraia Gosudarstvennaia Duma*, 316.
57. Pipes, *Struve*, 65.
58. Ascher, *The Revolution of 1905*, 2:353–55.
59. V. A. Maklakov, *Iz Vospominanii* (New York: Chekhov Publishing House [Izdatelstvo imeni Chekhova], 1954), 362.
60. See A. Ia. Avrekh, *Stolypin i Tretia Duma* [Stolypin and the Third Duma] (Moscow: Izdatelstvo Nauka, 1968), 85–86; GDSO, Third Duma, 5th Sess., pt. 1, Meeting 10, October 29, 1911, cols. 818–20.
61. V. Maklakov, "Zakonnost v Russkoi zhizni" [The Rule of law in Russian life], *Vestnik Evropy*, May 1909 [Public lecture delivered March 17, 1909], 238, 259–63.
62. See Anthony Kroner, *The Debate between Miliukov and Maklakov on the Chances for Russian Liberalism* (Amsterdam, 1998), 110–11; Anthony Kroner, "The Debate between Miliukov and Maklakov on the Chances for Russian Liberalism," *Revolutionary Russia* 7, no. 2 (1994): 239, 250 (citing *Vestnik Partii Narodnoi Svobody*, no. 1 [January 4, 1907], 48); Maklakov, "Sredi izbiratelnii" [Among the voters], *Russkie Vedomosti* [Russian news], March 26, 1906, 2; Maklakov, "Gde vykhod" [Where is there a way out?], *Russkie Vedomosti*, May 20, 1906, 2; Maklakov, "Zakoldovannyi krug" [A vicious circle], *Russkie Vedomosti*, August 27, 1906, 3.
63. V. A. Maklakov, *Pervaia Gosudarstvennaia Duma* [The First State Duma] (Moscow: Tsentrpoligraf, 2006), 94–95.
64. Tyrkova-Williams Diary and Letters, 282 (entry for September 29, 1950).

65. See Stephen F. Williams, "A Kadet's Critique of the Kadet Party: Vasily Maklakov," *Revolutionary Russia* 23 (2010), 29, 52–57.
66. P.N. Miliukov, "V.A. Maklakov mezhdu 'obshchestvennostiu i vlastiu, II,'" [V.A. Maklakov between society and the state, II] *Poslednie Novosti* [Recent news], May 30, 1937, col. 5.
67. P.N. Miliukov, "'Sovremennye Zapiski,' kn. 56," ["Contemporary notes," vol. 56] *Poslednie Novosti* [Recent news], July 16, 1939, col. 5; "Liberalizm, Radikalizm i Revolutsiia," in *Sovremennye Zapiski* (1935), 285, 312–13; "V.A. Maklakov mezhdu 'obshchestvennostiu i vlastiu, II,'" in *Poslednie Novosti* [Recent news], May 30, 1937, col. 3.
68. P.N. Miliukov, "V.A. Maklakov o knige prof. Pares," [V.A. Maklakov on Prof. Pares's book] *Poslednie Novosti* [Recent news], July 16, 1939, col. 3.
69. See Yuval Levin, *The Great Debate: Edmund Burke, Thomas Paine, and the Birth of Right and Left* (New York: Basic Books, 2013).

CHAPTER 8: THE THIRD AND FOURTH DUMAS AND MAKLAKOV'S FIGHT AGAINST GOVERNMENT ARBITRARINESS

1. GDSO, Third Duma, 5th Sess., pt. 2, February 29, 1912, col. 3420. See also Bakhmetev-Maklakov Correspondence, 1:458 (Maklakov to Bakhmetev, August 30, 1921).
2. Abraham Ascher, *P.A. Stolypin: The Search for Stability in Late Imperial Russia* (Stanford: Stanford University Press, 2001), 210–11; Ben-Cion Pinchuk, *The Octobrists in the Third Duma, 1907–1912* (Seattle: University of Washington Press, 1974), 31–34. C. Jay Smith, "The Russian Third Duma: An Analytical Profile," *Russian Review*, 17, no. 3 (July 1958), 201–10. As Ascher notes, the party classifications are uncertain because of the deputies' relatively frequent party switching. Ascher, P.A. Stolypin, 420n5.
3. Pinchuk, *The Octobrists in the Third Duma*, 42–43; V.A. Maklakov, *Iz Vospominanii* (New York: Chekhov Publishing House [Izdatelstvo imeni Chekhova], 1954), 384–86.
4. V.A. Maklakov, "L'Étape Actuelle du Bolshevisme," *Mercure de France*, May 1, 1922, 577, 606–7 (regarding Soviet talk of independent courts in the 1920s as meaningless until the peasants, whom he regarded as the country's sole productive force, acquired political power); see also Matthew Stephenson, "'When the Devil Turns . . .': The Political Foundations of Independent Judicial Review," *Journal of Legal Studies* 32 (2003), 59.
5. GDSO, Third Duma, 1st Sess., *Prilozheniia*, Item No. 13, 39–41 (reciting indictment).
6. Ibid., Item No. 69, 277–80 (reciting indictment).
7. GDSO, Third Duma, 1st Sess., pt. 3, May 19, 1908, cols. 954–56.
8. See Article 19 of the Statute Establishing the Duma (*Uchrezhdenie*

Gosudarstvennoi Dumy), cross-referencing Article 7 of the Statute on Elections to the Duma (*Polozhenie o vyborakh v Gosudarstvenuiu Dumu*), August 6, 1905. (Article 7 became Article 10 of the statute as amended by the Act of June 3, 1907. See GDSO, Third Duma, 2nd Sess., *Prilozheniia*, Item No. 80, 1.)

9. GDSO, Third Duma, 2nd Sess., pt. 4, April 27, 1909, cols. 49–52, 54–56, 58–59.
10. Ibid., col. 111 (Koliubakin); col. 126 (Kosorotov).
11. See generally Jonathan W. Daly, "On the Significance of Emergency Legislation in Late Imperial Russia," *Slavic Review* 54, no. 3 (1995), 602, 605.
12. GDSO, Third Duma, 1st Sess., pt. 2, April 29, 1908, col. 2390.
13. Richard J. Robbins, *The Tsar's Viceroys* (Ithaca: Cornell University Press, 1987).
14. GDSO, Third Duma, 1st Sess., pt. 2, April 29, 1908, col. 2397.
15. Ibid., col. 2401.
16. Ibid.; Third Duma, 2nd Sess., pt. 4, May 12, 1909, col. 1096.
17. Ibid., Third Duma, 1st Sess., pt. 2, April 29, 1908, cols. 2406–2407.
18. GDSO, Third Duma, 2nd Sess., pt. 1, October 15, 1908, cols. 22–24. See also ibid., 3rd Sess., pt. 2, February 18, 1910, col. 1779 (referring to police barring a deputy from reporting to his voters despite March 4 rules). Compare ibid. (suggesting that the March 4 rules assure freedom for unions) with Third Duma, 4th Sess., December 1, 1910, col. 2359 (arguing that all the government needs for its war on unions is the March 4 rules). And see Geoffrey A. Hosking, "P. A. Stolypin and the Octobrist Party," *Slavonic and East European Review* 47, no. 108 (January 1969), 137, 150–51 (discussing Octobrist use of interpellations to shed light on government violations of March 4 rules).
19. GDSO, Third Duma, 1st Sess., pt. 2, April 29, 1908, cols. 2402–2406.
20. Ibid., 5th Sess., pt. 1, November 18, 1911, cols. 2150–51.
21. Ibid., 3rd Sess., pt. 4, April 28, 1910, cols. 204–5. See also V. Maklakov, "III Sessiia Gosudarstvennoi Dumy" [The third session of (the Third) State Duma], *Russkaia Mysl* [Russian thought] (February 1911), 114.
22. GDSO, Third Duma, 1st Sess., pt. 2, April 29, 1908, cols. 2395–97; ibid., 2nd Sess., pt. 4, February 13, 1909, cols. 1494–96; GDSO, Fourth Duma, 1st Sess., pt. 1, March 13, 1913, cols. 2113–14.
23. GDSO, Third Duma, 1st Sess., pt. 1, February 15, 1908, cols. 1962–63, 1966.
24. GDSO, Third Duma, 2nd Sess., pt. 4, February 13, 1909, cols. 1486–87.
25. GDSO, Third Duma, 4th Sess., pt. 1, December 1, 1910, cols. 2365–66.
26. GDSO, Fourth Duma, 1st Sess., pt. 3, May 27, 1913, col. 114. See also ibid., Third Duma, 2nd Sess., pt. 4, February 13, 1909, col. 1494.
27. GDSO, Third Duma, 1st Sess., pt. 1, February 15, 1908, col. 1969.
28. Ibid., 3rd Sess., pt. 4, April 28, 1910, col. 210.

29. Hugh Seton-Watson, *The Decline of Imperial Russia, 1855–1914* (New York: Frederick A. Praeger, 1952), 269–71; Bernard Pares, *The Fall of the Russian Monarchy: A Study of the Evidence* (New York, 1939), 143; Dominic Lieven, *Nicholas II: Twilight of the Empire* (New York: St. Martin's Press, 1993), 183.
30. See, e.g., GDSO, Fourth Duma, 1st Sess., pt. 1, March 8, 1913, cols. 2106–19.
31. Ascher, *P.A. Stolypin*, 334–35; A. Ia. Avrekh, *P.A. Stolypin i Sudby Reform* [P. A. Stolypin and the fate of reform] (Moscow: Izdatelstvo politicheskoi literatury, 1991), 160.
32. Maklakov, *La Chute*, 19.
33. GDSO, Third Duma, 4th Sess., pt. 3, April 27, 1911, col. 2873.
34. Ibid., cols. 2874, 2878, 2880.
35. Ibid., cols. 2857–59. See also Ascher, *P.A. Stolypin*, 359–60.
36. GDSO, Third Duma, 4th Sess., pt. 3, April 27, 1911, cols. 2879–80. See chapter 5 for a discussion of Maklakov's use of the argument after the revolution.
37. The reference to government agents generating revolution echoes a common Maklakov theme—that government activity, especially its use of agents provocateurs, was what kept the embers of revolutionary activity from dying out. See, for example, GDSO, Third Duma, 1st Sess., pt. 1, February 15, 1908, col. 1967. The "precedent" referred to is presumably one of imperial inability to keep premiers and to keep working in harmony with them.
38. GDSO, Third Duma, 4th Sess., pt. 3, April 27, 1911, col. 2887.
39. Ascher, *P.A. Stolypin*, 360.
40. Since the exchange over the field courts martial, there had been a clash on November 16, 1907, over the government's priorities as between repression and reform and Stolypin's hint of possible future curtailments of judicial independence. See chapter 11; GDSO, Third Duma, 1st Sess., pt. 1, November 16, 1907, cols. 307–12 (Stolypin); cols. 343–48 (Maklakov); cols. 348–54 (Stolypin).
41. Georgii Adamovich, *Vasilii Alekseevich Maklakov: Politik, Iurist, Chelovek* [Vasily Alekseevich Maklakov: Politician, jurist, human being] (Paris, 1959), 182n*.

CHAPTER 9: RELIGIOUS LIBERTY

1. GDSO, Third Duma, 2nd Sess., pt. 4, May 12, 1909, col. 1006 (explanation of Karaulov, reporter for the committee on Old Believers issues).
2. Ibid., cols. 1006–10. A related but less developed argument occurred on a bill allowing members of the Orthodox Church to leave the church freely, without creating conflicts between the church's and the state's view of their status. The amendment Maklakov supported—

entitling a person exiting the faith to automatic government recognition of the exit—was included in the final bill, but, as with the Old Believer provision discussed below, the Duma failed to reach agreement with the State Council. See GDSO, Third Duma, 2nd Sess., pt. 4, May 22, 1909, cols. 1780–86; Ben-Cion Pinchuk, *The Octobrists in the Third Duma, 1907–1912* (Seattle: University of Washington Press, 1974), 87–92; Geoffrey A. Hosking, *The Russian Constitutional Experiment: Government and Duma, 1907–1914* (Cambridge: Cambridge University Press, 1973), 179; J. S. Curtiss, *Church and State in Russia* (New York: Columbia University Press, 1965), 325–26.

3. GDSO, Third Duma, 2nd Sess., pt. 4, May 12, 1909, cols. 1089–90, 1094.
4. Ibid., col. 1091.
5. Ibid., col. 1093.
6. Ibid., cols. 1404, 1606.
7. Ibid., cols. 1094–98.
8. GDSO, Third Duma, 4th Sess., pt. 1, October 20, 1910, cols. 131, 146–47; ibid., pt. 2, February 25, 1911, col. 2887 (Duma informed of reconciliation committee's results). See also Hosking, *The Russian Constitutional Experiment*, 179; Curtiss, *Church and State in Russia*, 322–26.
9. See Robert Geraci, "Pragmatism and Prejudice: Revisiting the Origin of the Pale of Settlement and Its Historiography," unpublished manuscript, used with permission (reviewing the explanations offered over the centures and arguing that prior treatments have understated the role of pure anti-Semitism and crude stereotypes of Jewish behavior).
10. GDSO, Third Duma, 4th Sess., pt. 2, February 9, 1911, cols. 1548–49.
11. Ibid., col. 1547.
12. For broader arguments about reactions to exceptionally hard-working minorities, see Thomas Sowell, *Migrations and Cultures: A World View* (New York: Basic Books, 1996).
13. GDSO, Third Duma, 4th Sess., pt. 2, February 9, 1911, cols. 1550–51.
14. Ibid., cols. 1551–52.
15. Ibid., col. 1553.
16. Maklakov used the term *gosudarstvennost*, a term that defies an exact and simple translation into English.
17. On August 10, 1789, the Abbé Sieyès said in the French National assembly, at the close of a speech defending the *dîme* (a tax on harvests collected for the clergy), that the French should not do things that will make the rest of Europe say, "*Ils veulent être libres et ils ne savent pas être justes!*"; see http://vdaucourt.free.fr/Mothisto/Sieyes1/Sieyes1.htm.
18. GDSO, Third Duma, 4th Sess., pt. 2, February 9, 1911, cols. 1554–55.
19. Ibid., cols. 1602, 1607 (deadline vote), 1609–14. Alexander Orbach, "The Jewish People's Group and Jewish Politics in Tsarist Russia, 1905–1914," *Modern Judaism* 10, no. 1 (February 1990), 1, 8, incorrectly

says the 208–138 vote embodied the idea of no time limit on the committee; in the end, of course, Duma inaction led to that result.

20. GDSO, Third Duma, 4th Sess., pt. 2, March 30, 1911, col. 1924.
21. Edmund Levin, *A Child of Christian Blood: Murder and Conspiracy in Tsarist Russia: The Beilis Blood Libel* (New York: Schocken Books, 2014), 12.
22. A.S. Tager, *The Decay of Czarism: The Beilis Trial* (Philadelphia: The Jewish Publication Society of America, 1935), 39–41.
23. Levin, *A Child of Christian Blood*, 230, 278.
24. See Charles A. Ruud and Sergei Stepanov, *Fontanka 16: The Tsars' Secret Police* (Montreal: McGill-Queen's University Press, 1999), 265–69, 271; Tager, *The Decay of Czarism*, 176–78.
25. Levin, *A Child of Christian Blood*, 63n24; Jacob Langer, *Corruption and Counterrevolution: The Rise and Fall of the Black Hundred* (PhD thesis, Duke University, 2007), 138; *Padenie tsarskogo rezhima*, 3:378–79 (May 15, 1917, testimony of S.P. Beletskii, director of the police).
26. *Delo Beilisa, Stenograficheskii otchet* [The Beilis affair, Stenographic record] (Kiev: Pechatniia S.P. Iakovleva, 1913) 3:123–55.
27. Levin, *A Child of Christian Blood*, 205, 288.
28. Ibid., 284.
29. "Dela istorii" [A matter of history], in *Novoe Russkoe Slovo* [New Russian word] (August 11, 1957), 3.
30. Vasily Maklakov, "Spasitelnoe predosterezhenie: smysl dela Beilisa" [A Saving lesson: The meaning of the Beilis case], *Russkaia Mysl* [Russian thought], no. 11 (November 1913), 135–43.
31. Langer, *Corruption and Counterrevolution*, 91–96, 138.
32. Hans Rogger, "The Beilis Case," *Slavic Review* 25, no. 4 (December 1966), 615, 626, 628.
33. Ibid., 620.
34. V.A. Maklakov, *Iz Vospominanii* (New York: Chekhov Publishing House [Izdatelstvo imeni Chekhova], 1954), 258–60.
35. Levin, *A Child of Christian Blood*, 304.
36. See Oleg Budnitskii, "The Russian Ambassador in Paris on the Whites and the Jews," *Jews in Eastern Europe*, no. 3(28) (1995), 55 ("it would be incorrect to conclude that Maklakov was a Judeophile").
37. *Spor o Rossii: V.A. Maklakov i V. V. Shulgin, Perepiska, 1919–1939* [Debate about Russia: V.A. Maklakov and V.V. Shulgin, correspondence, 1919–1939], ed. and introduction by Oleg Budnitskii (Moscow: ROSSPEN, 2012), 370–71 (Maklakov letter of December 23, 1929).
38. Tyrkova-Williams Diary and Letters, 162.
39. GDSO, Third Duma, 4th Sess., pt. 2, February 9, 1911, cols. 1544–46; A. Ia. Avrekh, *Stolypin i Tretia Duma* [Stolypin and the Third Duma] (Moscow: Nauka, 1968), 42.
40. Michael F. Hamm, "Liberalism and the Jewish Question: The Progressive Bloc," *Russian Review* 31, no. 2 (April 1972), 165–69.
41. GDSO, Fourth Duma, 4th Sess., February 11, 1916, cols. 1467–68.

42. *Sezdy i konferentsii*, 3:89–92 (June 7, 1915). See also O. Budnitskii, "V.A. Maklakov i evreiskoi vopros" [V.A. Maklakov and the Jewish question], *Vestnik Evreiskogo universiteta* [Bulletin of the Jewish University] no. 1(19) (1999), 42–94 (arriving at substantially similar conclusions).

CHAPTER 10: NATIONAL MINORITIES

1. V. Maklakov, "III Sessiia Gosudarstvennoi Dumy" [The third session of (the Third) State Duma], *Russkaia Mysl* [Russian thought] (February 1911), 96–125.
2. Ibid., 119.
3. Ibid., 119–20.
4. V.A. Maklakov, "F.I. Rodichev i A.R. Lednitskii," *Novyi Zhurnal*, no. 16 (1947), 246; V.A. Maklakov, *Vlast i obshchestvennost na zakate staroi Rossii (Vospominaniia sovremenika)* [State and society in the twilight of old Russia (Recollections of a contemporary)] (Paris: Izdanie zhurnala "Illustrirovanaia Rossiia," 1936), 362–64.
5. Maklakov, "F.I. Rodichev i A.R. Lednitskii," 247.
6. Abraham Ascher, *P.A. Stolypin: The Search for Stability in Late Imperial Russia* (Stanford: Stanford University Press, 2001), 331–36.
7. Maklakov, "III Sessiia Gosudarstvennoi Dumy," 123.
8. Ibid., 123–24.
9. GDSO, Third Duma, 5th Sess., pt. 2, January 20, 1912, cols. 643–46.
10. Ibid., cols. 647–52.
11. Ibid., cols. 652–53.
12. Ibid., cols. 653–55.
13. Ibid., col. 656.
14. Ibid., col. 658; GDSO, Third Duma, 5th Sess., pt. 4, col. 396.
15. GDSO, Fourth Duma, 4th Sess., pt. 1, February 11, 1916, col. 1465.
16. Joshua A. Sanborn, *Imperial Apocalypse: The Great War and the Destruction of the Russian Empire* (Oxford: Oxford University Press, 2014), 58 n.147.
17. Vaclav Lednitskii, "Vokrug V.A. Maklakova (lichnye vospominaniia)" [Around V.A. Maklakov (personal reminiscences)], *Novyi Zhurnal*, no. 56 (March 1959), 222, 243–44. The author was the son of Alexander Lednitskii.
18. GDSO, Third Duma, 3rd Sess., pt. 4, May 22, 1910, cols. 2128–30.
19. See Geoffrey A. Hosking, *The Russian Constitutional Experiment: Government and Duma, 1907–1914* (Cambridge: Cambridge University Press, 1973), 106–11.
20. Ibid., 111–12.
21. GDSO, Third Duma, 3rd Sess., pt. 4, May 22, 1910, cols. 2133–35, 2142, 2145.
22. Ibid., cols. 2136–38, 2144–46.
23. Ibid., cols. 2165–67 (A.A. Motovilov, nationalist); cols. 2201–2204 (V.V. Tenishev, Octobrist); cols. 2370–71 (Markov). See also

Maklakov's treatment of the issue in "III Sessiia Gosudarstvennoi Dumy," 120–22.

24. GDSO, Third Duma, 3rd Sess., pt. 4, May 28, 1910, col. 2582; Hosking, *The Russian Constitutional Experiment*, 112, 116.
25. *Sezdy i konferentsii*, 3:96, 107–9, 113; Bakhmetev-Maklakov Correspondence, 1:206 (Maklakov to Bakhmetev, May 6, 1920).

CHAPTER 11: JUDICIAL REFORM, CITIZEN REMEDIES

1. GDSO, Third Duma, 5th Sess., pt. 4, May 2, 1912, cols. 326–27.
2. Ibid., 2nd Sess., pt. 4, February 13, 1909, col. 1493; 3rd Sess., pt. 1, November 13, 1909, col. 1877.
3. GDSO, Fourth Duma, 2nd Sess., pt. 4, May 12, 1914, cols. 491, 495; Edmund Levin, *A Child of Christian Blood: Murder and Conspiracy in Tsarist Russia: The Beilis Blood Libel* (New York: Schocken Books, 2014), 184–85.
4. GDSO, Third Duma, 5th Sess., pt. 4, May 2, 1912, col. 319. No part of the Senate was a legislature; its first and cassation departments were judicial bodies (and are discussed later in this chapter).
5. *Padenie tsarskogo rezhima*, 2:364, 365–66. An 1885 statute empowered the minister of justice to demand explanations of a judge for his actions and to issue instructions relating to future or even completed cases. William G. Wagner, "Tsarist Legal Policies at the End of the Nineteenth Century: A Study in Inconsistencies," *Slavonic and East European Review* 54, no. 3 (July 1976), 371, 375. While the statute uses language broadly authorizing issuance of instructions, the occasions triggering the authority are an undue accumulation of cases, slowness, a halt in the court's activity, or deviation from legal order. *Polnoe Sobranie Zakonov* [Complete collection of laws], 3rd series, law of May 20, 1885, no. 2959. As the first three occasions clearly relate to the mechanics of the judicial process rather than to its substance, I think even the last phrase should be understood as equally limited. The statute seems not to have been seized upon to justify ministerial efforts to control judicial outcomes.
6. GDSO, Third Duma, 1st Sess., pt. 1, November 16, 1907, col. 308.
7. Ibid., col. 347.
8. Ibid., cols. 345–46. See also Maklakov's assault on Stolypin's hint at express curtailment of judicial tenure at GDSO, Third Duma, 2nd Sess., pt. 2, February 13, 1909, cols. 1485, 1493.
9. GDSO, Fourth Duma, 1st Sess., pt. 3, May 27, 1913, col. 120.
10. Ibid., 2nd Sess., pt. 2, February 18, 1914, col. 813.
11. Ibid., col. 824.
12. Dumas Malone, *Jefferson and His Time*, vol. 5, *Jefferson the President: The Second Term, 1805–1809* (1974), 305–6. See also William Rehnquist, "Jefferson and His Contemporaries," *Journal of Law and Politics* 9 (1993), 595, 605.

13. *Padenie tsarskogo rezhima,* 2:342 (April 24, 1917, testimony of Shcheglovitov).
14. GDSO, Third Duma, 5th Sess., pt. 4, May 2, 1912, col. 331.
15. GDSO, Fourth Duma, 2nd Sess., pt. 2, February 18, 1914, cols. 830–32.
16. Ibid., col. 831. Note that the judges of the first department did not have tenure. Natasha Assa, "How Arbitrary Was Tsarist Administrative Justice? The Case of the Zemstvos Petitions to the Imperial Ruling Senate, 1866–1916," *Law and History Review* 24 (Spring 2006), 1, 38.
17. GDSO, Third Duma, 5th Sess., pt. 4, May 2, 1912, col. 316.
18. Dominic Lieven, *Russia's Rulers under the Old Regime* (New Haven and London: Yale University Press, 1989), 211.
19. Jane Burbank, *Russian Peasants Go to Court: Legal Culture in the Countryside, 1905–1917* (Bloomington and Indianapolis: Indiana University Press, 2004), 54, 121; Vasilii Maklakov, "Local Justice in Russia," *Russian Review* 2, no. 4 (1913), 126–47; Catherine Frierson, "Rural Justice in Public Opinion: The Volost' Court Debate, 1861–1912," *Slavonic and East European Review* 64, no. 4 (October 1986), 526, 529. Frierson, ibid., 527–28, points out that the model for the township court was a system devised in the late 1830s for state serfs, for whom the "lord" was the tsar, who was obviously not going to manage justice on his estates directly.
20. See Thomas S. Pearson, "Russian Law and Rural Justice: Activity and Problems of the Russian Justices of the Peace, 1865–1889," *Jahrbücher für Geschichte Osteuropas* (1984), 67–70.
21. Ibid., 71.
22. See Gareth Popkins, "Code versus Custom? Norms and Tactics in Peasant Volost Court Appeals, 1889–1917," *Russian Review* 59, no. 3 (July 2000), 408–24; Gareth Popkins, "Peasant Experiences of the Late Tsarist State: District Congresses of Land Captains, Provincial Boards and the Legal Appeals Process, 1891–1917," *Slavonic and East European Review* 78, no. 1 (January 2000), 90–114; Maklakov, "Local Justice in Russia," 130; Frierson, "Rural Justice in Public Opinion," 529.
23. Burbank, *Russian Peasants Go to Court,* 166–73.
24. Frierson, "Rural Justice in Public Opinion," 539.
25. GDSO, Third Duma, 1st Sess., *Prilozheniia,* Item No. 457, 770–96.
26. GDSO, Third Duma, 3rd Sess., pt. 1, November 2, 1909, col. 1210; ibid., 1st Sess., *Prilozheniia,* Item No. 457, 777–78 (Art. 23).
27. GDSO, Third Duma, 3rd Sess., pt. 3, March 27, 1910, cols. 2083–84.
28. Ibid., 1st Sess., *Prilozheniia,* Item No. 457, 777–78. The Duma debated proposals for longer terms for judges, but rejected them in a voice vote. GDSO, Third Duma, 3rd Sess., pt. 2, cols. 286–308, January 25, 1910. Maklakov did not participate.
29. GDSO, Third Duma, 3rd Sess., pt. 3, March 27, 1910, col. 2086.
30. Ibid., cols. 2077–83.
31. Ibid., cols. 2136–42.

32. GDSO, Third Duma, 1st Sess., *Prilozheniia*, Item No. 457, p. 767 (Art. 17).
33. Ibid., 3rd Sess., pt. 1, December 7, 1909, cols. 3113–20.
34. GDSO, Third Duma, 1st Sess., *Prilozheniia*, Item No. 457, p. 717.
35. See also Daly's finding that the regime embarked in 1905 on deliberate enhancement of "leadership" in the provincial courts of appeal, doubtless measured by its own criteria. Jonathan W. Daly, "On the Significance of Emergency Legislation in Late Imperial Russia," *Slavic Review* 54, no. 3 (1995), 624.
36. GDSO, Third Duma, 3rd Sess., pt. 3, March 27, 1910, cols. 2067–68.
37. *Polnoe Sobranie Zakonov*, 3rd ser., no. 37328, Prilozhenie I (published in part 2 of volume 32 of the *Polnoe Sobranie Zakonov* at 212–20 (accessible at http://www.nlr.ru/e-res/law_r/search.php?part=1969®im=3), §§ 5–8, 29–40, 91–93. See also Maklakov, "Local Justice in Russia," 141–43; Geoffrey A. Hosking, *The Russian Constitutional Experiment: Government and Duma, 1907–1914* (Cambridge: Cambridge University Press, 1973), 175–77.
38. *Polnoe Sobranie Zakonov*, 3rd ser., no. 37328, 663; Maklakov, "Local Justice in Russia," 142.
39. *Polnoe Sobranie Zakonov*, 3rd ser., no. 37328, 667; Maklakov, "Local Justice in Russia," 142–43.
40. *Polnoe Sobranie Zakonov*, 3rd ser., no. 37328, 680, 683; *Polnoe Sobranie Zakonov*, 3rd ser., no. 37328, Prilozhenie I, § 54; Maklakov, "Local Justice in Russia," 142.
41. GDSO, Third Duma, 3rd Sess., pt. 2, February 1, 1910, col. 573.
42. V. Maklakov, "III Sessiia Gosudarstvennoi Dumy" [The third session of (the Third) State Duma], *Russkaia Mysl* [Russian thought] (February 1911), 104.
43. GDSO, Third Duma, 3rd Sess., pt. 1, November 2, 1909, cols. 1201–12; ibid., pt. 2, February 1, 1910, cols. 564–71.
44. Burbank, *Russian Peasants Go to Court*, 245–57; Corinne Gaudin, *Ruling Peasants* (DeKalb: Northern Illinois University Press, 2007).
45. Maklakov, "Local Justice in Russia," 139, 141.
46. GDSO, Third Duma, 3rd Sess., pt. 1, November 2, 1909, cols. 1201–1203.
47. Assa, "How Arbitrary Was Tsarist Administrative Justice?," 1, 38.
48. GDSO, Fourth Duma, 2nd Sess., pt. 2, February 18, 1914, cols. 818–37.
49. Ibid., cols. 823–24.
50. Ibid., cols. 831, 833–34; Ekaterina A. Pravilova, *Zakonnost i Prava Lichnosti: Administrativnaia Iustitsia v Rossii* [Legality and individual rights: Administrative justice in imperial Russia] (St. Petersburg: Obrazovanie-Kultura, 2000), 182–83. Maklakov also argued that nothing supplied the Senate with the authority to set aside administrative acts that violated the law. GDSO, Fourth Duma, 2nd Sess., pt. 2, February 18, 1914, col. 833. That was not actually true, as Count

Emmanuel Bennigsen pointed out later in the debate, without attempted refutation by Maklakov. Ibid., February 28, 1914, col. 1283.

51. Ibid., February 18, 1914, col. 825.
52. See, e.g., ibid., cols. 820, 825–26, 828, 829.
53. Ibid., col. 827.
54. Pravilova, *Zakonnost i Prava Lichnosti*, 182, 182–84.
55. See GDSO, Fourth Duma, 2nd Sess., pt. 2, February 28, 1914, col. 1283 (Count Bennigsen).
56. Ibid., February 28, 1914, cols. 1283–84, 1289–90; see also GDSO, Fourth Duma, 2nd Sess., *Prilozheniia*, Item No. 197 (committee report on Bill No. 813), 98–99 (text of Art. 75[1] as proposed by committee). Another amendment eliminated Senate review of ministerial and agency orders; Maklakov thought that review at publication would preempt review in a concrete case, thus likely neutering the latter review, which was potentially more valuable. GDSO, Fourth Duma, 2nd Sess., pt. 2, cols. 1287–88. Another amendment narrowed the Senate's authority to deny publication to rules of Duma and State Council to cases of non-compliance with the statutes or administrative rules governing those bodies' formal procedures, a change that Maklakov said followed from their not being subordinate to the Senate. Ibid., cols. 1279–80.
57. B. Maklakoff, "La Russie de 1900 à 1917, Vers la Révolution: Le Dénouement," *Revue de Paris* 5 (1924), 508, 512. This is the first of a series of three articles, all with the same title (except that the second and third bear the additional legend, "suite").
58. Maklakov, "III Sessiia Gosudarstvennoi Dumy," 98–100.
59. For an excellent general review, see Marc Szeftel, "Personal Inviolability in the Legislation of the Russian Absolute Monarchy," *American Slavic and East European Review* 17, no. 1 (February 1958), 1–24.
60. Pravilova, *Zakonnost i Prava Lichnosti*, 231–32.
61. Ibid., 229; GDSO, Third Duma, 5th Sess., pt. 1, November 18, 1911, col. 2149.
62. GDSO, Third Duma, 5th Sess., pt. 1, November 18, 1911, col. 2156; see also Szeftel, "Personal Inviolability in the Legislation of the Russian Absolute Monarchy," 5–6; Pravilova, *Zakonnost i Prava Lichnosti*, 220–24; Richard Wortman, "Russian Monarchy and the Rule of Law: New Considerations of the Court Reform of 1864," *Kritika: Explorations in Russian and Eurasian History* 6, no. 1 (Winter 2005), 154.
63. GDSO, Third Duma, 5th Sess., pt. 1, November 18, 1911, col. 2156.
64. Ibid., cols. 2159–60. See also GDSO, Third Duma, 4th Sess., *Prilozheniia*, Item No. 271, 19–20, pp. 71–74 (Art. 1096 as proposed by committee); GDSO, Third Duma, 5th Sess., pt. 1, November 18, 1911, col. 2296 (the Kadets' proposed text).
65. Ibid., November 19, 1911, cols. 2287–98; the vote is recorded at ibid., cols. 2296–97.

66. Pravilova, *Zakonnost i Prava Lichnosti*, 224–25.
67. GDSO, Third Duma, 5th Sess., pt. 1, November 22, 1911, cols. 2364–68. Under modern U.S. law officials are typically personally liable for violations of law—but only ones that a reasonable officer would have recognized as illegal at the time he acted. See *Harlow v. Fitzgerald*, 457 U.S. 800 (1982).
68. GDSO, Third Duma, 5th Sess., pt. 1, November 22, 1911, cols. 2366–69. See also Wortman, "Russian Monarchy and the Rule of Law," 154. Pravilova points out additional problems, such as (1) the agencies' ability, in cases where a private party seeks relief against an unlawful order, to drag matters out and keep the challenged order in place for years, (2) very broad concepts of official immunity, and (3) the likely inability to collect from relatively impecunious bureaucrats. Pravilova, *Zakonnost i Prava Lichnosti*, 56, 57–58. See also Szeftel, "Personal Inviolability in the Legislation of the Russian Absolute Monarchy," 6 (explaining absence of any relief for unlawful arrest and obstructions to relief when the unlawfully arrested person is later acquitted). Maklakov returned to these issues on March 21, 1914. See GDSO, Fourth Duma, 2nd Sess., pt. 3, March 21, 1914, cols. 15–25, 63–77.
69. GDSO, Third Duma, 5th Sess., pt. 1, November 22, 1911, col. 2387; Pravilova, *Zakonnost i Prava Lichnosti*, 230.
70. D.C.B. Lieven, "The Security Police, Civil Rights, and the Fate of the Russian Empire, 1855–1917," in *Civil Rights in Imperial Russia*, ed. Olga Crisp and Linda Edmondson (Oxford: Oxford University Press, 1989), 258–61.

CHAPTER 12: PEASANT RIGHTS

1. Bakhmetev-Maklakov Correspondence, 1:460 (Maklakov to Bakhmetev, August 30, 1921). The other great sin he identified in this passage was the monarchy's fear of and hostility to industrial capital.
2. V.A. Maklakov, *Vtoraia Gosudarstvennaia Duma* [The Second State Duma] (Moscow: Tsentrpoligraf, 2006), 171; V.A. Maklakov, *Iz Vospominanii* (New York: Chekhov Publishing House [Izdatelstvo imeni Chekhova], 1954), 395.
3. For the many ways in which the reform fell short of actually establishing private ownership, see Stephen F. Williams, *Liberal Reform in an Illiberal Regime: The Creation of Private Property in Russia, 1906–1915* (Stanford: Hoover Institution Press, 2006), 216–23, 243–48.
4. Victor Leontovitsch, *The History of Liberalism in Russia*, translated by Parmen Leontovitsch, with a foreword by Aleksandr Solzhenitsyn (Pittsburgh: University of Pittsburgh Press, 2012), 88.
5. V. Maklakov, "III Sessiia Gosudarstvennoi Dumy" [The third session of (the Third) State Duma], *Russkaia Mysl* [Russian thought] (February 1911), 106–9.

6. V. A. Maklakov, "Pereustroistvo krestianskago byta" ["Reconstruction of peasant life"], *Vestnik grazhdanskovo prava* [Bulletin of civil law], no. 8 (December 1916), 29–52; no. 1 (January 1917), 29–69.
7. V. Maklakov, *Rech na Sezd K-D* [*Speech to Kadet Conference*] (Moscow, 1917). This is a separately printed pamphlet containing only his speech. It is unclear who published it; given its deviation from Kadet orthodoxy, it is surely not one of the pamphlets of Maklakov speeches that the party often published and circulated.
8. Ingeborg Fleischhauer, "The Agrarian Program of the Russian Constitutional Democrats," *Cahiers du Monde russe et soviétique*, no. 20(2), (1979), 4–5. Article VI of the Kadet proposal specified that the recipients of redistributed land would receive only a long-term right to use the property, with no right of sale, exchange or gift ("assignment"). GDSO, First Duma, Meeting 6, May 8, 1906, 250. A maverick Kadet, L. I. Petrazhitskii, made a carefully honed argument that this approach would prevent transactions that could be expected to benefit sellers and buyers alike, and indirectly the public interest, ibid., 451–58, an argument that the major Kadet speaker (Mikhail Gertsenshtein) seemed not to fully grasp, much less rebut, ibid., 465–71.
9. George Tokmakoff, *P. A. Stolypin and the Third Duma: An Appraisal of the Three Major Issues* (Washington, DC: University Press of America, 1981), 34 and n.27 (citing GDSO, Third Duma, 1st Sess., pt. 1, November 16, 1907, cols. 343–48.
10. See A. A. Kaufman, *Agrarnyi vopros v Rossii* [The Agrarian Question in Russia] (Moscow: Moskovskoe Nauchnoe Izdatelstvo, 1918), 221; Peter Toumanoff, "Some Effects of Land Tenure Reforms on Russian Agricultural Productivity, 1901–1913," *Economic Development and Cultural Change* 32, no. 4 (July 1984), 861–72; and see the discussion in Williams, *Liberal Reform in an Illiberal Regime*, 102–3.
11. *Sezdy i konferentsii*, 3:610.
12. Ibid., 624. Rosenberg says that the conference adopted "the conservative position on almost every point," but he refers to rejection of proposals such as one under which landowners would receive no compensation whatever. See William G. Rosenberg, *Liberals in the Russian Revolution: The Constitutional Democratic Party, 1917–1921* (Princeton, NJ: Princeton University Press, 1974), 129.
13. Basil Maklakov, "The Peasant Question and the Russian Revolution," trans. Bernard Pares, *Slavonic Review* 2, no. 5 (December 1923), 244.
14. Maklakov, *La Chute*, 49.
15. Tyrkova-Williams Diary and Letters, 403 (letter of April 28, 1944).
16. "Doklad po zakonoproektu ob otmene nekotorykh ogranichenii v pravakh selskikh obyvatelei i lits byvshikh podatnykh sostoianii" (Vysochaishii Ukaz 5 Oktiabr 1906 g.) [Report on a bill for repeal of certain limits on the rights of village inhabitants and persons of former taxed status (Imperial Decree of October 5, 1906)], GDSO, Fourth Duma,

4th Sess., Prilozheniia, Item No. 235 (hereafter cited as "Report"); GDSO, Fourth Duma, 4th Sess., Meeting 53, June 9, 1916, col. 5011.

17. Bakhmetev-Maklakov Correspondence, 3:400 (Maklakov to Bakhmetev, February 23, 1928); Leo Tolstoy, *Anna Karenina*, trans. Richard Pevear and Larissa Volkhonsky (New York: Viking, 2001), part 8, chapter 16.
18. See the Kollontai-Maklakov letters at http://ru-lib.3dn.ru/publ/kollontaj_aleksandra_mikhajlovna_pisma_k_v_a_maklakovu/1-1-0-460, letter no. 14. See chapter 3.
19. GDSO, Fourth Duma, 4th Sess., Meeting 56, June 14, 1916, col. 5392. After reviewing the provisions on the Baltics, the Duma approved the bill as a whole. Ibid., Meeting 59, June 18, 1916, cols. 5665–68.
20. Ibid., Meeting 51, June 3, 1916, col. 4816.
21. Ibid., Meeting 55, June 13, 1916, cols. 5320–23.
22. Ibid.; see also V. A. Maklakov, *Vlast i obshchestvennost na zakate staroi Rossii (Vospominaniia sovremenika)* [State and society in the twilight of old Russia (Recollections of a contemporary)] (Paris: Izdanie zhurnala "Illustrirovanaia Rossiia," 1936), 579–80, 587–88, 593–95; Maklakov, *Vtoraia Gosudarstvennaia Duma*, 172–75.
23. Ivan Strakhovskii, *Peasant Law and Institutions* (*Krestianskie prava i uchrezhdeniia*) (St. Petersburg: Izdatelstvo Obshchestvennaia Polza, 1903).
24. This was an exaggeration, to be sure. In 1848, at long last, for example, peasants received the right to acquire land on their own, i.e., non-allotment land, held in the conventional manner. Leontovitsch, *The History of Liberalism in Russia*, 88.
25. Report, 11/1.
26. Ibid.
27. Ibid., 10/1–2.
28. Report, 7/2.
29. Ibid., 11/2.
30. GDSO, Fourth Duma, 4th session, Meeting 51, June 3, 1916, col. 4775.
31. Report, 12/1.
32. Ibid., 12/2; see also Basil Maklakov, "The Peasant Question and the Russian Revolution," 245–46.
33. See Report, 35/2 (explaining role of the Senate's 1904 judgment); ibid., 30 (text of Section XII, codifying the Senate decree and addressing the matter); ibid., 31 (text of Section XXII, allowing an official of village societies to refuse to perform in-kind obligations when his duties prevent his continuous presence in the village society).
34. Report, 40/1–2, 47/1–48/2; GDSO, Fourth Duma, 4th Sess., June 9, 1916, col. 5007; ibid., June 14, 1916, col. 5375.
35. Report, 13/1.
36. Neil B. Weissman, *Reform in Tsarist Russia: The State Bureaucracy and Local Government, 1900–1914* (New Brunswick: Rutgers Univer-

sity Press, 1981), 190–96, 202–4; Geoffrey A. Hosking, *The Russian Constitutional Experiment: Government and Duma, 1907–1914* (Cambridge: Cambridge University Press, 1973), 161–70; Don C. Rawson, *Russian Rightists and the Revolution of 1905* (New York: Cambridge University Press, 1995), 223; A. Ia. Avrekh, *Tsarizm i IV Duma, 1912–1914 gg.* [Tsarism and the Fourth Duma, 1912–1914] (Moscow: Izdaletsvo Nauka, 1981), 78.

37. P. A. Pozhigailo, ed., *P.A. Stolypin glazami sovremennikov* [P. A. Stolypin through his contemporaries' eyes] (Moscow: ROSSPEN, 2008), 640–41.
38. GDSO, Fourth Duma, 4th Sess., June 9, 1916, col. 5073; ibid., June 18, 1916, cols. 5669–72.
39. Ibid., June 3, 1916, col. 4769.
40. Ibid., col. 4810.
41. Ibid., June 9, 1916, col. 5011.
42. Ibid., cols. 5014–15.
43. Ibid., col. 4993.
44. Ibid., col. 4996.
45. GDSO, Fourth Duma, 4th Session, Meeting 53, June 9, 1916, cols. 5063–64.
46. Code of Laws of the Russian Empire (*Svod Zakonov Rossiikoi Imperii*), vol. 14, section 205.
47. See Alan Wood, "The Use and Abuse of Administrative Exile to Siberia," *Irish Slavonic Studies*, no. 6 (1985), 65–81.
48. Law on Termination of Permanent Exile and Restrictions on Temporary Exile Declared as a Sentence Pronounced by a Court or Community, in the *Polnoe Sobranie Zakonov Rossiikoi Imperii*, series 3 (1881–1913), vol. 20, Item 18839, at 758 (official publication), section II. See also Wood, "The Use and Abuse of Administrative Exile to Siberia."
49. GDSO, Fourth Duma, 4th session, Meeting 54, June 10, 1916, cols. 5135–36.
50. Ibid., col. 5262.
51. Ibid., cols. 5262–63.
52. Ibid., cols. 5263–66.
53. See Jonathan W. Daly, "On the Significance of Emergency Legislation in Late Imperial Russia," *Slavic Review* 54, no. 3 (1995), 602–29 (saying that peasants "considered indispensable their right to subject 'undesirables' to administrative exile").
54. Maklakov, *Vtoraia Gosudarstvennaia Duma*, 175.
55. GDSO, Fourth Duma, 4th Sess., June 3, 1916, cols. 4761, 4768, 4777.
56. Ibid., June 9, 1916, cols. 5041–42.
57. Ibid., col. 5043.
58. Ibid.
59. Ibid., col. 5012.
60. Ibid., June 3, 1916, col. 4759 (Kerensky's claim).
61. Ibid., col. 4763.

62. Ibid., June 9, 1916, cols. 5015, 5069–71.
63. Ibid., June 3, 1916, col. 4774 (Kerensky); ibid., June 9, 1916, col. 5016 (Maklakov).
64. Ibid., cols. 5016–18.

CHAPTER 13: REFORMS AND REFORM: AN APPRAISAL

1. V. Maklakov, "III Sessiia Gosudarstvennoi Dumy" [The third session of (the Third) State Duma], *Russkaia Mysl* [Russian thought] (February 1911), 96, 97.
2. Ibid., 119–24.
3. GDSO, Third Duma, 2nd Sess., pt. 1, December 10, 1908, col. 2487.
4. Ibid.
5. GDSO, Fourth Duma, 2nd Sess., pt. 4, May 12, 1914, col. 506.
6. Ibid., cols. 506–7.
7. V.A. Maklakov, *Vlast i obshchestvennost na zakate staroi Rossii (Vospominaniia sovremenika)* [State and society in the twilight of old Russia (Recollections of a contemporary)] (Paris: Izdanie zhurnala "Illustrirovanaia Rossiia," 1936), 14.
8. Ibid., 28.
9. Maklakov, *La Chute*, 64.
10. Ibid.
11. Bakhmetev-Maklakov Correspondence, 3:33 (Maklakov to Bakhmetev, July 4, 1923).
12. V.A. Maklakov, *Iz Vospominanii* (New York: Chekhov Publishing House [Izdatelstvo imeni Chekhova], 1954), 366.
13. See generally Wayne Dowler, *Russia in 1913* (DeKalb: Northern Illinois University Press, 2012).
14. Eric Lohr, "Patriotic Violence and the State: The Moscow Riots of May 1915," *Kritika* 4, no. 3, n.s. (Summer 2003), 607–26; William C. Fuller, Jr., *The Foe Within: Fantasies of Treason and the End of Imperial Russia* (Ithaca and London: Cornell University Press, 2006).

CHAPTER 14: NATIONAL LIBERALS

1. D.N. Shipov, *Vospominaniia i dumy o perezhitom* [Memoirs and reflections on the past] (Moscow: ROSSPEN, 2007), 520–24; Geoffrey A. Hosking, *The Russian Constitutional Experiment: Government and Duma, 1907–1914* (Cambridge: Cambridge University Press, 1973), 224–25.
2. V. Maklakov, *Moskovskii Ezhenedelnik* no. 42 (November 1, 1908), 6–13.
3. D.C.B. Lieven, *Russia and the Origins of the First World War* (London: Macmillan, 1983), 125–26.
4. Dominic Lieven, *Russia's Rulers under the Old Regime* (New Haven and London: Yale University Press, 1989), 228–30.
5. GDSO, Fourth Duma, 1st Sess., pt. 1, December 7, 1912, cols. 328–29. On the broad domestic aspects of the December 7 speech, see A. Ia.

Avrekh, *Tsarizm i IV Duma, 1912–1914 gg.* [Tsarism and the Fourth Duma, 1912–1914] (Moscow: Izdaletsvo Nauka, 1981), 42–43.

6. *Russkie Vedomosti* [Russian news], December 6, 1912, 3–4.
7. Hosking, *The Russian Constitutional Experiment*, 233–38; Christopher Clark, *The Sleepwalkers* (New York: Harper, 2012), 264–65; Andrew Rossos, *Russia and the Balkans* (Toronto: University of Toronto Press, 1981), 112–13.
8. *Protokoly*, 2:101 (A. S. Izgoev).
9. Ibid., 106, 109 (October 22, 1912).
10. See Valentin Valentinovich Shelokhaev, *Ideologiia i politicheskaia organizatsiia rossiiskoi liberalnoi burzhuazii, 1907–1914* [The Ideology and political organization of the Russian liberal bourgeoisie, 1907–1914] (Moscow: Nauka, 1991), 179–93 for a review of the intra-party debates; Melissa Kirschke Stockdale, *Paul Miliukov and the Quest for a Liberal Russia, 1880–1918* (Ithaca and London: Cornell University Press, 1996), 212–20.
11. Maklakov is presumably referring to Outer Manchuria, acquired by Russia pursuant to treaties with China in 1858 and 1860, and still Russian territory.
12. Marina Aleksandrovna Ivanova, "Rol V. A. Maklakova v Obshchestvenno-politicheskoi zhizni Rossii" [The role of V. A. Maklakov in the social-political life of Russia] (PhD thesis, Rossiiskii Universitet Druzhby Narodov, 1997), 108, 218, nn. 56–57 (citing GIM, fond 31, delo 148, ll. 143, 149).
13. Letter of Lucy Bresser to Maklakov, October 4, 1912 (n.s.), GIM, fond 31, delo 11, l. 54.
14. See V. I. Lenin, *Polnoe sobranie sochinenii* [Complete collected works] (Moscow: Gosudarstvennoe Izdatelstvo Politicheskoi literatury, 1961), 22:245.
15. Shelokhaev, *Ideologiia*, 179.
16. Avrekh, *Tsarizm i IV Duma*, 220.
17. *Protokoly*, 2:143.
18. Ibid.
19. Ibid., 143–44.
20. Bakhmetev-Maklakov Correspondence, 1:461 (Maklakov to Bakhmetev, August 20, 1921).
21. *Protokoly*, 2:146.
22. Ibid., 147–48.
23. Ibid., 153.
24. *Sezdy i konferentsii*, 2:508–9, 565–66 (March 23–25, 1914); *Protokoly*, 2:153.
25. *Protokoly*, 2:281–82.
26. Stockdale, *Paul Miliukov*, 198–200; V. S. Dyakin, *Burzhuaziya, dvoryanstvo i tsarizm v 1911–1914 gg.: Razlozhenie tretei-unskoi sistemy* [The Bourgeoisie, the nobility and tsarism in 1911–1914: The Break-up

of the June 3 system] (Leningrad: Nauka 1988), 218n130; Avrekh, *Tsarizm i IV Duma*, 211–13.

27. *Protokoly*, 2:283.
28. *Sezdy i konferentsii*, 2:405–9, 421–22, 427.
29. *Sezdy i konferentsii*, 2:429–32.
30. *Sezdy i konferentsii*, 2:441, 444.
31. Shipov, *Vospominaniia i dumy*, 524–26.
32. Shelokhaev, *Ideologiia*, 71–72.
33. On the intra-Kadet battles over strategy, see generally Dyakin, *Burzhuaziya, dvoryanstvo i tsarizm v 1911–1914 gg.*
34. Evgenii Efimovskii, "Odin iz Mogikan: Pamiati V. A. Maklakova" [One of the Mohicans: Memories of V. A. Maklakov], *Vozrozhdenie* 68 (1957), 122, 124.
35. Dyakin, *Burzhuaziya, dvoryanstvo i tsarizm v 1911–1914 gg.*, 205.
36. Tyrkova-Williams Diary and Letters, 153 (diary, July 19, 1915).
37. Ibid., 400 (letter to Maklakov, March 28, 1944); ibid., 167 (diary, February 6, 1916).
38. Avrekh, *Tsarizm i IV Duma*, 220–21.
39. Tyrkova-Williams Diary and Letters, 877–78 (Maklakov to Tyrkova-Williams, November 14, 1943). Maklakov put the last sentence into quotes because it is (with an immaterial variation) taken from a poem by N. A. Nekrasov, "Sasha": "*Delo vekov popravliat nelegko.*"

CHAPTER 15: WAR—AND THE MAD CHAUFFEUR

1. Dominic Lieven, *The End of Tsarist Russia* (New York: Viking, 2014), 304–7, 324.
2. Leopold Haimson's 1964 and 1965 articles appeared to suggest a view that a revolutionary outcome such as that of October 1917 was inevitable regardless of the war, but his 2000 take on the subject was far more nuanced, stressing the proposition that the effect of the war was not to "conceive" but merely to "accelerate" polarization that was well under before the war. Leopold Haimson, "The Problem of Social Stability in Urban Russia, 1905–17, Part I," *Slavic Review* 23 (1964), 619–42; Haimson, "The Problem of Social Stability in Urban Russia, 1905–17, Part II," *Slavic Review* 24 (1965), 1–22; Haimson, "'The Problem of Political and Social Stability in Urban Russia on the Eve of War and Revolution' Revisited," *Slavic Review* 59 (2000), 848–75.
3. See, e.g., Bakhmetev-Maklakov Correspondence, 3:38 (Maklakov to Bakhmetev, September 25, 1923).
4. Michael Melancon, *The Lena Goldfields Massacre* (College Station: Texas A&M University Press, 2006), 107.
5. GDSO, Third Duma, 5th Sess., pt. 3, April 18, 1912, cols. 2757–73.
6. Vladimir Kokovtsov, *Out of My Past* (Stanford: Stanford University Press, 1935), 454–55.

7. Lieven, *The End of Tsarist Russia*, 114–15, 294.
8. Michael Cherniavsky, ed., *Prologue to Revolution: Notes of A.N. Iakhontov on the Secret Meetings of the Council of Ministers, 1915* (Englewood Cliffs, NJ: Prentice-Hall, 1967), 7.
9. A.Ia. Avrekh, *Tsarizm i IV Duma, 1912–1914 gg.* [Tsarism and the Fourth Duma, 1912–1912] (Moscow: Izdaletsvo Nauka, 1981), 93. The "divine discontent" reference is a nod to Ralph Waldo Emerson.
10. GDSO, Fourth Duma, 2nd Sess., pt. 4, May 12, 1914, col. 506.
11. V.I. Burtsev, "Arest pri tsare i arest pri Lenine," *Novyi Zhurnal*, no. 69 (1962), 170, 180–85, 192–93.
12. Raymond Pearson, *The Russian Moderates and the Crisis of Tsarism, 1914–1917* (New York: Barnes and Noble, 1978), 29–31; V.A. Maklakov, *Iz Vospominanii* (New York: Chekhov Publishing House [Izdatelstvo imeni Chekhova], 1954), 260.
13. Norman Stone, *The Eastern Front, 1914–1917* (London: Penguin, 1998), 122–93.
14. Maklakov, *La Chute*, 66–67.
15. Tsuyoshi Hasegawa, *The February Revolution* (Seattle and London: University of Washington Press, 1981), 28–29.
16. GDSO, Fourth Duma, 4th Sess., pt. 1, August 1, 1915, cols. 291–94, 339–43; ibid., August 8, 1915, cols. 530–34.
17. Ibid., August 28, 1915, cols. 1123–24.
18. S.P. Melgunov, *Na putiakh dvortsovomu perevorotu (zagovory pered revoliutsiei 1917 goda)* [On the way to a palace coup (plots before the revolution of 1917)] (Paris: Librairie "La Source," 1931), 39n*.
19. *Sezdy i konferentsii*, 3:170 (Kokoshkin), 194–95 (party resolution); Hasegawa, *The February Revolution*, 29–30.
20. *Protokoly*, 3:152 (August 19, 1915). See also Hasegawa, *The February Revolution*, 53–54.
21. Tyrkova-Williams Diary and Letters, 883 (letter to Ariadne Tyrkova-Williams, January 8, 1944).
22. *Russkie Vedomosti* [Russian news], September 27, 1915, 2, trans. by George Katkov, *Russia 1917: The February Revolution* (New York: Harper and Row, 1967), 178–79.
23. Pearson, *The Russian Moderates*, 71.
24. Katkov, *Russia 1917*, 179. See also Melgunov, *Na putiakh dvortsovomu perevorotu*, 93.
25. Tyrkova-Williams Diary and Letters, 399 (letter dated March 16, 1944).
26. Hasegawa, *The February Revolution*, 34–39; Bernard Pares, *The Fall of the Russian Monarchy: A Study of the Evidence* (New York, 1939), 265.
27. Pearson, *The Russian Moderates*, 136–37.
28. Semion Lyandres, "Progressive Bloc Politics on the Eve of the Revolution: Revisiting P.N. Miliukov's 'Stupidity or Treason' Speech of November 1, 1916," *Russian History/Histoire Russe* 31, no. 4 (Winter 2004), 447–64; see also Hasegawa, *The February Revolution*, 54.

29. V. A. Maklakov, "Libo my, libo oni" [We or they], in *V. A. Maklakov, Rechi: Sudebniia, Dumskiia i Publichniia Lektsii, 1904–1926* [V. A. Maklakov, Speeches: Judicial, Duma and public lectures, 1904–1926] (Paris: Izdanie Iubileinogo Komiteta, 1869–1949), 205–12.
30. A. Ia. Avrekh, *Raspad treteiiuskoi sistemy* [The Fall of the June 3 System] (Moscow: Nauka, 1985), 119–20.
31. Martin Gilbert, *The First World War* (New York: Holt Paperbacks, 2004), 306.
32. V. Maklakov, "Zakonnost v Russkoi zhizni" ("The Rule of law in Russian life"), *Vestnik Evropy* (May 1909), 238, 260–61.
33. Melgunov, *Na putiakh dvortsovomu perevorotu*, 195.
34. GARF, fond 63, opis 47, delo 511(1), ll. 31–32. F. A. Gaida states that the person approached was Duma Chairman Rodzianko, but the letter does not say that, and Gaida offers no source for the proposition. See Gaida, *Liberalnaia oppozitsiia na putiakh vlasti (1914–vesna 1917 g.)* [The liberal opposition on the path to power (1914–Spring 1917)] (Moscow: ROSSPEN, 2003), 259; see also Marina Aleksandrovna Ivanova, "Rol V. A. Maklakova v Obshchestvenno-politicheskoi zhizni Rossii" [The role of V. A. Maklakov in the social-political life of Russia] (PhD thesis, Rossiiskii Universitet Druzhby Narodov, 1997), 142 (discussing another apparently unsubstantiated claim that Rodzianko was the subject).
35. See Hasegawa, *The February Revolution*, 173–74, 190–97.

CHAPTER 16: THE KILLING OF RASPUTIN

1. V. A. Maklakov, "Delo ob ubiistve Rasputina: V. A. Maklakov o svoem uchastii v zagovore" [The Rasputin murder case: V. A. Maklakov on his role in the plot], *Illiustrirovannia Rossiia*, no. 12 (358) (March 19, 1932), 1–6.
2. Prince Felix Youssoupoff, *Rasputin: His Malignant Influence and His Assassination*, trans. Oswald Rayner (London: Jonathan Cape, 1934 [reissue of 1927 edition]); Vladimir Mitrofanovich Purishkevich, *The Murder of Rasputin*, ed. Michael E. Shaw, trans. Bella Costello, with a reprint of Maklakov's introduction to the original (Ann Arbor: Ardis, 1985).
3. See Youssoupoff, *Rasputin*, 128 (receiving the truncheon), 181 (battering the body).
4. Maklakov, Introduction, in Purishkevich, *The Murder of Rasputin*, 60.
5. Ronald C. Moe, *Prelude to the Revolution: The Murder of Rasputin* (Chula Vista, CA: Aventine Press, 2011), 570; Edmund Levin, *A Child of Christian Blood: Murder and Conspiracy in Tsarist Russia: The Beilis Blood Libel* (New York: Schocken Books, 2014), 263–66.
6. Maurice Paléologue, *An Ambassador's Memoirs* (New York: Octagon, 1972), 3:188–89.

CHAPTER 17: FEBRUARY 1917

1. Tsuyoshi Hasegawa, *The February Revolution* (Seattle and London: University of Washington Press, 1981), 229. See generally ibid., 215–31 (events of February 23).
2. Ibid., 310.
3. Ibid., 227.
4. V. Maklakov, "Kanun revoliutsii" [The eve of the revolution], *Novyi Zhurnal*, no. 14 (1946), 306, 308–9.
5. Ibid., 309–10. See also Hasegawa, *The February Revolution*, 255–56.
6. Ibid., 265.
7. Vasily Shulgin, *Dni * 1920* [Days * 1920] (Moscow: Sovremenika, 1989), 167–71; Maklakov, "Kanun revoliutsii," 310.
8. Ibid. Paléologue confirms the encounter, though not the specific comment. He emphasizes that he had said to Maklakov that if a crisis should be precipitated he [Maklakov] would undoubtedly "be called on to play a part. In that case, let me beg of you not to forget the fundamental obligations the war has laid on Russia." Maklakov replied, "You can count on me." Maurice Paléologue, *An Ambassador's Memoirs* (New York: Octagon, 1972), 3:216–17.
9. Compare Maklakov, "Kanun revoliutsii," 310, with Hasegawa, *The February Revolution*, 274 (naming Savich, Balashov, and Dmitriukov but not Tereshchenko).
10. Maklakov, "Kanun revoliutsii," 310.
11. Ibid., 310–11.
12. Ibid., 311–12.
13. Maklakov's account (ibid., 312) appears to mix up dates. Rodzianko on Saturday the 25th spontaneously adjourned the Duma to the 27th (Hasegawa, *The February Revolution*, 256), but Maklakov specifies Sunday the 26th for the adjournment order.
14. Hasegawa, *The February Revolution*, 268–74.
15. Ibid., 276–80; Maklakov, "Kanun revoliutsii," 312–13; Semion Lyandres, *The Fall of Tsarism: Untold Stories of the February 1917 Revolution* (Oxford: Oxford University Press, 2013), 90, 98–99.
16. Maklakov, "Kanun revoliutsii," 313–14.
17. The "Senioren Konvent" or "Sovet stareishin."
18. Its "*Uchrezhdenie*."
19. Hasegawa, *The February Revolution*, 276, 349–53; Andrei Borisovich Nikolaev, *Gosudarstvennaia duma v Fevral'skoi revoliutsii: Ocherki istorii* [The State Duma in the February Revolution: Historical notes] (Riazan: Izdatel P. A. Tribunskii, 2002), 27–31; Lyandres, *The Fall of Tsarism*, 91–92, 99.
20. Melissa Kirschke Stockdale, *Paul Miliukov and the Quest for a Liberal Russia, 1880–1918* (Ithaca and London: Cornell University Press, 1996), 241.
21. Leonard Schapiro, *The Russian Revolutions of 1917: The Origins of Modern*

Communism (New York: Basic Books, 1984), 45. See also Hasegawa, *The February Revolution*, 352–53 (speaking of the creation of the Duma Committee as "noncommittal").

22. Hasegawa, *The February Revolution*, 367–69; Nikolaev, *Gosudarstvennaia duma v Fevralskoi revoliutsii*, 77; Schapiro, *The Russian Revolutions of 1917*, 45–46; N. G. Dumova, *Kadetskaia partiia v period pervoi mirovoi voiny i Fevralskoi revolutsii* [The Kadet party in the period of the First World War and the February Revolution] (Moscow: Nauka, 1988), 96. Nikolaev says that the Duma Committee also appointed Kerensky a commissar, but acknowledges that no such appointment is listed in the records and reports no activity by Kerensky as commissar. Nikolaev, *Gosudarstvennaia duma v Fevral'skoi revoliutsii*, 77–78.
23. Ibid., 110.
24. Ibid., 77–78.
25. V. A. Maklakov, *Iz Vospominanii* (New York: Chekhov Publishing House [Izdatelstvo imeni Chekhova], 1954), 259–61; Nikolaev, *Gosudarstvennaia duma v Fevralskoi revoliutsii*, 78, 85; B. Maklakoff, "La Russie de 1900 à 1917, Vers la Révolution: Le Dénouement," *Revue de Paris* 5 (1924), 511–12. Maklakov mentions only Adzhemov as a fellow commissar; perhaps their shared Kadet background made them the most aggressive.
26. See, e.g., Sarah Badcock, "Structures and Practices of Power: 1917 in Nizhegorod and Kazan' Provinces," in *Russia's Home Front in War and Revolution, 1914–22*, eds. Sarah Badcock, Liudmila G. Novikova, and Aaron B. Retish (Bloomington, Indiana: Slavica Publishers, 2015), 355–81; Ilya V. Gerasimov, *Modernism and Public Reform in Late Imperial Russia: Rural Professionals and Self-Organization, 1905–30* (New York: Palgrave Macmillan, 2009), 168–84.
27. Richard Pipes, *The Russian Revolution* (New York: Knopf, 1990), 300; see also Stockdale, *Paul Miliukov*, 243.
28. Semion Lyandres, "Conspiracy and Ambition in Russian Politics before the February Revolution of 1917: The Case of Prince Georgii Evgenevich Lvov," *Journal of Modern Russian History and Historiography* 8 (2015), 99–133; S. P. Melgunov, *Na putiakh dvortsovomu perevorotu (zagovory pered revoliutsieĭ 1917 goda)* [On the way to a palace coup (plots before the Revolution of 1917)] (Paris: Librairie "La Source," 1931), 177–78.
29. Hasegawa, *The February Revolution*, 520.
30. Ibid., 523; George Katkov, *Russia 1917: The February Revolution* (New York: Harper and Row, 1967), 391; Lyandres, *The Fall of Tsarism*, 162, 164–65. See also ibid., 182 (Matvei Skobelev, a Menshevik, in a 1917 interview, asserts without detail or identification of his source that Maklakov "turned [the ministry] down" in favor of Kerensky).
31. Hasegawa, *The February Revolution*, 526–27; Raymond Pearson, *The Russian Moderates and the Crisis of Tsarism, 1914–1917* (New York: Barnes and Noble, 1978), 171.

32. Georgii Adamovich, *Vasilii Alekseevich Maklakov: Politik, Iurist, Chelovek* [Vasily Alekseevich Maklakov: Politician, jurist, human being] (Paris, 1959), 205. Apart from Rodzianko and Maklakov, another interesting case is the nonselection of Ivan Efremov, a Progressive whom some had evidently contemplated for internal affairs but who had often clashed with Miliukov in the Progressive Bloc. Hasegawa, *The February Revolution*, 528; Pearson, *The Russian Moderates*, 171.
33. Hasegawa, *The February Revolution*, 526–27, 539–41. See also *The Russian Provisional Government 1917—Documents*, eds. R. P. Browder and A. F. Kerensky (Stanford, 1961), 1:191. It contains the text of a directive by Kerensky, dated March 2, 1917, confirming the instructions of deputy minister Chebyshev, of the tsarist government, who acted on instructions of Adzhemov and Maklakov.
34. See Bakhmetev-Maklakov Correspondence, 3:373 (Maklakov to Bakhmetev, December 19, 1927); see also Hasegawa, *The February Revolution*, 427 (predicting immediate counter-revolution if the Soviet had formed a government).
35. Hasegawa, *The February Revolution*, 425. This and the preceding paragraph draw heavily on Hasegawa, *The February Revolution*, 379–427.
36. Pipes, *The Russian Revolution*, 319; Hasegawa, *The February Revolution*, 558–59.
37. Compare Pipes, *The Russian Revolution*, 319, with Katkov, *Russia 1917*, 408.
38. Pipes, *The Russian Revolution*, 319–20.
39. Mark V. Vishniak, *"Sovremennye Zapiski": Vospominaniia redaktora* ["Contemporary Notes"; Recollections of the Editor] (St. Petersburg: Izdatelstvo Logos, 1993), 194. Nina Berberova, not a completely reliable witness, says that when word spread that Mikhail had declined the throne, Maklakov exclaimed, "All is lost." *Liudi i Lozhi* [People and lodges] (Moscow: Progress-Traditsiia, 1997), 298–99.
40. Maklakoff, "Le Dénouement," 524.
41. Maklakov, *La Chute*, 13.
42. V. D. Nabokov recounts the events surrounding the drafting of Mikhail's manifesto but does not address the issue of how the grand duke could grant the authority he purports to grant. See V. D. Nabokov, *V.D. Nabokov and the Russian Provisional Government, 1917*, eds. Virgil D. Medlin and Steven L. Parsons (New Haven: Yale University Press, 1976), 49–55.
43. Maklakoff, "Le Dénouement," 530.
44. V. A. Maklakov, *Vlast i obshchestvennost na zakate staroi Rossii (Vospominaniia sovremenika)* [State and society in the twilight of old Russia (Recollections of a contemporary)] (Paris: Izdanie zhurnala "Illustrirovanaia Rossiia," 1936), 559. See also Maklakov, *La Chute*, 13 ("A new 'autocracy,' with complete confusion of powers was established—an absolute power henceforth belonging to ten people chosen in secret party meetings in the Duma's palace."). I have not seen any contemporaneous writing of Maklakov voicing this criticism, but Vishniak's comment

that he lost hope in the February Revolution by the end of March 3, plus the priority that he had long given to rule-of-law and similar institutional concerns (e.g., the focus on his attack on the field courts martial), suggest that this was not just hindsight.

45. Witold S. Swarowski, "The Authorship of the Abdication Document of Nicholas II," *Russian Review* 30, no. 3 (July 1971), 277–86.
46. Ibid., 278–79.
47. Hasegawa, *The February Revolution*, 520.
48. Nikolaev, *Gosudarstvennaia duma v Fevral'skoi revoliutsii*, 227–28.
49. See Tsuyoshi Hasegawa, "The Duma Committee, the Provisional Government, and the Birth of 'Triple Power' in the February Revolution," in *A Companion to the Russian Revolution*, ed. Daniel Orlovsky (Chichester, UK, and Malden, MA: Wiley-Blackwell, forthcoming 2018); Lyandres, "Conspiracy and Ambition in Russian Politics before the February Revolution of 1917," 99, 132–33; Lyandres, *The Fall of Tsarism*, 285–90.
50. Hasegawa, "The Duma Committee"; Pearson, *The Russian Moderates*, 149.
51. Maklakoff, "Le Dénouement," 529.
52. Ibid., 530.
53. Ibid., 517–19; B. Maklakoff, "La Russie de 1900 à 1917, Vers la Révolution: Le Dénouement," *Revue de Paris* 6 (1924), 609, 610–13. See also Hasegawa, *The February Revolution*, 364 (describing the appearance of Grand Duke Kirill Vladimirovich [the tsar's cousin] with the crew of the ship of the First Guard Regiment at the Tauride Palace on February 28, and declaration of his allegiance to the Duma); Pipes, *The Russian Revolution*, 289 (describing groups of workers, soldiers, intellectuals, and officers marching to the Tauride Palace between February 27 and March 1, including a detachment of the Corps of Gendarmes singing the "Marseillaise" and sporting red flags).
54. R.B. McKean, *St. Petersburg between the Revolutions* (New Haven: Yale University Press, 1990), 497–98.
55. Shulgin, *Dni * 1920*, 174–75.
56. Nikolaev, *Gosudarstvennaia duma v Fevral'skoi revoliutsii*, 91–92, 226.
57. Maklakoff, "Le Dénouement," *Revue de Paris* 5 (1924), 518. See also *Rech* [Speech], May 5, 1917, 304 (Maklakov makes the same point in his speech of May 4, 1917, discussed below); Hasegawa, *The February Revolution*, 561 (agreeing on the moral necessity for the Duma of favoring the insurgents over the old regime).
58. Hasegawa, *The February Revolution*, 557–58.
59. Orlando Figes and Boris Kolonitskii, *Interpreting the Russian Revolution: The Language and Symbols of 1917* (New Haven and London: Yale University Press, 1999), 72. See also Boris Kolonitskii, *"Tragicheskaia erotika": obrazy imperatorskoi semi v gody Pervoi mirovoi voiny* ["Tragic Erotica": images of the imperial family in the years of the First World War] (Moscow: Novoe literaturnoe obozrenie, 2010).

60. Ibid., 71–103. See also Leonid Heretz, *Russia on the Eve of Modernity: Popular Religion and Traditional Culture under the Last Tsars* (Cambridge: Cambridge University Press, 2008), 191 (arguing that the war "involved the torrential infusion of ideas and information from the modern Russian/European civilization into the consciousness of the peasantry, which re- [or mis-]interpreted this flow of facts according the categories of the traditional culture and thereby produced a confused and highly volatile mental condition").
61. Kolonitskii, *"Tragicheskaia erotika,"* 26.
62. Maklakoff, "Le Dénouement," 531.
63. Ibid., 534.
64. Ibid., 532.
65. Michael T. Florinsky, *The End of the Russian Empire* (New York: Collier Books, 1961), 191.
66. On both the development of civil society and the government's clumsy but assiduous efforts to stifle it, see Wayne Dowler, *Russia in 1913* (DeKalb: Northern Illinois University Press, 2012).
67. *Rech*, May 5, 1917, 3–4.
68. Ibid.

CHAPTER 18: IN THE MAELSTROM: THE LIBERALS IN OFFICE

1. W.E. Mosse, "The Russian Provisional Government, 1917," *Soviet Studies* 15, no. 4 (April 1964), 408–19. See also Richard Pipes, *The Russian Revolution* (New York: Knopf, 1990), 326; and Melissa Kirschke Stockdale, *Paul Miliukov and the Quest for a Liberal Russia, 1880–1918* (Ithaca and London: Cornell University Press, 1996), 249–50.
2. William G. Rosenberg, *Liberals in the Russian Revolution: The Constitutional Democratic Party, 1917–1921* (Princeton, NJ: Princeton University Press, 1974), 148–49.
3. John L. Keep, *The Russian Revolution: A Study in Mass Mobilization* (New York: Norton, 1976), 70–71.
4. Ibid., 172–85.
5. Joshua A. Sanborn, *Imperial Apocalypse: The Great War and the Destruction of the Russian Empire* (Oxford: Oxford University Press, 2014); Joshua A. Sanborn, "Unsettling the Empire: Violent Migrations and Social Disaster in Russia in World War I," *Journal of Modern History* 77, no. 2 (June 2005), 290–324.
6. Pipes, *The Russian Revolution*, 321–22.
7. Kermit E. McKenzie, "Zemstvo Organization and Role within the Administrative Structure," in *The Zemstvo in Russia: An Experiment in Local Self-Government*, eds. Terence Emmons and Wayne S. Vucinich (Cambridge: Cambridge University Press, 1982), 31, 57–61, 65.
8. Boris I. Kolonitskii, "Antibourgeois Propaganda and Anti-'Burzhui' Consciousness in 1917," *Russian Review* 53, no. 2 (April 1994), 183–96.
9. See N. G. Dumova, *Kadetskaia partiia v period pervoi mirovoi voiny i*

Fevralskoi revolutsii [The Kadet party in the period of the First World War and the February Revolution] (Moscow: Nauka, 1988), 101–2; D. A. Chugaev, ed., *Revoliutsionnoe dvizhenie v Rossii v iiule 1917 g.* [The Revolutionary movement in Russia in July 1917] (Moscow: Izdatelstvo Akademii Nauk SSSR, 1959), 583; Basil Maklakov, "On the Fall of Tsardom," *Slavonic and East European Review* 18, no. 52 (July 1939), 77; F. A. Gaida, *Liberalnaia oppozitsiia na put akh k vlasti (1914–vesna 1917 g.)* [The liberal opposition on the path to power (1914–Spring 1917)] (Moscow: ROSSPEN, 2003), 339–40; *Protokoly*, 3:355–56; Maklakov, *La Chute*, 8–9, 16–18. Compare Leonard Schapiro, *The Russian Revolutions of 1917: The Origins of Modern Communism* (New York: Basic Books, 1984), 61–62 (commenting on the anomaly of the inquiry commission).

10. Rex A. Wade, *The Russian Search for Peace: February–October 1917* (Stanford: Stanford University Press, 1969), 64–69.
11. Sanborn, *Imperial Apocalypse*, 209–10, 218.
12. William C. Fuller, Jr., *The Foe Within: Fantasies of Treason and the End of Imperial Russia* (Ithaca and London: Cornell University Press, 2006), 240–41. For an overview of the Kerensky-Kornilov affair, see James D. White, "The Kornilov Affair: A Study in Counter-Revolution," *Soviet Studies* 20, no. 2 (1968), 187–205.
13. *Rech*, June 4, 1917, 2. See also Dumova, *Kadetskaia partiia*, 146.
14. Sanborn, *Imperial Apocalypse*, 201, 236.
15. Alexander Ivanovich Verkhovskii, *Rossiia na Golgof; iz pokhodnago dnevnika* [Russia at Golgotha: from a diary on the march] *1914–1918 gg.* (Petrograd: "Delo Naroda," 1918), 113–39.
16. V. D. Nabokov, *V.D. Nabokov and the Russian Provisional Government, 1917*, eds. Virgil D. Medlin and Steven L. Parsons (New Haven: Yale University Press, 1976), 152–55.
17. Semion Lyandres, *The Fall of Tsarism: Untold Stories of the February 1917 Revolution* (Oxford: Oxford University Press, 2013), 251, 263. See also S. P. Melgunov, *Na putiakh dvortsovomu perevorotu (zagovory pered revoliutsieĭ 1917 goda)* [On the way to a palace coup (plots before the Revolution of 1917)] (Paris: Librairie "La Source," 1931), 153.
18. Sanborn, *Imperial Apocalypse*, 173, 222, 257.
19. Verkhovskii, *Rossiia na Golgof*, 123–24.
20. Nabokov, *V.D. Nabokov and the Russian Provisional Government, 1917*, 153.
21. Ibid., 154.
22. Ibid., 152.
23. Ibid., 96.
24. https://ru.wikipedia.org/wiki/верховский, александр иванович.
25. For a general assessment of Kornilov's military prowess, see D. N. Collins, "Correspondence," *Soviet Studies* 4, no. 4 (April 1970), 528–32.
26. Pipes, *The Russian Revolution*, 442–46; Boris Savinkov, *K delu Kornilova* [The Kornilov Affair] (Paris: 1918), 6–23.

27. Richard Abraham, *Alexander Kerensky: The First Love of the Revolution* (New York: Columbia University Press, 1987), 261; Pavel D. Dolgorukov, *Velikaia razrukha: Vospominaniia osnovatelia partii kadetov, 1916–1926* [Great devastation: Memoirs of founder of the party of Constitutional Democrats, 1916–1926] (Moscow: Tsentrpoligraf, 2007) 44–45.
28. *Rech*, August 16, 1917, 2.
29. Savinkov, *K delu Kornilova* , 17; Paul N. Miliukov, *The Russian Revolution* (Gulf Breeze, FL: Academic International Press, 1978–1987), 2:114–15.
30. Pipes, *The Russian Revolution*, 440–41, 446–48; A. Kerenskii, *Delo Kornilova* [The Kornilov affair] (Ekaterinoslav, 1918), 20–21.
31. Maklakov, *La Chute*, 85–86.
32. Bakhmetev-Maklakov Correspondence, 3:347–48 (Maklakov to Bakhmetev, September 16, 1927).
33. Anton Ivanovich Denikin, *Ocherki russkoi smuty* [Notes of the Russian chaos] (Moscow, 1991; reprint of the same, published in Paris in 1922), 2:31.
34. Bakhmetev-Maklakov Correspondence 3:35 (Maklakov to Bakhmetev, September 16, 1927).
35. The above account, including the translation of the Hughes machine transcript, is drawn from Pipes, *The Russian Revolution*, 451–57.
36. Bakhmetev-Maklakov Correspondence, 3:348–49 (Maklakov to Bakhmetev, September 16, 1927).
37. Winston Churchill, *Great Contemporaries* (London: Thornton Butterworth, 1937), 126.
38. The full text of the transcript appears at D. A. Chugaev, ed., *Revoliutsionnoe dvizhenie v Rossii v avguste 1917 g.* [The Revolutionary movement in Russia in August 1917] (Moscow: Izdatelstvo Akademii Nauk SSSR, 1959), 448–52.
39. See Dumova, *Kadetskaia partiia*, 198, for a version of this conversation edited to erase the difference between a coup against Kerensky and an effort to have the Provisional Government take a stronger line against the prevailing centrifugal tendencies.
40. Pipes, *The Russian Revolution*, 458–63.
41. See, e.g., V. A. Maklakov, *Vlast i obshchestvennost na zakate staroi Rossii (Vospominaniia sovremenika)* [State and society in the twilight of old Russia (Recollections of a contemporary)] (Paris: Izdanie zhurnala "Illustrirovanaia Rossiia," 1936), 244–46, 414–16, 457–60, 472–73, 602, 607, 609–10.

CHAPTER 19: EXILE

1. Oleg Budnitskii, "Posly nesushchestvuiushchei strany" [Ambassadors of a nonexistent country], introduction to Bakhmetev-Maklakov Correspondence, 1:16.
2. Ibid., 2:547 (letter of April 24, 1923).

3. Georgii Adamovich, *Vasilii Alekseevich Maklakov: Politik, Iurist, Chelovek* [Vasily Alekseevich Maklakov: Politician, jurist, human being] (Paris, 1959), 207.
4. Bakhmetev-Maklakov Correspondence, 1:197 (Maklakov to Bakhmetev, April 10, 1920).
5. Bakhmetev-Maklakov Correspondence, 1:366–67 (Maklakov to Bakhmetev, April 15, 1921). Later, in an echo of his 1909 discussion of the way history may turn an illegal coup d'état into a lawful regime, he observed that the émigrés had had to give up the practice of calling the Soviets usurpers; see V. Maklakov, "Zakonnost v Russkoi zhizni" [The rule of law in Russian life], *Vestnik Evropy*, May 1909. Tyrkova-Williams Diary and Letters, 906 (Maklakov to Tyrkova-Williams, April 6, 1945).
6. Bakhmetev-Maklakov Correspondence, 2:90 (Maklakov to Bakhmetev, November 8, 1921).
7. Leon Aron, *Roads to the Temple: Truth, Memory, and Ideals in the Makings of the Russian Revolution, 1987–1991* (New Haven: Yale University Press, 2012), 11–35.
8. Tyrkova-Williams replies to him (quite vociferously) in her letter of November 14, 1944, Tyrkova-Williams Diary and Letters, 406; the Maklakov writing to which she responds, evidently undated, appears at ibid., 767n1198.
9. Tyrkova-Williams Diary and Letters, 906 (Maklakov to Tyrkova-Williams, April 6, 1945). See also Hoover 16-3 ("Les paragraphes de A.K.," noting that World War II forced Stalin to allow Russians to return to their Russian roots).
10. V. A. Maklakov, "Sovetskaia vlast i emigratsiia," [Soviet power and the emigration], *Russkie Novosti*, May 25, 1945, 2, in Hoover 20-3.
11. Hoover 10-24 (June 25, 1934).
12. See Hoover 19-31 (typed copy of text of a June 14, 1946, Soviet decree on re-admitting refugees to Soviet citizenship, published in the June 22, 1946, issue of the pro-Soviet *Russkie Novosti*). See also Robert Harold Johnston, *New Mecca, New Babylon: Paris and the Russian Exiles, 1920–1945* (Kingston and Montreal: McGill-Queen's University Press, 1988), 172–74.
13. Robert H. Johnston, "The Great Patriotic War and the Russian Exiles in France," *Russian Review* 35, no. 3 (July 1976), 303, 309–12.
14. Ibid., 314–15.
15. Maklakov's account is in a seven-page single-spaced typewritten memo in Hoover 19-31.
16. Johnston, "The Great Patriotic War," 314.
17. Richard Abraham, *Alexander Kerensky: The First Love of the Revolution* (New York: Columbia University Press, 1987), 274.
18. Brian Boyd, *Vladimir Nabokov: The American Years* (Princeton, NJ: Princeton University Press, 1991), 84–85.
19. Evgenii Efimovskii, "Odin iz Mogikan: Pamiati V. A. Maklakova"

[One of the Mohicans: Memories of V. A. Maklakov], *Vozrozhdenie* 68 (1957), 123–24.

20. Tyrkova-Williams Diary and Letters, 445 and 778 n.1266 (letter of Tyrkova-Williams to Bakhmetev, June 1, 1951).
21. Johnston, "The Great Patriotic War," 318, 320.
22. Johnston, *New Mecca*, 33–34.
23. John M. Thompson, *Russia, Bolshevism and Versailles Peace* (Princeton, NJ: Princeton University Press, 1966), 65.
24. With the agreement of the United States State Department, the work of the conference, including its experts, was financed out of credits of the Provisional Government in the West. Budnitskii, Bakhmetev-Maklakov Correspondence, 1:59.
25. Ibid., 76; and see ibid., 65–81, for the formation of the group. See also Budnitskii, Bakhmetev-Maklakov Correspondence, 1:57–59, 490n3.
26. Thompson, *Russia, Bolshevism*, 73.
27. Constantine Nabokoff, *The Ordeal of a Diplomat* (London: Duckworth and Co., 1921), 188.
28. Thompson, *Russia, Bolshevism*, 81.
29. Ibid., 78–79.
30. Adamovich, *Vasilii Alekseevich Maklakov*, 209–10. Although there is ample documentation of Maklakov's speech to the foreign ministers of the Big Five (the Big Four plus Japan) or their delegates, see Svetlana Suveica, "'Russkoe Delo' and the 'Bessarabian Cause': The Russian Political Émigrés and the Bessarabians in Paris (1919–1920)," Institute for East and Southeast European Studies (IOS), no. 64, February 2014, http://www.dokumente.ios-regensburg.de/publikationen/mitteilun gen/mitt_64.pdf; *The Roumanian Occupation in Bessarabia: Documents*, https://archive.org/stream/roumanianoccupatooparirich#page/124 /mode/2up/search/Appendix+No.+37, the discussion with the Big Four, assuming Adamovich's sources are correct that it occurred at all, is alluded to in formal records (though with a questionable date) but appears to have generated no transcript. See *The Case for Bessarabia: A Collection of Documents on the Rumanian Occupation* at 20, 26, https:// archive.org/stream/caseforbessarabiooruss#page/n3/mode/2up.
31. Budnitskii, Bakhmetev-Maklakov Correspondence, 1:63.
32. Jonathan D. Smele, *Civil War in Siberia: The Anti-Bolshevik Government of Admiral Kolchak, 1918–1920* (Cambridge: Cambridge University Press, 1996), 183–84.
33. Thompson, *Russia, Bolshevism*, 296–303.
34. Oleg Budnitskii, *Russian Jews between the Reds and the Whites, 1917–1920* (Philadelphia: University of Pennsylvania Press, 2012), 269.
35. Ibid., 165–66.
36. Ibid., 446n142.
37. Ibid., 169–71.
38. Bakhmetev-Maklakov Correspondence, 1:256–58 (Maklakov to Bakhmetev, October 21, 1920); Oleg Budnitskii, "The Russian

Ambassador in Paris on the Whites and the Jews," *Jews in Eastern Europe* no. 3(28) (1995), 62–64 (which contains translations into English of portions of the October 21, 1920, letter); Budnitskii, *Russian Jews*, 212–15.

39. Ibid., 311.
40. Budnitskii, Bakhmetev-Maklakov Correspondence, 1:87; see also Hoover 7-12 (letter to Maklakov from the French foreign ministry dated May 5, 1939, using his and the office's exact titles); Johnston, *New Mecca*, 66–69.
41. Adamovich, *Vasilii Alekseevich Maklakov*, 213–14.
42. Roman Petroff, *Novembre blanc* (St. Malo: Editions L'Ancre de Marine, 2012), 419–20.
43. Adamovich, *Vasilii Alekseevich Maklakov*, 214–15.
44. Marc Raeff, *Russia Abroad: A Cultural History of the Russian Emigration, 1919–1939* (Oxford University Press, 1990), 35–36; Vaclav Lednitskii, "Vokrug V. A. Maklakova (lichnye vospominaniia)" [Around V. A. Maklakov (personal reminiscences)], *Novyi Zhurnal*, no. 56 (March 1959), 239–43.
45. Budnitskii, Bakhmetev-Maklakov Correspondence, 1:88–89; Johnston, *New Mecca*, 162; Adamovich, *Vasilii Alekseevich Maklakov*, 222.
46. Budnitskii, Bakhmetev-Maklakov Correspondence, 1:90.
47. Johnston, *New Mecca*, 178; Hoover 14-11 (March 1, 1945 letter from Maklakov to Alexandra Tolstoy reporting on resumption of efforts); R. L. Uritskaia, *Oni liubili svoiu stranu: Sudba russkoi emigratsii vo Frantsii s 1933 po 1948 g.* [They loved their country: Destiny of Russian emigration in France from 1933 to 1948] (St. Petersburg: Dmitrii Bulanin, 2010), 205–7.
48. Budnitskii, Bakhmetev-Maklakov Correspondence, 1:91–92; Tyrkova-Williams Diary and Letters, 1006–1007 (Maklakov to Tyrkova-Williams, August 21, 1955); Lednitskii, "Vokrug V. A. Maklakova," 247–48.
49. Adamovich, *Vasilii Alekseevich Maklakov*, 216, 220; http://goslitmuz.ru/media/videos/.
50. Berberova, *Liudi i lozhi*, 301; Johnston, *New Mecca*, 86.
51. Lednitskii, "Vokrug V. A. Maklakova," 246–50; Adamovich, *Vasilii Alekseevich Maklakov*, 232.
52. Ibid., 234.
53. Ibid., 237.
54. Ibid., 238.

CHAPTER 20: CODA: THE RULE OF LAW AS THE THIN END OF THE WEDGE

1. The Federalist, No. 51.
2. See 28 U.S.C. § 453 (part of the oath required for judges appointed under Article III of the U.S. Constitution).
3. See Joseph Raz, *The Authority of Law*, 2nd ed. (Oxford, New York:

Oxford University Press, 2009), 211 (arguing that use of very broad concepts turns "rule of law" into a proxy for ideal government).

4. C.L. Stevenson, *Ethics and Language* (New York: AMS Press, 1979 [reprint]).
5. Not for all audiences. For some the idea sounds narrow, or rigid, or formulaic, perhaps because of confusion as to what it means.
6. See, e.g., The World Justice Project, *Rule of Law Index* (Washington, DC: World Justice Project, 2011), 12 and n8 (scoring "the elimination of discrimination," and specifically its elimination "in respect of employment and occupation," as aspects of the rule of law).
7. For a description of that regime, see Marc Szeftel, "The Form of Government of the Russian Empire Prior to the Constitutional Reforms of 1905–06," in *Essays in Russian and Soviet History in Honor of Geroid Tanquary Robinson*, ed. John Shelton Curtiss (New York: Columbia University Press, 1963), 105–19.
8. See, e.g., Randall Peerenboom, *China's Long March toward Rule of Law* (New York: Cambridge University Press, 2002), 397–99. For the concept of "policy drift," see Matthew D. McCubbins, Roger G. Noll, and Barry R. Weingast, "Structure and Process, Politics and Policy: Administrative Arrangements and the Political Control of Agencies," *Virginia Law Review* 75 (1989), 431, 439, 444; McCubbins, Noll, and Weingast, "Administrative Procedures as Instruments of Political Control," *Journal of Law, Economics, and Organization* 3 (1987), 243, 255, 262.
9. See, e.g., Francis Spufford, *Red Plenty* (Minneapolis: Graywolf Press, 2010) (an account in fictionalized form of the ubiquitous back-scratching, deal-making, and principal-agent abuses that developed under the Soviet regime). Of course in a regime as rigid as Soviet economic planning, elimination of these devices would likely make the system still less effective at meeting consumer desires.
10. Martin Shapiro, "Courts in Authoritarian Regimes," in Tom Ginsburg and Tamir Moustafa, *Rule by Law: The Politics of Courts in Authoritarian Regimes* (Cambridge and New York: Cambridge University Press, 2008), 326, 334–35, discusses the problem in relation to legitimacy.
11. Pierre Landry, "The Institutional Diffusion of Courts in China: Evidence from Survey Data," in Ginsburg and Moustafa, *Rule by Law*, 207–8. The data supplied here do not answer the question about the duration of the associated stability, in either democracies or authoritarian systems.
12. The Federalist, No. 78.
13. Matthew Stephenson, "'When the Devil Turns . . . .': The Political Foundations of Independent Judicial Review," *Journal of Legal Studies* 32 (2003) (considering feasibility of an independent judiciary in the absence of political constraints on the executive). This is not to preclude the possibility of polities where (for a time) the rule of law is strong but civil society is weak, as is widely considered true of Singapore.

14. Neysun Mahboubi, "Suing the Government in China," in *Democratization in China, Korea, and Southeast Asia?: Local and National Perspectives*, eds. Kate Xiao Zhou, Shelly Rigger, and Lynn T. White III (New York: Routledge, 2014), 141–55.
15. See, e.g., He Weifang, *In the Name of Justice: Striving for the Rule of Law in China* (Washington, DC: Brookings Institution Press, 2012), 71–72 (celebrating congressional debate in the United States).
16. Alexis de Tocqueville, *The Old Regime and the Revolution*, ed. François Furet and Françoise Mélonio, trans. Alan S. Kahan, vol. 1 [The Complete Text] (Chicago: University of Chicago Press, 1998), 243.
17. "Article 1 Being loyal and resolute. A judge shall give priority to the cause of the Party, the interests of the people, and the supremacy of the Constitution and the law, be consistent with the CPC Central Committee in respect of ideology and behaviors, and shall not say any word or commit any conduct in violation of the basic policy of the Party and the state and the socialist judicial system." Notice of the Supreme People's Court on Issuing the Code of conduct for Judges (2010 Revision). Translated by the ChinaLawInfo, a database managed by the Peking University Law School.
18. Shmuel Galai, *The Liberation Movement in Russia, 1900–1905* (Cambridge: Cambridge University Press, 1973), 242–43; V. A. Maklakov, *Vlast i obshchestvennost na zakate staroi Rossii (Vospominaniia sovremenika)* [State and society in the twilight of old Russia (Recollections of a contemporary)] (Paris: Izdanie zhurnala "Illustrirovanaia Rossiia," 1936), 355–60.
19. See Eva Pils, "Charter 08 and Violent Resistance: The Dark Side of the Chinese *Weiquan* Movement," in Jean-Philippe Béja, Fu Hualing, and Eva Pils, *Liu Xiaobo, Charter 08, and the Challenges of Political Reform in China* (Hong Kong: Hong Kong University Press, 2012), 229–49 (noting division of protester community between those hewing closely to nonviolent methods and those embracing violence).
20. D. C. B. Lieven, "The Security Police, Civil Rights, and the Fate of the Russian Empire, 1855–1917," in *Civil Rights in Imperial Russia*, eds. Olga Crisp and Linda Edmondson (Oxford: Oxford University Press, 1989) 258–61.

Selected Bibliography

Frequently cited works are listed separately by both their Russian and translated titles.

Abraham, Richard. *Alexander Kerensky: The First Love of the Revolution.* New York: Columbia University Press, 1987.

Acemoglu, Daron, and James A. Robinson. *Why Nations Fail: The Origins of Power, Prosperity, and Poverty.* New York: Crown, 2012.

Adamovich, Georgii. *Vasilii Alekseevich Maklakov: Politik, Iurist, Chelovek* [Vasily Alekseevich Maklakov: Politician, jurist, human being]. Paris: Friends of Maklakov, 1959.

Aldanov, Mark. "P. N. Durnovo—Prophet of War and Revolution." *Russian Review* 2, no. 1 (Autumn 1942), 31–45.

Aronov, Dmitrii Vladimirovich. *Pervyi spiker* [First speaker]. Moscow: Iurist, 2006.

Ascher, Abraham. *P. A. Stolypin: The Search for Stability in Late Imperial Russia.* Stanford, CA: Stanford University Press, 2001.

———. *The Revolution of 1905: Authority Restored.* 2 vols. Stanford, CA: Stanford University Press, 1992.

Assa, Natasha. "How Arbitrary Was Tsarist Administrative Justice? The Case of the Zemstvos Petitions to the Imperial Ruling Senate, 1866–1916." *Law and History Review* 24, no. 1 (Spring 2006), 1–43.

Avrekh, A. Ia. *P. A. Stolypin i sudby reform v Rossii* [Stolypin and the fate of reform in Russia]. Moscow: Izdatelstvo politicheskoi literatury, 1991.

———. *Raspad treteiiunskoi sistemy* [The Fall of the June 3 System]. Moscow: Nauka, 1985.

———. *Stolypin i Tretia Duma* [Stolypin and the Third Duma]. Moscow: Nauka, 1968.

———. *Tsarizm i IV Duma, 1912–1914 gg.* [Tsarism and the Fourth Duma, 1912–1914]. Moscow: Nauka, 1981.

Bakhmetev-Maklakov Correspondence. *See* Abbreviations.

Balzer, Harley D., ed. *Russia's Missing Middle Class: The Professions in Russian History*. Armonk, NY: M.E. Sharpe, 1996.

Berman, Harold. "The Rule of Law and the Law-Based State (Rechtsstaat)." In *Toward the "Rule of Law" in Russia? Political and Legal Reform in the Transition Period*, edited by Donald D. Barry, 43–60. Armonk, NY: M.E. Sharpe, 1992.

Bhat, Girish N. "The Moralization of Guilt in Late Imperial Russian Trial by Jury: The Early Reform Era." *Law and History Review* 15, no. 1 (Spring 1997), 77–113.

Bradley, Joseph. "Subjects into Citizens: Societies, Civil Society and Autocracy in Tsarist Russia." *American Historical Review* 107, no. 4 (October 2002), 1094–1123.

———. *Voluntary Associations in Tsarist Russia: Science, Patriotism and Civil Society*. Cambridge, MA: Harvard University Press, 2009.

Budnitskii, Oleg V. "Netipichnyi Maklakov" [Atypical Maklakov]. *Otechestvennaia Istoriia* no. 3 (1999), 17–22.

———, ed. "The Russian Ambassador in Paris on the Whites and the Jews." *Jews in Eastern Europe* no. 3(28) (1995), 53–66.

———. *Russian Jews between the Reds and the Whites, 1917–1920*. Translated by Timothy J. Portice. Philadelphia: University of Pennsylvania Press, 2011.

———. "V.A. Maklakov i evreiskoi vopros" [V.A. Maklakov and the Jewish question]. *Vestnik Evreiskogo universiteta* [Bulletin of the Jewish University] no. 1(19) (1999), 42–94.

Burbank, Jane. "Legal Culture, Citizenship, and Peasant Jurisprudence: Perspectives from the Early Twentieth Century." In Solomon, *Reforming Justice in Russia, 1864–1894*.

———. *Russian Peasants Go to Court: Legal Culture in the Countryside, 1905–1917*. Bloomington and Indianapolis: Indiana University Press, 2004.

Burtsev, V.L. "Arest pri tsare i arest pri Lenine" [Arrest under the tsar and arrest under Lenin]. *Novyi Zhurnal* no. 69 (1962), 170–207.

Chamberlain, William Henry. "The Short Life of Russian Liberalism." *Russian Review* 26, no. 2 (April 1967), 144–52.

Chugaev, D.A., et al., eds. *Revoliutsionnoe dvizhenie v Rossii v avguste 1917 g.: Razgrom Kornilovskogo miatezha*. Moscow: Izdaletsvo Akademii Nauk SSSR, 1959.

———. *Revoliutsionnoe dvizhenie v Rossii v iiule 1917 g.; iiulskii crizis*. Moscow: Izdatelstvo Akademii Nauk SSSR, 1959.

———. *Revoliutsionnoe dvizhenie v Rossii v mae-iiune 1917 g.: iiunskaia demonstratsia*. Moscow: Izdatelstvo Akademii Nauk SSSR, 1959.

Churchill, Winston S. *Great Contemporaries*. London: Thornton Butterworth, 1937.

Clowes, Edith W., Samuel D. Kassow, and James L. West, eds. *Between Tsar and People: Educated Society and the Quest for Public Identity in Late Imperial Russia*. Princeton, NJ: Princeton University Press, 1991.

Crisp, Olga. "The Russian Liberals and the 1906 Anglo-French Loan to Russia." *Slavonic and East European Review* 39, no. 93 (June 1961), 497–511.

Crisp, Olga, and Linda Edmondson, eds. *Civil Rights in Imperial Russia*. Oxford: Oxford University Press, 1989.

Czap, Peter, Jr. "Peasant Class Courts and Peasant Customary Justice in Russia, 1861–1912." *Journal of Social History* 1, no. 2 (Winter 1967), 149–78.

Daly, Jonathan W. "On the Significance of Emergency Legislation in Late Imperial Russia." *Slavic Review* 54 (Autumn 1995), 602–629.

———. "Political Crime in Late Imperial Russia." *Journal of Modern History* 74, no. 1 (March 2002), 62–100.

———. *The Watchful State*. DeKalb: Northern Illinois University Press, 2004.

Davies, David Arwyn. *V.A. Maklakov and the Problem of Russia's Westernization*. PhD thesis, University of Washington, 1967.

Davies, R. W. *From Tsarism to the New Economic Policy*. Ithaca, NY: Cornell University Press, 1991.

Dedkov, N. I. *Konservativnyi liberalizm Vasiliia Maklakova*. Moscow: Seriia "AIRO-XX—Pervaia Monografiia," 2005.

Delo Beilisa, Stenograficheskii otchet [The Beilis affair, Stenographic record]. Kiev: Pechatniia S. P. Iakovleva 1913. Available at http://ldn-knigi.lib.ru/JUDAICA/StenBeil/Beilis_Steno.htm.

Denikin, Anton Ivanovich. *Ocherki russkoi smuty* [Notes on the Russian chaos]. Moscow, 1991; reprint of the same, published in Paris in 1922.

Dolgorukov, Pavel D. *Velikaia razrukha: Vospominaniia osnovatelia partii kadetov, 1916–1926* [Great devastation: Memoirs of founder of the party of Constitutional Democrats, 1916–1926]. Moscow: Tsentrpoligraf, 2007.

Dowler, Wayne. *Russia in 1913*. DeKalb: Northern Illinois University Press, 2012.

Dumova, N. G. *Kadetskaia partiia v period pervoi mirovoi voiny i Fevralskoi revoliutsii* [The Kadet party in the period of the First World War and the February Revolution]. Moscow: Nauka, 1988.

Dyakin, V. S. *Burzhuaziya, dvorianstvo i tsarizm v 1911–1914 gg.: Razlozhenie tretei-unskoi sistemy* [The Bourgeoisie, the nobility and tsarism in 1911–1914: The Break-up of the June 3 system]. Leningrad: Nauka, 1988.

Edelman, Robert. *Proletarian Peasants: The Revolution of 1905 in Russia's Southwest*. Ithaca, NY, and London: Cornell University Press, 1987.

Efimovskii, Evgenii. "Odin iz Mogikan: Pamiati V. A. Maklakova" [One of the Mohicans: Memories of V. A. Maklakov]. *Vozrozhdenie* [Revival] 68 (1957), 119–24.

Emmons, Terence. "The Beseda Circle, 1899–1905." *Slavic Review* 32 (September 1973), 461–90.

———. *The Formation of Political Parties and the First National Elections in Russia.* Cambridge, MA: Harvard University Press, 1983.

———. "The Zemstvo in Historical Perspective." In Emmons and Vucinich, *The Zemstvo in Russia*, 423–46.

Emmons, Terence, and Wayne S. Vucinich, eds. *The Zemstvo in Russia: An Experiment in Local Self-Government.* Cambridge and New York: Cambridge University Press, 1982.

Enticott, Peter. *The Russian Liberals and the Revolution of 1905.* London and New York: Routledge, 2016.

Ferenczi, Caspar. "Freedom of the Press under the Old Regime." In Crisp and Edmondson, *Civil Rights in Imperial Russia*, 191–214.

Figes, Orlando, and Boris Kolonitskii. *Interpreting the Russian Revolution: The Language and Symbols of 1917.* New Haven and London: Yale University Press, 1999.

Fischer, George. *Russian Liberalism: From Gentry to Intelligentsia.* Cambridge, MA: Harvard University Press, 1958.

Fitzpatrick, Sheila. *Stalin's Peasants: Resistance and Survival in the Russian Village after Collectivization.* Oxford: Oxford University Press, 1994.

Fleischhauer, Ingeborg. "The Agrarian Program of the Russian Constitutional Democrats." *Cahiers du Monde russe et soviétique* [Notes on the Russian and Soviet world] 20, no. 2 (1979), 173–201.

Florinsky, Michael T. *The End of the Russian Empire.* New York: Collier Books, 1961.

Frierson, Catherine. "Rural Justice in Public Opinion: The Volost' Court Debate, 1861–1912." *Slavonic and East European Review* 64, no. 4 (1986), 526–45.

Fuller, Lon L. *The Morality of Law.* Rev. ed. New Haven and London: Yale University Press, 1977.

Fuller, William C., Jr. "Civilians in Military Courts, 1881–1904." *Russian Review* 41, no. 3 (July 1982), 288–305.

———. *Civil-Military Conflict in Imperial Russia, 1881–1914.* Princeton, NJ: Princeton University Press, 1985.

———. *The Foe Within: Fantasies of Treason and the End of Imperial Russia.* Ithaca, NY, and London: Cornell University Press, 2006.

Gaida, F. A. *Liberalnaia oppozitsiia na putiakh k vlasti (1914–vesna 1917 g.)* [The liberal opposition on the road to power (1914–Spring 1917)]. Moscow: ROSSPEN, 2003.

Galai, Shmuel. "The Impact of the Vyborg Manifesto on the Fortunes of the Kadet Party." *Revolutionary Russia* 20, no. 2 (December 2007), 197–224.

———. "The Jewish Question as a Russian Problem: The Debates in the First State Duma." *Revolutionary Russia* 17, no. 1 (June 2004), 131–67.

———. "Kadet Domination of the First Duma and Its Limits." In Smele and Heywood, *The Russian Revolution of 1905*, 196–217.

———. "The Kadet Quest for the Masses." In McKean, *New Perspectives in Modern Russian History*, 80–98.

———. "The Kadets in the Second Duma." *Revolutionary Russia* 23, no. 1 (June 2010), 1–28.

———. "Konstitutsionalisty-demokraty i ikh kritiki" [The Constitutional Democrats and their critics]. *Voprosy istorii* no. 12 (1991), 3–13.

———. *The Liberation Movement in Russia, 1900–1905*. Cambridge: Cambridge University Press, 1973.

———. "The True Nature of Octobrism." *Kritika* n.s. 5, no. 1 (Winter 2004), 137–47.

Galili, Ziva. *The Menshevik Leaders in the Russian Revolution: Social Realities and Political Strategies*. Princeton, NJ: Princeton University Press, 1989.

GARF. *See* Abbreviations.

Gatrell, Pater. *Russia's First World War: A Social and Economic History*. Harlow, Eng.: Pearson Longman, 2005.

———. *A Whole Empire Walking: Refugees in Russia during World War I*. Bloomington: Indiana University Press, 1999.

Gatrell, Peter, and Mark Harrison. "The Russian and Soviet Economies in the Two World Wars: A Comparative View." *Economic History Review* 46, no. 3 (1993), 425–52.

Gaudin, Corrine. *Ruling Peasants: Village and State in Late Imperial Russia*. DeKalb: Northern Illinois University Press, 2007.

GDSO. *See* Abbreviations.

Geifman, Anna. *Thou Shalt Kill: Revolutionary Terrorism in Russia*. Princeton, NJ: Princeton University Press, 1993.

Gessen, Iosif (I. V.). *V Dvukh vekakh: Zhiznennyi otchet* [In two centuries: A life's account]. *Arkhiv Russkoi Revoliutsii* 22 (1937). Berlin: Speer and Schmidt.

GIM. *See* Abbreviations.

Ginsburg, Tom, and Tamir Moustafa, eds. *Rule By Law: The Politics of Courts in Authoritarian Regimes*. Cambridge and New York: Cambridge University Press, 2008.

Gleason, William. "Alexander Guchkov and the End of the Russian Empire." *Transactions of the American Philosophical Society* 73, part 3 (1983). Philadelphia: American Philosophical Society.

Goldenbeizer, A. A. "Vospominaniia o V. A. Maklakove." *Novoe Russkoe Slovo* [New Russian word], July 28, 1957, 2.

Goldman, L. I. *Politicheskie protsessy v Rossii, 1901–1917* [Political trials in Russia, 1901–1917]. Moscow: [Publishing House of the All-Union Society of Political Prisoners and Exiles], 1932.

Gregory, Paul. *Before Command.* Princeton, NJ: Princeton University Press, 1994.

Greif, Avner. *Institutions and the Path to the Modern Economy: Lessons from Medieval Trade.* New York: Cambridge University Press, 2006.

Gruzenberg, O. O. *Yesterday: Memoirs of a Russian Jewish Lawyer.* Translated by D. Rawson and T. Tipton. Berkeley: University of California Press, 1981.

Guchkov, Alexander. "Iz Vospominanii." *Poslednie Novesti,* nos. 5647 and 5651, September 9 and 13, 1936.

Haimson, Leopold, ed. *The Politics of Rural Russia, 1905–1914.* Bloomington: Indiana University Press, 1979.

———. "'The Problem of Political and Social Stability in Urban Russia on the Eve of War and Revolution' Revisited." *Slavic Review* 59, no. 4 (Winter 2000), 848–75.

———. "The Problem of Social Stability in Urban Russia, 1905–17." *Slavic Review* 23 (1964), 619–42, and 24 (1965), 1–22.

Hamm, Michael F. "Liberalism and the Jewish Question: The Progressive Bloc." *Russian Review* 31, no. 2 (April 1972).

Hasegawa, Tsuyoshi. "The Duma Committee, the Provisional Government, and the Birth of 'Triple Power' in the February Revolution." In *A Companion to the Russian Revolution,* edited by Daniel Orlovsky. Chichester, UK, and Malden, MA: Wiley-Blackwell, forthcoming 2018.

———. *The February Revolution: Petrograd, 1917.* Seattle: University of Washington Press, 1981.

———. "The Problem of Power in the February Revolution in Russia." *Canadian Slavonic Papers* 14, no. 4 (1972), 622–32.

Hassell, James E. *Russian Refugees in France and the United States between the World Wars.* Philadelphia: American Philosophical Society, 1991.

Heretz, Leonid. *Russia on the Eve of Modernity: Popular Religion and Traditional Culture under the Last Tsars.* New Studies in European History. Cambridge: Cambridge University Press, 2008.

Heywood, Anthony. "Socialists, Liberals and the Union of Unions in Kyiv during the 1905 Revolution: An Engineer's Perspective." In Smele and Heywood, *The Russian Revolution of 1905,* 177–95.

Hickey, Michael C. "Discourses of Public Identity and Liberalism in the February Revolution: Smolensk, Spring 1917." *Russian Review* 55, no. 4 (October 1996), 615–37.

Holquist, Peter. "Violent Russia, Deadly Marxism? Russia in the Epoch of Violence, 1905–21." *Kritika: Explorations in Russian and Eurasian History* n.s. 4, no. 3 (Summer 2003), 627–52.

Hoover. *See* Abbreviations.

Hosking, Geoffrey A. "P. A. Stolypin and the Octobrist Party." *Slavonic and East European Review* 47, no. 108 (January 1969), 137–60.

———. *Russia: People and the Empire.* Cambridge, MA: Harvard University Press, 1997.

———. *The Russian Constitutional Experiment: Government and Duma, 1907–1914*. Cambridge: Cambridge University Press, 1973.

Johnston, Robert Harold. "The Great Patriotic War and the Russian Exiles in France." *Russian Review* 35, no. 3 (July 1976), 303–321.

———. *New Mecca, New Babylon: Paris and the Russian Exiles, 1920–1945*. Kingston, Canada: McGill-Queen's University Press, 1988.

Karpovich, M. "Two Types of Russian Liberalism: Maklakov and Miliukov." In *Continuity and Change in Russian and Soviet Thought*, edited by Ernest J. Simmons, 129–43. Joint Committee on Slavic Studies of the American Council of Learned Societies and the Social Science Research Council. Cambridge, MA: Harvard University Press, 1955, 1967.

Katkov, George. *The Kornilov Affair: Kerensky and the Break-Up of the Russian Army*. New York: Longman, 1980.

———. *Russia 1917: The February Revolution*. New York: Harper and Row, 1967.

Kazantsev, Sergei M. "The Judicial Reform of 1864 and the Procuracy in Russia." In Solomon, *Reforming Justice in Russia, 1864–1894*, 44–60.

Keep, John L. *The Russian Revolution: A Study in Mass Mobilization*. New York: Norton, 1976.

Kerensky, Alexander. *Russia and History's Turning Point*. New York: Duell, Sloan, and Pearce, 1965.

Kizevetter, A. A. *Na rubezhe dvukh stoletii: Vospominaniia* [On the border of two centuries: Memoirs]. Moscow: Iskusstvo, 1996.

Kokovtsov, Vladimir Nikolaevich. *Iz Moego Proshlago*. The Hague and Paris: Mouton, 1969. Reprint of 1933 edition.

———. *Out of My Past: The Memoirs of Count Kokovtsov*. Stanford, CA: Stanford University Press; London: H. Milford, Oxford University Press, 1935.

Kolonitskii, Boris Ivanovich. "Antibourgeois Propaganda and Anti-'Burzhui' Consciousness in 1917." *Russian Review* 53, no. 2 (April 1994), 183–96.

———. "'Democracy' in the Political Consciousness of the February Revolution." *Slavic Review* 57, no. 1 (Spring 1998), 96–106.

———. *"Tragicheskaia erotica": Obrazy imperatorskoi semi v gody Pervoi mirovoi voiny* ["Tragic Erotica": Images of the imperial family in the years of the First World War]. Moscow: Novoe literaturnoe obozrenie, 2010.

Korros, Alexandra. "Activist Politics in a Conservative Institution: The Formation of Factions in the Russian Imperial State Council, 1906–1907." *Russian Review* 52 (January 1993), 1–19.

———. *Stolypin, Nationalism, and the Politics of the Russian Imperial State Council, 1906–1911*. Lanham, MD: Rowman and Littlefield, 2002.

Kroner, Anthony Willem. *The Debate between Miliukov and Maklakov on the Chances for Russian Liberalism*. Amsterdam, 1998.

———. "The Debate between Miliukov and Maklakov on the Chances for Russian Liberalism." *Revolutionary Russia* 7, no. 2 (1994), 239–71.

———. "The Influence of Miliukov and Maklakov on Current Views of Russian Liberalism." *Revolutionary Russia* 9, no. 2 (1996), 143–63.

Kucherov, Samuel. "The Case of Vera Zasulich." *Russian Review* 11, no. 2 (April 1952), 86–96.

———. *Courts, Lawyers, and Trials under the Last Three Tsars*. New York: F. A. Praeger, 1953.

Landmarks Revisited: The Vekhi Symposium One Hundred Years On. Edited by Robin Aizlewood and Ruth Coates. Brighton, MA: Academic Studies Press, 2013.

Lednicki [Lednitskii], Waclaw. "Vokrug V. A. Maklakova (lichnye vospominaniia)" [Around V. A. Maklakov (personal reminiscences)]. *Novyi Zhurnal* 56 (March 1959), 222–50.

Leiken, Ezekiel. *The Beilis Transcripts: The Anti-Semitic Trial That Shook the World*. Northvale, NJ : Jason Aronson, 1993.

Leonard, Carol. *Agrarian Reform in Russia: The Road from Serfdom*. Cambridge: Cambridge University Press, 2010.

Leontovitsch, Victor. *The History of Liberalism in Russia*. Translated by Parmen Leontovitsch, with a foreword by Aleksandr Solzhenitsyn. Pittsburgh: University of Pittsburgh Press, 2012.

Lieven, Dominic C. B. *Nicholas II: Twilight of the Empire*. New York: St. Martin's Press, 1993.

———. *Russia and the Origins of the First World War*. London: Macmillan, 1983.

———. *Russia's Rulers under the Old Regime*. New Haven and London: Yale University Press, 1989.

Lohr, Eric. *Nationalizing the Russian Empire: The Campaign against Enemy Aliens during World War I*. Cambridge, MA: Harvard University Press, 2003.

———. "Patriotic Violence and the State: The Moscow Riots of May 1915." *Kritika* n.s. 4, no. 3 (Summer 2003), 607–26.

Lohr, Eric, and Marshall Poe, eds. *The Military and Society in Russia, 1450–1917*. Leiden: Brill, 2002.

Long, James William. "Organized Protest against the 1906 Russian Loan." *Cahiers du monde Russe et soviétique* 13, no. 1 (1972), 24–39.

Lunacharskii, A., K. Radek, and L. Trotsky. *Siluety: Politicheski portrety*. Moscow: Izd-vo polit. Lit-ry, 1991.

Macey, David A. J. *Government and Peasant in Russia, 1861–1906: The Prehistory of the Stolypin Reforms*. Dekalb: Northern Illinois University Press, 1987.

Mahboubi, Neysun. "Suing the Government in China." In *Democratization in China, Korea, and Southeast Asia?: Local and National Perspectives*, edited by Kate Xiao Zhou, Shelly Rigger, and Lynn T. White III, 141–55. New York: Routledge, 2014.

Maklakov, Vasily A. [Vasilii; Basil]. "The Agrarian Problem in Russia before the Revolution." *Russian Review* 9, no. 1 (January 1950), 3–15.

———. Beilis summation. See *Delo Beilisa.*
———. *La Chute. See* Abbreviations.
———. "Delo ob ubiistve Rasputina: V.A. Maklakov o svoem uchastii v zagovore" [The Rasputin murder case: V.A. Maklakov on his role in the plot]. *Illiustrirovannia Rossiia* no. 12(358) (March 19, 1932), 1–6.
———. "Ereticheskie mysli" [Heretical thoughts]. *Novyi Zhurnal* 19 (1949?), 141–64, and 20 (1949?), 131–49.
———. "L'Ėtape Actuelle du Bolshevisme" [The present condition of Bolshevism]. *Mercure de France,* May 1, 1922, 577–608.
———. "F.I. Rodichev i A.R. Lednitskii." *Novyi Zhurnal* no. 16 (1947), 240–51.
———. *Iz Vospominanii* [Out of my recollections]. New York: Chekhov Publishing House, 1954.
———. "Kanun Revoliutsii" [The Eve of the revolution]. *Novyi Zhurnal* 14 (1946), 306–14.
———. *L.N. Tolstoi kak obshchestvennyi deiatel* [L.N. Tolstoy as a public figure]. In V.A. Maklakov, *Rechi,* 129–56.
———. "Local Justice in Russia." *Russian Review* 2, no. 4 (1913), 127–46.
———. "1905–1906 gody." In *Vinaver i russkaia obshchestvennost nachala XX veka: Sbornik stateĭ* [Vinaver and Russian society at the start of the twentieth century: Collection of articles], 53–96. Paris: Imp. Cooperative Ėtoile, 1937.
———. *O Lve Tolstom: Dve Rechi* [On Leo Tolstoy: Two speeches]. Paris: Annales contemporaines, 1929.
———. "On the Fall of Tsardom." *Slavonic and East European Review* 18, no. 52 (July 1939), 73–92.
———. "The Peasant Question and the Russian Revolution." *Slavonic and East European Review* 2, no. 5 (December 1923), 225–48.
———. "Pereustroistvo krestianskago byta" [Reconstruction of peasant life]. *Vestnik grazhdanskovo prava* no. 8 (December 1916), 29–52; no. 1 (January 1917), 29–69.
———. *Pervaia Gosudarstvennaia Duma: Vospominaniia Sovremennika* [The First State Duma: Recollections of a contemporary]. Moscow: Tsentrpoligraf, 2006.
———. *Rechi: Sudebniia, Dymskiia i Publichniia Lektsii, 1904–1926* [Speeches: Judicial, Duma and public lectures, 1904–1926]. Paris: Izdanie Iubileinogo Komiteta, 1949.
———. *Rech na Sezd K-D* [Speech to Kadet Conference]. Moscow, 1917.
———. "Serbia i slavianksii vopros" [Serbia and the Slav question]. *Moskovskii Ezhenedelnik* no. 42 (November 1, 1908), 6–13.
———. "Spasitelnoe predosterezhenie: Smyl dela Beilisa" [Salutary warning: The meaning of the Beilis affair]. *Russkaia Mysl* [Russian thought] no. 11 (November 1913), 135–43.
———. *Speeches: Judicial, Duma and Public Lectures, 1904–1926. See* Maklakov, V.A. *Rechi: Sudebniia, Dymskiia i Publichniia Lektsii, 1904–1926.*
———. *State and Society. See* Maklakov, V.A. *Vlast i obshchestvennost.*

———. "III Sessiia Gosudarstvennoi Dumy" [The Third Session of [the Third] State Duma]. *Russkaia Mysl* [Russian thought] 2 (1911), 96–125.
———. *Tolstoi i bolshevizm*. Paris: Russkiia zemlia, 1921.
———. "Tolstoi i sud" [Tolstoy and the courts]. In V. A. Maklakov, *Rechi*, 157–93.
———. "Vers la Révolution. La Russie de 1900 à 1917, Le dénouement." *Revue de Paris* 5 (October 1, 1924), 508–534; 6 (November 15, 1924), 271–91; and 6 (December 1, 1924), 609–631.
———. *Vlast i obshchestvennost na zakate staroi Rossii (Vospominaniia sovremenika)* [State and society in the twilight of old Russia (Recollections of a contemporary)]. Paris: Izdanie zhurnala "Illustrirovanaia Rossiia," 1936. [Often cited as 3 vols., but published in 1 vol.]
———. *Vtoraia Gosudarstvennaia Duma* [The Second State Duma]. Moscow: Tsentrpoligraf, 2006.
———. "Zakonnost v Russkoi zhizni" [Lawfulness in Russian life]. In *Vestnik Evropy* (May 1909), 238–75.
Maklakov, V. A., and V. V. Shulgin. *Spor o Rossii. V. A. Maklakov—V. V. Shulgin. Perepiska 1919–1939 god* [Dispute over Russia. V. A. Maklakov—V. V. Shulgin Correspondence, 1919–1939]. Moscow: ROSSPEN, 2012.
Mandelshtam, M. L. *1905 god v politicheskikh protsessakh* [The year 1905 in political trials]. Moscow: Izdatelstvo polikatorzhan, 1931.
Margolis, A. D. "Sistema Sibirskoy ssylki i zakon ot 12 iyunya 1900 goda" [The system of Siberian exile and the law of June 12, 1900]. In *Ssylka i obshchestvenno-politicheskaia zhizn v Sibiri (XVIII–nachalo XX v.)*, 126–40. Novosibirsk, Russia, 1978.
McCloskey, Deirdre. *Bourgeois Dignity: Why Economics Can't Explain the Modern World*. Chicago: University of Chicago Press, 2011.
———. *Bourgeois Equality: How Ideas, Not Capital or Institutions, Enriched the World*. Chicago: University of Chicago Press, 2016.
———. *The Bourgeois Virtues: Ethics for an Age of Commerce*. Chicago: University of Chicago Press, 2006.
McDaniel, Tim. *Autocracy, Capitalism, and Revolution in Russia*. Berkeley: University of California Press, 1988.
McDonald, David. *United Government and Foreign Policy in Russia, 1900–1917*. Cambridge, MA: Harvard University Press, 1992.
McKean, Robert B. "The Bureaucracy and the Labour Problem, June 1907–February 1917." In McKean, *New Perspectives in Modern Russian History*, 222–49.
———, ed. *New Perspectives in Modern Russian History*. New York: St. Martin's Press, 1992.
———. *St. Petersburg between the Revolutions*. New Haven: Yale University Press, 1990.
McKenzie, Kermit E. "Zemstvo Organization and Role within the Administrative Structure." In Emmons and Vucinich, *The Zemstvo in Russia*, 31–78.

Medlin, Virgil D., and Steven L. Parsons, eds. *V. D. Nabokov and the Russian Provisional Government, 1917*. Introduction by Robert P. Browder. New Haven: Yale University Press, 1976.

Melancon, Michael. *The Lena Goldfields Massacre and the Crisis of the Late Tsarist State*. Eugenia & Hugh M. Stewart '26 Series on Eastern Europe. College Station: Texas A&M University Press, 2006.

Melgunov, S. P. *Na putiakh k dvortsovomu perevorotu: Zagovory pered revoliutsiei 1917 goda* [On the way to the palace coup: Conspiracies before the revolution of 1917]. Series: Belaia Rossiia [White Russia]. Moscow: Airis-press, 2007.

Menashe, Louis. "'A Liberal with Spurs': Alexander Guchkov, a Russian Bourgeois in Politics." *Russian Review* 26, no. 1 (1967), 38–53.

Miliukov, Paul [Pavel N.]. *God borby, publitsisticheskaia khronika, 1905–1906* [Year of struggle, a journalistic chronicle]. St. Petersburg, 1907.

———. "Liberalizm, Radikalizm i Revolutsiia" [Liberalism, radicalism and revolution]. *Sovremennye Zapiski* 57 (1935), 285.

———. *Political Memoirs, 1905–1917*. Edited by Arthur P. Mendel. Translated by Carl Goldberg. Ann Arbor: University of Michigan Press, 1967.

———. "Politika v 'Sovremennykh Zapiskakh'" [Politics in "Contemporary Notes"]. *Poslednie Novosti* [Recent news], April 4, 1929.

———. "Politika v 'Sovremennykh Zapiskakh'" [Politics in "Contemporary Notes"]. *Poslednie Novosti* [Recent news], July 8, 1930.

———. "Publitsistika 'Sovremennykh Zapiskakh'" [The opinion journalism of "Contemporary Notes"]. *Poslednie Novosti* [Recent news], July 16, 1931.

———. "Rokovye Gody" [Fateful years]. In *Russkiia Zapiski* 109 (April 1938).

———. *The Russian Revolution*. 3 vols. Edited by Richard Stites. Translated by Tatyana and Richard Stites. Vol. 1: introduction by Richard Stites; vols. 2 and 3, introductions by G. M. Hamburg. Gulf Breeze, FL: Academic International Press, 1978–1987.

———. "Russkie 'liberalizm' i zaem 1906 g." [Russian "liberalism" and the 1906 loan]. *Poslednie Novosti* [Recent news], March 5, 1936.

———. "'Sovremennye Zapiski,' kn. 56." *Poslednie Novosti* [Recent news], November 22, 1934.

———. "Sud nad Kadetskim 'Liberalizmom'" [Judging Kadet "Liberalism"]. *Sovremennye Zapiski* 41 (1930), 347.

———. *Tri Popytki* [Three tries]. Paris, 1921.

———. "V. A. Maklakov mezhdu 'obshchestvennostiu i vlastiu, I'" [V. A. Maklakov between "society and the state" I]. *Poslednie Novosti* [Recent news], May 28, 1937.

———. "V. A. Maklakov mezhdu 'obshchestvennostiu i vlastiu, II'" [V. A. Maklakov between "society and the state" II]. *Poslednie Novosti* [Recent news], May 30, 1937.

———. "V. A. Maklakov o knige prof. Pares" [V. A. Maklakov and Professor Pares's book]. *Poslednie Novosti* [Recent news], July 16, 1939.

———. *Vospominaniia* [Memoirs]. Moscow: Sovremennik, 1990.

Mironov, Boris. *The Standard of Living and Revolutions in Russia, 1700–1917*. London and New York: Routledge, 2012.

Moe, Ronald C. *Prelude to Revolution: The Murder of Rasputin*. Chula Vista, CA: Aventine Press, 2011.

Nabokoff, Constantine. *The Ordeal of a Diplomat*. London: Duckworth and Co., 1921.

Nasledie Ariadny Vladimirovny Tyrkovoi. See Tyrkova-Williams Diary and Letters *in* Abbreviations.

Nathans, Benjamin. *Beyond the Pale: The Jewish Encounter with Late Imperial Russia*. Berkeley: University of California Press, 2002.

Neuberger, Joan. "Popular Legal Cultures: The St. Petersburg *Mirovoi Sud*." In *Russia's Great Reforms, 1855–1881*, edited by Ben Eklof, John Bushnell, and Larissa Zakharova, 132–46. Bloomington: Indiana University Press, 1994.

Nikolaev, Andrei Borisovich. *Gosudarstvennaia duma v Fevralskoi revoliutsii: Ocherki istorii* [The State Duma in the February Revolution: Historical notes]. Riazan, Russia: Izdatel P. A. Tribunskii, 2002.

Olson, Mancur. "Dictatorship, Democracy and Development." *American Political Science Review* 87, no. 3 (1993), 567–76.

Orbach, Alexander. "The Jewish People's Group and Jewish Politics in Tsarist Russia, 1905–1914." *Modern Judaism* 10, no. 1 (February 1990), 1–15.

Orlovsky, Daniel T. "Professionalism in the Ministerial Bureaucracy on the Eve of the February Revolution of 1917." In Balzer, *Russia's Missing Middle Class*, 267–92.

Owen, Thomas C. "Autocracy and the Rule of Law in Russian Economic History." In *The Rule of Law and Economic Reform in Russia*, edited by Jeffrey D. Sachs and Katharina Pistor, 23–40. Boulder, CO: Westview, Perseus Books, 1997.

———. *Capitalism and Politics in Russia: A Social History of the Moscow Merchants, 1855–1905*. Cambridge: Cambridge University Press, 1981.

———. *The Corporation under Russian Law, 1800–1917: A Study in Tsarist Economic Policy*. Cambridge and New York: Cambridge University Press, 1991.

———. "Impediments to a Bourgeois Consciousness in Russia, 1880–1905: The Estate Structure, Ethnic Diversity, and Economic Regionalism." In Clowes, Kassow, and West, *Between Tsar and People*, 75–89.

———. "The Russian Industrial Society and Tsarist Economic Policy, 1867–1905." *Journal of Economic History* 45, no. 3 (September 1985), 587–606.

Padenie tsarskogo rezhima. See Abbreviations.

Paléologue, Maurice. *An Ambassador's Memoirs*. 3 vols. New York: Octagon, 1972.

Pares, Bernard. "Alexander Guchkov." *Slavonic and East European Review* 15, no. 43 (July 1936), 121–34.

———. *The Fall of the Russian Monarchy: A Study of the Evidence*. New York: Knopf, 1939.

———. "The Second Duma." *Slavonic and East European Review* 2, no. 4 (June 1923), 36–55.

Parthé, Kathleen. "Who Speaks the Truth? Writers vs. Lawyers." *Universals and Contrasts* (St. Petersburg Institute of Linguistics, Cognition, and Culture) no. 1 (Spring 2012), 1.

Pearson, Raymond. *The Russian Moderates and the Crisis of Tsarism, 1914–1917*. New York: Barnes and Noble, 1978.

Pinchuk, Ben-Cion. *The Octobrists in the Third Duma, 1907–1912*. Seattle: University of Washington of Press, 1974.

Pipes, Richard. *Karamzin's Memoir on Ancient and Modern Russia: A Translation and Analysis*. New ed. Ann Arbor: University of Michigan Press, 2005.

———. *Russia under the Old Regime*. New York: Scribner's, 1974.

———. *Struve: Liberal on the Left, 1870–1905*. Cambridge, MA: Harvard University Press, 1970.

———. *Struve: Liberal on the Right, 1905–1944*. Cambridge, MA: Harvard University Press, 1980.

Pomeranz, William E. *The Emergence and Development of the Russian Advokatura: 1864–1905*. PhD dissertation, University of London, 1990.

Pozhigailo, P. A., ed. *P. A. Stolypin glazami sovremennikov* [P. A. Stolypin through a contemporary's eyes]. Moscow: ROSSPEN, 2008.

Pravilova, Ekaterina A. *Zakonnost i Prava Lichnosti: Administrativnaia Iustitsia v Rossii* [Legality and individual rights: Administrative justice in Imperial Russia]. St. Petersburg: "Obrazovanie-Kultura," 2000.

Procaccia, Uriel. *Russian Culture, Property Rights, and the Market Economy*. Cambridge: Cambridge University Press, 2007.

Protokoly. *See* Abbreviations.

Purishkevich, Vladimir Mitrofanovich. *Comment j'ai tué Raspoutaine*. Paris: J. Povolozky et cie, 1924.

———. *The Murder of Rasputin*. Edited and introduced by Michael E. Shaw. Translated by Bella Costello. With an Introduction by V. A. Maklakov. Ann Arbor: Ardis, 1985.

———. *Ubiistvo Rasputina* [The Murder of Rasputin]. 1923.

Rabinowitch, Alexander. *The Bolsheviks Come to Power: The Revolution of 1917 in Petrograd*. New York: W. W. Norton, 1976.

———. *The Bolsheviks in Power: The First Year of Soviet Rule in Petrograd*. Bloomington: Indiana University Press, 2007.

———. *Prelude to Revolution: The Petrograd Bolsheviks and the July 1917 Uprising*. Bloomington: Indiana University Press, 1968.

Radkey, Oliver H. *Russia Goes to the Polls: The Election to the All-Russian Constituent Assembly, 1917*. Ithaca, NY: Cornell University Press, 1989.

Raeff, Marc. *Russia Abroad: A Cultural History of the Russian Emigration, 1919–1939*. New York: Oxford University Press, 1990.

———. "Some Reflections on Russian Liberalism." *Russian Review* 18 (July 1959), 218–30.

Raleigh, Donald J. *Revolution on the Volga*. Ithaca, NY, and London: Cornell University Press, 1986.

Rappaport, A. Iu. "Russkii sud do revoliutsii" [Russian courts before the revolution]. *Novyi Zhurnal* no. 112 (1973), 149–62.

Rawson, Don C. "Rightist Politics in the Revolution of 1905: The Case of Tula Province." *Slavic Review* 51, no. 1 (Spring 1992), 99–116.

———. *Russian Rightists and the Revolution of 1905*. New York: Cambridge University Press, 1995.

Raz, Joseph. *The Authority of Law*. 2nd ed. Oxford: Oxford University Press, 2009.

Read, Christopher. *From Tsar to Soviets: The Russian People and Their Revolution, 1917–21*. New York: Oxford University Press, 1996.

Robbins, Richard J. *The Tsar's Viceroys*. Ithaca, NY: Cornell University Press, 1987.

Rogger, Hans. "The Beilis Case." *Slavic Review* 25, no. 4 (December 1966), 615–29.

———. "Government, Jews, Peasants, and Land in Post-Emancipation Russia." *Cahiers du Monde russe et soviétique* 17, no. 1 (January–March 1976), 2–25; no. 2/3 (April–September 1976), 171–211.

———. *Jewish Policies and Right-Wing Politics in Imperial Russia*. Berkeley and Los Angeles: University of California Press, 1986.

———. "Russia in 1914." *Journal of Contemporary History* 1 (1966), 95–119.

———. *Russia in the Age of Modernization and Revolution, 1881–1917*. London and New York: Longman, 1983.

———. "Was There a Russian Fascism? The Union of the Russian People." *Journal of Modern History* 36, no. 4 (December 1964), 398–415.

Roosa, Ruth A. "Russian Industrialists and 'State Socialism,' 1906–17." *Soviet Studies* 23 (January 1972), 395–417.

Rosenberg, William G. "The Democratization of Russia's Railroads in 1917." *American Historical Review* 86, no. 5 (December 1981), 983–1008.

———. *Liberals in the Russian Revolution: The Constitutional Democratic Party, 1917–1921*. Princeton, NJ: Princeton University Press, 1974.

———. "The Russian Municipal Duma Elections of 1917: A Preliminary Computation of Returns." *Soviet Studies* 21, no. 2 (October 1969), 131–63.

Rosenberg, William G., and Diane P. Koenker. "The Limits of Formal Protest: Worker Activism and Social Polarization in Petrograd and Moscow." *American Historical Review* 92, no. 2 (April 1987), 296–326.

Rossiiskii liberalizm serediny XVIII–nachala XX veka: entsiklopediia. Edited by V. V. Shelokhaev, N. I. Kanishcheva, V. V.. Zhuravlev, A. N. Medushevskii, et al. Moscow: ROSSPEN, 2010.

Rossos, Andrew. *Russia and the Balkans: Inter-Balkan Rivalries and Russian Foreign Policy, 1908–1914*. Toronto, Canada, and Buffalo, NY: University of Toronto Press, 1981.

The Russian Provisional Government 1917—Documents. Edited by R. P. Browder and A. F. Kerensky. 3 vols. Stanford, CA: Stanford University Press, 1961.

Ruud, Charles A. *Fighting Words: Imperial Russian Censorship and the Russian Press, 1804–1906*. Toronto: University of Toronto Press, 1982.

Ruud, Charles A., and Sergei Stepanov. *Fontanka 16: The Tsars' Secret Police.* Montreal: McGill-Queen's University Press, 1999.

Samuel, Maurice. *Blood Accusation: The Strange History of the Beilis Case.* New York: Knopf, 1967.

Sanborn, Joshua A. *Drafting the Russian Nation.* DeKalb: Northern Illinois University Press, 2003.

———. *Imperial Apocalypse: The Great War and the Destruction of the Russian Empire.* Oxford: Oxford University Press, 2014.

———. "Unsettling the Empire: Violent Migrations and Social Disaster in Russia in World War I." *Journal of Modern History* 77, no. 2 (June 2005), 290–324.

Savinkov, B. V. *K delu Kornilova.* Paris, 1918.

Sazonov, S. *Les années fatales.* Paris: Payot, 1927.

Schapiro, Leonard. *The Russian Revolutions of 1917: The Origins of Modern Communism.* New York: Basic, 1984.

———. *Russian Studies.* Edited by Ellen Dahrendorf. New York: Viking, 1986.

Schleifman, Nurit. *Undercover Agents in the Russian Revolutionary Movement, 1902–1914.* New York: Palgrave, Macmillan, 1988.

Senin, A. S. *Aleksandr Ivanovich Guchkov.* Moscow: Scriptori, 1996.

Service, Robert. *Lenin: A Biography.* Cambridge, MA: Harvard University Press, 2000.

Seton-Watson, Hugh. *The Decline of Imperial Russia, 1855–1914.* New York: Frederick A. Praeger, 1952.

Sezdy i konferentsii. See Abbreviations.

Shanin, Teodor. *Russia, 1905–1907: Revolution as a Moment of Truth.* New Haven: Yale University Press, 1986.

Shelokhaev, S. V. *D. N. Shipov: Lichnost i obshchestvenno-politicheskaia deiatelnost* [D. N. Shipov: The Person and the public and political activity]. Moscow: ROSSPEN, 2010.

Shelokhaev, V. V. "Agrarnia programma kadetov v pervoi Russkoi revoliutsii." *Istoricheskie Zapiski* 86 (1970), 172–230.

———, ed. *Gosudarstvennaia Duma Rossiiskoi Imperii, 1906–1917: Entsiklopediia.* Moscow: ROSSPEN, 2008.

———. *Ideologiia i politicheskaia organizatsiia rossiiskoi liberalnoi burzhuazii.* Moscow: Nauka, 1991.

———, ed. *Petr Arkadevich Stolypin: Entsiklopediia.* Moscow: ROSSPEN, 2011.

Shilov, D. N. *Gosudarstvennye deiateli rossiiskoi imperii, 1802–1917: Biobibliograficheskii spravochnik.* St. Petersburg: Dmitrii Bulanin, 2001.

Shipov, D. N. *Vospominaniia i dumy o perezhitom* [Memoirs and reflections on the past]. Moscow: ROSSPEN, 2007.

Shulgin, Vasilii Vitalevich. *Dni * 1920* [Days * 1920]. Moscow: Sovremenika, 1989.

Siegelbaum, Lewis H. *The Politics of Industrial Mobilization in Russia, 1914–1917: A Study of the War Industrial Committees.* New York: St. Martin's Press, 1983.

Smele, Jonathan D. *Civil War in Siberia: The Anti-Bolshevik Government of Admiral Kolchak, 1918–1920*. Cambridge: Cambridge University Press, 1996.

Smele, Jonathan D., and Anthony Heywood, eds. *The Russian Revolution of 1905: Centenary Perspectives*. London: Routledge, 2005.

Smith, C. Jay. "The Russian Third Duma: An Analytical Profile." *Russian Review* 17, no. 3 (July 1958), 201–210.

Smith, Scott B. *Captives of Revolution: The Socialist Revolutionaries and the Bolshevik Dictatorship, 1918–1923*. Pittsburgh: Pittsburgh University Press, 2013.

Solomon, Peter H., Jr. "Courts and Their Reform in Russian History." In Solomon, *Reforming Justice in Russia, 1864–1894*, 3–20.

———, ed. *Reforming Justice in Russia, 1864–1894: Power, Culture, and the Limits of Legal Order*. Armonk, NY: M.E. Sharpe, 1997.

Solovev, K.A. *Kruzhok "Beseda": V poiskakh novoi politicheskoi realnosti, 1899–1905*. [The "Beseda" circle: In search of a new political reality, 1899–1905]. Moscow: ROSSPEN, 2009.

Sovershenno Lichno i doveritelno! See Bakhmetev-Maklakov Correspondence *in* Abbreviations.

Spence, Richard B. *Boris Savinkov: Renegade on the Left*. New York: East European Monographs, 1991.

Steinberg, Mark D. *Voices of Revolution, 1917*. New Haven and London: Yale University Press, 2003.

Stockdale, Melissa Kirschke. *Paul Miliukov and the Quest for a Liberal Russia, 1880–1918*. Ithaca, NY, and London: Cornell University Press, 1996.

Stone, Norman. *The Eastern Front, 1914–1917*. New York: Scribner, 1975.

Sukhanov, N.N. *The Russian Revolution: A Personal Record*. Edited, abridged, and translated by Joel Carmichael from *Zapiski o revolutsii*; with new addendum by the editor. Princeton, NJ: Princeton University Press, 1984.

Swarowski, Witold S. "The Authorship of the Abdication Document of Nicholas II." *Russian Review* 30, no. 3 (July 1971), 277–86.

Szeftel, Marc. "The Form of Government of the Russian Empire Prior to the Constitutional Reforms of 1905–06." In *Essays in Russian and Soviet History in Honor of Geroid Tanquary Robinson*, edited by John Shelton Curtiss, 105–19. New York: Columbia University Press, 1963.

———. "Personal Inviolability in the Legislation of the Russian Absolute Monarchy." *American Slavic and East European Review* 17, no. 1 (February 1958), 1–24.

———. *The Russian Constitution of April 23, 1906: Political Institutions of the Duma Monarchy*. Brussels: Éditions de la Librarie encyclopédique, 1976.

Tager, A.S. *The Decay of Czarism: The Beilis Trial*. Philadelphia: The Jewish Publication Society of America, 1935.

Thurston, Robert W. *Liberal City, Conservative State: Moscow and Russia's Urban Crisis, 1906–1914*. New York: Oxford University Press, 1987.

Timberlake, Charles E., ed. *Essays on Russian Liberalism*. Columbia, MO: University of Missouri Press, 1972.

———. "The Zemstvo and the Development of a Russian Middle Class." In Clowes, Kassow, and West, *Between Tsar and People*, 164–79.

Tokmakoff, George. *P.A. Stolypin and the Third Duma: An Appraisal of the Three Major Issues*. Washington, DC: University Press of America, 1981.

Tolstoi, Lev N. [Leo Tolstoy]. *Polnoe Sobranie sochinenii* [Complete works]. Edited by G. Chertkov. 90 vols. Moscow: Gos. izd-vo khudozh. lit-ry, 1928–58.

Tyrkova-Williams, Ariadna V. *From Liberty to Brest-Litovsk: The First Year of the Russian Revolution*. Westport, CT: Hyperion Press, 1977.

———. *Na putiakh k svobode* [On the way to freedom]. Moscow: Moskovskaia shkola politicheskikh issledovanii, 2007.

———. "Russian Liberalism." *Russian Review* 10, no. 1 (January 1951), 3–14.

Tyrkova-Williams Diary and Letters. *See* Abbreviations.

Uritskaia, R. L. *Oni liubili svoiu stranu: Sudba russkoi emigratsii vo Frantsii s 1933 po 1948 g.* [They loved their country: Destiny of Russian emigration in France from 1933 to 1948]. St. Petersburg: Dmitrii Bulanin, 2010.

Verkhovskii, Alexander Ivanovich. *Rossiia na Golgof: Iz pokhodnago dnevnika, 1914–1918 g.* [Russia at Golgotha: From a diary on the march, 1914–1918]. Petrograd: "Delo Naroda," 1918.

Vinaver, M. M. *Nedavnee: Vospominaniia i kharakteristiki*. Paris, 1926.

Vishniak, M. V. "O russkoi revolutsii" [On the October Revolution]. *Sovremennye Zapiski* no. 38 (1929), 314–51.

———. *"Sovremennye Zapiski": Vospominaniia redaktora* ["Contemporary Notes": Recollections of the editor]. St. Petersburg: Izdatelstvo Logos, 1993.

Von Laue, Theodore H. *Sergei Witte and the Industrialization of Russia*. New York: Columbia University Press, 1963.

Vucinich, Wayne S., ed. *The Peasant in Nineteenth-Century Russia*. Stanford, CA: Stanford University Press, 1968.

Wade, Rex A. *The Russian Search for Peace, February to October 1917*. Stanford, CA: Stanford University Press, 1969.

Wagner, William G. *Marriage, Property, and Law in Late Imperial Russia*. Oxford: Clarendon Press; New York: Oxford University Press, 1994.

———. "Tsarist Legal Policies at the End of the Nineteenth Century: A Study in Inconsistencies." *Slavonic and East European Review* 54, no. 3 (July 1976), 371–94.

Waldron, Peter. "Religious Toleration in Late Imperial Russia." In Crisp and Edmondson, *Civil Rights in Imperial Russia*, 103–19.

———. "States of Emergency: Autocracy and Extraordinary Legislation, 1881–1917." *Revolutionary Russia* no. 8 (1995), 1–25.

———. "Stolypin and Finland." *Slavonic and East European Review* 63, no. 1 (January 1985), 41–55.

Walicki, Andrzej. *A History of Russian Thought from the Enlightenment to Marxism*. Stanford, CA: Stanford University Press, 1979.

———. *Legal Philosophies of Russian Liberalism*. Notre Dame and London: University of Notre Dame Press, 1992.

Walkin, Jacob. "Government Controls over the Press." *Russian Review* 13 (1954), 203–9.

———. *The Rise of Democracy in Pre-Revolutionary Russia*. New York: Praeger, 1962.

Wcislo, Francis W. *Reforming Rural Russia: State, Local Society, and National Politics, 1855–1914*. Princeton, NJ: Princeton University Press, 1990.

———. *Tales of Imperial Russia: The Life and Times of Sergei Witte, 1849–1915*. Oxford: Oxford University Press, 2011.

Weinberg, Robert. *Ritual Murder in Late Imperial Russia: The Trial of Mendel Beilis*. Bloomington: Indiana University Press, 2013.

Weissman, N.B. *Reform in Tsarist Russia*. New Brunswick, NJ: Rutgers University Press, 1981.

Wilson, Colin. *Rasputin and the Fall of the Romanovs*. London: Granada Publishing, 1977.

Wood, Alan. "The Use and Abuse of Administrative Exile to Siberia." *Irish Slavonic Studies* no. 6 (1985), 65–81.

Worobec, Christine. *The Human Tradition in Imperial Russia*. Lanham, MD: Rowman and Littlefield, 2009.

Wortman, Richard. *The Development of a Russian Legal Consciousness*. Chicago: University of Chicago Press, 1976.

———. "Property Rights, Populism, and the Russian Political Culture." In Crisp and Edmondson, *Civil Rights in Imperial Russia*, 13–32.

Yaney, George L. "Social Stability in Prerevolutionary Russia: A Critical Note." *Slavic Review* 24, no. 3 (September 1965).

———. *The Urge to Mobilize: Agrarian Reform in Russia, 1861–1930*. Champaign: University of Illinois Press, 1982.

Yusupov, Felix F. [Prince Felix Youssoupoff]. *Konets Rasputina: Vospominaniia*. Paris, 1927.

———. *Lost Splendor*. Translated from the French by Ann Green and Nicholas Katkoff. New York: Putnam, 1954.

———. *Rasputin: His Malignant Influence and His Assassination*. Translated from the Russian by Oswald Rayner. London: Jonathan Cape, 1934. Reissue of 1927 edition.

Index

Illustrations are indicated by bold page numbers.

Permission has been granted for the use of ideas and language expressed by Stephen F. Williams in the following publications:

"Antidote to Revolution: Vasilii Maklakov's Advocacy of the Rule of Law and Constitutionalism," in *Russia's Home Front in War and Revolution, 1914–22*, Book 4: *Reintegration: The Struggle for the State* (Bloomington, IN: Slavica Publishers, forthcoming 2017).

"A Kadet's Critique of the Kadet Party: Vasily Maklakov," *Revolutionary Russia* 23 (2010), 29–65 (Abingdon, UK, and Philadelphia: Taylor & Francis).

"Liberalism," in *A Companion to the Russian Revolution*, edited by Daniel Orlovsky (Chichester, UK, and Malden, MA: Wiley-Blackwell, forthcoming 2018).

"The Rule of Law as the Thin End of the Wedge," in *A Revolution in the International Rule of Law: Essays in Honor of Don Wallace, Jr.*, edited by Borzu Sabahi, Nicholas J. Birch, Ian A. Laird, and José Antonio Rivas, 49–58 (Huntington, NY: JurisNet LLC, 2014).